D1179492

Sustainable Culinary Systems

There is increasing public and academic interest in local and sustainable foods and food tourism. These interests have been reflected in such diverse elements as the growth of farmers' markets, green restaurants, food miles, carbon and sustainability labelling, concerns over food supply and security, Slow Food, Fair Trade, and a desire to buy and 'eat locally'. Food-related hospitality and tourism are integral to this process because of the way in which they simultaneously act to globalise and localise food consumption and create new foodways and commodity chains. This book therefore aims to provide an integrated understanding of the contemporary interest in food and food tourism through the use of an international collection of illustrative case study chapters as well as the provision of a novel integrative framework for the book, a sustainable culinary system.

This is the first volume to examine the concept of sustainable culinary systems, particularly with specific reference to tourism and hospitality. Divided into two parts, the book explores firstly the notion of the local, reflecting the increased interest in the championing of local food production and consumption. Second, treatment of sustainability in food and food tourism and hospitality in settings that reach beyond the local in a business and socio-economic sense is reviewed. The book, therefore, reflects much of the contemporary public interest in the ethical consumption and production of food, as well as revealing the inherent tensions between local and broader goals in both defining and achieving sustainable culinary systems and the environmental, social and economic implications of food production and consumption.

This book provides the reader with an integrated approach to understanding the subject of how culinary systems may be made more sustainable. It will be valuable reading to all those interested in sustainable food and food tourism.

C. Michael Hall is a Professor in the Department of Management, University of Canterbury, New Zealand; Docent in the Department of Geography, University of Oulu and a Visiting Professor at the University of Eastern Finland and Linnaeus University, Sweden.

Stefan Gössling is a Professor at the Department of Service Management, Lund University, and the School of Business and Economics, Linnaeus University, both in Sweden. He is also research coordinator at the Research Centre for Sustainable Tourism, Western Norway Research Institute.

Routledge studies of gastronomy, food and drink
Series Editor: C. Michael Hall
University of Canterbury, New Zealand

This groundbreaking series focuses on cutting-edge research on key topics and contemporary issues in the area of gastronomy, food and drink to reflect the growing interest in this as academic disciplines as well as food movements as part of economic and social development. The books in the series are interdisciplinary and international in scope, considering not only culture and history but also contemporary issues facing the food industry, such as security of supply chains. By doing so, the series will appeal to researchers, academics and practitioners in the fields of gastronomy and food studies, as well as related disciplines such as tourism, hospitality, leisure, hotel management, cultural studies, anthropology, geography and marketing.

Published:

The Business of Champagne
A delicate balance
Edited by Steven Charters

Alternative Food Networks
Knowledge, practice, and politics
David Goodman, Michael Goodman and Melanie DuPuis

Sustainable Culinary Systems
Local foods, innovation, tourism and hospitality
Edited by C. Michael Hall and Stefan Gössling

Forthcoming:

Social, Cultural and Economic Impacts of Wine in New Zealand
Peter Howland

Sustainable Culinary Systems

Local foods, innovation, tourism and hospitality

**Edited by C. Michael Hall and
Stefan Gössling**

Routledge
Taylor & Francis Group

LONDON AND NEW YORK

First published 2013
by Routledge
2 Park Square, Milton Park, Abingdon, Oxon OX14 4RN

Simultaneously published in the USA and Canada
by Routledge
711 Third Avenue, New York, NY 10017

Routledge is an imprint of the Taylor & Francis Group, an informa business

British Library Cataloguing in Publication Data
A catalogue record for this book is available from the British Library

Library of Congress Cataloging in Publication Data
Hall, Colin Michael, 1961–
Sustainable culinary systems: local foods, innovation, tourism and
hospitality/C. Michael Hall and Stefan Gössling.
   p. cm.
   Includes bibliographical references and index.
   1. Local foods. 2. Sustainable agriculture. 3. Farmers' markets.
   4. Agritourism. 5. Sustainable tourism. 6. Hospitality industry.
   I. Gössling, Stefan. II. Title.
   HD9000.5.H343 2012
   338.1'9–dc23

                      2012024984

ISBN: 978-0-415-53370-6 (hbk)
ISBN: 978-0-203-11407-0 (ebk)

Typeset in Times New Roman
by Wearset Ltd, Boldon, Tyne and Wear

Printed and bound in Great Britain by
TJ International Ltd, Padstow, Cornwall

Contents

Illustrations

Figures

Tables

Contributors

Tim Baird, Department of Management, College of Business and Economics, University of Canterbury, Christchurch, New Zealand.

Paul W. Ballantine, Department of Management, College of Business and Economics, University of Canterbury, Christchurch, New Zealand.

Paul Cleave, Business School, University of Exeter, Exeter, UK.

Sally Everett, Division of Tourism and Leisure, University of Bedfordshire, Faculty of Education, Sport and Tourism, Luton, Bedfordshire, LU1 3JU, UK.

Stefan Gössling, School of Business and Economics, Linnaeus University, Kalmar, Sweden, and Research Centre for Sustainable Tourism, Western Norway Research Institute, Sogndal, Norway.

C. Michael Hall, Department of Management, University of Canterbury, Christchurch, New Zealand; Department of Geography, University of Oulu, Finland; Centre for Tourism, University of Eastern Finland, Savonlinna, Finland; Freiburg Institute of Advanced Studies, Freiburg, Germany; and School of Business and Economics, Linnaeus University, Kalmar, Sweden.

Atsuko Hashimoto, Department of Tourism and Environment, Brock University, 500 Glenridge Avenue, St Catharines, ON L2S 3A1, Canada

Carrie Herzog, College of Management and Economics, School of Hospitality and Tourism Management, University of Guelph, Guelph, Ontario, Canada.

Amy Hughes, Department of Geography, Planning and Recreation, Northern Arizona University, Flagstaff, Arizona 86011–5016, USA.

Johannes Idsø, Sogn og Fjordane University College, P.O. Box 133, N-6851 Sogndal, Norway.

Shinichi Kurihara, Department of Food and Resource Economics, Chiba University, 864 Matsudo, Matsudo, Chiba, 271–8510, Japan.

Marte Lange-Vik, Vestlandsforsking, Box 163, 6851 Sogndal, Norway.

Alan A. Lew, Department of Geography, Planning and Recreation, Northern Arizona University, Flagstaff, Arizona 86011–5016, USA.

Karin Malm, School of Business and Economics, Linnaeus University, Kalmar, Sweden.

Iain P. Murray, College of Management and Economics, School of Hospitality and Tourism Management, University of Guelph, Guelph, Ontario, Canada.

Jan Henrik Nilsson, Lund University, Department of Service Management, Box 882, Helsingborg, 25108, Sweden.

Yasuo Ohe, Department of Food and Resource Economics, Chiba University, 864 Matsudo, Matsudo, Chiba, 271–8510, Japan.

Josefine Østrup Backe, Lund University, Department of Service Management, Box 882, Helsingborg, 25108, Sweden.

Amos S. Ron, Department of Tourism and Hotel Management, Kinneret College on the Sea of Galilee, Israel, and Department of Tourism and Leisure Studies, Ashkelon Academic College, Israel.

Susan L. Slocum, Division of Tourism and Leisure, University of Bedfordshire, Faculty of Education, Sport and Tourism, Luton, Bedfordshire, LU1 3JU, UK.

Sharifah Zannierah Syed Marzuki, Faculty of Business Management, Universiti Teknologi MARAKampus Pahang, Bandar Pusat Jengka, Malaysia.

David J. Telfer, Department of Tourism and Environment, Brock University, 500 Glenridge Avenue, St Catharines, ON L2S 3A1, Canada.

Dallen J. Timothy, School of Community Resources and Development and Global Institute of Sustainability, Arizona State University, 411 N. Central Avenue, Suite 550, Phoenix, Arizona 85004, USA.

Acknowledgements

The links between sustainability, food and tourism constitute both an academic and a practical interest of the editors. On the day the manuscript was completed Michael was managing the impacts of his gaggle of geese on the banks of his pond in the icy depths of a South Island winter while Stefan was about to deal with his own management issues on his property for the Swedish *midsommar*. We are not gentlemen farmers. Those who know us may debate whether we are gentlemen at all! However, what we are deeply interested in is where our food comes from, how the food we produce fits into the food chain and fits in with tourism and hospitality in particular, and the delights and vagaries of low-carbon organic farming and lifestyles. We also recognise that these extremely personal and localised concerns are intimately related to the 'larger' issues that occupy much of our academic lives, for example global environmental change, climate change adaptation and mitigation, sustainable tourism development and consumption, and the politics of mobility and tourism. When we are at Solberga Gård or Riverstones we know that we are able to walk outside and harvest our own meals; we are also very deeply aware that most people cannot do so, and that a large number of the world's population do not have the luxury of regular nutritional meals.

Interest in the role of alternative food networks in tourism as well as the potentially sustainable interrelationships between food and tourism led to the commencement of this project in 2009. Critical to its success have been a number of meetings, most important of which were a conference and workshops on sustainable food and tourism in Kalmar, Sweden, in September 2010 at which a number of contributors to this volume were able to discuss and get feedback on their papers. The editors would like express their gratitude to Anneli Andersson for organising all practical details of the meeting, and for requesting the use of regional foodstuffs during all dinners, as well as the assistance of Christoph Tiedtke. A number of colleagues also contributed as members of the Scientific Advisory Board, including David J. Telfer, Melissa Wan Hassan, Liz Sharples, Kevin Fields, Dallen Timothy, Anne-Mette Hjalager, Paul Ballantine, Gerrie du Rand, Dieter Müller, Lee Jolliffe and Bernard Lane; and, as members of the Organising Committee, Carlo Aall, Anneli Andersson, MaxMikael Björling, Christer Foghagen, Johan Hultman, Per Petterson-Löfquist and Hans Wessblad, at Linnaeus University, Lund University and Western Norway Research Institute. Support for the project also came from Sven Lindgren, County Governor, and Stephen Hwang, Rector of Linnaeus University.

Stefan would like to express his gratitude to the team at Linnaeus University for their great company, and the blind eye they turn to longer periods of absence in the name of the science. He is also thankful to those trying to understand our food structures, and acting to prevent our remaining on the path of agricultural industrialisation and concentration. Lastly, he would like to thank Meike and Linnea – who have put up with his own farming ambitions for three years now.

Michael would like to thank those who have assisted in the recovery from the impacts of the Canterbury and Christchurch earthquakes since September 2010, without whom this book would never have been completed. He would also like to be able to extol the virtues of living in a city where a temporary sports stadium can be built faster than public social housing or the decision-making on earthquake-affected property, but he can't. This book is therefore definitely not dedicated to Minister Gerry Brownlee or the Key-led government, but he remains reassured that the Christchurch Recovery has its goals as appropriately set on track as the country's climate change policy.

A number of colleagues with whom Michael has undertaken food research or discussed food- and tourism-related issues over the years have also contributed to this volume. In particular, thanks to Tim Baird, Richard Butler, Tim Coles, David Duval, Anna Grundén, Johan Hultman, John Jenkins, Richard Mitchell, Ghazali Musa, Dieter Müller, Stephen Page, Jarkko Saarinen, Anna Dóra Sæþórsdóttir, Liz Sharples, Brian and Delyse Springett, David J. Telfer, Sandra Wall, Melissa Wan Hassan, Sandra Wilson and Allan Williams for their thoughts, as well as for the stimulation of Beirut, Nick Cave, Bruce Cockburn, Elvis Costello, Stephen Cummings, Chris Difford and Glenn Tilbrook, Dimmer, Ebba Forsberg, Hoodoo Gurus, The Kills, Ed Kuepper, Jackson Code, Vinnie Reilly, David Sylvian, Twinemen, Jennifer Warnes, Chris Wilson, and the *Guardian* and the BBC – without whom the four walls of a hotel room would be much more confining. Finally, Michael would like to thank the many people who have supported his work over the years, and especially the Js and the Cs who stay at home, or whatever we now call home.

We would all like to extend our thanks to our editor Emma Travis at Routledge as well as to the rest of the team who have supported us over the project, particularly Carol Barber.

Part I
Introductory context

1 Sustainable culinary systems

An introduction

Stefan Gössling and C. Michael Hall

Eating, more than any other single experience, brings us into a full relationship with the natural world. This act itself calls forth the full embodiment of our senses – taste, smell, touch, hearing and sight. We know nature largely by the various ways we consume it. Eating establishes the most primordial of all human bonds with the environment ... [it] is the bridge that connects culture with nature....

(Rifkin 1992: 234)

Introduction

In April 2012, German newspapers reported that discounter Aldi, one of the largest retail chains in the world, had reduced the price of standard milk by almost 15 per cent to €0.48 per litre, and to €0.42 per litre for low fat milk (*Spiegel* 2012). German farmers protested, as in previous years, when the price of milk had been reduced by the discounter, and the spokesperson for agriculture of the Green Party suggested that 'consumers don't want [price-]dumped milk' (*Stern* 2012). As a reaction to the national news, *Badische Zeitung*, a regional newspaper with a specific children's page, unexcitedly informed its young readers that cows are now producing amounts of milk several orders of magnitude more than in historical times, while their life expectancy has – because of the strain of intensive milk production – massively declined. In the EU15, average per cow milk production is now 6,709 kg per year, reaching its highest level of 8,569 kg per cow per year in Denmark (EU 2012). This level has increased constantly since 2001, when the EU15 average was 5,998 kg per cow per year, with 7,070 kg per cow per year in Denmark, the EU's leader in agro-engineering in this sector. Milk production has for a long time been moving towards industrialization, equivalent to the full-scale industrialization of chicken and pig rearing, and animal welfare is clearly not relevant in this trend. It thus remains doubtful whether price-conscious consumers care about the background of price-dumped products: it is in particular the 'price aggressive retailers' that have continued to grow rapidly, according to Planet Retail (2011).

The example illustrates one of the many frictions between consumer expectations, retail concentration and increasing demands on sustainability in today's food production, with related sustainability implications including land conversion and the associated loss of biodiversity and ecosystems (Lawton and May 1995; Pimm *et al.* 1995; Vitousek *et al.* 1997a; Sage 2012); changes in global biogeochemical processes, such as nitrogen cycles (Vitousek *et al.* 1997b); water consumption (Chapagain and Hoekstra 2007, 2008; Hoekstra and Chapagain 2007); the use of substances potentially harmful to human health, such as pesticides, herbicides and fungicides (Koutros *et al.* 2008; Bhalli *et al.* 2009); and ethical questions, such as those relating to genetically modified organisms (Zollitsch *et al.* 2007). Another significant problem is the sector's contribution to global emissions of greenhouse gases (GHGs) from agriculture, food processing, storage, transport and the preparation of meals (Gössling *et al.* 2011) as well as the global contribution of processed foods to increasing levels of diet-related diseases and risk factors (cardiovascular, diabetes, obesity) (Hawkes 2008).

These issues will gain in importance in the future, as a growing world population and demand for high-protein food create pressure on farmers to produce increasing volumes of (protein-rich) food at declining unit costs. At the same time, oil prices, land availability and water competition are likely to make production more expensive, while extreme weather events related to climate change will increase the vulnerability of production, potentially aggravating the effects of biofuel production on agricultural lands (e.g. Royal Society 2008). Notably, there is now a rapid expansion of discounter chains from the developed countries in the emerging economies, leading to further concentration in the food sector. Of course, some will claim that the global commercial food and agriculture industry has actually contributed to a great food success story with respect to feeding the world. For example,

> World population has doubled while the available calories per head increased by 25 percent. Worldwide, households now spend less income on their daily food than ever before, in the order of 10–15 percent in the OECD countries, as compared to over 40 percent in the middle of the last century. Even if many developing countries still spend much higher but declining percentages, the diversity, quality and safety of food have improved nearly universally and stand at a historic high.
>
> (Fresco 2009: 379)

As Sage (2012: 2) observes, 'we have arrived as a point where food has become a highly contested arena of competing paradigms' (see also Lang and Heasman 2004). As a counterpoint to Fresco (2009), Sage (2012) notes a number of current shortcomings and weaknesses of the global agricultural and food system:

- Market mechanisms cannot ensure equitable access to food. An estimated one billion people around the world are experiencing hunger and malnutrition.
- The profit-seeking behaviour of food companies has encouraged the promotion of convenience, confectionary and snack products that are high in salt,

sugar and fat. Over one billion people in the world are overweight or obese and susceptible to diet-related disease.

- The declining share of food in household budgets

> does not reflect the true economic, social or environmental cost of its production, distribution and consumption. What we pay for food at the supermarket checkout does not take into account the loss of ecological services, the depletion of resources, the impairment of Earth system processes, and the rising medical costs of poorer human health.
>
> (Sage 2012: 3)

- Questions of delivering global food security to an increasingly urbanized and growing global population will require new approaches to ensure appropriate developmental, environmental and social justice outcomes.

Virtually all of these issues have direct and indirect links to tourism and hospitality. Tourism is of relevance in food consumption because of the enormous amounts of food prepared in both leisure and business tourism contexts, including the food consumed in restaurants, cafeterias and canteen kitchens as well as on board trains, aircraft, ferries or cruise ships. According to one estimate, some 75 billion meals per year, or just over 200 million meals per day, might be consumed in tourism (Gössling *et al.* 2011). In a broader setting, the food service sector (also known as catering), which includes the businesses and institutions responsible for any meal prepared outside the home, is responsible for a very high proportion of food sales. In 2002 the value of global sales of food was estimated at US$4.096 trillion, of this US$1.803 trillion or a little over 44 per cent of total sales by value was in the service sector, with the remainder in retail (Gehlhar and Regmi 2005). According to Gehlhar and Regmi (2005: 5), 'With consumers increasingly demanding convenience, it is likely that the value of global foodservice sales will overtake global retail food sales in the future.' Data for the UK (Table 1.1) indicate that although the relative proportion of consumer expenditure on catering services declined between 2008 and 2011 as a result of the economic climate, it still accounted for over 43 per cent of total sales. In addition, the catering sector employed 1.415 million people compared to 1.139 million people working in food retail (Department for Environment, Food and Rural Affairs (DEFRA) 2011).

Consumption of food is associated with both production and waste. It is estimated that total UK food and drink waste is around 15 million tonnes per year, with households generating 7.2 million tonnes/year of which 4.4 million tonnes are avoidable (DEFRA 2011). In 2009 the UK hospitality sector disposed of around 600,000 tonnes of food waste to landfill, of which almost two-thirds was avoidable. It is estimated that UK hospitality businesses pay approximately £1.02 billion a year for food that is subsequently wasted (DEFRA 2011). However, levels of food and drink waste generated by the hotels and catering sector had dropped by over 40 per cent between 2002–3 and 2009 (DEFRA 2011) (Table 1.2 illustrates UK food hospitality waste going to landfill).

Table 1.1 Consumer expenditure on catering services in the UK as proportion of total food expenditure, 2008–11

Food expenditure category	2008 £bn	%	2009 £bn	%	2010 £bn	%	2011 £bn	%
Consumer expenditure on catering services	82	47.7	81	46.8	78.7	45.2	74.9	43.1
Household expenditure on food and drink	90	52.3	92	53.2	95.1	54.8	98.7	56.9
Total consumer expenditure on food, drink and catering	172	100.0	173	100.0	174	100.0	173.6	100.0

Source: derived from DEFRA (2008, 2009, 2010, 2011).

Table 1.2 UK food hospitality waste going to landfill in 2009

Category	Avoidable '000 tonnes	% avoidable	Unavoidable '000 tonnes	Total waste '000 tonnes
Restaurants	167	69.6	73	240
Pubs	154	63.9	87	241
Hotels	40	63.5	23	63
Quick service restaurants	39	72.2	15	54
Total	400	66.9	198	598

Source: derived from DEFRA (2011).

Depending on the choices made by those responsible for purchases, this may increase or decrease the sustainability of the global food industry, in particular with regard to three issues. First, sustainability in food consumption is in the hands of a few decision makers. For instance, the initiative by hotel chain Scandic to purchase only organic and fairly traded coffee affects 20 million cups of coffee served per year (Scandic 2012). In contrast, the German railways company (Deutsche Bahn) sources its foodstuffs from all over the world, with chicken and beef being imported from South America. Second, food service establishments can potentially cook food more efficiently, as the simultaneous preparation of many meals typically entails lower energy use per meal (Carlsson-Kanyama *et al.* 2003). At the same time, restaurants may offer more complex and hence energy-intense food creations, also generating higher amounts of food waste (e.g. Swedish Environmental Protection Agency 2008). Third, food purchases have considerable influence on the globalization of the food industry. Evidence suggests, for instance, that purchasing strategies are generally characterized by a focus on the lowest per-unit costs, leading to growing pressure on food producers. This, in turn, encourages the industrialization of food production, which Vos (2000) argues has led to many of its current problems, including outbreaks of swine fever and bovine spongiform encephalopathy.

Over the longer term, tourism and hospitality also influence foodways, food value chains and distribution channels. Globalization not only affects contemporary foodways and food systems but also has an important historical context.

> Single, local ecology food, is a peculiarly twenty-first-century construct. Sugar, the potato, the tomato, maize and many other 'New World' foods transformed the range and scope of culinary expression, but in distinct and uneven ways in different European food provisioning and culinary systems.
>
> (Harvey *et al.* 2004: 202)

The globalization of some foods to the extent that they are integral to the cuisine of regions far away from their natural ecological range is testimony to the complexity of the interactions between agricultures, food consumption, trade and tourism as well as the development of food media (Mintz 1986; Zuckerman 1999; Hall and Mitchell 2000; Green *et al.* 2003; Harvey *et al.* 2003). As Probyn (1998: 161) commented, the global–local tension of localization is

> compellingly problematized by food. Whether overly politicized or not, eating scrambles neat demarcations and points to the messy interconnections of the local and the global, the inside and the outside. Food systems (from production to consumption) highlight the singular and current ways in which the private is becoming public, and the public is being privatized.

This book does not focus on all these issues, but it aims to develop a range of related perspectives so as to initiate awareness and debate about the role of tourism and hospitality in the global food system and, ultimately, its sustainability. Firstly, food consumption is widely recognized to be an essential part of the tourism experience (Hjalager and Richards 2002; Boniface 2003; Hall *et al.* 2003; Hall and Sharples 2008). For instance, locally distinctive food can be important both as a tourism attraction in itself and in helping to shape the image of a destination (Hall *et al.* 2003; Cohen and Avieli 2004; du Rand and Heath 2006). Since the 1990s a number of articles have emphasized the potential for local food experiences to contribute to sustainable development, help maintain regional identities and support agricultural diversification, particularly through the support of particular products and the creation and maintenance of backward linkages (Telfer and Wall 1996; Knowd 2006; Clark and Chabrel 2007; Everett and Aitchison 2008; Sims 2009). Other writers have identified the market potential for 'gastronomic tourism', arguing that it potentially has strong sustainability credentials if grounded in local foods (Hjalanger and Richards 2002; Hall 2003; Hall *et al.* 2003; du Rand and Heath 2006; Nummedal and Hall 2006). These findings suggest that both the production and the consumption of food are important aspects in the development of sustainable tourism and sustainable culinary systems.

Culinary systems

Although the utility of a systems approach to integrate the various elements of travel and the simultaneous consumption and production of tourism experiences and products has been well established in tourism for many years (Hall 2008), the notion of a culinary system is not so well recognized. In food studies the concept of a culinary system has historically tended to be interpreted as another way of describing foodways and food styles (Clark 1975; Murcott 1982; London 2000; Parasecoli 2001; Hegarty 2006; van Esterik 2006), rather than being one way of also describing how food consumption is linked to supply and value chains and environmental factors (Horng and Lee 2009). For example, Rozin (1990) argues that culinary systems are mainly comprised of rules about appropriate contexts for eating foods. A broader perspective, which is more in keeping with the approach taken in this volume, although still with an anthropological base, comes from Mintz (2006) who observes with respect to the changes to local cuisines as a result of modernization:

> The progressive emergence of a global system has worn away at local culinary systems ... even as it has provided certain benefits. In the West, local or regional cuisines have been modified – occasionally even eliminated in large measure – by freezers, new processing and preservation techniques such as irradiation, packaged foods, improved transport and the like. Similar changes are rapidly unfolding in the non-Western world as well.
>
> (Mintz 2006: 6)

Such cultural economy approaches (Wilks 2006) highlight the importance of a stronger dialectical articulation of the relationship between the material (e.g. products, design, transport networks, technology) and the immaterial (place branding, marketing, identity, image) dimensions of the way in which food is produced and consumed. In the case of tourism for example, such an approach may help shed light on the 'symbolic economy' of food and its role in regional competitiveness strategies as well as the way in which food, and cultural discourses of food difference and otherness, become part of entrepreneurial place strategies. For example, Tschofen (2008) traces the use of 'culinary heritage' as a concept in regional practices and European politics, and analyses how everyday food practices are transformed first into cultural heritage, and then into cultural property via EU regulatory structures with respect to the intellectual property of place and the food quality assurance system. This perspective is also somewhat shared by Clark (1975) in one of the first uses of the culinary system concept: 'the production of cuisine is both a culinary and a cultural process, which involves what may be termed a culinary system. This system has distinct sectors for the creation, production, diffusion and consumption of cuisine' (Clark 1975: 198).

Important to the culinary systems perspective adopted in the present work is the interaction of different ecologies of food production and consumption with socio-cultural differences. 'Different ecologies clearly have a major impact on food provisioning systems, in terms of variety, aesthetic characteristics, nutritional value and content' (Harvey *et al.* 2004: 201). However, most ecologies of food are best understood as cultivated ecologies in that the ecologies of production have been socially constructed in both perception and reality. It is these cultivated ecologies that form the basis of interactions between environments and natural capital and socio-economic and cultural processes that affect not only food in tourism and hospitality but also broader issues of food security. Indeed, Harvey *et al.* (2004: 202) note that

> transfers from one ecology to another involved both a cultivation and a consumption transformation, new agricultural processes and hybrids, as well as new cuisines and culinary hybrids. It is difficult to think of quality transformations in other domains that involve this kind of complex interaction with ecologies.

Arguably the most significant ecology of food overall for environmental sustainability, in which tourism and hospitality are deeply embedded, is that configured by mass urbanization. As Harvey *et al.* (2004: 202) observe, 'this ecosystem is one in which the quality and sustainability of mass urban food has become the irreversibly dominant feature, and has generated issues of standardization, aesthetics, nutrition and hygiene that are quite specific to the quality of food.' If there is to be a more sustainable alternative to the ecological modernization of food, what is often referred to as part of the process of McDonaldization (Ritzer 1998), then there will have to be a response to the implications for food systems of mass urbanization.

Sustainable culinary systems

The notion of 'sustainability' in its broadest sense, as opposed only to the reduction in the environmental impact of individual products or agricultural or industrial processes on a productivist per capita or per unit of output basis, 'requires thinking in "systemic terms"' (Green *et al.* 2003: 146: see also Lifset and Graedel 2002; Hall 2008, 2010a). Food consumption and production systems are therefore defined to 'include the whole "chain" of human-organized activities concerned with the production, processing, transport, selling, cooking and eating of food and the disposal of the wastes of such activities' (Green *et al.* 2003: 146: see also Tansey and Worsley 1995; Millstone and Lang 2008; Sage 2012). These include:

*   the inputs to farming (including water, chemicals, seeds and machinery);
*   the agricultural sector (including fishing and commercial hunting and gathering);
*   the food processing and packaging industries;
*   food distribution (including wholesaling and retailing and the transport associated with these);
*   equipment for food storage and preparation;
*   hospitality and food 'service' (i.e. restaurants, catering and institutional food providers);
*   the household activities of shopping, cooking and clearing up;
*   the disposal and recycling of food, water and packaging wastes;
*   resource inputs into the food system including water, energy, material for packaging, chemicals and storage; and
*   outputs from the system such as emissions and other pollutants that are not recycled.

Figure 1.1 provides an illustration of the flow of food materials and some of the inputs and outputs of the system that highlight resources use and potential waste and environmental impacts. The system is shown as being embedded in a natural resource base which provides the basis for the system but is also affected by the rate of use as well as the pollutants from the food system. At each stage of the

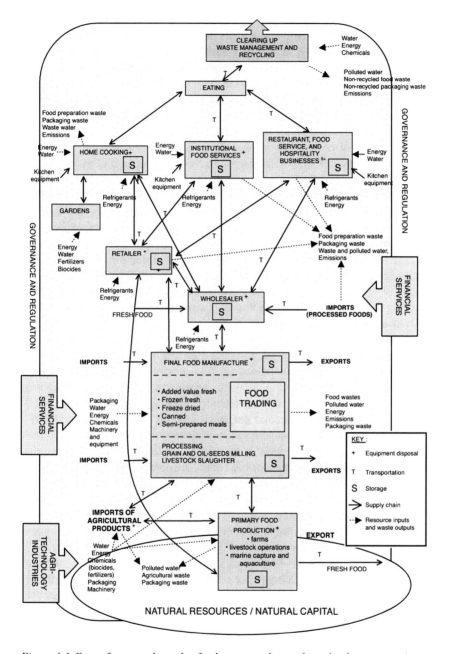

Figure 1.1 From farm to plate: the food consumption and production system (source: After Green *et al.* 2001, 2003; Green 2003, Von Braun and Diaz-Bonilla 2008; Sage 2012).

system from farm to plate there are significant environmental and resource use impacts. The system is also in part structured by the provision of financial services, governance and regulation, as well as the role of the agro-food industry.

Nevertheless, as Green *et al.* (2003) themselves identified, 'there is of course a problem in partitioning the complex of human–human and human–ecology interactions into such "systems".... Food production is often combined with non-food agriculture.... Moreover, agricultural production in general cannot be seen as autonomous.' However, perhaps most significantly, the consumption of food is also socially constructed. This means that culture and history, as well as the economic and political dimensions of food systems, also need to be considered in order to understand better how food systems have developed and may be transformed. Therefore, this book uses the concept of a culinary system the better to express the importance of the cultural economy of food and foodways and their consumption and production as well as the cultivated ecologies on which they are based. In addition, the notion of a culinary system also brings to the fore the major role that tourism- and hospitality-related food services play in the food system. Indeed, given their centrality to food production and consumption processes, and therefore to the sustainability of food resources, it is remarkable that so little attention has been given to this role and its contribution to food-related global change.

Bearing in mind the needs of present and future generations, *a sustainable culinary system must be able to demonstrate that it can optimize food output and consumption without compromising the stock of natural capital and ecosystem services.* In order to achieve this, the analysis and understanding of culinary systems need to include all aspects of the system extending from agricultural and aquacultural production and fishing, hunting and foraging through to all subsequent stages of processing, distribution and transport, retailing, cooking and presentation to the consumption of food and the management of waste. Following Sage (2012), implicit in the notion of a sustainable culinary system is that each stage must seek to minimize the use of non-renewable resources, e.g. fossil fuels, and ensure that the utilization of renewable resources is within their stock regeneration capacity, e.g. wild salmon fisheries. In addition, waste streams should be kept to a minimum and pollution levels, including emissions, need to be within the capacity of ecosystems to remediate them. Finally, Sage (2012: 5) argues that any sustainable food system should also be 'committed to the principle of social justice, which means working to ensure the achievement of food [and] ... nutritional ... security for all'.

Before moving to an assessment of the different ways in which different stakeholders assess sustainability in the culinary system, the chapter will discuss some of the major global food issues that provide a context for the need to develop more sustainable culinary systems.

Food security

Over the past 60 years, the global population has almost tripled from 2.5 billion in 1950 to about seven billion in 2010 (UN 2011). By 2050, it is anticipated that the world population may reach at least eight billion (low fertility variant), with an upper-range scenario of 10.5 billion (high fertility variant). While there might be a marked decline in the world population over the second half of the century, the likely scenario is that there will be some nine billion people by mid-century, with a concomitant increase in average wealth. This, in turn, will lead to higher consumption and greater demand for high-protein foods such as meat, dairy products and fish, as well as processed foods, all of which are known to add pressure on the food supply system. These trends are already visible. For instance, over the past 50 years there has been a 1.5-fold increase in global cattle, sheep and goat numbers, and 2.5- to 4.5-fold increases in the number of pigs and chicken respectively (FAOSTAT 2009). Overall, it is anticipated that by 2050, world food demand will be 70–100 per cent higher than it is today (World Bank 2008; Royal Society 2009).

As outlined by Godfray *et al.* (2010: 812), feeding about nine billion people will require radical changes in the way food is produced, stored, processed, distributed and accessed. There have been considerable productivity gains, with for instance grain production more than doubling since 1960, compared to growth in arable land by only 9 per cent. In the future, however, Godfray *et al.* (2010) suggest that options to take further land into agricultural use are limited, as competition from other human activities is too significant, and they conflict with other objectives, such as carbon storage in rainforests or the conservation of biodiversity. Vice versa, considerable land areas have been lost to urbanization and other human uses, as well as environmental change including desertification, salinization or soil erosion. In order to increase productivity, Godfray *et al.* (2010) suggest that it will be necessary to close yield gaps (the difference between actual and possible production); to increase production limits, for which biotechnology and GM technologies would have to be accepted by consumers; to reduce waste, given that some 30–40 per cent of food in both developed and developing worlds is lost to waste; to change diets, i.e. reduce the share of meat and in particular red meat in food consumption; and to expand aquaculture.

Global food production is characterized by industrialization and concentration, with a few large-scale actors having power over a considerable share of overall food production. Concentration processes appear to be followed up in particular by critical non-governmental organizations, with for instance Erklärung von Bern (2011) suggesting that 16 per cent of global animal feed production, 55 per cent of global fertilizer production, 74 per cent of global seed production, and 90 per cent of global pesticide production are in the hands of the 10 largest agri-businesses. Similar concentrations are suggested to exist in meat production, with for instance 99 per cent of the world's poultry production apparently being managed by just four companies (Figure 1.2).

Furthermore, 75 per cent of the world's trade in wheat and soya is managed by four businesses, and 28 per cent of all food processing (in commercial value) by 10 businesses. Almost 11 per cent of all food retail is in the hands of 10 large corporations, Walmart, Carrefour, Schwarz Group, Tesco, Aldi, Kroger, AEON, Edeka, Rewe Group and Ahold. Vertical linkages exist between many of the largest companies, such as those involved in seed production and pharmaceuticals/

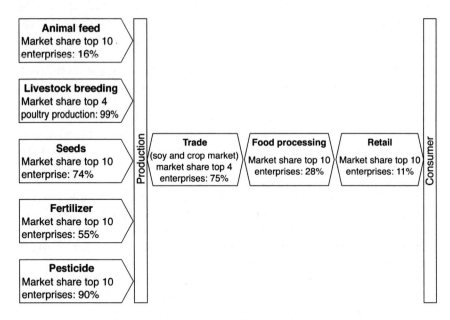

Figure 1.2 Share of largest corporations in food production (source: adapted from Erklärung von Bern 2011).

pesticides. For instance, Monsanto produces 27 per cent of all seeds (in terms of commercial value), and owns some 25 associated pharmaceutical/chemical businesses (see also UNCTAD 2006, 2009). Aggressive price pressing strategies are now also becoming evident in non-related retail sectors, with for instance furniture retailer IKEA offering a growing assortment of extremely cheap processed foods. As prices for the processed foods offered are in many cases not even likely to cover purchasing and preparation (staff) costs, these need to be seen as strategies to attract consumers by offering subsidized food. A secondary effect of such retail strategies is that they distort the consumers' understanding of what can be considered 'normal', 'low' or 'acceptable' prices for food, as well as of which foods are 'trendy'. Notably, IKEA does not reveal where its foods are sourced, other than to mention cooperation with 44 suppliers and its strong commitment to sustainability (IKEA 2011).

Changing diets and trends in consumption

A growing world population demands more food, and changes in dietary preferences towards higher-order foods, with trends towards more intensive production of beef, poultry and pork being observable in many parts of the developing world (Smith *et al.* 2009). Alexandratos (2006) shows, for instance, that per capita food consumption has been growing from 2,411 kcal per person per day around 1970 to 2,789 kcal per person per day in the year 2000, with further growth expected by 2050 (3,130 kcal per person per day). Average values conceal considerable differences between per capita per day food consumption values in developing countries (2,111 kcal, 1970) and industrialized nations (3,046 kcal, 1970); these, however, will become more equitable towards 2050 (3,540 kcal in industrialized and 3,070 kcal in developing countries).

Table 1.3 also shows that there has been a large increase in the consumption of calories from meat, with the most dramatic changes visible in China, i.e. the most populous country in the world. Consumption of meat has grown by 349 per cent over the 40-year period covered by statistics, and vegetable oil consumption by 680 per cent (Kearney 2010). Notably, diet change in a two-stage pattern: an expansion effect, where the main change in calorie consumption stems from additional cheap foodstuffs of vegetable origin, is followed by a substitution effect, where carbohydrate-rich staples (cereals, roots, tubers) are replaced by vegetable oils, animal products (meat and dairy products) and sugar. While the first stage of change has been observed globally, the second is influenced by culture and religious traditions, and is regionally different.

Kearney (2010) suggests that the main drivers of food consumption are income, urbanization, trade liberalization, transnational food corporations (franchises and manufacturers), retailing, food industry marketing, and consumer attitudes and behaviour. While income as a variable is self-evident, 'urbanization' entails marketing, distribution infrastructures, large supermarkets owned by multinational corporations, and better transport systems and imports of food supplies, leading to a greater range of food choices and higher calorific intake despite lower physical actvitity. In the UK the eating out diet contributed 10.8 per cent of energy intake in 2010, excluding energy from alcohol. It contains more fat and protein but less carbohydrate and non-milk extrinsic sugar than the household diet (DEFRA 2011). Both mono-unsaturated and poly-unsaturated fatty acids are higher in the eating out diet while saturated fatty acids are lower (DEFRA 2011).

Trade liberalization can affect the food consumption of the poor; in particular it is affected by foreign investment in food distribution and retail, and greater availability of processed foods, meat and dairy products – most of which imply changes in diets towards calorie-rich and nutrient-poor choices. Transnational food corporations include in particular fast-food outlets and producers of processed foods, also fostering less healthy and less sustainable diets. With regard to retailing, Kearney (2010: 2804) notes the rapid expansion of supermarkets in Latin America, concluding that 'where supermarkets have made major inroads into the food retailing system, the entire food economy from farm to fork is affected'. Food industry marketing has influenced consumption, a notable example being the change in milk consumption in the USA, which switched from four times more milk than carbonated soft drinks in 1945 to two and a half times more carbonated beverages than milk in 1995 (Kearney 2010: 2804).

Several other trends of relevance, including organic, functional and genetically modified foods, will drive the development of diets (Kearney 2010).

Table 1.3 Changes in food calories

	Meat	% change 1963–2003	Sugar	% change 1963–2003	Pulses	% change 1963–2003	Roots and tubers	% change 1963–2003	Vegetable oils	% 1963–2003	Wheat	% change 1963–2003	Rice	% change 1963–2003
Developing countries														
1963	147		75		167		178		80		245		580	
1983	210		128		113		157		145		453		694	
2003	369	119	170	127	99	–41	154	–13	239	199	457	87	655	13
Industrialized countries														
1963	833		349		40		145		241		592		188	
1983	929		337		29		112		385		559		145	
2003	958	15	328	–6	37	–75	112	–23	494	105	627	6	153	–19
China														
1963	90		18		143		255		35		194		637	
1983	192		54		50		222		95		534		962	
2003	644	349	73	305	17	–88	176	–31	273	680	448	131	790	24

Source: Kearney (2010).

Organic farming is characterized by strong growth trends, with some 30 million hectares being certified worldwide, mostly in Australia (12.3 million ha), China (2.3 million ha), Argentina (2.2 million ha) and the USA (1.5 million ha) (Paull 2008). Demand for certified foods is highest in the EU, and in particular the UK, Italy and Germany. This demand is expected to grow, though scepticism has been voiced regarding the options of extending organic agriculture in a world with sharply increasing food demands, as it gives lower yields per hectare (Kearney 2010). Functional foods refer to consumer demand focusing on both convenience and health, and even in this area market shares are expected to increase. Genetically modified foods, on the other hand, face considerable scepticism in some markets, but are seen as an essential component of feeding a larger world population. Food consumption drivers and the sustainability of the system are summarized in Figure 1.3.

Emissions and climate change

Climate change is a key issue for food production and consumption, because agriculture and food production chains are major contributors to emissions of greenhouse gases. At the same time, agriculture will be affected by climate change, as increasing temperatures will, beyond a certain threshold, increase production vulnerabilities. An even greater risk comes from potential changes in weather patterns, i.e. heat waves, storms, heavy rainfall, or outbreaks of pests and the introduction of invasive species (Schneider *et al.* 2007).

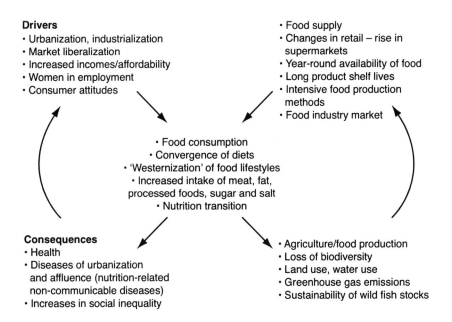

Figure 1.3 Drivers of food consumption changes (source: modified from Kearney 2010).

Agriculture accounted for between 10 and 12 per cent of total anthropogenic GHG emissions in 2005 (Smith *et al.* 2009). Most problematic are the sector's emissions of methane (CH_4) and nitrous oxide (N_2O), to which agriculture contributes 47 per cent and 58 per cent respectively of the global anthropogenic total (Smith *et al.* 2009). Both methane and nitrous oxide are potent GHGs, with one molecule of CH_4 having a global warming potential (GWP) 21 times that of carbon dioxide (CO_2) and the GWP of N_2O corresponding to 310 times that of CO_2 (time horizon: 100 years; IPCC 1995). Emissions from global fisheries would have to be added to those from agriculture, accounting for an estimated 50 billion litres of fuel per annum, corresponding to about 1.2 per cent of global oil consumption (Tyedmers 2001; Tyedmers *et al.* 2005). Food production and consumption also include packaging, retailing, transport and preparation, all of which add considerably to overall emissions from this sector. Tukker *et al.* (2006) estimate that what people eat has more impact on climate change than any other aspect of daily life, with the EU food supply chain accounting for 31 per cent of the global warming potential of products consumed within the then EU15 (also see Tukker and Jansen 2006). A calculation made on an end-use-consumption basis revealed that food consumption accounts for more than 20 per cent of Norway's total GHG emissions (Hille *et al.* 2008). This figure might be considered representative of a large number of industrialized countries. For example, around 115 million tonnes of CO_2 equivalent GHGs (CO_2e) were emitted within the UK from domestic food chain activity in 2009, excluding emissions from non-fertilizer pre-farm production, overseas production, food packaging, food waste and land use change. Of this six million tonnes came directly from catering services. The UK farming and fishing sector was the largest contributor, accounting for 53 million tonnes CO_2e. It is estimated that a further 59 million tonnes CO_2e per year are attributable to overseas emissions as a result of the production of imported food (DEFRA 2011). Catering accounts directly for almost 10 per cent (2.7 million tonnes oil equivalent) of the total energy use (28.4 million tonnes oil equivalent) in the UK food chain. However, as with the emissions figure provided this does not include the food service-related proportion of fertilizer production, farming and fishing, food manufacturing and transport.

In the future, emissions from the culinary system will increase unless there is a dramatic transformation. A growing demand for meat, for instance, requires greater use of irrigation and fertilizer for animal feed production, which in turn increases the demand for energy. It also induces changes in land use, for instance from forest to grassland: a process that inevitably leads to CO_2 emissions (Smith *et al.* 2009). Food production and its analogue, food consumption, are consequently of critical importance in the current and future development of GHG emissions.

Climate change will also affect agriculture. Under various climate change scenarios, food security is a key concern. Low-latitude areas are most at risk of seeing decreased crop yields, while mid- and high-latitude areas may see increases in crop yields under temperature increases of up to 3°C. Notably, the impact of climate change will vary by location. According to the IPCC, there is some evidence (low to medium confidence) that beyond 3°C, global production will decline because of climate change and that this decline would continue as global mean temperatures increase (Schneider *et al.* 2007). It is also important to note that most studies of the effects of climate change on agriculture have not incorporated critical factors such as changes in extreme events or the spread of pests and diseases.

The climate change dimension of food has not been covered in great depth in the tourism literature. No study has yet been published that considers in detail the interrelationships implicit in tourism-related food consumption, energy use and GHG emissions. A few studies have attempted to incorporate food into the total ecological footprint of tourism at a specific destination, or in particular hotels (e.g. WWF-UK 2002; Peeters and Schouten 2006). However, such studies tend to be limited by the vast amount of data required to develop sophisticated food management carbon inventories.

In an analysis of the greenhouse gas intensity of various meats, only studies that included production on the farm have been compared (Gössling *et al.* 2011). Table 1.4, for instance, compares potatoes, carrots, onions, lettuce, tomatoes and cucumbers on a farming lifecycle basis. Several conclusions can be drawn from

Table 1.4 Greenhouse gas intensity of various vegetables

Vegetable	$kgCO_2e/kg$	$kgCO_2e/1000kcal$	Country	Source
Potatoes	0.158	0.247	UK	DEFRA (2007)
	0.160	0.250	Denmark	LCA Food (2003)
	0.261–0.274	0.442–0.464	Netherlands	Kok *et al.* (2001)[a,b]
	0.073–0.083	0.114–0.130	Sweden	Cederberg *et al.* (2005)[a]
	0.100	0.156	Sweden	Mattsson *et al.* (2001)
Carrots	0.046	0.144	UK	DEFRA (2007)
	0.122–0.234	0.381–0.730	Denmark	Miljøstyreisen (2006)[a,c]
	0.036	0.112	Sweden	Cederberg *et al.* (2005)
Onions	0.060	0.201	Sweden	Cederberg *et al.* (2005)
	0.079	0.265	UK	DEFRA (2007)
	0.382	1.28	Denmark	Miljøstyreisen (2006)
Lettuce	0.602	5.46	UK	DEFRA (2007)
Tomatoes (greenhouse)	0.082 (unheated)	0.456 (unheated)	Spain	Antón *et al.* (2005)[d]
	1.30	7.20	Sweden	Möller Nielsen (2007)
	5.90–28.50	33.00–158.00	UK	Williams *et al.* (2006)[e]
	3.45–4.92	19.10–27.30	Denmark	Miljøstyreisen (2006)[a]
Cucumber (greenhouse)	4.37	45.00	Denmark	Miljøstyreisen (2006)

Source: Gössling *et al.* (2011).

Notes
System boundary: farm production including all greenhouse gases based on lifecycle analysis.
a Lower value: conventional, higher value: organic production.
b Own calculation to include other GHGs.
c Organic production.
d Greenhouse, unheated.
e Higher values relate to cocktail tomatoes.

the comparison. First, even though only a few vegetables are considered, there are considerable differences in emissions. For example, the production of cucumbers in heated greenhouses leads to emissions up to 180 times higher per calorie than the production of tomatoes, onions or potatoes in the field. Imports are not necessarily better, as the implications of transport distance and transport mode have to be considered.

Table 1.5 shows that figures for meat production are less variable than, for vegetable production. Thus beef production per 1,000 kcal will lead to emissions of about 10 kg CO_2 equivalent, lamb about 8 kg CO_2e, chicken and turkey 7 kg CO_2e, and pork 2 kg CO_2e. Note, however, that various assumptions have been

Table 1.5 Greenhouse gas intensity of various meats

Meat	kgCO₂e/kg	kgCO₂e/1,000 kcal	Country	Source
Beef	29.00	16.10	Denmark	LCA Food (2003)[b]
	15.00	8.30	Sweden	LRF (2002)
	19.00–22.00	10.60–12.20	Sweden	Cederberg and Darelius (2000)[c]
	24.00	13.30	Sweden	Cederberg and Nilsson (2004)
	18.00–28.00	10.00–15.60	Ireland	Casey and Holden (2006)
	11.60–18.40	6.40–10.20	Germany	Hirschfeld *et al.* (2008)
	22.30–22.90	12.40–12.70	Germany	Hirschfeld *et al.* (2008)[d]
	18.00	10.00	Netherlands	Kok *et al.* (2001)[b]
	13.40	7.40	Sweden	LRF (2002)
Lamb	*c.*19.00	8.30	UK	DEFRA (2007)[b]; Williams *et al.* (2006)
Pork	3.75	1.50	Denmark	LCA Food (2003)
	4.80	1.90	Sweden	Cederberg and Darelius (2001)
	5.10–8.80	2.00–3.50	France	Basset-Mens and van der Werf (2005)[a,b]
	2.70–4.00	1.10–2.60	Germany	Hirschfeld *et al.* (2008)[a]
	4.25	1.70	Sweden	LRF (2002)
Chicken	*c.*3.70	6.90	Denmark	LCA Food 2003
	8.17	7.60	Netherlands	Kok *et al.* 2001[b]
	1.35	1.25	Sweden	LRF 2002
Chicken and turkey	*c.*7.10–10.30	6.60–9.50	UK	Williams *et al.* 2006[a]

Source: Gössling *et al.* (2011).

Notes
Conversion factors used: 1 kg beef = 1,800 kcal, 1 kg lamb = 2,300 kcal, 1 kg pork = 2,500 kcal, and 1 kg chicken = 1,080 kcal.
a Lower value refers to conventional, higher value to organic production.
b Own calculation, involving other sources.
c Organic production.
d Higher values relate to conventional production, lower value to organic production.

made to allow for comparison, and these are less consistent in the case of chicken. Overall, the studies seem to imply that pork is climatically more favourable than chicken, which again is more favourable than lamb and beef. Beef is found to be around five times more GHG emissions-intense than pork.

Table 1.6 illustrates the energy use entailed in transporting 1 kg of various foodstuffs by various means of transport. While imports of melons from Brazil have a comparative small footprint, imports of grapes by aircraft from South Africa imply the greatest kg CO_2/kg. Transport by air is generally most CO_2-intensive. The table also allows for a direct comparison between two modes of transporting tomatoes to Germany from Spain, suggesting that their transport by road may be nine times more CO_2-intensive than their transport by rail. This effect is entirely due to the different fuel efficiencies of these two modes of transporting tomatoes.

Similar results have also been reported in a Swedish case study presented by Carlsson-Kanyama and González (2009), who found that differences in emissions per kg of edible product vary between 0.4 and 30 kg CO_2e (case study involving 20 food items). For protein-rich foods, there is a difference of up to a factor of 30 in emission intensity, comparing for instance legumes, poultry and eggs to beef, cheese or pork. Lowest emissions are found for foods rich in carbohydrates, and the authors suggest that changes in diets towards more plants, meat from animals with little enteric fermentation to avoid CH_4 emissions, and towards foods processed energy-efficiently may make a considerable contribution to emission reductions. In the UK it is estimated that although air freight of food accounts for only 1 per cent of food tonne kilometres, it produces 12 per cent of the food transport CO_2e emissions (DEFRA 2011).

Seafood has a small carbon footprint in comparison to meat, even though Tyedmers *et al.* (2005; italics added) highlight that '*From an efficiency perspective, the energy content of the fuel burned by global fisheries is 12.5 times greater than the edible-protein energy content of the resulting catch.*' Fuel consumption in global fisheries depends to a considerable degree on how the fish are caught, as lifecycle analysis suggests that 75–90 per cent of energy use is related to harvesting (Tyedmers 2001). For example, per tonne of deep-sea fish, including important commercial species such as cod, fuel use for ships can vary between 230 and 2,724 litres. For pelagic species, including herring and mackerel, values are lower at 19 to 159 litres/tonnes. The highest fuel use is entailed in shrimp fisheries, with per-tonne fuel use varying between 331 and 2,342 litres (Tyedmers 2001). These values affect emissions per calorie of food, which vary between 0.085 kg CO_2e/1,000 kcal for mackerel (Tyedmers 2001) and 109 kg CO_2e/1,000 kcal for lobster (LCA Food 2003). The variation is by a factor of 1,280, which is by more than three orders of magnitude. High-energy input values have also been reported for aquaculture, with for instance shrimp production in China requiring 38 GJ of energy per ton of live weight. However, reported emissions of greenhouse gases are considerably lower at 0.4 tonnes CO_2e per tonne of shrimp (Cao *et al.* 2011; for a national comparison (Norway) see also Winther *et al.* 2009). As most of these may be for long-distance export and even processing, considerable emissions may arise from transport.

Table 1.6 Emissions involved in transporting various foodstuffs in Germany

Food transported (1 kg)	Distance		Distance source	CO₂	
	Great circle (km)	Corrected (km)[a]		kg CO₂/tkm[b]	kg CO₂/kg food
1 Grapes by aircraft from South Africa	8,690	9,125	www.webflyer.com/travel/milage_calculater/	0.725	6.62
2 Nile perch by aircraft from Tanzania	6,980	7,329	www.webflyer.com/travel/milage_calculater/	0.725	5.31
3 Strawberries by aircraft from Egypt	2,910	3,056	www.webflyer.com/travel/milage_calculater/	0.725	2.22
4 Melons by ship from Brazil		9,723	www.portworld.com/map/	0.015	0.15
5 Tomatoes by truck from Spain		2,333	www.maps.google.com/	0.160	0.37
6 Tomatoes by train from Spain		2,441	www.maps.google.com/ (shortest rail route)	0.015	0.04

Source: Gössling *et al.* (2011).

Notes
a Aircraft cannot usually fly directly between two points, so a detour factor has been used to correct for this.
b Emission factors based on Gilbert and Perl (2008), Léonardi and Baumgartner (2004) and Zachariadis and Kouvaritakis (2003).

Water use

Only 3 per cent of the water on Earth is fresh water suitable for drinking and agriculture (Sage 2012), yet human water use has tripled over the past 50 years on a global scale (Carbon Disclosure Project 2010). Depending on our diet it is estimated that we *eat* between 1,600 and 5,000 litres of water per day (Sage 2012). The most water-consuming activity is irrigation for agriculture, which accounts for 70 per cent of total water withdrawals and more than 90 per cent of consumptive water use (Bates *et al.* 2008). Agriculture is also the most important factor in the future growth of water consumption (Bates *et al.* 2008), a trend that is in conflict with the decline of available water resources in many regions due to the depletion of non-renewable fossil water resources (both groundwater and glacial ice), pollution of water bodies and groundwater sources, and climate change leading to declining precipitation levels and increased frequency of drought, increased evaporation, and changes in patterns of runoff (IPCC 2007; Parry *et al.* 2009a, 2009b). Specifically, anticipated changes in large-scale hydrological cycles under climate change include:

- Climate models project annual increases in precipitation in the high latitudes and parts of the tropics, and decreases in sub-tropical and lower mid-latitude regions.
- Climate models also project an increase in annual average river runoff and water availability in high latitudes and some wet tropical areas, and decreases over dry regions at mid-latitudes and in the dry tropics.
- Increased precipitation intensity and variability are also projected, resulting in greater likelihood of flooding and drought in many areas.
- Higher water temperatures and changes in extremes, including floods and droughts, will affect water quality and exacerbate many forms of water pollution.
- Changes in water quantity and quality would also affect food availability, stability, access and utilization.
- The operation of existing water infrastructure, including hydropower, structural flood defences, drainage and irrigation systems, and water supply and treatment systems will be affected by these on-going and future climate-induced hydrological changes (Bates *et al.* 2008).

Food production is consequently contributing to large-scale water abstractions, and will also be affected by changes in the availability of water for agriculture. Over the past decade, considerable advances in the assessment of the water content of various foodstuffs have been made (Hoekstra 2003, 2008; Hoekstra *et al.* 2012). To produce 1 kg of wheat may require between 500 and 4,000 litres of water, while 1 kg of beef takes at least 10,000 litres (Hoekstra and Chapagain 2007). Table 1.7 gives water requirements for selected foods: 1 kg of fruit, for instance, may entail water use of 700–880 litres, while the production of 1 kg of chocolate consumes 24,000 litres (Hoekstra 2008).

More detailed studies have investigated the food sectors of nations or specific foods. For instance, Liu and Savenije (2008) estimate that in the case of China, per capita water requirements for food have increased from 255 m³ per capita per year in 1961 to 860 m³ per capita per year in 2003, with a total national water requirement of 1.127 km³ per year in 2003. Based on scenario analysis, the authors conclude that an additional 407–515 km³ per year will be required in 2030 compared to 2003, adding pressure on the country's limited water resources. A considerable amount of the water footprint of the culinary system is also lost in the form of waste. In the UK the water footprint of avoidable and possibly avoidable household food waste is 6,200 million m³ per year, representing nearly 6 per cent of all UK water requirements. Only a quarter of this water footprint represents water used to grow and process food in the UK (DEFRA 2011).

Aldaya and Hoekstra (2010) analyse the water footprint of pizza and pasta products in Italy. They conclude that a pizza with a weight of 0.725 kg entails a water footprint of 1.215 litres, 73 per cent of this a result of mozzarella cheese, 24 per cent related to wheat flour, and 3 per cent to tomato puree. In this case,

Table 1.7 Water footprint of various foodstuffs

Food item	Unit	Global average water footprint (litres)
Apple or pear	1 kg	700
Banana	1 kg	860
Beef	1 kg	15,500
Beer (from barley)	1 glass of 250 ml	75
Bread (from wheat)	1 kg	1,300
Cabbage	1 kg	200
Cheese	1 kg	5,000
Chicken	1 kg	3,900
Chocolate	1 kg	24,000
Coffee	1 250 ml glass	140
Cucumber or pumpkin	1 kg	240
Dates	1 kg	3,000
Groundnuts (in shell)	1 kg	3,100
Lettuce	1 kg	130
Maize	1 kg	900
Mango	1 kg	1,600
Milk	1 250 ml glass	250
Olives	1 kg	4,400
Orange	1 kg	460
Peach or nectarine	1 kg	1,200
Pork	1 kg	4,800
Potato	1 kg	250
Rice	1 kg	3,400
Sugar (from sugar cane)	1 kg	1,500
Tea	1 250 ml glass	30
Tomato	1 kg	180
Wine	1 250 ml glass	120

Source: Hoekstra (2008).

the pizza is nevertheless considered sustainable, as most of the water used during production is rainwater, which is sourced in an area with large renewable water resources.

In tourism, a considerable share of overall water use appears to be a result of food consumption (Table 1.8). A recent estimate suggests, for instance, that accommodation, traditionally seen as the major factor in water consumption (including water use in hotel rooms and swimming pools, and for cleaning and gardens), is small in comparison to the water footprint of food (Gössling *et al.* 2012).

Biodiversity

Tourism is increasingly being recognized as a significant beneficiary of biodiversity. Biological diversity (biodiversity) refers to the total sum of biotic variation, ranging from the genetic level, through the species level and on to the ecosystem level. The concept indicates diversity within and between species as well as the diversity of ecosystems. The extent or quantity of diversity can be expressed in terms of the size of a population and the abundance of different species, as well as the size of an ecosystem (area) and the number of ecosystems in a given area. The integrity or quality of biodiversity can be expressed in terms of the extent of diversity at the genetic level, and resilience at the species and ecosystem levels (Martens *et al.* 2003). According to the Secretariat of the Convention on Biological Diversity (CBD) (2010: 9), 'There are multiple indications of continuing decline in biodiversity in all three of its main components — genes, species and ecosystems.' Furthermore, the five principal pressures directly driving biodiversity loss – habitat change, overexploitation, pollution, invasive alien species and climate change – are all factors to which tourism is a significant contributor (Hall 2011), and 'are either constant or increasing in intensity.... The ecological footprint of humanity exceeds the biological capacity of the Earth by a wider margin than at the time the 2010 target was agreed' (Secretariat of the CBD 2010: 9).

Table 1.8 Water use categories and estimated use per tourist per day

Water use category – direct	*Litres per tourist per day*
Accommodation	84–2,000
Activities	10–30
Water use category – indirect	*Litres per tourist per day*
Infrastructure	n.a.
Fossil fuels	750 (per 1,000 km by air/car)
Biofuels	2,500 (per 1 L)
Food	2,000–5,000
Total per tourist per day	Estimated range: 2,000–7,500

Source: Gössling *et al.* (2012).

The world's food supply is based on a narrow plant and animal base. According to Pimental and Pimental (2008), 90 per cent of the world's food supply comes from only 15 crop plant species and eight livestock species. However, as Sage (2012) notes, not only is the superstructure of the global food system built upon rather limited genetic foundations, 'these are narrowing further as a result of agricultural modernisation and intensification' (2012: 100). The genetic base of commercial livestock and plant seed supply is far smaller than the traditional farming base. For example, commercial seed supply is geared towards the availability of increased farming technologies, high water and energy inputs, chemical fertilizers and biocides and a high degree of mechanization in order to gain short-term crop or livestock maximization. The top five transnational seed companies also control 47 per cent of global commercial seed sales (Sage 2012: 103). In contrast, traditional agriculture was often extremely diverse and marked by multifunctional operations and based on a much more diverse range of seed supplies. Such traditional farming strategies served at least two major functions:

> First, maintaining varieties was a strategy to minimise risk and make the best use of uncertainty (poor or late rains) and hazards (outbreaks of pest or disease). Consequently, practices such as polycultures, intercropping, staggered planting times and so on had the advantages of reducing total crop losses, spreading labour demands, diversifying food sources and ensuring some degree of food security over the year. Second, different varieties were cultivated for different culinary and cultural purposes.
>
> (Sage 2012: 100–1)

The loss of genetic diversity carries with it substantial risks for food security. For example, in 1970 a corn blight wiped out more than 15 per cent of the entire US corn crop because a single gene that had been inserted into all the common commercial corn varieties was highly blight-susceptible (Watson 1996). Risks to food security for many locations have also been increased as a result of intellectual property rights being attached to new seed varieties; the long-term implications of transgenic seeds to cultivated and natural ecologies; and the high cost of energy, water, fertilizer and biocide inputs for commercial seeds. In addition, food production affects environment and biodiversity as a result of changed farming methods and practices such as the increased use of biocides, chemical fertilizers and deep ploughing; as well as the clearing of natural vegetation for agriculture, as in the Amazon basin (Brannstrom 2009), or removal and neglect of hedgerows and semi-natural vegetation on farms (Sánchez *et al.* 2010). All of these activities result in the loss of biodiversity (Green *et al.* 2005), and may also affect the attractiveness of rural locations for tourism (Hall and Sharples 2008).

Responses to the loss of biodiversity include the development of seed-saving networks as well as the development of alternative farming systems, e.g. organic and biodynamic farming, and networks. Much of this occurs under the rubric of local food systems and the relocalization of food. Indeed, many of the chapters in this volume focus on the interrelationships between tourism, hospitality and the development of local food systems.

A local food system refers to deliberately formed systems that are characterized by a close producer–consumer relationship within a designated place or local area. Local food systems support long-term connections; meet economic, social, health and environmental needs; link producers and markets via locally focused infrastructure; promote environmental health; and provide competitive advantage to local food businesses (Food System Economic Partnership 2006; Buck *et al.* 2007; Hall and Sharples 2008). Buck *et al.* (2007) argue that the potential benefits of such a system include

- bolstering the local economy as less money is diverted to corporations based outside the region and local businesses satisfy unmet demands or create new or more efficient systems for the production and movement of foods: 'These opportunities help to strengthen the local economy by growing the agricultural sector, creating jobs, providing more choices for consumers, contributing to the local tax base, and reinvesting local money exchanged for food back into local farms and businesses' (Buck *et al.* 2007: 3);
- producers and consumers are linked via efficient infrastructures, which can provide a competitive advantage for local farmers, processors, distributors, retailers and consumers alike, meaning that farmers receive a greater return for their produce as there are fewer intermediaries: 'By sharing the risks and rewards of food production, processing, distribution, and retail with other local partners, farmers and businesses can explore opportunities to produce new varieties of foods or expand existing ventures to meet a local or regional need' (Buck *et al.* 2007: 3);
- positive effects on community development and revitalization, with consumers receiving fresher, healthier food and the opportunity to develop a relationship with the farmers;
- supporting the viability of small and medium-sized family farms and fostering a sense of place, culture, history and ecology within a region as well as helping to combat urban sprawl, obesity and hunger; and
- generating environmental benefits particularly as a result of decreased energy and fuel consumption

Food citizenship and social justice

Arguably, the final overarching issue with respect to the development of sustainable culinary systems is the development of food citizenship and the growing awareness of the importance of social justice as an issue in the food supply chain. Although citizenship is a politically contested and evolving term, the notion of food citizenship and related concepts such as 'ecological citizenship' refers to the development of an environmentally informed morality that provides a 'rationale for changing behaviour towards more sustainable lifestyles' (Seyfang 2011: 58). This is expressed in a number of different food chains including the growth of farmers' markets; the development of short food chains from producer to consumer; the growth of organic, ethically produced and free-range food products; and fair trade (Cohen 2006; Parkins and Craig 2006; Hall 2010b, 2012), all of which have had an impact on notions of food sustainability in the tourism and hospitality industries. With respect to the relationship between food citizenship, consumer activism and the relocalization of food, Anderson and Cook (2000: 237) comment:

> The major advantage of localizing food systems, underlying all other advantages, is that this process reworks power and knowledge relationships in food supply systems that have become distorted by increasing distance (physical, social, and metaphorical) between producers and consumers ... [and] gives priority to local and environmental integrity before corporate profit-making.

Although much of the focus of food citizenship is on the development of new culinary systems that rely on face-to-face or spatially proximate food chains, Sage (2007) also identifies the development of spatially extended short supply chains for Fair Trade products. Fair Trade is a social and economic movement with respect to the trading of commodities between the developed and developing nations. Originally primarily a European social justice movement that sought to ensure a fair and equitable price for products imported by the West (often from former colonies), the notion of fair trade has since expanded to include concern for the environment as well as general principles of sustainable development (Fridell 2007; Grankvist *et al.* 2007; Hall 2010b). Fair Trade was defined by FINE (the four major international groups associated with fair trade: International Fair Trade Association/International Federation for Alternative Trade (IFAT, now renamed the World Fair Trade Organization (WFTO)), Fair Trade Labelling Organizations International (FLO), Network of European Worldshops (NEWS!) and the European Fair Trade Association (EFTA)), as 'a trading partnership, based on dialogue, transparency and respect, that seeks greater equity in international trade. It contributes to sustainable development by offering better trading conditions to, and securing the rights of, marginalized producers and workers – especially in the South' (FINE 2001). Although there are a large number of internationally traded food and non-food Fair Trade products, coffee is the main food product and is found in many different hospitality and food service businesses (Hall 2010b). In 2007 Fair Trade global sales equated to the support of 1.5 million producers and workers in 58 developing countries (Fairtrade Labelling Organizations International 2008).

The final social justice dimension of the food system of course is that there are over a billion people without access to enough nourishing food who 'are experiencing hunger and malnutrition because of their lack of entitlements through which to express a demand for food' (Sage 2012: 3). Juxtaposing such a figure with the food dimensions of the world's tourism and hospitality industry may seem almost callous to some readers. But instead it actually strikes to the heart of understanding the ways in which culinary systems are developed and may possibly be transformed, given that major international tourism institutions, such as the UN World Tourism Organization and the World Travel and Tourism Council, advocate the advancement of market-based solutions to development issues and promote tourism as a mechanism for poverty relief in particular (Hall 2007). Different stakeholders in culinary systems not only have different understandings of sustainability but also promote different ways in which it may be achieved.

Transforming the culinary system?

Despite the term 'sustainability' being widely used in the lexicon of tourism and hospitality, as well as agri-food systems, there is no single accepted definition of what it means (Aiking and de Boer 2004; Hall 2010a; Sage 2012). Three main approaches to the sustainability of culinary systems can be identified in developed countries: 'business as usual' (BAU), 'green growth', and steady-state/ sustainable consumption (Table 1.9). In addition, a fourth approach to sustainable food systems, which Green *et al.* (2003) term 'traditional sustainable', is also included but is regarded as applying primarily to rural areas in the less developed countries (Pretty 1995; see also Pretty 2007). The divisions of the table relate to the core elements of the food system identified in Figure 1.1 above. Clearly such categorizations should be interpreted as idealized versions of approaches to sustainability. Yet they provide a useful set of frames with which to consider culinary and agri-food systems in general and the role of tourism and hospitality within them. For example, although focused on issues of sustainability in winegrowing, Chapter 12 below by Hall and Baird highlights the divergence of perspectives among New Zealand winegrowers as to the value of sustainable approaches which in the New Zealand case are as much an appeal to branding as they are to reduction of environmental impact. Indeed, the role of sustainability as a branding mechanism is a frequent theme in many of the chapters in this volume.

This chapter, as well as this book overall, is seeking to come to terms with achieving the development of sustainable culinary systems in the face of the significant problems facing food supply discussed in the previous section, not least of which is growing world population levels and concerns over the effects of climate change and energy costs. In reflecting on the relationships between global environmental change and sustainable agri-food systems, Green *et al.* (2003: 157) argue that the problems of industrialized agriculture and its consumption patterns need to be confronted, while in the developing countries

> sustainability must mean slowing down, if not reversing, the adoption of the environmentally degrading impacts of [industrialized agri-food] systems in those countries whose living standards are approaching those of the developed world. But it must also recognize the needs for food security of the rural poor and, crucially ... the 'urban' people.

Table 1.9 Approaches to sustainable culinary systems

Elements of consumption and production	'business as usual' (BAU)	'Green growth'	'Traditional sustainable'	'Steady-state'/sustainable consumption
Concept of sustainability	The sustainability 'problem' is defined in economic terms and the need for the reduction of regulatory barriers to the development of international food trade in order allow market solutions to operate.	Although the approach seeks to balance the economic, environmental and social foundations of sustainability, sustainability is primarily defined in technical-rational economic terms that seek to encourage greater efficiency. Promotion of 'green' economic growth via market and technological solutions.	Based on the development of 'traditional' methods of food production in less developed countries in order to encourage food security for rural poor. 'Sustainable agriculture' as an alternative model for rural development. Limited attention to urban issues. Promotes sufficiency as well as efficiency.	Sustainability is understood as being grounded in the constraints of natural capital/ natural systems. Includes aspects of sustained yield approaches together with environmental conservation (degrowth). Recognized as dependent on natural capital. Sufficiency more important than efficiency for sustainable consumption.
General characteristics	Based on 'Fordist' principles of seeking high labour productivity and economies of scale in all elements of the culinary system. Food consumption is based on a wide variety of mass commodities and is especially high in meat products. It is also characterized by high scientific input into food product and process innovation, including genome modification.	Responds to criticisms of the environmental effects of BAU approaches by looking to use technological and scientific approaches to encourage greater efficiencies in the industrial ecology of food thereby reducing waste per capita as well as maintaining or increasing food output per capita. Genome modification is regarded as the most economically and environmentally solution in many cases.	Emphasis on small-scale agricultural production and innovation that is culturally and ecologically sensitive to local needs and foodways.	Focused on food production that engages with natural systems and cycles in agriculture and processing in order to achieve social and economic sustainability goals. Cultural significance is given to 'natural' and 'organic' products and production methods as a means of ensuring human, plant, animal and ecosystem health. Strategy is focused on local food systems/foodsheds regarding production–consumption relations although spatially extended short supply chains may be appropriate for some products, such as Fair Trade.

Energy use	High energy use along with high energy efficiency in crop production	High energy use along with high energy efficiency in crop production	Renewable energy use wherever possible.	Renewable energy use wherever possible. Renewable energy is subsidized and non-renewables taxed to reduce GHG emissions.
Control of pests and diseases	Application of pesticides or other agrochemicals, use of genome knowledge in development of new strains.	Application of pesticides or other agrochemicals, use of genome knowledge in development of new strains. Biological methods employed where economically viable or regulation or public pressure requires its use.	Non-chemical solutions encouraged and use of natural pests.	Use of non-chemical solutions including overall management of cultivated ecology so as to encourage natural pests.
Overcoming soil fertility constraints	Application of chemical fertilizers	Application of chemical fertilizers. Organic farming methods used for high-end niche markets only.	Limited chemical inputs together with nutrient recycling, natural nitrogen fixation, and soil regeneration.	Closed nutrient cycles with much waste recycling.
Solving water problems	Construction of large-scale water storage, supply and irrigation systems and genetic manipulation of crops and stock	Construction of irrigation systems and genetic manipulation of crops and stock. Use of grey water where economically viable and public perceptions allow.	Small-scale water storage along with selection of appropriate local food species	Small-scale water storage along with selection of appropriate food species for climate. Strong focus on water management.
Biodiversity	Loss of genetic diversity unless immediately economically valuable.	Potential long–term economic value of genetic diversity recognized for private sector innovation and wealth generation. Market approaches favoured for biodiversity conservation.	Substantial emphasis on maintaining and increasing local biodiversity; GM seeds based on local seed improvements and local genome ownership.	High emphasis on maintaining and increasing natural and cultivated biodiversity; no GM seeds or livestock.

continued

Table 1.9 Continued

Elements of consumption and production	'business as usual' (BAU)	'Green growth'	'Traditional sustainable'	'Steady-state'/sustainable consumption
Farm size	Large with small labour forces and high productivity of uniform products for mass markets. Animal welfare not a focus. Extremely high meat production. Potential transfer of farming approach to biofuel production.	Large with small labour forces and high productivity of a range of mass customized products. Animal welfare issue only when affects brand values. High levels of meat production as well as non-food production, such as biofuels and pharmaceuticals.	Small farms, based on traditional rural communities; high labour inputs, and local intellectual capital. Limited meat production.	Smaller farms than BAU or green economy and more labour intensive. Production is primarily for local food system although some may be exported. Strong focus on animal welfare. Limited meat production.
Food manufacture, processing and packaging	High levels of automation and processes. Focused on mass markets and increasing use of packaging to attract consumers.	High levels of innovation in food products, e.g. functional foods, processing methods, energy reduction, and packaging. Focussed on a large increase in demand for processed foods and meat products in developing countries. Quality developed via branding and industry self-regulation.	Primary focus on production improvement for local consumption, with limited processing. Regional food surpluses are exported.	Focus on certification and regulation throughout the food chain; as well as food quality, criteria include waste management, packaging systems and energy-saving and emissions reduction systems in processing and transport.

| Food distribution, wholesaling, retail and transport | Distribution based on flexible and intelligent *production-led* supply chains. Extended supply chains based on air, sea, rail and road transport. Increasing growth of supermarkets. | Distribution based on flexible and intelligent *co-produced* supply chains. Extended supply chains based on air, sea, rail and road transport. Limited changes for niche markets only. Increasing growth of supermarkets along with a small number of specialist food stores. Both supermarkets and specialist stores respond to highly specialized *consumption-led* supply chains, e.g. organic and local foods. | Distribution is localized with accompanying job creation and skills development. Use of traditional farmers' markets. Surplus can be distributed to other regions. | Emphasis on environmental costs. Growth in organic products and more *local* food distribution. Shift to seasonal and regional foods with reductions in international trade in food products. Where international trade does occur social justice principles are a major consideration. |
| Food storage and preparation | High capital and energy intensity, with dependence on packaging and refrigeration. | High capital and energy intensity, with dependence on packaging and refrigeration. Some high-end market-driven intelligent energy-saving devices | Improvements in local storage by better pest management. Limited use of food storage and preparation equipment run on renewable energy. | Seeks to reduce energy intensity and therefore environmental and resource impacts while preserving nutritional quality. |

continued

Table 1.9 Continued

Elements of consumption and production	'business as usual' (BAU)	'Green growth'	'Traditional sustainable'	'Steady-state'/sustainable consumption
Tourism, hospitality and food service	Continued rise in out-of-home consumption of food in all countries. Continued encouragement of mass international tourism and hospitality. Significant standardization. High levels of media promotion of food service products.	Continued rise in out-of-home consumption of food in all countries. Mass customization of food and hospitality. Development of niche food tourism experiences, including international 'slow tourism' and gastronomic tourism to high-end markets. Branding that links food and tourism used for regional promotion. High levels of media convergence between food and tourism as part of lifestyle promotion	Limited development of food services based on local foodways and notions of hospitality. International tourism encouraged as part of pro-poor tourism strategies.	Growth of organic and other appropriate specialized hospitality services encouraged. High levels of local leisure-related mobility tied to food and lifestyle. Strong domestic tourism focus. Some international tourism encouraged but with costs of emissions accounted.

Household food activities	High capital and energy intensity in food preparation and clearing up. Continued growth in use of prepared foods as well as internationalization of food products. Majority of shopping based on car-dependent supermarkets as well as supermarket-based internet shopping.	High capital and energy intensity in food preparation and clearing up. Continued growth in use of prepared foods as well as growing internationalization of food products but little increase in overall food consumption. Majority of shopping based on car-dependent supermarkets as well as supermarket-based internet shopping.	Improvements in household cooking and storage practices, including more fuel and energy efficiency. Encouragement of regional markets.	Focus on local food system and short supply chains means an emphasis on direct sales, farmers' markets, locally owned stores, and retail diversity. Cooperative and community-owned supermarkets supported. Opposition to transnational food retail and food service chains. Internet use encouraged to promote food localism.
Disposal and recycling of food and packaging wastes.	Limited recycling for packaging where economically viable for market to operate. Household food waste recycling limited to home composting.	Installation of good systems of packaging and household recycling. Some subsidy of private initiatives or managed under public–private partnerships.	Food wastes recycled for agriculture.	Strong focus on reduced packaging of foods, although recycling is integral along with waste food disposal for agriculture/home composting.

Sources: Pretty (1995); Tansey and Worsley (1995); Green *et al.* (2003); Lang and Heasman (2004); Fernandes *et al.* (2005); Hall (2010a); Sage (2012).

These are worthy sentiments. However, what might new transformations of the culinary system look like, and what role do the hospitality and tourism industries play, given their substantial economic, social and environmental significance to culinary systems? These are issues that this book aims to address.

The book is divided into two main sections. The first section (Chapters 2 to 9) examines a number of cases from around the world where the notion of the local is reinforced in food and tourism. The chapters draw on studies from Canada, Japan, New Zealand, Norway, Sweden, the UK and the USA. A key issue in a number of the chapters is the difficulties of defining local and the fluidity of the concept. As several authors argue, this is not just an academic issue but has significant implications for regulation, branding and even the intellectual property of place. The second section (Chapters 10 to 15) examines the notion of what constitutes sustainable food in a number of different contexts. Sustainable food is identified in the various chapters as having economic, authentic, business development, network and even religious contexts. The divergence of perspectives also highlights issues of food regulation and governance as well as the way in which these not only help provide certainty to customers but may also serve to stymie innovation in certain cases. Nevertheless, many of the cases in this volume are regarded as innovative in their particular context and serve as initiatives or models that others study because of the possibilities they raise with respect to other food and tourism business, community and system initiatives. The final chapter of the book reflects back on the issues faced in creating sustainable culinary systems as evidenced in this book as well as outlining concerns for the future.

Despite the massive proportion of food provided by the hospitality, tourism and food service industries there is a surprising dearth of material on their contribution to the sustainability of food systems, what we refer to here as culinary systems given the way in which food consumption and production are socially constructed. This is not to suggest that research on alternative food networks and short supply chains is lacking, or that the research on the relationship between food and tourism is not recognized, far from it. However, while there have been many statements about the sustainability of tourism (Hall 2010a), what has been relatively absent is the examination of how tourism does or can contribute to the sustainability of food and foodways. If, as discussed above, sustainability necessitates the adoption of a systems approach, then the understanding of tourism and sustainability should focus not just immediately on tourism and hospitality but on the interconnections between tourism and other categories of economic and social activity as part of the global system.

In considering the case of the American food system, what is potentially the exemplar of future directions in the global agri-food system, Mintz (2006: 3) observed that,

> an impasse has been created for us by the forces of what's called 'progress', and so far, no one has found a way to escape it. Yet I must also wonder whether we, who like to think that we care greatly – both about what we eat, and about the health and environmental consequences of our food system – have thought seriously enough about what it is that we confront.

In the same way we would like to confront our readers and encourage them to think about the prospects of more sustainable culinary systems in tourism and hospitality and whether the future of food lies, as some argue, in a choice between McDonaldization or Slow Food, or whether it will be in a culinary path that lies between the two.

References

Aiking, H. and de Boer, J. (2004) 'Food sustainability: diverging interpretations', *British Food Journal*, 106(5): 359–65.

Aldaya, M.M. and Hoekstra, A.Y. (2010) 'The water needed for Italians to eat pasta and pizza', *Agricultural Systems*, 103(6): 351–60.

Alexandratos, N. (ed.) (2006) *World Agriculture: towards 2030/50, Interim Report. An FAO Perspective*. London and Rome: Earthscan and FAO.

Anderson, M.D. and Cook, J.T. (2000) 'Does food security require local food systems?' In J.M. Harris (ed.) *Rethinking Sustainability: Power, Knowledge and Institutions*. Ann Arbor: University of Michigan Press.

Antón, A., Montero, J.I. and Muñoz, P. (2005) 'LCA and tomato production in Mediterranean greenhouses', *International Journal of Agricultural Resources Governance and Ecology*, 4(2): 102–12.

Askegaard, S. and Kjeldgaard, D. (2007) 'Here, there, and everywhere: place branding and gastronomical globalization in a macromarketing perspective', *Journal of Macromarketing*, 27(2): 138–47.

Basset-Mens, C. and van der Werf, H.M.G. (2005) 'Scenario-based environmental assessment of farming systems: the case of pig production in France', *Agriculture, Ecosystems and Environment*, 105(1–2): 127–44.

Bates, B.C., Kundzewicz, Z.W., Wu, S. and Palutikof, J.P. (2008) *Climate Change and Water. Technical Paper of the Intergovernmental Panel on Climate Change*. Geneva: IPCC Secretariat.

Bhalli, J.A., Ali, T., Asi, M.R., Khalid, Z.M., Ceppi, M. and Khan, Q.M. (2009) 'DNA damage in Pakistani agricultural workers exposed to mixture of pesticides', *Environmental and Molecular Mutagenesis*, 50(1): 37–45.

Boniface, P. (2003) *Tasting Tourism: Travelling for Food and Drink*. Burlington: Ashgate.

Brannstrom, C. (2009) 'South America's neoliberal agricultural frontiers: places of environmental sacrifice or conservation opportunity', *AMBIO: A Journal of the Human Environment*, 38(3): 141–9.

Buck, K., Kaminski, L.E., Stockmann, D.P. and Vail, A.J. (2007) *Investigating Opportunities to Strengthen the Local Food System in Southeastern Michigan, Executive Summary*. Ann Arbor: University of Michigan – School of Natural Resources and Environment.

Cao, L, Diana, J.S., Keoleiant, G.A. and Lai, Q. (2011) 'Life cycle assessment of Chinese shrimp farming systems targeted for export and domestic sales', *Environmental Science and Technology*, 45(15): 6531–8.

Carbon Disclosure Project (2010) *CDP Water Disclosure 2010 global report. On behalf of 137 Investors with assets of US$16 trillion*. Report written for Carbon Disclosure Project by ERM. London: Carbon Disclosure Project.

Carlsson-Kanyama, A. and González, A.D. (2009) 'Potential contributions of food consumption patterns to climate change', *American Journal of Clinical Nutrition*, 89: 1704–9S.

Carlsson-Kanyama, A., Pipping Ekström, M. and Shanahan, H. (2003) 'Food and life cycle energy inputs: consequences of diet and ways to increase efficiency', *Ecological Economics*, 44(2–3): 293–307.

Casey, J.W. and Holden, N.M. (2006) 'Quantification of GHG emissions from sucker-beef production in Ireland', *Agricultural Systems*, 90(1–3): 79–98.

Cederberg, C. and Darelius, K. (2001) Livscykelanalys (LCA) av griskött [Lifecycle analysis of pork). Naturresursforum, Landstinget Halland. Online. Available: www. regionhalland.se/dynamaster/file_archive/041011/783f1b18fe599c66cafeb5ac66d3c7fc/ Rapport%20griskott.pdf (accessed 21 October 2009).

Cederberg, C. and Nilsson, B. (2004) *Livscykelanalys (LCA) av ekologisk nötköttsproduktion i ranchdrift. MAT 21.* Report 718 from SIK, Göteborg.

Cederberg, C., Wivstad, M., Bergkvist, P., Mattsson, B. and Ivarsson, K. (2005) *Hållbart växtskydd. Analys av olika strategier för att minska riskerna med kemiska växtskyddsmedel* [Sustainable plant protection. Analysis of different strategies to reduce the risks of chemicals]. Rapport MAT21 6/2005.

Chapagain, A.K. and Hoekstra, A.Y. (2007) 'The water footprint of coffee and tea consumption in the Netherlands', *Ecological Economics*, 64(1): 109–18.

Chapagain, A.K. and Hoekstra, A.Y. (2008) 'The global component of freshwater demand and supply: an assessment of virtual water flows between nations as a result of trade in agricultural and industrial products', *Water International*, 33(1): 19–32.

Clark, G. and Chabrel, M. (2007) 'Measuring integrated rural tourism', *Tourism Geographies*, 9(4): 371–86.

Clark, P.P. (1975) 'Thoughts for food II: culinary culture in contemporary France', *The French Review*, 49(2): 198–205.

Cohen, E. and Avieli, N. (2004) 'Food in tourism: attraction and impediment', *Annals of Tourism Research*, 31: 755–78.

Cohen, M.J. (2006) 'Sustainable consumption research as democratic expertise', *Journal of Consumer Policy*, 29(1): 67–77.

Department for Environment, Food and Rural Affairs (DEFRA) (2007) Environmental footprint and sustainability of horticulture (including potatoes): A comparison with other agricultural sectors. University of Warwick. Online. Available: http://randd.defra.gov.uk/ Document.aspx?Document=WQ0101_6748_FRA.pdf (accessed 21 October 2009).

Department for Environment, Food and Rural Affairs (DEFRA) (2008) *Food Statistics Pocketbook 2008.* York: Food Statistics Branch, Department for Environment, Food and Rural Affairs.

Department for Environment, Food and Rural Affairs (DEFRA) (2010) *Food Statistics Pocketbook 2009.* York: Food Statistics Branch, Department for Environment, Food and Rural Affairs.

Department for Environment, Food and Rural Affairs (DEFRA) (2010) *Food Statistics Pocketbook 2010.* York: Food Statistics Branch, Department for Environment, Food and Rural Affairs.

Department for Environment, Food and Rural Affairs (DEFRA) (2011) *Food Statistics Pocketbook 2011 (In year update).* York: Food Statistics Branch, Department for Environment, Food and Rural Affairs.

du Rand, G.E. and Heath, E. (2006) 'Towards a framework for food tourism as an element of destination marketing', *Current Issues in Tourism*, 9: 206–34.

Erklärung von Bern (2011) *Agropoly. Wenige Konzerne beherrschen die weltweite Lebensmittelproduktion* [Agropoly. A few businesses rule global food production]. Zurich: Erklärung von Bern.

EU (2005) Dairy herds and yield. Online. Available: http://ec.europa.eu/agriculture/agrista/2005/table_en/42001.pdf (accessed 15 May 2012).

EU (2012) The 2011 agricultural year: Overview. Online. Available: http://ec.europa.eu/agriculture/statistics/agricultural/2011/pdf/tables-maps-graphs_en.pdf (accessed 15 May 2012).

Everett, S. and Aitchison, C. (2008) 'The role of food tourism in sustaining regional identity: a case study of Cornwall, South West England', *Journal of Sustainable Tourism*, 16: 150–67.

Fairtrade Labelling Organizations International (2008) Global Fairtrade sales increase by 47%, Fairtrade Labelling Organizations International. Online. Available: www.fairtrade.net/single_view.html?&cHash=d6f2e27d2c&tx_ttnews[backPid]=104&tx_ttnews[tt_news]=41 (Accessed 24 May 2008).

FAOSTAT (2009) FAOSTAT. Online. Available: http://faostat.fao.org/default.aspx (accessed 15 May 2012).

FINE Fernandes, E., Pell, A. and Upkoff, N. (2005) Rethinking agriculture for real opportunities', in J. Pretty (ed.) *The Earthscan Reader in Sustainable Agriculture*. London: Earthscan. (IFAT, (International Fair Trade Association; FLO, Fair Trade Labelling Organizations International; NEWS!, Network of European Worldshops) and EFTA (European Fair Trade Association)] (2001) Fair trade definition and principles as agreed by FINE in December 2001, European Observatory on Fair Trade Public Procurement, European Fair Trade Association. Online. Available: www.european-fair-trade-association.org/observatory/index.php/en/fairtrade (accessed 1 April 2012).

Food System Economic Partnership (2006) *Alternative Regional Food System Models: Successes and Lessons Learned: A Preliminary Literature Review*. Ann Arbor, Mich.: Food System Economic Partnership.

Fresco, L. (2009) 'Challenges for food system adaptation today and tomorrow', *Environment Society and Policy*, 12(4): 378–85.

Fridell, G. (2007) *Fair Trade Coffee: The Prospects and Pitfalls of Market-Driven Social Justice*. Toronto: University of Toronto Press.

Gehlhar, M. and Regmi, A. (2005) 'Factors shaping global food markets', in A. Regmi and M. Gehlhar (eds) *New Directions in Global Food Markets*, Agricultural Information Bulletin No. 794, Washington DC: United States Department of Agriculture.

Godfray, H.C.J., Beddington, J.R., Crute, I.R., Haddad, L., Lawrence, D., Muir, J.F., Pretty, J., Robinson, S., Thomas, S.M. and Toulmin, C. (2010) 'Food security: The challenge of feeding 9 billion people', *Science*, 327: 812–18.

Grankvist, G., Lekedal, H. and Marmendal, M. (2007) 'Values and eco- and fair-trade labelled products', *British Food Journal*, 109(2): 169–81.

Green, K. (2003) 'Give peas a chance: transformations in food consumption and production systems', paper presented to the IHDP Open Science Conference, Montreal, October 2003.

Green, K., Harvey, M. and McMeekin, A. (2001) 'Transformations in food consumption and production systems', paper prepared for presentation at the Workshop on 'Integrating Food Systems and GEC Research', open meeting of the Human Dimensions of Global Environmental Change Research Community, Rio de Janeiro, 6–8 October, 2001.

Green, K., Harvey, M. and McMeekin, A. (2003) 'Transformations in food consumption and production systems', *Journal of Environmental Policy & Planning*, 5(2): 145–63.

Green, R.E., Cornell, S.J., Scharlemann, J.P.W. and Balmford, A. (2005) 'Farming and the fate of wild nature', *Science*, 307: 550–5.

Gössling, S., Garrod, B., Aall, C., Hille, J. and Peeters, P. (2011) 'Food management in tourism. Reducing tourism's carbon "foodprint"', *Tourism Management*, 32: 534–43.

Gössling, S., Peeters, P., Hall, C.M., Dubois, G., Ceron, J.P., Lehmann, L. and Scott, D. (2012) 'Tourism and water use: supply, demand, and security. An international review', *Tourism Management*, 33: 1–15.

Hall, C.M. (ed.) (2003) *Wine, Food and Tourism Marketing*. Binghampton: Haworth.

Hall, C.M. (2007) 'Pro-poor tourism: do "tourism exchanges benefit primarily the countries of the South"?' *Current Issues in Tourism*, 10: 111–18.

Hall, C.M. (2008) *Tourism Planning*, 2nd edn. Harlow: Pearson.

Hall, C.M. (2010a) 'Tourism and biodiversity: more significant than climate change?', *Journal of Heritage Tourism*, 5: 253–66.

Hall, C.M. (2010b) 'Blending fair trade coffee and hospitality', in L. Joliffe (ed.) *Coffee Culture, Destinations and Tourism*, Bristol: Channelview.

Hall, C.M. (2011) 'Policy learning and policy failure in sustainable tourism governance: from first and second to third order change?', *Journal of Sustainable Tourism*, 19(4–5): 649–71.

Hall, C.M. (2012) 'The contradictions and paradoxes of slow food: environmental change, sustainability and the conservation of taste', in S. Fullagar, K. Markwell and E. Wilson (eds) *Slow Tourism: Experiences and Mobilities*, Bristol: Channel View.

Hall, C.M. and Mitchell, R. (2000) 'We are what we eat: food, tourism and globalization', *Tourism, Culture and Communication*, 2(1): 29–37.

Hall, C.M. and Sharples, L. (eds) (2008) *Food and Wine Festivals and Events Around the World*. Oxford: Butterworth-Heinemann.

Hall, C.M., Sharples, L., Mitchell, R., Macionis, N. and Cambourne, B. (eds) (2003) *Food Tourism Around the World: Development, Management and Markets*. Oxford: Butterworth-Heinemann.

Harvey, M., McMeekin, A. and Warde, A. (2004) 'Conclusion: quality and processes of qualification', in M. Harvey, A. McMeekin and A. Warde (eds) *Qualities of Food*. Manchester: Manchester University Press.

Harvey, M., Quilley, S. and Beynon, H. (2003) *Exploring the Tomato: Transformations of Nature, Economy and Society*. Cheltenham: Edward Elgar.

Hawkes, C. (2006) 'Uneven dietary development: linking the policies and processes of globalisation with the nutrition transition, obesity and diet-related chronic diseases', *Globalization and Health*, 2(4), 28 March. Online.

Hegarty, J.A. (2006) 'Developing "subject fields" in culinary arts, science, and gastronomy', *Journal of Culinary Science & Technology*, 4(1): 5–13.

Hille, J., Sataøen, H.L., Aall, C. and Storm, H.N. (2008) Miljøbelastningen av norsk forbrukogproduksjon 1987–2007 (Environmental impacts of Norwegian consumption and production 1987–2007). Vestlandsforsking, Sogndal. Online. Available: www.vestforsk.no/www/show.do?page=12&articleid=2201 (accessed 15 May 2012).

Hirschfeld, J., Weiß, J., Preidl, M. and Korbun, T. (2008). *Klimawirkungen der Landwirtschaft in Deutschland* [German agriculture's impacts on climate change]. Berlin: Institut für Ökologische Wirtschaftsforschung. www.foodwatch.de/foodwatch/content/e10/e17197/e17201/e17220/IOEW_Klimawirkungen_der_Landwirtschaft_SR_186_08_ger.pdf (accessed 21 October 2009).

Hjalager, A.-M. and Richards, G. (eds) (2002) *Tourism and Gastronomy*. Abingdon: Routledge.

Hoekstra, A.Y. (ed.) (2003) Virtual water trade: proceedings of the International Expert Meeting on Virtual Water Trade. Value of Water Research Report Series No. 12,

UNESCO-IHE, Delft Netherlands. Online. Available: www.waterfootprint.org/Reports/Report12.pdf (accessed 15 May 2012).

Hoekstra, A.Y. (2008) The water footprint of food. Online. Available: www.waterfootprint.org/Reports/Hoekstra-2008-WaterfootprintFood.pdf (accessed 15 May 2012).

Hoekstra, A.Y. and Chapagain, A.K. (2007) 'Water footprints of nations: water use by people as a function of their consumption pattern', *Water Resources Management*, 21: 35–48.

Hoekstra, A.Y., Chapagain, A.K., Aldaya, M.M. and Mekonnen, M.M. (2012) *The Water Footprint Assessment Manual. Setting the Global Standard*. London and Washington: Earthscan. Online. Available: www.waterfootprint.org/downloads/TheWaterFootprintAssessmentManual.pdf (accessed 15 May 2012).

Horng, J.-S. and Lee, Y.-C. (2009) 'What environmental factors influence creative culinary studies?', *International Journal of Contemporary Hospitality Management*, 21(1): 100–17.

IKEA (2011) Sustainability Report 2011. Online. Available: www.ikea.com/ms/sv_SE/about_ikea/pdf/sustainability_report_fy11.pdf (accessed 20 May 2012).

IPCC (1995) *Climate Change 1995, The Science of Climate Change: Summary for Policymakers and Technical Summary of the Working Group I Report.* Cambridge: Cambridge University Press.

IPCC (2007) *Summary for Policymakers. Intergovernmental Panel on Climate Change: Fourth Assessment Report: Climate Change 2007: Synthesis Report.* Cambridge: Cambridge University Press.

Kearney, J. (2010) 'Food consumption trends and drivers', *Philosophical Transactions of the Royal Society B*, 365: 2793–807.

Knowd, I. (2006) 'Tourism as a mechanism for farm survival', *Journal of Sustainable Tourism*, 14: 24–42.

Kok, R., Benders, R.M.J. and Moll, H.C. (2001) *Energie-intensiteiten van de nederlandse consumptieve bestedingen anno 1996* [The energy intensity of consumption in the Netherlands in 1996]. Groningen: IVEM, Rijksuniversiteit Groningen.

Koutros, S., Lynch, C.F., Ma, X., Lee, W.J., Hoppin, J.A., Christensen, C.H., Andreotti, G., Freeman, L.B., Rusiecki, J.A., Hou, L., Sandler, D.P. and Alavanja, M.C.R. (2008) 'Heterocyclic aromatic amine pesticide use and human cancer risk: results from the US Agricultural Health Study', *International Journal of Cancer*, 124(5): 1206–12.

Lang, T. and Heasman, M. (2004) *Food Wars: The Global Battle for Mouths, Minds and Markets*. London: Earthscan.

Lawton, J.H. and May, R.M. (1995) *Extinction Rates.* Oxford: Oxford University Press.

LCA Food (2003) LCA food database. www.lcafood.dk (accessed 21 October 2009).

Lifset, R. and Graedel, T.E. (2002) 'Industrial ecology: goals and definitions', in R.U. Ayres and L.W. Ayres (eds) *A Handbook of Industrial Ecology*. Cheltenham: Edward Elgar.

Liu, J. and Savenije, H.H.G. (2008) 'Food consumption patterns and their effect on water requirements in China', *Hydrolology and Earth System Sciences*, 12: 887–98.

London, G. (2000) 'Ethnoarchaeology and interpretations of the past', *Ethnoarchaeology*, 163(1): 2–8.

LRF (Lantbrukarnas riksförbund) (2002) *Maten och miljön – Livscykelanalys av sju livsmedel.* [Food and environment – a lifecycle analysis of seven foodstuffs]. Stockholm: LRF. www.svensktsigill.com/website2/1.0.2.0/466/maten%20o%20miljon.pdf (accessed 21 October 2009).

Martens, P., Rotmans, J. and Groot, D. de (2003) 'Biodiversity: luxury or necessity?' *Global Environmental Change*, 13: 75–81.

Miljøstyrelsen (2006). *Miljøvurdering af konventionel og økologisk avl af grøntsager.* [Environmental consequences of conventional and organic vegetable choices]. Arbejdsrapport nr. 5/2006, Miljøstyrelsen, Copenhagen. http://www2.mst.dk/common/ Udgivramme/Frame.asp?http://www2.mst.dk/Udgiv/publikationer/2006/87–7614–960–9/ html/default.htm (accessed 21 October 2009).

Millstone, E. and Lang, T. (2008) *The Atlas of Food: Who Eats What, Where and Why,* 2nd edn. London: Earthscan.

Mintz, S.W. (1986) *Sweetness and Power: The Place of Sugar in Modern History.* London: Penguin.

Mintz, S.W. (2006) 'Food at moderate speeds', in R. Wilks (ed.) *Fast Food/Slow Food: The Cultural Economy of the Global Food System,* Lanham, Md.: Altamira.

Möller Nielsen, J. (2007) *Energin i svensk växthusodling 2007. Tomat* [Energy use in Swedish greenhouse production 2007. Tomatoes.]. Cascada AB. www.svensktsigill.se/ website2/1.0.2.0/466/Sammanfattning%20Tomat%20&%20energi.pdf. (accessed 21 October 2009).

Murcott, A. (1982) 'The cultural significance of food and eating', *Proceedings of the Nutrition Society,* 41: 203–10.

Nummedal, M. and Hall, C.M. (2006) 'Local food in tourism: an investigation of the New Zealand South Island's bed and breakfast sector's use and perception of local food', *Tourism Review International,* 9(4): 365–78.

Parasecoli, F. (2001) 'Deconstructing soup: Ferran Adrià's culinary challenges', *Gastronomica: The Journal of Food and Culture,* 1(1): 60–73.

Parkins, W. and Craig, G. (2006) *Slow Living.* London: Berg.

Parry, M., Lowe, J. and Hanson, C. (2009b) 'Overshoot, adapt and recover', *Nature,* 485: 1102–3.

Parry, M., Arnell, N., Berry, P., Dodman, D., Fankhauser, S., Hope, C. *et al.* (2009a) *Assessing the Costs of Adaptation to Climate Change: A Review of the UNFCCC and Other Recent Estimates.* London: International Institute for Environment and Development and Grantham Institute for Climate Change.

Paull, J. (2008) 'Organics Olympiad 2007 – perspectives on the global state of organic agriculture', *Acres Australia,* 16: 36–8.

Peeters, P. and Schouten, F. (2006) 'Reducing the ecological footprint of inbound tourism and transport to Amsterdam', *Journal of Sustainable Tourism,* 14(2): 157–71.

Pimental, D. and Pimental, M. (eds) (2008) *Food, Energy, and Society,* 2nd edn. Baton Rouge, La.: CRC Press.

Pimm, S.L., Russell, G.J., Gittleman, J.L. and Brooks, T.M. (1995) 'The future of biodiversity', *Science,* 269(5222): 347–50.

Planet Retail (2011) Top 20 ranking, 2011. When the strong grow stronger. Top 20 rankings, 2011. Online. Available: www.planetretail.net (accessed 12 September 2011).

Pretty, J. (1995) *Regenerating Agriculture: Policies and Practice for Sustainability and Self-reliance.* London: Earthscan.

Pretty, J. (2007) *The Earth Only Endures: On Reconnecting with Nature and our Place in it.* London: Earthscan.

Probyn, E. (1998) 'McIdentities: food and the familial citizen', *Theory, Culture & Society,* 15(2): 155–73.

Rifkin, J. (1992) *Beyond Beef: The Rise and Fall of the Cattle Culture.* London: Thorsons.

Ritzer, G. (1998) *The McDonaldization Thesis,* London: Sage.

Royal Society of London (2008) *Sustainable Biofuels: Prospects and Challenges.* London: Royal Society.

Royal Society of London (2009) *Reaping the Benefits: Science and the Sustainable Intensification of Global Agriculture*. London: Royal Society.

Rozin, P. (1990) 'Development in the food domain', *Developmental Psychology*, 26: 555–62.

Sage, C. (2007) 'Trust in markets: economies of regard and spaces of contestation in alternative food networks'. In J. Cross and A. Morales (eds) *Street Trade: Commerce in a Globalising World*. London: Routledge.

Sage, C. (2012) *Environment and Food*. London: Routledge.

Sánchez, I.A., Lassaletta, L., McCollin, D. and Bunce, R.G.H. (2010) 'The effect of hedgerow loss on microclimate in the Mediterranean region: an investigation in Central Spain', *Agroforestry Systems*, 78(1): 13–25.

Scandic (2012) Vi serverar gärna ekologisk mat (We love to serve organic food). Online. Available: www.scandichotels.se/settings/Sidfot/About-us-Container-/Omtanke-om-varlden/Vart-miljoarbete/Hallbara-hotell/Ekologisk-mat/ (accessed 20 May 2012).

Schneider, S.H., Semenov, S., Patwardhan, A., Burton, I., Magadza, C.H.D., Oppenheimer, M., Pittock, A.B., Rahman, A., Smith, J.B., Suarez, A. and Yamin, F. (2007) 'Assessing key vulnerabilities and the risk from climate change'. In M.L. Parry, O.F. Canziani, J.P. Palutikof, P.J. van der Linden and C.E. Hanson (eds) *Climate Change 2007: Impacts, Adaptation and Vulnerability. Contribution of Working Group II to the Fourth Assessment Report of the Intergovernmental Panel on Climate Change*. Cambridge: Cambridge University Press.

Secretariat of the Convention on Biological Diversity (2010) *Global Biodiversity Outlook 3*. Montreal: Secretariat of the Convention on Biological Diversity.

Seyfang, G. (2011) *The New Economics of Sustainable Consumption*. London: Palgrave Macmillan.

Sims, R. (2009) 'Food, place and authenticity: local food and the sustainable tourism experience', *Journal of Sustainable Tourism*, 17: 321–36.

Smith, P., Martino, D., Cai, Z., Gwary, D., Janzen, H., Kumar, P., McCarl, B., Ogle, S., O'Mara, F. Rice, C. Scholes, B. and Sirotenko, O. (2009) 'Agriculture'. In B. Metz, O.R. Davidson, P.R. Bosch, R. Dave and L.A. Meyer (eds) *Climate Change 2007: Mitigation. Contribution of Working Group III to the Fourth Assessment Report of the Intergovernmental Panel on Climate Change*. Cambridge: Cambridge University Press.

Spiegel (2012) Aldi senkt Milchpreise radikal [Aldi reduces milk prices radically]. Online. Available: www.spiegel.de/wirtschaft/0,1518,622789,00.html (accessed 15 May 2012).

Stern (2012) Sinkende Milchpreise trotz steigender Kosten erwartet [Declining milk prices despite increasing production costs expected]. 20 April. Online. Available: www.stern.de/news/ (accessed 20 April 2012).

Swedish Environmental Protection Agency (2008) *Svinn I livsmedelskedjan. Möjligketer, till minskade mängder, Rapport 5885*. Stockholm: Swedish Environmental Protection Agency.

Tansey, G. and Worsley, T. (1995) *The Food System: A Guide*. London: Earthscan.

Telfer, D.J. and Wall, G. (1996) 'Linkages between tourism and food production', *Annals of Tourism Research*, 23(3): 635–53.

Tschofen, B. (2008) 'On the taste of the regions: culinary praxis, European politics and spatial culture – a research outline', *Anthropological Journal of European Cultures*, 17(1): 24–53.

Tukker, A., Huppes, G., Guinée, J., Heijungs, R., de Koning, A., van Oers, L., Suh, S., Geerken, T., Van Holderbeke, M., Jansen, B. and Nielsen, P. (2006) *Environmental*

Impact of Products (EIPRO). Analysis of the Life Cycle Environmental Impacts Related to the Final Consumption of the EU-25. Technical Report EUR 22284 EN. Brussels: European Commission Joint Research Centre (DG JRC), Institute for Prospective Technological Studies.

Tukker, A. and Jansen, B. (2006) 'Environmental impacts of products: a detailed review of studies', *Journal of Industrial Ecology*, 10: 159–82.

Tyedmers, P. (2001) Energy consumed by North Atlantic Fisheries. Online. Available: http://sres. management.dal.ca/Files/Tyedmers/Energy_Tyedmers1.pdf.

Tyedmers, P.H., Watson, R. and Pauly, D. (2005) 'Fuelling global fishing fleets', *Ambio*, 34(8): 619–22.

UN (United Nations) (2011) *World Population Prospects: The 2010 Revision.* New York: United Nations.

UNCTAD (2006) Tracking the Trend Towards Market Concentration: The Case of the Agricultural Input Industry. Online. Available: www.unctad.org/en/docs/ditccom200516_en.pdf (accessed 1 April 2012).

UNCTAD World Investment Report (2009) *UNCTAD World Investment Report: Transnational Corporations, Agricultural Production and Development*, Geneva: UNCTAD.

van Esterik, P. (2006) 'From hunger food to heritage foods: challenges to food localization in Lao PDR', in R. Wilks (ed.) *Fast Food/Slow Food: The Cultural Economy of the Global Food System*, Lanham, Md.: Altamira.

Vitousek, P.M., Mooney, H.A., Lubchenco, J. and Melillo, J.M. (1997a) 'Human domination of Earth's ecosystems', *Science*, 277(5325): 494–9.

Vitousek, P.M., Aber, J.D., Howarth, R.W., Likens, G.E., Matson, P.A., Schindler, D.W., Schlesinger, W.H. and Tilman, D.G. (1997b) 'Human alteration of the global nitrogen cycle: sources and consequences', *Ecological Applications*, 7(3): 737–50.

von Braun, J. and Diaz-Bonilla, E. (2008) 'Globalization of agriculture and food: causes, consequences and policy implications'. in J. von Braun and E. Diaz-Bonilla (ed.) *Globalization of Food and Agriculture and the Poor.* Oxford: Oxford University Press.

Vos, E. (2000) 'EU food safety regulation in the aftermath of the BSE crisis', *Journal of Consumer Policy*, 23(3): 227–55.

Watson, B. (1996) *Taylor's Guide to Heirloom Vegetables.* Boston: Houghton Mifflin.

Wilks, R. (2006) 'From wild weeds to artisanal cheese'. In R. Wilks (ed.) *Fast Food/Slow Food: The Cultural Economy of the Global Food System*, Lanham, Md.: Altamira.

Williams, A.G., Audsley, E. and Sandars, D.L. (2006) *Determining the environmental burdens and resource use in the production of agricultural and horticultural commodities.* Defra project report IS0205.

Winther, U., Ziegler, F., Skontorp Hognes, E., Emanuelsson, A., Sund, V. and Ellingsen, H. (2009) Carbon footprint and energy use of Norwegian seafood products. Online. Available: https://nbl.sintef.no/upload/Fiskeri_og_havbruk/Fiskeriteknologi/Filer%20fra%20Erik%20Skontorp%20Hognes/Carbon%20footprint%20and%20energy%20use%20of%20Norwegian%20seafood%20products%20-%20Final%20report%20-%2004_12_09.pdf (accessed 21 October 2009).

World Bank (2008) *World Development Report. Agriculture for Development.* Washington DC: World Bank.

WWF-UK (2002) Holiday footprinting: A practical tool for responsible tourism. Online. Available: www.wwf.org.uk/filelibrary/pdf/holidayfootprintingfull.pdf (accessed 20 October 2009).

Zollitsch, W., Winkler, C., Waiblinger, S. and Haslberger, A. (2007) *Sustainable Food Production and Ethics.* Wageningen: Wageningen Academic Publishers.

Zuckerman, L. (1999) *The Potato.* London: Macmillan.

Part II
Reinforcing the local in food and tourism

2 Culinary networks and rural tourism development – constructing the local through everyday practices

Josefine Østrup Backe

Introduction

The focus on local food and local food products in relation to rural tourism experiences has increasingly gained attention, and destinations as well as their various actors are to a wider extent recognising the economic benefits of stressing the local origins and qualities of culinary products (Murdoch *et al.* 2000; Woods and Deegan 2003; DuPuis and Goodman 2005; Mossberg and Svensson 2009). As a consequence of the enhanced competition between tourism destinations, combined with changes in the perception of food products and food production, some of the new ways of selling the rural through food-related experiences include farm stays, farmers' markets, food events and festivals (Hall and Sharples 2003, 2008; Hall *et al.* 2009). Also, the use of local food networks has become an effective instrument for rural areas to mediate a sustainable culinary profile (Marsden *et al.* 2000; Venn *et al.* 2006).

New efforts have recently been made by Nordic governments and various organisations to enhance the interest and knowledge of Nordic food and highlight the qualities of locally produced food. Further to this, rural areas are of particular importance as the actual sources of the raw materials (Jordbruksverket 2010; Claus Meyer 2010; Laurin 2010). As terms such as 'locally sourced' and 'locally produced' become ever more popular in the planning and promotion of culinary experiences, the notion of sustainability seems to be an obvious discourse when talking of the combination of food and rural tourism development. Rural tourism is often connected to sustainability, as activities to a wide extent are executed within the same premises, i.e. with respect to the natural environment and the small-scale nature of local business (George *et al.* 2009; Hall *et al.* 2009).

Within the context of rural tourism development, this chapter seeks to explore how the local is constructed through culinary network practices, in order to enhance the understanding of the use of local values in the creation of culinary experiences. The chapter investigates a specific case study involving a culinary network situated in the Ystad/Österlen area of southern Sweden. In this regard, different dimensions of the local are considered – that is, how the phenomenon is constructed, negotiated and mediated through the practices of a culinary network.

From local food traditions to culinary tourism

Within academic research a number of studies have been focusing on food in relation to destination development (Henderson 2009; Mossberg and Svensson 2009) as well as image and identity formation (Bessière 1998; Everett and Aitchison 2008; Gunnarsdottir and Haraldsdottir in Hall *et al.* 2009) and sustainability (Marsden and Smith 2005; Sims 2009). Culinary tourism has become a well-established phenomenon which is used to a still wider extent when branding regions, cities or specific communities. Departing from Richards's (2002) definition, culinary tourism involves tourists visiting restaurants, markets and local producers as a significant part of their holiday activities. In this context, the actual meal does not have to be the primary aim of an experience, but is one of several activities. Accordingly, Long (2004) and Laurin (2010) point out that the food experience comprises a number of surrounding factors, such as the place, its physical setting, people, history and traditions. In this context, the local has received broader attention, as some tourists tend to value locally sourced products over standardised or globalised products.

The trend to the local seems to be a result of a rising interest in rural areas as potential tourism markets, as well as consumers having become more oriented towards knowledge-based holiday experiences and nature-based activities (Cochrane 2009), and different and authentic experiences (Bessière 1998; Hultman 2006). Accordingly, food and food-related experiences in rural areas are becoming increasingly important, and the possibility to eat 'local' meals or visit 'local' food producers has become the motive for more and more tourists' choice of destination (Sims 2009; Laurin 2010). In this sense, more and more destinations have recognised the power of culinary products and, according to du Rand *et al.* (2003: 98), 'a nation's identity is reflected and strengthened by the food experiences that it offers'. Kirshenblatt-Gimblet (2004: xi) argues that the food experience comprises much more than just the actual meal; while, obviously, all tourists must eat at some point, 'Making experiences memorable is a way the travel industry adds value – and profit – to an essential service such as food.' The focus on the *local* in food tourism may also contribute to strengthening the identity of particular regions. It enhances their uniqueness within their diverse communities (Telfer and Wall 1996; du Rand *et al.* 2003; Long 2004; Everett and Aitchison 2008), and awareness and development of a more sustainable environment (Everett and Aitchison 2008).

Localising the global

As the world is globalised, food products and the ways they are marketed, packed and provided are also being subjected to greater standardisation (Atkins and Bowler 2005). Cook and Crang (1996) argue that the 'local globalisation' of culinary culture means that it becomes harder to identify the actual origins of food and food products. Yet, on the other hand, a perception seems to exist in today's society that local food and food products are safer and of better quality than food and food products which are imported or originate from other regions or countries. Accordingly, the traditional values and uses of food products and food production are being highlighted, both by consumers and producers (Murdoch *et al.* 2000; DuPuis and Goodman 2005; Heldt Cassel 2006), and therefore it becomes still more important to emphasize the origin of food and food products (Burstedt *et al.* 2006).

Within wine-making, *terroir* is well known but the term is even gaining ground in the context of food and its ability to enhance the importance of specific places. In short, *terroir* refers to a certain product's connection to the soil and the soil's properties that infuse the product in terms of quality, taste and character (Gade 2004; Lagnevik 2010). But the producer's personal skills and methods when processing the product are also embedded in the *terroir*. In this sense, the local is given further meaning, as the product in question is loaded with place-specific values, such as local culture, traditions, history and authenticity (Bowen 2010; Lagnevik 2010). Emphasising local territory and food products' place-specific characteristics can thus be seen as a reaction to the globalisation and standardisation of food products and product handling processes (Burstedt 2004; Gade 2004). However, Robertson (1995: 28) claims that the global (homogenisation) and the local (heterogenisation) should not be treated separately, but rather synthesised into the merging term 'glocalisation' – because 'we appear to live in a world in which the expectation of uniqueness has become increasingly institutionalized and globally widespread'. That is, the global trend of offering place-unique food experiences is being applied and adapted in a local context, in accordance with the social and cultural prerequisites of the place. As Bell and Valentine (2005: 19) concluded: 'Perhaps more than any other process, globalisation (or glocalisation) is shaping and reshaping patterns of food consumption.'

Although culinary tourism has gained ground as a destination marketing tool in recent years, studies concerning the role of local food in relation to tourism and the tourism experience are limited (Long 2004; Nummedal and Hall 2006; Sims 2009). In addition, George *et al.* (2009) call for further examination of the relations between sustainable rural development, tourism and different economic, social and cultural aspects. Such relations can be expressed as the role of local food products and experiences in the development of rural tourism, as well as the role of culinary networks.

Culinary networks

Culinary tourism can be organised and arranged in a number of different ways, i.e. through niched efforts at the local, regional or national level. According to Buhalis (2000), tourists' total perception of a destination is constructed through various impressions provided by the different suppliers combined with the destination's attractions. This means that the marketing of a destination builds upon the marketing of each actor and the ability of these actors to mediate a common profile. Thus, a central factor in the making of a culinary destination is the ability among local suppliers to cooperate and find ways to promote a common 'product' (Holloway *et al.* 2006). One way to enhance the attraction of a specific area is through the establishment of culinary networks involving providers of local food products and food-related experiences (Marsden and Smith 2005; Venn *et al.* 2006). Such initiatives are perceived to contribute considerably to the development of rural communities in terms of social, cultural, environmental and economic sustainability (Lordkipanidze *et al.* 2005; Marsden and Smith 2005; Dredge 2006).

Culinary networks are subject to various definitions. Marsden and Smith (2005), for instance, use the notion of *ecological entrepreneurship*, which comprises the collaborations between key actors in local rural areas with the aim of achieving the common goals of sustainability and competitiveness. These networks have resulted from the crisis in European agriculture, which has forced many of those working in the resource industries to find new ways of positioning themselves. Ecological entrepreneurship plays an important role in rural development, creating motivation and new opportunities for other actors in local communities to form new networks, thereby strengthening a certain area's position and competitiveness. Similarly, Holloway *et al.* (2006) emphasise the positive contribution of *alternative food networks* to the development of tourism in rural areas. For instance, such networks help to bring local food products closer to consumers and reinforce the authentic experience (Marsden *et al.* 2000).

Accordingly, Bessière (1998) argues that collective initiatives are established in order to contribute to the development of rural tourism, linking local products and culinary traditions with the visitors' interest in quality. Furthermore, culinary heritage is used within a specific place or community as 'a kind of banner beneath which the inhabitants of a given area recognize themselves' (Bessière 1998: 23; see also Chapter 15 below). Bessière exemplifies this by referring to the use of labelling, which not only ensures the quality of the product, but 'gives the consumer a comfortable feeling about the history, identity and nature of the product' (Bessière 1998: 25). The various collaborations between local producers can thus be an important contributing factor in the process of constructing the local in terms of identity and community development (Østrup Backe 2010).

While culinary networks in general are of great value to rural communities, little attention is given to the actual processes of their development, and in particular to the practices by which they are shaped. By exploring how culinary networks emerge and develop it is also possible to achieve a broader understanding of the role of local food products and experiences in this process.

Studying culinary network practices

According to Reckwitz (2002) and Schatzki (2001), *the practice approach* considers how social life and phenomena are constituted through human practices. That is, the understanding of a specific phenomenon is centred on a shared practical understanding, including components such as 'knowledge, meaning, human activity, science, power, language, social institutions, and historical transformation' (Schatzki 2001: 2). A similar perspective is presented by Sztompka

(1991), who developed the theory of social becoming as an attempt to understand the various dimensions of 'the social'. In short, the theory of social becoming comprises the shift from a focus on structures (macro perspective) to a focus on individuals and their actions (micro perspective), and seeks to eliminate the division between the micro and macro perspectives. Hence, practice constitutes the meta-level on which the micro and macro perspectives are synthesised. The theory of social becoming relies on the perception that society is continuously constructed by human beings at the same time as human beings are shaped by society. Consequently, it is very likely that the process of social becoming – whether it concerns the social and individual actions of a group, an organisation or a network – will meet controversies of some kind, as its members will inevitably try to change the pre-given structures in different ways (Sminia 2003). However, some potential outcomes of the process of social becoming, Sztompka argues, are that conflicts might lead to change, power may cause development, and creativity might lead to production (Sztompka 1991). According to this perspective, tourism development can be understood as a process where places, people and tourism products are constantly interacting and changing in different ways. Furthermore, the local is constructed not solely at the micro- and the macro-level, but through different negotiation processes between the levels.

A common understanding of the practice term seems to be that it is of an interpretative nature and embraces everyday life. Sztompka (2008) defines everyday life as consisting of observable manifestations – social events – that embed collective acts and relations between people. Social events can comprise usual daily routines, like grocery shopping or watching television; but less frequent activities such as going to church, attending a concert, or visiting an event fall within an understanding of everyday life. The 'criterion' for definition as a social event is that an activity is not unique, but will be repeated at certain moments – every day, every month or every year. Thus, studying social events can contribute to the understanding of how everyday practices are related and connected not only to the formation of culinary tourism networks but also to the construction of the local and the networks' role in rural tourism development on a more general level.

Approaching the field

The case study involved the culinary network *Matrundan*, situated in the Ystad-Österlen area of southern Sweden. The practices of the Matrundan network were studied according to the micro- and macro-perspectives presented by Sztompka (1991). The integration of the micro- and macro-perspectives is important because it is not possible to understand the relationship between culinary networks, the local, and rural tourism development by exclusively studying the practices of a network exclusively. Rather, one needs to assess the interrelationships between them in order to understand how they are linked in relation to local and global aspects. That is, to understand the formation of a culinary network, the surrounding factors affecting this formation must also be considered.

The focus of the empirical study rested on an actual description of the Matrundan network; that is, identifying the different network members and their roles, as well as the products and activities provided. Observations and informal conversations took place in different settings (e.g. private and public meetings, seminars, events) so as to understand how products and activities were presented and conveyed, as well as how actions were performed (e.g. gestures, expressions, attitudes). In addition, three qualitative interviews were carried out with a network representative, a project organiser, and a representative of a financing stakeholder organisation. The interviews were carried out in order to obtain background information about the establishment and development of the Matrundan network. Finally, the network's website and marketing brochures were examined in order to further understand the network and, in particular, how it used the local. In order to identify the role of culinary networks in rural tourism, the overall tourism and development strategy for Scania as well as other relevant reports and documents were also examined.

The Ystad-Österlen area and the Matrundan network

The Ystad-Österlen area is characterised by small, rural communities, with Ystad, the largest city, having only approximately 28,000 inhabitants (Boiystad 2010). Since most businesses are small scale and often family-owned, tourism and business development in the area are limited. There has been little management of economic development in the area and, as a consequence, a more focused strategy for the region was introduced by the regional tourism board, a local bank and a foundation for growth. The primary aim of the strategy is to find new forms of engagement and collaboration in order to create a more dynamic region with better educational and business opportunities. Tourism is an important aspect in this regard. At the practical level, the new strategy for Ystad-Österlen concerns product development, focusing on specific niche activities such as the arts, food and movies (for example, Ystad is the centre for the growing 'Wallander tourism'). Another part of the development strategy is the emphasis on all-year activities. Due to the rural nature of the area, seasonality is a big issue, and one important prerequisite for attracting visitors and investors is a vibrant region with a broad variety of activities and attractions. Therefore, it is crucial to involve communities as well as local entrepreneurs and businesses, so that a large number of different activities can be offered throughout the year.

The Matrundan network is one such activity, initiated in late 2006 by two external project organisers. The idea of establishing a culinary tourism profile in Scania was based on a rising global interest in the connections between food and tourism. However, this had not affected Sweden. In fact, the Nordic countries have never really been recognised as culinary destinations, due to the perception among visitors that Nordic meals and food products are heavy, uninteresting and expensive, though this is about to change, thanks to newly initiated efforts regarding local food products and tourism development (Claus Meyer 2010; Jordbruksverket 2010; Laurin 2010).

According to the project organisers, the focus on local food products and their increasing role in the marketing of destinations created an opportunity for Scania to develop new strategies in order to become a culinary destination. Hence, Ystad-Österlen was perceived to be an ideal place for the development of culinary tourism due to its overall rural characteristics and other significant factors such as a strong local culture and financial support from local stakeholders. It was also assumed that the Matrundan project would inspire new business opportunities in the area and reinforce its competitive advantages (Marsden and Smith 2005). Some inspiration for the culinary tourism project was found in well-established events such as Konstrundan (Art Tour) and Ölands Skördefest (Harvest Feast of Öland), as well as the UK's various food trails. The fact that Konstrundan was already established in the same area meant that both potential network members and visitors would be able to relate to this event, and it was thus presumed that the idea of a food tour would be easier to implement.

The most important point from the project organisers' point of view was that the Matrundan network should be heterogeneous and include not only restaurants but also a mix of producers and companies with the common interest of working with culinary experiences in some way. The intention was to ensure a wide and diverse range of products which would be interesting for visitors. At the time of writing, the network comprises approximately 30 members representing restaurants, B&Bs, inns, farm shops and various producers and cultivators of different culinary products. Apart from the network's internal activities, an annual food event is arranged during one week in spring and one weekend around harvest time in autumn. During this event visitors are offered a range of activities and experiences related to food, such as an apple safari, mustard tasting, herb field walks and chocolate courses. In most places the visitors participate actively or learn about the history and traditions of the products through exhibitions, lectures or demonstrations.

Culinary tourism in practice: the making of a network

The Matrundan network is based on a number of aspects, which can be identified according to the micro- and macro-levels of social structure (cf. Sztompka 1991). Seen from a macro-perspective, the local is the general discourse within which the network is being shaped in order to contribute to a regional culinary tourism profile. Likewise, the micro-perspective comprises the actual network, the activities and interactions of its members, and the use of the local in this respect. Further to the practice perspective, Matrundan can thus be seen as a social event manifested by the network members' interactions and performances (Sztompka 2008). The practices of the network seem to take on different dimensions according to the nature of these interactions and performances, the value of collective engagement, and both internal and external network activities. In the following these practices will be examined in more detail.

First, members run their business individually on a daily basis as it is their professional occupation from which they make their living. Collaboration is an important way of strengthening the business, and many of the Matrundan network members sell each other's products or hand out brochures which advertise the products and activities of other members. For instance, the owner of a spice farm claims that contact with the nearby mustard farm is fruitful: 'It is fun to be able to use and sell their products and benefit from each other.' But other network members do not interact particularly with each other at the daily level, as expressed by one inn owner:

> We don't see them much, really, we just focus on getting this place going.... We do sell the wines from the local vineyard, but we even have the lamb from the guy next door – and he is not part of the network.
>
> (inn owner 2010, author's translation)

Hence, at the daily level, the practices performed seem to be mainly business-oriented and collaboration is not directly connected to the membership of the network. Rather it appears to be related to who and what can support and contribute to economic profit. Furthermore, physical distance from other actors seems to be more important than actual participation in the Matrundan network.

Second, members partake in internal network activities such as meetings, workshops and other arrangements which have to do with the practical planning and development of the network. The practices executed in these contexts are the building blocks for the network; for example this is where the purpose of the network and membership criteria are discussed and decisions concerning events and activities are taken. This is also where the meaning of the local is being negotiated and tensions and conflicts become visible. One issue that has been subject to numerous discussions among existing network members is the criteria for membership. For example, at a workshop held in the start-up phase of the Matrundan network, participants discussed how members should be selected. While some wanted to establish certain criteria for membership – such as geographical position, degree of localness, business size (only small-scale businesses), and personal and economic engagement – others argued that everyone who wished to should become a member. It was further questioned who should be in charge of setting such criteria and how, for example, the degree of localness should be valued. As one participant asked, if the local hot dog man sells sausages made from locally produced pork but buys the bread from Germany, should he be part of the network or not? Here, the complexities of the network interactions become visible, revealing tensions related to members' roles as well as the power to define network structures (Buhalis 2000; Dredge 2006). In terms of negotiations of the local, each member has different perceptions of what the local holds, which makes the setting of criteria more or less impossible. Despite the conflicting perceptions of the network members, a common aim has been formulated, leaving space for individual interpretation, however (see also Chapter 5 below). Accordingly, the purpose of Matrundan is to contribute to the development of a culinary tourism profile in south-eastern Scania by offering culinary experiences, and by spreading the interest and knowledge of the area's products and the way they are processed (Matrundan 2010).

A third dimension of the network practices comprises the annual Matrundan event, where the members represent their own businesses and the network simultaneously. During the event, ideas and visions discussed internally are implemented and sold to visitors through culinary products and experiences. The making of the network happens through interactions with visitors, and in the presentation and execution of products and activities. Accordingly, the Matrundan network is shaped through a number of different performances and practices in different contexts, which over time turn into fixed routines or series of social rituals (Sztompka 2008). That is, the event and the internal network activities are held each year, at a certain time and certain place, involving more or less the same members and activities each time. The various activities and interactions taking place in different parts of the network are all components that construct the network and contribute to its development. Through the continuous process of interactions, performances and activities the Matrundan network and event are shaping specific practices for the network itself and its activities, but also eventually for the surrounding society.

Constructing and negotiating the local through everyday practices

As indicated above, the notion of the local is present at all levels of the Matrundan network. In the everyday practices of the network members, the local is expressed through different activities, both within the network and in interactions with visitors. The following examples illustrate how the practices of Matrundan and its members contribute to the construction of the local according to three different dimensions: the local as a structural tool; the local as a link between history and tourism; and the local as creator of 'glocalisation'.

The local as a structural tool

In the spring of 2010 a symposium was held for Matrundan members and other interested actors such as press and researchers. Under the title '*Terroir* – the soul of the place – provides the taste' (author's translation), the symposium was aimed at discussing the role of local food in relation to place and tourism, and particularly how this idea could be implemented in the network's efforts. The keynote speaker was the Danish celebrity chef and entrepreneur behind the 2010 number one restaurant in the world (Noma), Claus Meyer. Meyer is also one of the founders of the *New Nordic Kitchen*, a manifesto which focuses on Nordic *terroir* and how Nordic food products can convey their special qualities and values and be integrated in and outside northern countries, like obvious culinary destinations such as France, Spain and Italy (Claus Meyer 2010).

During the symposium it was discussed how Matrundan can preserve and develop the specialities of Ystad-Österlen and highlight the unique food products of the area that differentiate it from other regions. Hence, the local plays a central part in the establishment of projects such as Matrundan, as it shapes structures and practices for culinary tourism and the food experience. The role of the local in relation to the Matrundan network (and a more general culinary tourism strategy in Scania) was negotiated in several ways at the symposium. During a panel debate, for instance, perceptions of the local were expressed, such as the use of traditional products of the area: 'there is a treasure chest of old recipes and preparation methods' (Matrundan member 2010), which should be valued and used in new ways. Further, it was stressed that in order to attract visitors and make them purchase Matrundan products, it is important to emphasise the products, history: 'a history that can be inscribed with the place and provide an explanation of why it [the food] tastes good' (Matrundan member 2010). Hence, several members found that it was important to mediate the name and origin of each product, and accordingly a common key value was identified: the concept of 'nearby', which should embrace a number of connotations, such as place, products, producers, experiences, traditions, soil, ecology and localness.

The local was further manifested in practice at a mingle event prior to the symposium; the members of Matrundan had created a miniature market hall, offering small samples of their products – some raw or coming directly from the soil, and some prepared as small dishes. All dishes and products were presented with small labels stating their name and/or origin; or the producer would explain the dish when handing it out: raw asparagus, reaped the same day; smoked sausages from Svinaberga's farm; different types of homemade herb butter; and Österlen chocolates, to mention some. The example of the market hall shows how the local is being negotiated in practice – that is, through each producer's choice of product and their presentation and labelling. The discussions and activities related to the symposium also show how *terroir* is used in relation to food; apart from the significance of their being grown and processed in the particular area, the products are loaded with unique meanings according to their place-specific characteristics, their cultural, traditional and historical values, as well as the skills of the people handling them (Burstedt 2004; Gade 2004; Bowen 2010; Lagnevik 2010).

The notion of the local is also clearly integrated in the Matrundan event, expressed through products and activities, and in the various marketing material. In the event programme for 2010, an inn announces: 'Every day during Matrundan at 12–15 o'clock. *Äggakaka* [omelette], a Scanian cultural heritage made from new-laid Österlen eggs, served with stirred lingonberries and smoked bacon' (*Matrundan Österlen* 2010: 3; author's translation). Here, the typical traditional Scanian dish *äggakaka* is advertised (directly translated, it means 'cake of eggs'). In other parts of Sweden one would use the ordinary word for 'omelette'; however, in this context the word in itself – with its dialectal emphasis – becomes a clear manifestation of the local. That the dish is served in the traditional way with smoked bacon and lingonberries, as well as the ingredients of the dish being from Österlen, further stresses the 'place-boundedness' of the dish as well as the *terroir* of the ingredients (Bessière 1998; Burstedt 2004; Gade 2004; Claus Meyer 2010). A similar example from a guesthouse connects the notion of the local with the nature and culture of Österlen:

Come and live and eat in beautiful and calm settings with a magnificent view of the mighty Östersjön with its straight unbroken horizon. At 19 o'clock we serve locally produced beef and spring vegetables (*primörer*). And if the asparagus is ready … mmmmmm. Must be booked in advance! Vernissage at 12–16 o'clock. Works by Christian Lewin, Marie Englund and Magnus Åkersson (www.maknusakesson.se) [*sic*]. We serve small delicacies and good wine at Matrunde prices. …

(*Matrundan Österlen* 2010: 4; author's translation)

Not only does the place offer a beautiful environment; the guest will also be able to experience food and food products from nearby producers and enjoy the work of local artists. The local food is put into a setting, which should be easy for potential visitors to imagine. Thus this example illustrates how the local is used to mediate a certain place, a place for culinary experiences and other cultural activities (Murdoch *et al.* 2000; Kirshenblatt-Gimblett 2004; DuPuis and Goodman 2005; Laurin 2010).

The local as a link between history and tourism

In a tourism context, places and destinations often stress the local by connecting specific food products or dishes to local traditions, in order to make the product unique and create a feeling of authenticity (Bessière 1998; Sims 2009). All landscapes in Sweden have their own traditional place-specific food products, meals or seasoning known in just that area. In many cases, these products are connected to different benefits (health, luck, wealth) or emphasised in a historical context. In the Matrundan network, the emphasis on connecting the tourism experience with history was brought out at the symposium, as described above – but it is also clearly manifested through the different activities offered during the Matrundan event. For instance, the connection between local traditions and the tourism experience is shown at the spice farm, where the owner arranges 'herb-field safaris', taking the visitors on a guided tour of the cultivated lands. Practical information about specific herbs, spices and reaping methods is enriched with stories and anecdotes about the plants' function and use in cooking or beverages. In between, the owner tells a short tale about to a specific crop, linking it to medieval myths or the personal history of her family. For instance, her grandmother always used southernwood (which is also used for schnapps) when mopping floors. Since the herb stuck to the cracks in the floor the house would smell good for a long time after. And, in the Middle Ages, for instance, the soldiers would always have a thyme-flavoured bath before going out to war because it was believed that the thyme would give them extra strength. Also, according to an old legend, an elderberry tree must be planted by every house to give strength and protection to the people living there.

The above example shows how the local is produced and negotiated in the practices of the Matrundan members. Accordingly, as well as being a commercial tool to sell a tourist experience, the tales also connect the herbs and spices with the place and display a historical value, as they emphasise the food products' connection to the local heritage and traditions of the visited area (Bessière 1998; Burstedt 2004; Long 2004). Additionally, in combination the stories can be seen as a latent way of communicating a sustainable profile, as they stress the localness of products and activities in terms of traditions and local heritage, but also through the use of locally sourced food products (Lordkipanidze *et al.* 2005; Marsden and Smith 2005; Sims 2009).

Localising the global

During the Matrundan event the general store in a small community offers a number of different local products from some of the Matrundan members. Visitors get the opportunity to taste bread, charcuterie, chocolate, mustard, cheeses and olive or rape-seed oil – and eventually they should be persuaded to buy their favourites to take home. The products clearly represent the local specialities of the area – confirmed by their labels, which almost without exception name their place of origin: Österlen chocolates, Petersborgsgård mustard, Kivik apple juice. The olive oil from Crete is conspicuous, placed with other 'local' products, making one wonder how this foreign product comes to be presented as an Österlen product. The reason is fascinating: a man living in the community has a second home in Crete and belongs to the village's olive oil cooperative. Oil which he and his Greek neighbours cannot consume is packaged neatly in glass bottles and given a fine label that states its exact origin. In Österlen the bottles are sold in the general store as a local product. The exotic olive oil from a small unheard-of Cretan village has suddenly become local because the man who imports it happens to live in the community.

The example has two dimensions with regard to the notion of the local: first, the labels of the products offered in the general store all emphasise the origins of each product, boasting a certain quality as well as their connection to local traditions (Bessière 1998). Second, the olive oil illustrates 'glocalisation' (Robertson 1995). The notion of the global being localised is also found at a local vineyard:

> Imagine if the new champagne is found in Österlen, we think and hope so. When you visit us you will get the feeling of how a Swedish vineyard works. We want to give you as nice a time you would have as in France, Italy or South Africa.
>
> (*Matrundan Österlen* 2010: 7; author's translation)

By referring to acknowledged wine countries, the little-known product from the Österlen-based vineyard is put into a global context, signalling that the products and related experiences are of similar quality. But the visitor will be able to experience a global product in a local context, produced and packed according to local prerequisites (Robertson 1995; Cook and Crang 1996; Atkins and Bowler 2005; Bell and Valentine 2005). But the process of 'glocalisation' can also take place the other way round, as in the example of an asparagus farm, situated just outside a small village in Österlen, which has become an established company since its humble start some 14 years ago. Today, the company is a large provider of asparagus around the country, delivering to individuals, small grocery stores and even a few large supermarkets. The farm has long received a large number of visitors each year during the very short season, and since the introduction of the Matrundan event, the number has increased dramatically. On rainy days many have come in vain, as there has simply not been enough asparagus to pick and sell.

The small, family-owned asparagus farm has slowly turned into a producer of a high-quality local product, well known not only in southern Sweden but even in other parts of the country as well as in the eastern part of neighbouring Denmark. In addition, the origin of the asparagus has recently gained wider rec-ognition, since the above-mentioned chef and entrepreneur Meyer brought the crop to his Noma restaurant. At the *terroir* symposium he was offered a spear of raw asparagus and, after a certain initial scepticism, he stated that he had never tasted better asparagus – and ordered a few kilos for his restaurant. Hence, from being a local provider with enough visitors to ensure day-to-day profits, the Österlen asparagus became globalised through representation in the world's number one restaurant. Guests are introduced to a sample of the Österlen *terroir* and its potential food experiences, and in this sense one might argue that the local is reinforcing the process of 'glocalisation'.

Conclusions

This chapter has explored the making of a culinary network through the prac-tices of its members, and in particular the notion of the local embedded within this process. Hence, the formation of the Matrundan network seems to be a complex process, offering many challenges to the actors involved. That is, the network is formed and structured continuously as its members and activities change, but also according to surrounding cultural, social and economic factors. This creates tensions when aspects such as members' roles and responsibilities, definitions of membership criteria, and network purposes and activities are being defined and negotiated. Despite the fact that the common goal of the network is to create a strong, common brand which can mediate a culinary tourism profile for the region, each member acts differently according to his or her own every-day situation. Matrundan may not be very important in the daily activities of each network member; however, there seems to be a high degree of engagement in the common network activities (and the annual event in particular), and in this perspective the Matrundan members seem to recognise and appreciate the value of the network.

The Matrundan event emphasises how different practices can actually con-tribute to the mediation of culinary tourism in rural areas. While the Matrundan network plays an important role for its individual actors and in the local com-munities of Ystad/Österlen, the network is still just one, albeit a significant one, of several initiatives in the all-year-round string of events which are a central element of the Scanian destination strategy. Hence, the synthesising of micro- and macro-levels essential in the theory of social becoming can be illustrated through the Matrundan network: the micro through the establishment of a specific network and its development through everyday interactions and performances; the macro is understood in a wider perspective, the network being an attempt to shape new structures (locally and regionally) but also emerging from a more global idea of highlighting local food products.

Culinary networks as an instrument of sustainable rural tourism development?

As was pointed out in the analysis above, the local is of great significance to the Matrundan network, and is present throughout the entire process of its formation. The notion of the local is embedded in the everyday activities of the network members and reigns as a general discourse within which the network acts. However, defining what is actually local is not clear-cut, as it has been suggested here. The local is socially constructed, understood according to the prerequisites and previous experiences of the network members and other actors (see Chapter 5 below). The perceptions of what or who is *not* local seem to have a particular influence on the negotiation process. Nevertheless, the local is of great importance to the Matrundan members as a mediator of the specific history and traditions of each product offered, and as an indicator of high-quality products and experiences.

While the local is clearly expressed in the various interactions and activities of the Matrundan network, the notion of sustainability remains more latent. In the network, sustainability is embedded with localness, expressed through the use of 'locally sourced', 'ecological' and 'traditional' food products, or as an integrated part of the 'nearby' concept. The term in itself is hardly mentioned by the network members; rather, it seems to be an obvious context of their interactions and activities. It is interesting that 'being local' and 'being sustainable' seem to be perceived as more or less equivalent, although – despite common features – the terms differ remarkably. The local is but one aspect of sustainability and selling locally produced and ecological products does not automatically create sustainability (see Chapter 1 above).

However, the discourse that seems to exist in today's society – that local and ecological products automatically entail sustainability – proves that phenomena such as culinary tourism will gain an increasing role in the marketing of destinations and rural areas in particular. Although the story of Matrundan is just one example of a larger phenomenon and should not be generalised, I would dare to argue that culinary networks can be used as a tool for sustainable tourism development in rural areas, as such initiatives involve small-scale producers, highlight locally sourced products, and enhance local traditions and cultural values. Further studies should therefore focus on the relationship between localness and sustainability in the development of rural tourism and the food experience, in order to catch the different nuances of discourses on the local and 'sustainability'.

References

Atkins, P. and Bowler, I. (2005) *Food in Society: Economy, culture, geography*, New York: Oxford University Press.

Bell, D. and Valentine, G. (2005) *Consuming Geographies: We are where we eat*, London: Routledge.

Bessière, J. (1998) 'Local development and heritage: traditional food and cuisine as tourist attraction in rural areas', *Sociologia Ruralis*, 38(1): 21–34.

Boiystad (2010) www.boiystad.nu/boiystad.nsf/AllDocuments/2622B21997A8E604C125 75D100491C44 (accessed 13 August 2010).

Bowen, S. (2010) 'Embedding local places in global spaces: geographical indications as a territorial development strategy', *Rural Sociology*, 75(2): 209–43.

Buhalis, D. (2000) 'Marketing the competitive destination of the future', *Tourism Management*, 21: 97–116.

Burstedt, A. (2004) 'The place on the plate!', *Ethnologia Europea*, 32(2): 145–58.

Burstedt, A., Fredriksson, C. and Jönsson, H. (2006) 'Inledning', in A. Burstedt, C. Fredriksson and H. Jönsson (eds) *Mat. Genealogi och gestaltning*, Lund: Studentlitteratur.

Burstedt, A., Fredriksson, C. and Jönsson, H. (eds) (2006) *Mat. Genealogi och gestaltning*, Lund: Studentlitteratur.

Claus Meyer (2010) Online. Available: www.clausmeyer.dk/da/faglige_engagementer/ det_nye_nordiske_koekken/nordisk_terroir_.html (accessed 26 August 2010).

Cochrane, J. (2009) 'Changing landscapes and rural tourism', in R. Thomas (ed.) *Managing Regional Tourism: A case study of Yorkshire, England*, Ilkley: Great Northern Books.

Cook, I. and Crang, P. (1996) 'The world on a plate: culinary culture, displacement and geographical knowledges', *Journal of Material Culture*, 1(2): 131–53.

Dredge, D. (2006) 'Networks, conflict and collaborative communities', *Journal of Sustainable Tourism*, 14: 562–81.

DuPuis, E.M. and Goodman, D. (2005) 'Should we go "home" to eat?: toward a reflexive politics of localism', *Journal of Rural Studies*, 21: 359–71.

du Rand, G.E., Heath, E. and Alberts, N. (2003) 'The role of local and regional food in destination marketing: a South African situation analysis', *Wine, Food and Tourism Marketing*, 14(3–4): 97–112.

Everett, S. and Aitchison, C. (2008) 'The role of food tourism in sustaining regional identity: a case study of Cornwall, South West England', *Journal of Sustainable Tourism*, 16: 150–67.

Gade, D.W. (2004) 'Tradition, territory, and terroir in French viniculture: Cassis, France, and appellation contrôlée', *Annals of the Association of American Geographers*, 94: 848–67.

George, E.W., Mair, H. and Reid, D.G. (2009) *Rural Tourism Development. Localism and Cultural Change*, Bristol: Channel View Publications.

Hall, C.M. and Sharples, E. (2003) 'The consumption of experiences or the experience of consumption? An introduction to the tourism of taste', in C.M. Hall, E. Sharples, R. Mitchell, N. Macionis and B. Cambourne (eds) *Food Tourism Around the World: Development, management and markets*, Oxford: Butterworth-Heinemann.

Hall, C.M. and Sharples, E. (ed.) (2008) *Food and Wine Festivals and Events Around the World: Development, management and markets*, Oxford: Butterworth-Heinemann.

Hall, C.M., Müller, D.K. and Saarinen, J. (2009) *Nordic Tourism: Issues and cases*, Bristol, Buffalo, NY, and Toronto: Channel View Publications.

Heldt Cassel, S. (2006) 'Regionen för finsmakare. Regional profilering och varumärkes-byggande i skärgården', in A. Burstedt, C. Fredriksson and H. Jönsson (eds) *Mat. Genealogi och gestaltning*, Lund: Studentlitteratur.

Henderson, Joan C. (2009) 'Food tourism reviewed', *British Food Journal*, 111(4): 317–26.

Holloway, L., Cox, R., Venn, L., Kneafsy, M., Dowlers, E. and Tuomanenm, H. (2006) 'Managing sustainable farmed landscape through "alternative" food networks: a case study from Italy', *The Geographical Journal*, 172(3): 219–29.

Hultman, J. (2006) 'Från jord till ord. Maten i Skåne', in A. Burstedt, C. Fredriksson and H. Jönsson (eds) *Mat. Genealogi och gestaltning*, Lund: Studentlitteratur.

Jordbruksverket (2010) Online. Available: www.jordbruksverket.se (accessed 28 July 2010).

Kirshenblatt-Gimblett, B. (2004) 'Foreword', in L.M. Long (ed.) *Culinary Tourism*, Lexington, Ky: University Press of Kentucky.

Lagnevik, M. (2010) 'Absolut terroir', in H. Sandberg (ed.) *Skåne, mat och medier*, Lund: Media Tryck och Skånes Livsmedelsakademi.

Laurin, U. (2010) *Den Svenska Turistmåltiden, En internationell bild av mat och måltider*, Rapport 0044, Tillväxtverket.

Long, L.M. (ed.) (2004) *Culinary Tourism*, Lexington, Ky: University Press of Kentucky.

Lordkipanidze, M., Brezet, H. and Backman, M. (2005) 'The entrepreneurship factor in sustainable tourism development', *Journal of Cleaner Production*, 13: 787–98.

Marsden, T. and Smith, E. (2005) 'Ecological entrepreneurship: sustainable development in local communities through quality food production and local branding', *Geoforum*, 36: 440–51.

Marsden, T., Banks, J. and Bristow, G. (2000) 'Food supply chain approaches: exploring their role in rural development', *Sociologia Ruralis*, 40(4): 424–38.

Matrundan (2010) Online. Available: www.matrundan.se.

Matrundan Österlen (2010) *Matrundan på Österlen 8–16 maj*, event programme, Österlen Matrundan.

Mossberg, L. and Svensson, I. (2009) *Boken om Måltidsturism i Västra Götaland*, Göteborg: Västsvenska Turistrådet.

Murdoch, J., Marsden, T. and Banks, J. (2000) 'Quality, nature, and embeddedness: some theoretical considerations in the context of the food sector', *Economic Geography*, 76(2): 107–25.

Nummedal, M. and Hall, C.M. (2006) 'Local food in tourism: an investigation of the New Zealand South Island's bed and breakfast sector's use and perception of local food', *Tourism Review International*, 9(4): 365–78.

Reckwitz, A. (2002) 'Toward a theory of social practices: a development in culturalist theorizing', *European Journal of Social Theory*, 5(2): 243–63.

Richards, G. (2002) 'Gastronomy: an essential ingredient in tourism production and consumption?', in A.-M. Hjalager and G. Richards (eds) *Tourism and Gastronomy*, London: Routledge.

Robertson, R. (1995) 'Glocalization: time – space and homogeneity – heterogeneity', in M. Featherstone, S. Lash and R. Robertson (eds) *Global Modernities*, London: Sage.

Schatzki, T.R. (2001) 'Introduction: practice theory', in T.R. Schatzki, K.K. Cetina and E. von Savigny (eds) *The Practice Turn in Contemporary Theory*, London: Routledge.

Sims, R. (2009) 'Food, place and authenticity: local food and the sustainable tourism experience', *Journal of Sustainable Tourism*, 17: 321–36.

Sminia, H. (2003) 'The failure of the Sport7 TV-channel: controversies in a business network', *Journal of Management Studies*, 40(7): 1621–49.

Sztompka, P. (1991) *Society in Action: The theory of social becoming*, Chicago: The University of Chicago Press.

Sztompka, P. (2008) 'The focus on everyday life: a new turn in sociology', *European Review*, 16(1): 23–37.

Telfer, D.J. and Wall, G. (1996) 'Linkages between tourism and food production', *Annals of Tourism Research*, 23(3): 635–53.

Venn, L., Kneafsy, M., Holloway, L., Cox, R., Dowler, E. and Tuomainen, H. (2006) 'Researching European "alternative" food networks: some methodological considerations', *Area*, 38(3): 248–58.

Woods, M. and Deegan, J. (2003) 'A warm welcome for destination quality brands: the example of the Pays Cathare region', *International Journal of Tourism Research*, 5(4): 269–82.

Østrup Backe, J. (2010) 'Från äggakaka till coq au vin de Köpingsberg', in H. Sandberg, (ed.) *Skåne, mat och medier*, Lund: Media Tryck och Skånes Livsmedelsakademi.

3 Real food in the US

Local food initiatives, government and tourism

Amy Hughes and Alan A. Lew

Introduction

Food is a politically and economically complex and contentious topic. In the US, city planners have recognized this since at least the late 1990s (Pothukuchi and Kaufman 1999), though more recently they have begun to understand better how the dominant industrial food system permeates human use of the built environment and directly influences variations in community health and well-being (American Planning Association (APA) 2007). Food is a public policy issue to the degree that it affects public health and the general well-being of the community. These, in turn, impact how residents and visitors perceive, interact with, and feel about a local community. Like poverty and illness, food-related problems in one part of a community can degrade the broader population through added costs for social and medical services, reduced efficiency in the local labor force, difficulties for educators in affected schools, and a variety of other social and economic challenges. If the goal of local government is to address the common and shared welfare and safety needs of a community, then food policies and planning should play an important part in that.

This chapter's focus is on the specific role of local government planning departments in food policy development and implementation, and how this might relate to tourism and hospitality. Planning in the US usually incorporates community development and is the branch of local government that is most involved in community outreach and support (though not always). In addition, planners tend to have a broader perspective on the issues and needs of a community, from transportation to land use, and from economic development to neighborhood design. This holistic view makes planning a logical nexus for the intersection of local food policy and development efforts.

Probably the most significant public planning and policy issues related to food are access and security. Food access is the ability for consumers to purchase affordable, nutritious food and is directly related to the local food geography (Walker *et al.* 2010). This includes the presence or absence of local food stores and the transportation options that are available to get to an adequate food outlet. Many small local stores are not able to compete with large supermarkets that have longer business hours, large parking lots, and discounted prices to attract a larger market. In addition, mergers among food retail outlets can create inequities in food access, as smaller inner-city stores are closed in favor of larger supermarkets on the outskirts of cities (APA 2007; Breitbach 2007). Plus, the lack of adequate food access can exacerbate food security issues.

Food security, as defined by the US Department of Agriculture (USDA), means having access at any time to enough food for an active and healthy life (Nord and Coleman-Jensen 2011). More than 14 percent of households in the US have been identified as experiencing food insecurity (US Congress 2010). To assist food-insecure households, the USDA spends $60 billion annually on domestic food and nutrition assistance programs (US Congress 2010). The National School Lunch Program is the second largest nutrition assistance program in the US, providing free and reduced-price lunches to children from food-insecure households. Ironically, the National School Lunch Program is influenced by the nation's farm bill, which determines what children will have for lunch (Pollan 2006a). Because of the interdependence of these economic and social welfare programs, the resulting policies have tended to disregard their impacts on human and environmental health, in favor of the country's industrial food system.

The industrial food system contributes substantially to global and national economies, and provides basic levels of food access that reach most of the world's ever growing population. Local and regional economies, however, are paying a price for this economic efficiency. Caton-Campbell (2004: 345) argued that corporate food production "drives diversified farming operations out of business, and forces farmers into contract farming that leaves them vulnerable to layoffs." Additionally, the costs of food production and distribution are externalized, enabling food prices to remain low, yet creating negative environmental and human health consequences (Pollan 2006b).

Environmental pollution is one of the externalized costs prevalent in communities where Concentrated Animal Feeding Operations (CAFOs) are present (Foer 2009). Labao and Stofferahn's (2008) research showed that close to 60 percent of communities located near an industrial farm suffered degradation of their environment, socioeconomic well-being, and their social fabric. A study of the effects of industrial farming in North Carolina showed that "children within three miles of an industrial farm operation had higher rates of asthma diagnosis and experienced more asthma-related emergency room visits than children living farther away" (Krisberg 2008: 22). According to the National Agricultural Law Center, nine states have laws that prohibit or limit corporate food production (Pittman 2005). However, the industrial food system, through a network of political support and economic influences, has created a society that is highly dependent on it.

Through modernization and economies of scale, industrial agriculture has become a profit-driven business influenced by corporate and political ideologies with little concern for communities (Breitbach 2007). Many communities are realizing that alternatives to the industrial food system exist, as is evidenced in the growing tensions and conflicts between industrial and alternative food systems (Caton-Campbell 2004). Support for community food systems is increasing due to these tensions, as well as a belief that community food systems can contribute to a community's overall health. "Not only does an adequate, varied diet contribute to individual health, but the way food is grown, distributed and eaten also profoundly affects the environmental, social, spiritual and economic well-being of the community" (Feenstra 1997: 28).

Broadly, there are two approaches to breaking away from the industrial food system. The first consists of a variety of *local food systems*. Localness refers to a single community or a small geographical region within which foods are produced and consumed. The second approach includes organic and related *alternative foods* that are produced and distributed to a much larger regional, national, or even international market. We define these two food systems together as *real food* because of the greater care taken to grow and make products that are not mass-produced out of unpronounceable ingredients from unknown sources.

The tourism and hospitality sector of a local economy is especially well situated to support real foods because community foods, in particular, reflect and strengthen a greater sense of place and identity, and that can be a market strength for tourists in search of real-place experience. In light of the growing interest in alternative food systems, this chapter explores the characteristics of community food systems in the US today, the current and potential role of city planners in helping plan for community food systems, and potential involvements of the hospitality and tourism sector in supporting local alternative foods.

Urban planning and food systems

More than a decade ago, two papers were published that marked a turning point in the significance of American planners' participation in food planning. The authors, Pothukuchi and Kaufman (1999, 2000), identified four areas related to food issues that would benefit from professional city planning involvement: (1) agricultural land preservation, (2) land use and zoning, (3) integrating food issues into economic development activities, and (4) documenting the environmental impacts of the industrial food system. Prior to these publications, food planning had been mostly ignored in planning literature (Pothukuchi and Kaufman 1999). Responding to this situation, in 2004 the *Journal of Planning Education and Research* dedicated a special issue to planning for food, helping to launch food planning as a major issue among planners (Hammer 2004). Several years later, in 2007, the adoption of the *Policy Guide on Community and Regional Food Planning* by the American Planning Association (APA) further asserted the significance of food planning. The *Policy Guide* advocates for the inclusion of food planning among other major city planning functions, such as efficient land use, economic development, poverty alleviation, reducing fossil fuel consumption, farmland preservation, and controlling environmental pollution (Table 3.1). In addition, the *Guide* identified ecological sustainability, social equity, cultural conservation, and public health as community goals that food planning could support.

From this perspective, city planners are in a unique position, "linked to decision makers and decision arenas in public, private, and nonprofit sectors" (Pothukuchi 2004: 361). They are able to mediate processes and recommend policies based on knowledge gained from the community. In this role, planners can encourage a food systems discourse and ultimately help facilitate this process for communities (Caton-Campbell 2004). The skills, knowledge, and position of planners within the community are advantageous for groups desiring to develop and expand alternative local food systems (Clancy 2004). And yet, while the benefits of having local government planners participate in community and regional food planning are numerous, very few planners work with communities on this issue.

Table 3.1 Justifications and goals for city planner involvement in local food planning

Planning justifications

1 Recognition that food system activities take up a significant amount of urban and regional land

2 Awareness that planners can play a role to help reduce the rising incidence of hunger on the one hand, and obesity on the other

3 Understanding that the food system represents an important part of community and regional economies

4 Awareness that the food Americans eat takes a considerable amount of fossil fuel energy to produce, process, transport, and dispose of

5 Understanding that farmland in metropolitan areas, and therefore the capacity to produce food for local and regional markets, is being lost at a strong pace

6 Understanding that pollution of ground and surface water, caused by the overuse of chemical fertilizers and pesticides in agriculture, adversely affects drinking water supplies

7 Awareness that access to healthy foods in low-income areas is an increasing problem for which urban agriculture can offer an important solution

8 Recognition that many benefits emerge from stronger community and regional food systems

Community goals

1 Support comprehensive food planning process at the community and regional levels

2 Support strengthening the local and regional economy by promoting local and regional food systems

3 Support food systems that improve the health of the region's residents

4 Support food systems that are ecologically sustainable

5 Support food systems that are equitable and just

6 Support food systems that preserve and sustain diverse traditional food cultures of Native American and other ethnic minority communities

7 Support the development of state and federal legislation to facilitate community and regional food planning discussed in general policies #1 through #6

Source: APA 2007: online.

Food Policy Councils in the US

One of the primary ways that alternative food systems awareness has expanded in the US has been through Food Policy Councils (FPCs). FPCs are collaborative organizations that support alternative community food systems and food security issues (CDC 2010). The first FPC in the US was established in Knoxville, Tennessee, in 1982 in response to a study conducted by graduate students and faculty in an urban planning class at the University of Tennessee, Knoxville (Haughton 1987). The study revealed severe inequities in the local food system, including nutritional deficiencies among the young and elderly due to the lack of access to food. By 1999, there were 15 FPCs in the US and Canada (Pothukuchi and Kaufman 1999). Less than 10 years later, 35 to 50 FPCs were either in the process of forming or already established. At present, there are more than 100 FPCs across the US.

FPCs convene multiple stakeholders from community members and local businesses to government and non-profit agencies, to examine food system issues comprehensively. The non-partisan councils conduct research and make policy recommendations. An example of policy change may involve an agricultural inventory, in which city-owned land is identified and made available for community gardens or other agricultural use. Many of these alternative food systems are initiated by concerned citizens and non-profit organizations, though a few have been launched through local, county, regional, and state governments (Dahlberg 1994). Pothukuchi and Kaufman (1999) emphasize that government-sanctioned FPCs are often better supported and thus more effective in influencing change.

A review of FPCs was undertaken to understand the objectives of alternative food system organizations. A list of 113 FPCs at the state, regional, county, and local levels was compiled from information available from the websites of two non-profit organizations, the Community Food Security Coalition (www.foodsecurity.org/) and the State Food Policy Council (www.statefoodpolicy.org/). The latter is an archive of the state and local food policy project operated by the Agricultural Law Center at Drake University.

According to the sources that were consulted, there are at least 113 FPCs across the US. A survey of those FPCs suggested that 36 were either currently forming or lacked an online presence, resulting in 86 FPCs with an active web presence. Of those 86 FPCs, 21 were state-level councils, eight were regional-level councils, 30 existed at the county level and 27 at the local level. The majority of the state-level FPCs were established after 2006. Eight were established between 2000 and 2005. Thirteen of the state-level FPCs originated through government, either by a governor mandate or through a Department of Agriculture or a Department of Health. The majority had an organizational structure with key members listed. Also listed was evidence of public and private partnerships and sources of funding. Many of these FPCs were funded by government. The remaining state-level FPCs, on the contrary, started through non-profit organizations or grassroots efforts. Overall, these councils showed little evidence of public–private partnerships. The regional FPCs differed slightly. The biggest distinction was the total number of councils at the regional level; only eight regional-level councils currently exist. The majority of councils were formed within the past three years. All of the regional councils began independently, through non-profit organizations or community activists.

There were several more county and local FPCs than councils at the state and regional level. Thirty-six FPCs exist at the county level and 43 exist at the local level. Of the 36 county-level FPCs, six lacked enough information or were not able to conduct an analysis. The majority of the county-level councils started within the past 10 years. In fact, only two began prior to 2002. Two of the county-level councils included restart dates, and had re-started in 2008. Nineteen started through community organizations or non-profits. All but two of the county-level councils analyzed showed evidence of an organizational structure, and 12 showed evidence of public–private partnerships.

Finally, at the local level, 16 FPCs were either currently being formed or did not have enough information available to conduct an analysis. The local-level FPCs more often began through a mandate by the mayor or by direction from city council. Four of the local-level FPCs began prior to 2002. While the majority of the local-level councils are young, they have an organizational structure and show evidence of public–private partnerships. Overall, the majority of the FPCs benefit from donations, grants, and volunteers. Other sources of funding come from government budgets. To assess these FPCs, beyond administrative characteristics, predetermined categories based on community food system projects, programs, and policies were extracted from the literature. The categories included:

• food access
• food security
• public health concerns
• benefits to the local economy
• environmental concerns
• community health
• food safety
• community education and food systems and nutrition
• farm-to-school programs and
• food justice.

The issues that concerned the majority of councils were community health and education, followed closely by impacts to the economy (Figure 3.1). Six of the regional and 21 of the county-level councils mentioned community health, while 17 of the state and 24 local-level councils specifically mentioned community health (Table 3.2). Similarly, 19 state-level councils, five regional-level, 21 county-level, and 21 local-level councils had goals to improve the economy. Overall, the local-level food policy councils addressed more issues and were actively engaged in a greater number of projects. In fact, more than half of all the local-level councils addressed issues related to food security, the environment, the local economy, community health, education, and food justice, and were involved in farm-to-school initiatives.

The issues least addressed were food safety and food justice. Across all FPCs, only 12 addressed food safety. Food justice was a goal in three state-level, two regional-level, and nine county-level councils. Interestingly, an exception for food justice was found in local-level councils, more than half of which addressed the issue. One observation related to the local-level councils was the dedication to education, which was generally associated with farm-to-school programs; 26 local food policy councils were engaged in or had a mission to encourage and support education and farm-to-school programs.

Based on the analysis, very few urban planners were actively involved in food planning with communities. Only nine FPCs mentioned working with a planning department. While the benefits have been explored, challenges also exist which may suggest reasons why planners are not more active. For the most part, the priorities set forth by the city government dictate the job responsibilities of the planner. Second, the awareness of benefits that planners offer in food planning is still growing, and tensions related to food systems may restrict planners from becoming involved in food planning. A third suggestion stems from the analysis

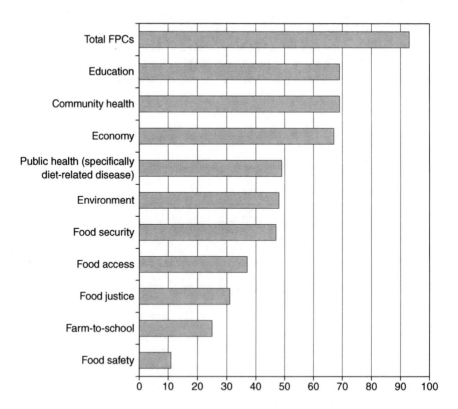

Figure 3.1 Issues addressed by Food Policy Councils in the United States.

of FPCs. Evidence located on websites indicates that several of the FPCs are staffed by individuals who volunteer to serve on the council. It was noted in meeting minutes that three councils specifically desired to remain completely independent from government, which may suggest that food planning is less related to community planners and better suited for a non-governmental social services venue.

The issues that planners face in relation to FPCs seem to exist for the tourism and hospitality sector in many communities. While some specialized, niche restaurants and caterers may participate in a local, community-level FPC, the emphasis on social welfare services is not very well aligned with the more commercial interests of the hospitality industry. As with city planners and city government in general, however, there is considerable potential for greater involvement and support for local food systems by tourism and hospitality interests.

Overall, many challenges exist to providing a healthy and robust local food system. If communities were interested in having the support of a city planner, many of the challenges could be better addressed. A major first step in overcoming some of the challenges is to become aware of the relationship that food systems have with the community, through health, the natural environment, and the built environment.

Community food in Flagstaff, Arizona

Located at the base of the San Francisco Peaks in northern Arizona and roughly 80 miles from the Grand Canyon, the city of Flagstaff is well known for its scenic beauty and convenient access to outdoor recreation activities. Historically,

Table 3.2 Issues addressed by Food Policy Councils in the United States by FPC level

	Food Policy Councils in the United States			
	State level	Regional level	County level	Local level
	21	8	30	27
Issues addressed				
Education	15	5	22	26
Community health	17	6	21	24
Economy	19	5	21	21
Public health (specifically diet-related diseases)	16	5	15	13
Environment	12	3	16	17
Food security	11	4	12	20
Food access	7	4	11	15
Food justice	3	2	9	18
Farm-to-school programs	7	0	4	26
Food safety	4	0	3	5

ranchers settled Flagstaff in the late 1800s, and were able to take advantage of the area's natural resources, notably water and timber (Hardy 2010). The railroads followed soon after, creating an opportunity to transport goods to markets, and within a few years Flagstaff was an established town with railroad access, livestock, lumber, and service industries.

The city of Flagstaff is a growing community. The 2010 population of Flagstaff was 65,870, which reflected an increase of 24.5 percent over 10 years (Ferguson 2011). The city averages 82 days of rain per year, with rainfall occurring primarily during July and August. At an elevation of nearly 7,000 feet (2100 meters), snow accumulation in the winter months can be heavy, with an average annual snowfall of 99.5 inches, and the cool climate makes for a relatively short frost-free growing season of about 100 days. Together, the elevation and weather patterns make Flagstaff a unique environment, particularly for agriculture.

To better understand the role of local government planning departments in food policy development and implementation, 12 interviews were conducted over three months and included six individuals from the public sector and six from the private sector (Table 3.3). Specifically, the interview questions explored individual food-shopping behaviors and examined individuals' awareness and beliefs about alternative food systems, and the role of planners in food policy development. In the event that the interviewees were unaware of food planning and the professional responsibilities of planners, a brief explanation of the American Planning Association's (APA) *Policy Guide on Community and Regional Food Planning* (2007) was introduced and discussed during the interview.

Table 3.3 Interview participants and their affiliations

Participant	Affiliation	Date of interview
A. Babbott (public sector)	Council member, City of Flagstaff	March 14, 2011
R. Emmons (private sector)	Resident and member of Flagstaff Foodlink	March 3, 2011
M. Jones (public sector)	Sustainability specialist, City of Flagstaff	February 14, 2011
J. Netzky (private sector)	Owner, local alternative catering	January 20, 2011
K. Otten (private sector)	Executive director, Flagstaff Community Supported Agriculture (FCSA) store	January 28, 2011
S. Overton (public sector)	Council member, City of Flagstaff	March 29, 2011
P. Pynes (private sector)	Gardener and beekeeper	February 17, 2011
K. Sharp (public sector)	Neighborhood planner, City of Flagstaff	March 1, 2011
S. Sopori (private sector)	Director, Willow Bend Environmental Education Center	February 18, 2011
C. Taylor (public sector)	Coconino County Supervisor	March 31, 2011
J. Tingerthal (private sector)	Resident	January 21, 2011
N. Woodman (public sector)	Sustainability manager, City of Flagstaff	February 14, 2011

The city of Flagstaff's government web pages served as the primary access point to procure interviews with individuals from the public sector. Public sector informants included Flagstaff council members, Flagstaff city employees and a member of the Coconino County Board of Supervisors. Private sector inform- ants were selected on the basis of their affiliation with or interest in community food systems. A key informant was used to gain access to other informants in the private sector. The key informant used for this research had exceptional knowledge of community food systems and food planning in general.

According to Gillham (2005: 54), an informant who has extensive knowledge about the research subject is described as an "elite" interviewee, and is likely part of a network of other well-informed individuals. This was indeed the case with the elite informant (see Hall 2011). As the Executive Director of Flagstaff's Community Supported Agriculture (FCSA) program and market, the key inform- ant maintains close connections with many area farmers and local initiatives to support community food systems. These interviews proved to be a rich source of information, specifically regarding ongoing efforts in support of alternative food systems in Flagstaff. While there are numerous benefits to interviewing elite informants, it should be noted that these interviewees represent a unique subset of the community; this in turn had the propensity to create a biased analysis of beliefs and behaviors for the community.

Several themes emerged throughout the interview, including the significance of education, establishing partnerships, and food accessibility issues related to transportation. Concerns about public health and food safety were also noted. Finally, many of the individuals interviewed believed that the alternative food systems could benefit local economies.

Education

Education was the prominent theme throughout all of the interviews. In total, 10 out of the 12 interviewees mentioned the lack of and need for community aware- ness and education, including public education, on food issues, and education or professional development for planners specifically related to food issues. K. Otten, Executive Director of the Flagstaff Community Supported FCSA store, discussed education comprehensively. She suggested that educating the public about the city's zoning plan was a good place to start, primarily due to its com- plexity: "The zoning plan might as well be in Latin. How do you make some- thing like that accessible, especially to someone who can't speak English?"

Furthermore, she suggested initiatives such as community gardens, cooking classes, and teaching about nutrition and its relationship to the economy. Several respondents mentioned that the local school gardens are helping to teach chil- dren how to grow food. One respondent noted that it had to be part of the curric- ulum for it to be a viable learning experience for students. The same respondent indicated that she teaches by example whenever she shops at the FCSA store.

The need for education is prominent in the community food systems liter- ature. Hopkins (2000: 209) asserts that "involving children in food production is very important" for environmental education and to promote life skills such as healthy eating. A similar strategy, the "farm-to-school" movement also promotes improving the health and nutrition of school-aged children (Vallianatos *et al.* 2004). Outreach as it relates to educating the public was a recurring theme, as explained by K. Otten who discussed an experience with a community garden initiative: "We go into a community, into people's lives and we think that we are helping, but we are not including them in the process. We need to create forums to make education and inclusion more accessible."

Overall, nine of the respondents recommended greater public awareness and suggested public awareness campaigns, to include information on nutrition and cooking. Other comments related to education included the need to educate planners and provide professional development opportunities for them to learn about food issues and food planning. A few of the respondents discussed education for planners:

> I'm not sure that contemporary issues such as food planning are covered in the planning curricula. There are a lot of people in the community that know about growing food here and that dialogue needs to open up.
>
> (R. Emmons)

> Planners need practical knowledge of farming and gardening, social knowledge of how communities create food systems, and political knowledge; and they need to be able to weave these knowledges together.
>
> (P. Pynes)

> I need to learn more and I am learning more. Planners would support it, but don't fully understand it. We need to understand the difference it would make to the community.
>
> (K. Sharp)

Partnerships

An awareness of the benefits of creating partnerships between public and private domains was a strong theme among interview responses. Levy (2010: 7) suggests that "being able to understand the political environment around oneself" is a useful ability for planners who want to effect positive change. Similarly, Caton-Campbell (2004) recommends that planners conduct a stakeholder analysis to determine how community stakeholders are part of the community food system, emphasizing that planners have specific skills which could contribute to the development of a food systems discourse. She suggests the need to "apply the standard tools of planning practice to food systems issues, making them more transparent to decision makers; agency officials; local, state, and federal funders; the broader planning community; and the general public" (2004: 349). Recommendations from both public and private sector interview respondents suggested that creating partnerships and developing a common language were necessary foundations for supporting alternative food systems: "We can use people in the community to obtain the language, maps and details. And to get an understanding of all the stakeholders" (K. Sharp).

Many respondents believed that planners could help develop relationships among stakeholders, acting as a "representative voice." In a similar vein, it was suggested that "Planners can be conduits between the city and the community, and help create relationships" (K. Otten). Pothukuchi (2004: 360) lists identical descriptions as rationales for planners' involvement in community food assessments.

Beyond partnerships, there were a number of recommendations made for the role of city planners in helping to provide opportunities for alternative food systems in the Flagstaff community. Respondents from the private sector made suggestions including removing obstacles and lifting restrictions "to make sure that people can grow food within the municipality," and taking advantage of opportunities through zoning (J. Netzky). A related suggestion was to help organize relevant studies, such as "a study of microclimates in Flagstaff to find the best places to grow food" (P. Pynes). Other suggestions included: (1) promote gardening, (2) promote local businesses that use local foods, (3) serve in a leadership role, and (4) set examples particularly through landscape practice on city property. While not all of these suggestions are realistic for planners, the responses illustrate individual perceptions of a planner's responsibilities.

Similar suggestions were made by informants from the public sector and included: (1) removing barriers and restrictions, (2) taxes, (3) land use and zoning, (4) addressing food security issues, (5) giving better direction to the city council, and (6) adopting the appropriate language in the regional plan, such as "including urban agriculture as a component of open space" (M. Jones). Throughout the literature it is evident that planners have impact through land use development and zoning. De la Salle and Holland (2010) illustrate how planners can participate in supporting alternative food systems through land use and growth management, transportation, parks and open spaces, and waste management. Many of the informants mentioned zoning, which may have been influenced by the recent draft zoning revision put forward by the city.

Accessibility, noted as a suggestion for planners, was another prominent theme throughout the interviews. Informants discussed food access through multiple perspectives including: (1) making alternative food systems accessible through community gardens, (2) helping to provide subsidies, (3) ensuring that food stamps for low-income people are accepted at the farmers' markets, and, as mentioned by one informant, (4) working with the Arizona Game and Fish Department to manage permits. The last suggestion was discussed in relation to valuing the local food supply and providing an advantage, through access, to local hunters over hunters from other states. Many of the suggestions made were outside of a planner's purview but are nonetheless important to consider with regard to the overall role of government in community food systems.

The term accessibility was also used to describe transportation issues. In fact, in many cases transportation planning is directly related to food security (Clifton 2004). However, informants discussed transportation into the city as opposed to routes throughout the city. The issue of transportation was discussed in relation to local and regional food systems and specifically the need to transport food into the community. As noted by one informant, the transportation issue has to be discussed: "it is a challenge, and it directs issues for us. There are a limited number of routes into Flagstaff" (S. Overton).

Public health

Although public health concerns dominated the literature in purporting the significance of food planning, only two respondents mentioned public health as a reason for planners' involvement in local food planning. Caton-Campbell (2004) explains that many consumers enjoy the convenience, low cost, and taste of food produced by the industrial food system despite the negative health and environmental consequences. Ultimately this relates to education and awareness of the public health benefits. S. Sopori, Director of the Willow Bend Environmental Education Center in Flagstaff, discussed the potential health benefits of people being able to use food stamps at the Flagstaff Community Market, noting that "small changes lead to better lifestyles." K. Otten also mentioned the ability for people to use food stamps at the Flagstaff Community Market and at New Frontiers Natural Marketplace. Both informants discussed the value of food stamps as a way for individuals with low incomes to have access to healthy food options. In addition to the perceived costs associated with alternative food systems, both of these respondents spoke of challenges to changing lifestyle behaviors: "It is hard for us to look at our lives and think about how we are doing something that we've done all of our lives and accept that it is wrong" (K. Otten).

Although the literature discussed food safety as a public health concern, this relationship was not evident in the interview data, and in fact the opposite was mentioned. Two informants commented on food safety issues related to farmers' markets.

Food safety

Food safety generally conjures up thoughts of food recalls by the federal government and images of Escherichia coli (E-coli) and Salmonella, two of the most common microorganisms that cause illness and food-borne diseases (CDC 2011). This was the case for one respondent who would not purchase eggs from a farmers' market because of the lack of safety standards. A second respondent discussed the risks associated with any type of food system from industrial to alternative, but distinguished that smaller-scale production has less risk because farmers have a deep commitment to what they are doing, there is minimal or no use of pesticides, and the food is less processed.

Food contamination can be either biological or from a chemical agent. Chemical agents from pollution, toxic substances, pesticides, animal drugs or other agrochemicals have opportunities to enter food during several food-processing stages and contribute to illnesses and disease (Frost and Sullivan 2006). Illnesses resulting from agrochemicals are often not listed on the safety page of the United States Food and Drug Administration's website, which lists recalls, market withdrawals, and safety alerts.

Economy

Fewer than half of the respondents discussed the potential benefits that alternative food systems could create for the local and regional economy. One informant discussed the need for a regional meat-processing facility or mobile butchering unit, thereby creating jobs. She explained further that state and federal regulations require on-site inspectors, which makes this option expensive and challenging. A few respondents mentioned supporting local businesses that utilized alternative food systems and two respondents mentioned shopping at farmers' markets to support local and regional farmers. Instead, comments related to economy stemmed primarily from food costs. Cost was mainly discussed as a potential deterrent for purchasing foods from alternative systems. In short, alternative food systems were presumed to be more expensive and less lucrative than industrial food systems. While this may be a common assumption, a report prepared for the USDA's Sustainable Agriculture Research and Education Center showed that sustainable community food systems can be competitive with the industrial food system and serve as a viable component of a community economic development strategy (Wilkinson and Van Seters 1997).

A noted opportunity is homestead chicken production, which is one of the fastest-growing small-scale agricultural ventures. According to the USDA report, "many farmers have found that they can earn good supplemental income" from small homestead chicken production (Wilkinson and Van Seters 1997). It should be noted that small-scale chicken production facilities are not allowed within the city of Flagstaff. Three respondents discussed the city's recent decision to allow a limited number of backyard chickens in some areas of the city. Another economic opportunity is evident in outdoor food facilities, including cart vendors, which are "making economically productive use of public spaces, and making them more active, colorful and fun" (Iams 2010: 8). According to two public sector informants, the city of Flagstaff already supports several outdoor food facilities that are mostly seasonal. Overall, informants suggested that growth in the local and regional economy were related to lifting restrictions for growing and producing food rather than developing new infrastructure.

Several other themes mentioned in the literature were only briefly discussed in the interviews. In fact, access to food due to poverty was not mentioned in any of the interviews even though some people may lack access to healthy foods because of inadequate transportation, the "grocery gap," and reliance upon "cheap eats" (Shenot and Salomon 2006). The grocery gap refers to scenarios where larger grocery stores, able to provide more options at lower prices, are predominantly located in more affluent areas. The presence of more than a dozen supermarkets within the city of Flagstaff may have influenced these perceptions of food accessibility.

Food security may be an issue for the city. In Flagstaff, the two area food banks have both seen an increase in assistance over the past several years. Less than two years ago, an article from the *Arizona Daily Sun* reported on several families who rely upon the food banks to get through a month and "help stretch their budget a bit farther" (Hendricks 2009). As cited in the article, Northern Arizona Food Bank's first-time customers receive a free box of food, but "subsequent visits require an agency referral and proof of income that the customer meets the 200 percent federal poverty guideline" (Hendricks 2009). In all of the interviews only two respondents mentioned hunger and specifically food security as important reasons why planners should be involved in food planning. While this issue is not limited to alternative food systems, one suggestion that was made was to help families by providing tools for creating a front or backyard garden.

Real food and tourism and hospitality

Based on the discussion above, the relationship of tourism and hospitality to alternative community food systems in general, and Food Policy Councils in particular, appears to be mixed. Community food advocates tend to focus on the local community first, and may only consider outside tourists in a peripheral manner, if at all. However, from a comprehensive city planning perspective, the food system that serves a community also serves visitors to the community. In addition, as noted above, it is an integral part of the local economy, public health and social welfare of a place, all which contribute to the image that both local residents and temporary visitors have of a community.

The hospitality industry could be supportive of food education, as it influences eating habits and can develop more sophisticated food choices by consumers. In addition, the broader impacts of education can positively influence the culinary image of a destination. Interesting and diverse culinary options can be part of the economic diversification of a community as well, which can make a place more attractive for both tourists and locals alike. Food security is an area that the hospitality industry could contribute to in a major way. The donation of excess food to food banks, for example, is a way that many restaurants already help the less advantaged populations in their communities.

Food safety concerns might be among the largest barriers to hospitality industry involvement in alternative and local food systems. The hospitality industry is responsible for the care of visiting guests and must make every effort to ensure their comfort and well-being. No one wants to intentionally cause harm to guests; however, the hospitality industry has a legal obligation to avoid potential dangers that may arise through the operation of hotels and restaurants.

Interview respondents in Flagstaff, Arizona, were asked to identify the alternative food systems and related businesses that are available in the community. The results show a considerable mix of alternative food activities in Flagstaff itself (Table 3.4), as well as regionally beyond the city (Table 3.5). The tables show that Flagstaff residents participate in considerably more non-commercial

Table 3.4 Community and alternative food activities in Flagstaff, Arizona

	Non-commercial/informal			Commercial	
	Private	Non-profit/NGO	Government	Individual	Company
1 Bountiful Baskets Cooperative		x			
2 Community gardens		x	x		
3 Flagstaff Community Supported Agriculture (FCSA)		x			
4 The Flagstaff CSA Store[a]		x			
5 Flagstaff Community Farmers' Market		x	x		
6 Home gardens	x				
7 Local Alternative Catering					x
8 Local honey producers				x	
9 Neighborhood coop delivery of organic foods					x
10 New Frontiers Natural Foods					x
11 Organic produce in supermarkets					x
12 Restaurants that use alternative foods[b]		x			
13 School gardens			x		
14 Students for Sustainable Living & Urban Gardening[c]		x			
15 Trading and purchasing local eggs, chickens, and raw goat milk	x				

Notes
a The Flagstaff Community Supported Agriculture (FCSA) Store is part of the weekly CSA program, but provides produce on a daily basis from supported farms in the Phoenix area.
b Restaurants that were identified included: Brix, Cottage Place, Criollo Latin Kitchen, Diablo Burger, Morning Glory Café, and New Jersey's Pizza.
c SSLUG is a student organization at Northern Arizona University.

Table 3.5 Community and alternative food activities outside of the Flagstaff, Arizona, city limits

	Non-commercial/informal			Commercial	
	Private	Non-profit/NGO	Government	Individual	Company
1 Camp Verde farms[a]					x
2 Cottonwood Community Farmers' Market[a]		x	x		
3 Dairy farms in Glendale[b]					x
4 The Diablo Trust[c]					x
5 Flying M Ranch[d]					x
6 Hunting wild game	x				
7 Harvesting wild mushrooms	x				
8 Online sellers of alternative foods					x
9 Pick your own farms[a]					x
10 Roadside farm stands[a]					x
11 Sedona Community Farmers' Market[a]		x	x		
12 Trout Farm at Page Springs[a]					x

Notes
a These communities and establishments are in the Verde Valley area, approximately 40 miles south of Flagstaff.
b Glendale is in the Phoenix metropolitan area, approximately 140 miles south of Flagstaff.
c The Diablo Trust supports traditional ranching techniques that integrate wildlife and environmental conservation with livestock husbandry.
d The Flying M Ranch is an alternative producer of local beef that is also sold at the Flagstaff Community Farmers' Market.

and informal alternative food activities in the urban area of Flagstaff. In more distant locations, they are more likely to participate in commercial enterprises that cater to the alternative food market. This most likely reflects different sizes in the market areas served by non-commercial and commercial interests. The pattern also reflects the geography of this part of northern Arizona.

Non-commercial food providers are more narrowly focused on the local community. They include cooperatives, farmers' markets and local government-run programs. These truly are the *community food* activities and services. Commercial food providers, on the other hand, are more likely to serve a larger market area to ensure economies of scale for an acceptable level of income. This is especially true for a rural area, such as northern Arizona, where the population is widely dispersed. In addition, these providers distinguish themselves by being alternatives to the industrial food system. These regional food providers are, therefore, the *alternative food* makers, a concept which might also apply to organic and similar food providers who market at multi-state and even national levels. Thus, in the US many supermarkets today have their local and organic foods sections, which typically demand higher prices than the industrial foods that overwhelm the remainder of the store shelves.

While the pattern of community foods in the form of farmers' markets and niche restaurants in the city and alternative food producers and "u-pick" farms beyond can be found in most other regional economies, the geography of northern Arizona is distinct in that Flagstaff is located at an elevation of 7,000 feet (2100 meters), giving it a short summer growing season, whereas the nearby Verde Valley is some 3,500 feet (1,000 meters) lower in elevation and has a correspondingly better climate for agriculture. These differences contribute to a regional food tourism and recreation pattern which has common corollaries throughout the world. For at least some residents of Flagstaff, the local farms in the Verde Valley, 30 to 40 miles (50 to 65 km) away, offer an opportunity for a day or overnight trip to a different climate and different experience. Agricultural tourism (or agritourism) is common at many different geographic levels, from the local to the international, but not many other places have such an extreme change in climate over so short a distance.

On the other hand, the relatively large number of community and alternative food activities and services in Flagstaff are part of the image of the city, even if it is not specifically stated in city policy. Flagstaff is a university town, with the Northern Arizona University being the largest employer and its more than 17,000 students representing a large part of the population of the city (about half of the students claim Flagstaff as their home for census purposes). The community and alternative food systems support the city's other socially liberal and alternative cultural values, as can be seen in the city's entertainment venues, political leadership, land use policies (light controls, tree protection, and historic preservation), and outdoor recreation ethic. Tourists and locals alike enjoy the city's historic downtown district, which happens to be where all of the six alternative food restaurants identified by the interviewees are located. Most of these restaurants explicitly identify themselves as serving local and alternative foods.

For example, to emphasize its local branding, the Diablo Burger restaurant, which serves hamburgers made from Flying M Ranch-grown meat, sells a souvenir automobile license plate with the word "LOCAL" in large letters at the center and the restaurant's name in small letters on the side.

Conclusions

In summary, the review of Food Policy Councils across the US, along with the interviews with key respondents in Flagstaff, Arizona, revealed that both the private sector and the public sector believed that the community members are the primary movers in influencing a city's food policy priorities. For Flagstaff, the majority of private sector respondents, in fact all but one, indicated that food planning was important and had numerous benefits. The public sector respondents felt that food planning was not a priority for the community at this time. Overwhelmingly, respondents felt that planners could play a role in food planning and that support for food planning was not unrealistic for the Flagstaff community. As mentioned previously, many of the respondents agreed that community members supported the existing alternative food system in Flagstaff because it was well suited to the culture and lifestyle of the town. Two respondents from the private sector specifically used the word "fear" to describe some reluctance in the community to support alternative food systems that were counter to the mainstream American culture.

Discussions about the potential role of local governments in fostering policies to encourage food planning elicited different responses, which illustrated different levels of knowledge about city planners and their job functions, specifically among individuals from the private sector. Above all, respondents believed that community education about food and nutrition was necessary, as well as creating partnerships between the public and private sectors. Many respondents believed that food planning could be incorporated into land use and zoning by lifting restrictions and removing barriers that impede food planning activities. Recommendations related to lifting restrictions and removing barriers may not be feasible due to the existing land use plan and zoning codes. There are legal issues involved in many matters related to planning and some recommendations made by respondents may not have considered those limitations, such as restrictions from neighborhood covenants.

The majority of respondents believed that it was important to take advantage of existing knowledge about food systems within the community in order to learn from each other and develop a useful language for the city's regional plan. Other practical recommendations included promoting community gardens and promoting local businesses that utilize local foods. The latter suggestion may also involve legal issues. In this case, the suggestion is better suited for the Chamber of Commerce than for a planner.

Thus, there is a potential role for the tourism and hospitality sector to play in the development and promotion of alternative community and regional food systems. Motivations for doing this include creating a more sophisticated food consumer who would appreciate niche food products that the hospitality industry can provide. Alternative food systems can also make a place more economically diverse and interesting for both locals and visitors. And finally, the hospitality industry could contribute in a major way to helping alleviate local food security challenges, which makes for both good citizenship and a more environmentally and socially sustainable society.

References

American Planning Association (APA) (2007) Policy Guide on Community and Regional Food Planning. Online. Available: www.planning.org/policy/guides/adopted/food.htm (accessed July 23, 2011).

Breitbach, C. (2007) "The geographies of a more just food system: building landscapes for social reproduction," *Landscape Research*, 32(5): 533–57.

Caton-Campbell, M. (2004) "Building a common table: the role for planning in community food systems," *Journal of Planning Education and Research*, 23(4): 341–55.

Centers for Disease Control and Prevention (CDC) (2010) Overweight and Obesity. Online. Available: www.cdc.gov/obesity/data/index.html (accessed July 23, 2011).

CDC (2011) Food Safety at CDC. Online. Available: www.cdc.gov/foodsafety/ (accessed July 23, 2011).

Clancy, K. (2004) "Potential contributions of planning to community food systems," *Journal of Planning Education and Research*, 23(4): 435–8.

Clifton, K. (2004) "Mobility strategies and food shopping for low-income families: A case study," *Journal of Planning Education and Research*, 23(4): 402–13.

Dahlberg, K. (1994) "Food policy councils: the experience of five cities and one county," paper presented at the Joint Meeting of the Agriculture, Food and Human Values Society and the Society for the Study of Food and Society, Tucson, Arizona, June 11.

de la Salle, J. and Holland, M. (2010) *Agricultural Urbanism*, Winnipeg: Green Frigate Books.

Feenstra, G. (1997) "Local food systems and sustainable communities," *American Journal of Alternative Agriculture*, 12(1): 28–36.

Ferguson, J. (2011) "2010 Census: Flag population surges," *Arizona Daily Sun*, March 11, 2011.

Foer, J. (2009) *Eating Animals*, New York: Little, Brown.

Frost & Sullivan (2006) *Advances in Food Safety: Technical Insights*, San Antonio, Tex.: Frost & Sullivan.

Gillham, B. (2005) *Research Interviewing: The Range of Techniques*, Milton Keynes: Open University Press.

Hall, C.M. (2011) "Researching the political in tourism: where knowledge meets power," in C.M. Hall (ed.) *Fieldwork in Tourism: Methods, Issues and Reflections*, London: Routledge.

Hammer, J. (2004) "Community food systems and planning curricula," *Journal of Planning Education and Research*, 23(4): 424–34.

Hardy, J. (2010) The early history of Flagstaff. History of Flagstaff Series' Flagstaff Visitor's Center Website. Online. Available: www.flagstaffarizona.org/downloads/visitors/flagstaff_history.pdf (accessed July 23, 2011).

Haughton, B. (1987) "Developing local food policies – one city's experiences," *Journal of Public Health Policy*, 8(2): 180–91.

Hendricks, L. (2009) "Restocking their lives – recession lifelines stretched thin: area food banks are struggling to shore up family budgets as the recession batters the working poor," *Arizona Daily Sun*, November 1.

Hopkins, R. (2000) "The food producing neighborhood," in H. Barton (ed.) *Sustainable Communities: The Potential for Eco-neighbourhoods*, London: Earthscan.

Iams, A. (2010) Food without Walls, *News & Views*. Online. Available: www.pgavplanners.com/images/uploads/PDF/News_Views_reduced.pdf (accessed July 23, 2011).

Krisberg, K. (2008) "Report: U.S. industrial farming endangers health, environment," *Nation's Health*, 38(6): 1–22.

Labao, L. and Stofferahn, C.W. (2008) "The community effects of industrialized farming: social science research and challenges to corporate farming laws," *Agriculture and Human Values*, 25(2): 219–40.

Levy, J.M. (2010) *Contemporary Urban Planning*, Boston: Longman.

Nord, M. and Coleman-Jensen, A. (2011) Food Security in the United States: Definition of Hunger and Food Security. Online. Available: www.ers.usda.gov/Briefing/FoodSecurity/labels.htm (accessed July 23, 2011).

Pittman, H.M. (2005) Market Concentration, Horizontal Consolidation, and Vertical Integration in the Hog and Cattle Industries: Taking Stock of the Road Ahead, *The Nationals Agricultural Law Center*. Online. Available: www.nationalaglawcenter.org/assets/articles/pittman_marketconcentration.pdf (accessed July 23, 2011).

Pollan, M. (2006a) "One thing to do about food," *Nation*, 283(7): 14–21.

Pollan, M. (2006b) *The Omnivore's Dilemma*, New York: Penguin.

Pothukuchi, K. (2004) "Community food assessment: a first step in planning for community food security," *Journal of the American Planning Association*, 23(4): 356–77.

Pothukuchi, K. and Kaufman, J. (1999) "Placing the food system on the urban agenda: the role of municipal institutions in food systems planning," *Agriculture and Human Values*, 16: 213–24.

Pothukuchi, K. and Kaufman, J. (2000) "The food system: a stranger to the planning field," *Journal of the American Planning Association*, 66(2): 113.

Shenot, C. and Salomon, E. (2006) Community Health and Food Access: The Local Government Role. Online. Available: http://bookstore.icma.org/freedocs/E43398.pdf (accessed July 23, 2011).

United States Congress (2010) "Food insecurity in the United States," *Congressional Digest*, 89(10): 301–6.

Vallianatos, M., Gottlieb, R., and Haase, M. (2004) "Farm-to-school: strategies for urban health, combating sprawl, and establishing a community food systems approach," *Journal of Planning Education and Research*, 23: 414–23.

Walker, R.E., Keane, C.R., and Burke, J.G. (2010) "Disparities and access to healthy food in the United States: a review of food deserts literature," *Health & Place*, 16: 876–84.

Wilkinson, F. and Van Seters, D. (1997) Adding Value to our Food System: An Economic Analysis of Sustainable Community Food Systems. Online. Available: www.ibiblio.org/farming-connection/foodsys/addval.htm (accessed July 23, 2011).

4 Rørosmat

The development and success of a local food brand in Norway

Marte Lange-Vik and Johannes Idsø

Introduction

Over the last decade, increased value creation in the agricultural sector has moved up on the Norwegian political agenda. Political strategies and documents have emerged, among them a valorisation programme for food, which has been operating for 10 years (LMD 2001). The objectives of this programme have been to stimulate and increase food entrepreneurship and local food production. Agricultural diversification strategies have also included farm tourism (LMD 2007), and the more recent national Norwegian tourism strategy emphasises that tourism is an important arena for marketing of Norwegian food culture and that synergies may be achieved by introducing local food into tourism (LMD 2008; NHD 2007). Against the background of these policy goals – and supported by considerable funds from the valorisation programme – production of local food has appeared as a niche in contemporary Norwegian agriculture. This is similar to developments in several Western European countries in the last decade (see for example Sims 2009, 2010).

In the same period, studies on food tourism have become an important part of tourism research. Scholars emphasise the potential of local food in the development of tourism (e.g. Hall *et al.* 2003; Hall and Sharples 2008), and the possible synergies between local primary production and the tourism industry (Telfer and Wall 1996).

This chapter will concentrate on Rørosmat ('Røros food'), which is one of the most successful local food brands in Norway. The chapter has two parts. The first part focuses on Rørosmat, its historical development, its effects for producers and its regional economic impact. The second part of the chapter discusses the integration of Rørosmat into both large and small-scale tourism enterprises.

In the following, we will first give an outline of the methodology which has been applied in this study before approaching the field of Røros and Rørosmat. This approach starts with a general introduction to the area. We then present our findings regarding the historical development and regional economic effect of Rørosmat. Towards the end of the chapter, there will be a discussion of the integration of Rørosmat into the tourism sector. Thus, the theoretical content of this chapter appears mainly in the second part, and concentrates on a discussion of the barriers to integration of Rørosmat as a local food brand and the tourism sector. In the conclusion, we draw some practical and theoretical implications from the research.

Røros and Rørosmat

The town of Røros is situated inland in eastern Norway and has a long history as a mining town. Røros's copper industry was founded in 1644 and the mines operated for 333 years. In the beginning, there were only a few scattered farms in the area, and the town grew around the mines. When the last mine closed in 1977, conservation of the cultural heritage had already commenced, and the town of Røros was the first Norwegian site to enter the UNESCO World Heritage (WH) list in 1980 (Verdensarven Røros 2010). The WH site has since been extended to a larger area, *Circumferensen*, including several mining sites and valuable landscapes in the region (Riksantikvaren 2010). Today, there are 3,500 inhabitants in Røros.

The town and its region have been an important tourism destination for several decades, and the town receives around 1 million tourists per year. The Røros area is a popular destination both in summer (several summer farms receive visitors and other outdoor activities are offered) and in winter, when cold weather offers a wide range of traditional activities such as cross-country skiing and horse or dog sledging. In addition, Røros is known for traditional handicrafts, and as a tourism destination the Røros area generally has a good position as a region with strong traditions. There are two hotels in the town, as well as several smaller *pensions* and possibilities for cabin rental in the area. For eating, there are several opportunities at all price levels (Destinasjon Røros 2010).

The local food corporation, Rørosmat, was established in 2003. The brand includes 20 producers, with a product spectrum ranging from crisp bread and game products to cheeses and herbs. The producers vary in size from limited companies with around 10 employees to sole proprietorships. One of the largest and most well-known producers is the local dairy, producing butter, sour cream and fresh cheese. The brand is distributed throughout Norway, particularly its dairy products which are distributed through the national dairy. The local organic thick sour milk, *Økologisk Tjukkmjølk*, is also a designated Protected Geographical Indication (PGI; *Beskyttet geografisk betegnelse*) (Rørosmat 2010; Rørosmeieriet 2010); and several other products are labelled as 'Speciality', *Spesialitet*, according to official Norwegian standards (KSL Matmerk 2010). These labels and designations all contribute to the emerging status of Rørosmat as a *terroir* brand (Amilien *et al.* 2005, 2008).

The Rørosmat area covers nine full municipalities and parts of another municipality (Lovdata 2011; see Figure 4.1). The borders for the area were set according to the regulation for PGI of Økologisk Tjukkmjølk in order to prevent future discussion. Today, there are only a few exceptions to the rule that both raw material production and food processing should take place within the area's borders (I. Galåen, personal communication, 5 February 2010).

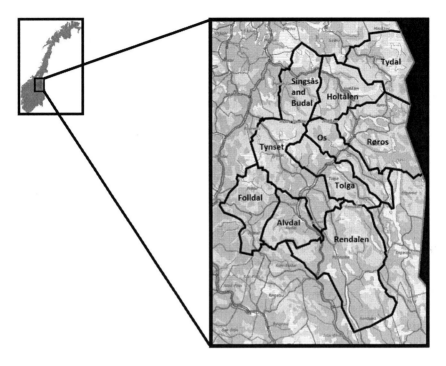

Figure 4.1 Map of the Rørosmat area, covering areas in 10 municipalities in eastern
Norway.

Methodology

The study uses both qualitative and quantitative methods. Qualitative data have
been gathered through document studies, interviews and observations. Document
studies have covered newspaper and magazine bulletins from 1990 to 2008,
including local, regional and national media, together with information, promotional material and prior studies on Rørosmat. On three occasions from October
2008 to February 2010, semi-structured interviews were conducted following a
standard format (Kvale 2009). All together, the authors conducted two pilot
interviews with key representatives from the early initiatives of what is now
Rørosmat; two interviews with restaurant chefs; and four with small-scale food
producers who were also tourist hosts. Our interviews covered both small- and
large-scale businesses involved in food production and tourism. As a supplement
to the interviews, the authors visited hotels and restaurants in the town of Røros
as guests, paying special interest to the menus. The document study was mainly
carried out with the purpose of describing the development of the local food
movement in the Røros region, and mapping critical success factors which have
been pointed out. Analysis of the interviews focused on issues such as identity,
ownership and network.

Quantitative data were obtained through national economic registers during the winter of 2009. From the Register of Business Enterprises, *Brønnøysundregistrene*, profit and loss statements them the private limited companies were available for the previous five years. From this information, the authors were able to calculate the value creation of these companies. Due to limited data availability, studies of the regional economic significance of Rørosmat were carried out solely by using data from the private limited companies. However, because these are the largest and economically strongest enterprises in Rørosmat, it is unlikely that data from sole proprietorships would have affected the overall results significantly.

Figure 4.2 presents the analytical model for the assessment of the regional economic significance of Rørosmat and illustrates that both internal and external sources generate investment capital for the region. External capital sources comprise exports to other regions or income from external investors, Innovation Norway, and other organisations and grants. From internal sources it is possible to raise investment capital through companies' retained profit, private savings, sale of property, local investors, local banks or the municipality or county.

Capital available in the region may circulate in two ways. It may leak out of the region either as dividend, to external investors, as payment for intermediate goods used in production or imported consumer goods, or as capital invested outside the region. Alternatively, the capital may be invested in the region as a driver for regional economic growth. The final direction of the capital is influenced by clusters, entrepreneurs, innovative companies and taxes and regulations.

The development of Rørosmat

The historical development of Rørosmat was grounded in two independent strategies. First, an ideological movement emerged at the beginning of the 1990s aimed at increased use of local and organic food products in the interests of improved consumer health and environmental impacts. This movement founded the Food-Health-Environment Alliance, *Mat-Helse-Miljø-alliansen*, and organised several meetings at the local and international levels (Røe 1995). The most important measures taken to achieve their aims were consumer awareness campaigns and networking between organic farmers. At the same time there has been a business development focus for local food products. The aim of this work has been to find suitable channels for marketing and distribution in order to generate increased sales of locally produced food. These strategies and movements have been concurrent, but independent of each other. The founding of the Northern Østerdal Organic Farming Association, Nord-Østerdal Økologiske Landbrukslag (NØØL), in 1989, may thus be seen as the first step towards the movement that has developed into Rørosmat. This association worked closely with the Food-Health-Environment Alliance, while at the same time working for the establishment of a network for distribution:

NØØL established an arrangement for the common purchase of organic goods from other suppliers. Thus, the unit was ready, and we had a certain customer base that were known to us at the moment when our own products came to be distributed on the market.

(Bjørn Huseklepp in Jortveit 2007)

After some years of operation with a focus on consumer campaigns, the Food-Health-Environment Alliance expanded its activities to include production. In 1997 the Association brand for local food, Food from the mountain region

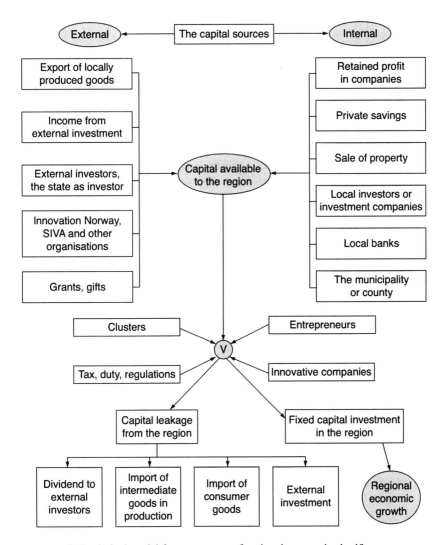

Figure 4.2 Analytical model for assessment of regional economic significance.

(Mat fra fjellregionen), was founded as the first brand of local food. The Association was formed to help local food producers with marketing, distribution and branding of products. The name was chosen in order for the brand to be inclusive and for all producers in the region to be able to identify with it (R. Roland, personal communication, 26 October 2008). In the beginning, 28 shareholders and six producers from three municipalities joined the Association, but it was extended to cover producers in nine municipalities the following year. At the same time, the main grocery store in Røros established a special shelf for local food, gathering all local products in one place and making these products more visible to customers. Several of the producers reported positive effects from becoming part of the brand (Roland and Hanssen 1999).

Food from the Mountain Region was replaced by the new organisation *Rørosmat* (Røros food) in 2003. The decision to rename the brand was taken on account of the associations to history and traditions that 'Røros' evokes and because the name is known outside the mountain region. This also marked a change in strategy for the entire brand, implying that the products were no longer to be sold just locally, but everywhere in Norway.

The movement towards increased local food production and consumption in the Røros region has depended on some important factors for success. Large non-hierarchical networks soon developed both on the consumer and the producer sides. The strategies mentioned above had broad appeal and support, and the networks worked as a stimulus to further developments. Historically, the network of consumers in the Food-Health-Environment Alliance preceded the network of producers and stimulated and encouraged initiatives and innovations from key individuals (Stuen 2007). A central characteristic of both these movements is the dependence on dedicated individuals, *ildsjeler*. Initially, three people launched the initiative which became the Food-Health-Environment Alliance. One of these was also central in NØØL, which was the first step towards a producer network. On the production side there have been a small number of key individuals who have been important for moving the development forward. One farmer worked as a pioneer for organic farming in the region, and another farmer pioneered farm food. At a larger scale, two or three individuals played a leading role in *Rørosmeieriet*, Røros dairy, and *Rørosmat*. They stimulated and encouraged others to take part in the developments, forming the above-mentioned networks.

A structural factor that played an important role in speeding up the development was the decision in 2000 by TINE, the national dairy company, to shut down its local factory in Røros. This dairy factory had been an important actor in Food from the Mountain Region and was a national pioneer in the production of organic milk. This decision provoked a reaction among the local population, and negotiations were carried out with the result that local actors were entitled to carry on production in the factory without regulations on quarantine, contrary to the general rules for factories shut down by TINE. Several local actors came together and founded the Røros dairy, *Rørosmeieriet*, which started production of the local organic thick sour milk, *Tjukkmjølk frå Røros*. This dairy soon became a significant actor, and because of the advantage of making use of the national distribution system of TINE, the products were on sale all over the country. Nationally, *Rørosmeieriet* has played the role of pioneer in the production of locally branded food products (Vik 2010). Several other Rørosmat products have also been designated national quality label products. This has been well documented and covered in the media, and it is also considered to be an important criterion for the success of Rørosmat (Enget 2006).

Regional economic development from Rørosmat

The importance of the organic farming association in the development of Rørosmat is still clear through the high level of involvement of organic producers. In economic terms value added for organic farming is higher than for conventional farming due to input level, and this positively affects the value added from Rørosmat. Moreover, the survival rate among Rørosmat producers is far higher than the Norwegian average. While national statistics show that only one-third of Norwegian enterprises are still operating five years after start-up, none of the Rørosmat producers have shut down since the start-up in 2003. An important advantage of the Rørosmat association is the removal of entry barriers to the market for new producers. Since Rørosmat is liberal regarding minimum production quantity, local producers can start small without major investment in production facilities or marketing efforts. Hence, new producers do not need access to large amounts of risk-seeking financial capital, and the economic risk related to production and sales of new products is thereby eliminated. Furthermore, the cost for the services provided by Rørosmat is low, and because sales and marketing are done by the Rørosmat office, the entrepreneurs can focus on production and product innovations.

At a regional scale, the assessment of economic flows (Figure 4.2) revealed two main external capital sources. First, Rørosmat contributes to capital inflow by the export of locally produced food. Figures show that around 90 per cent of the production is exported from the region. Second, Innovation Norway has given economic support to several of the companies. Internal capital is commonly gained through retained profit. Most enterprises started with little loan debt. Hence, profits from production are used directly for investments.

With respect to capital outflow, the leakage to external investors is limited because most of the enterprise owners in Rørosmat live within the region. Moreover, Rørosmat contributes to reduced capital leakage from the import of consumer goods since 10 per cent of the production is consumed locally. The members of Rørosmat may be called a cluster, and certainly there are some innovative forces among these which positively affect the share of capital used for investment in the region. All these results indicate a positive effect on regional economic development from Rørosmat.

Local food and tourism in Røros

Despite the positive findings regarding regional economic impact, we find an opposite trend when it comes to the possible synergies with the local tourism industry. Figures show that as much as 90 per cent of the produce is exported from the region to all of Norway, implying that merely 10 per cent remains for sale and consumption within the region, including the tourism sector.

In interviews, chefs from the larger hotels and restaurants all affirm their interest in local food. This is evident in their marketing, which strongly emphasises local and traditional food experiences. We found that the chefs use the local products as a means of impressing their customers, creating what they call a 'wow effect'. However, to a certain degree it is also important for each restaurant to keep a unique profile which distinguishes it from the rest. This may imply a challenge to the use of local food because not all restaurants want to focus on it. Consequently, one or two restaurants have a high profile on local and traditional food, using a high proportion of local food products, but the overall proportion of local food in restaurants and hotels is low. In small-scale and farm tourism the food is integrated into the tourism product in a much more consistent way. One important reason for this may be that the farms both produce food and provide tourism services.

Theoretical issues

Several studies on local food and tourism emphasise the potential for regional economic development from local brands (Telfer and Wall 1996; Hall 2005; Nummedal and Hall 2006; Everett and Aitchison 2008). Everett and Aitchison (2008) list three potential sources of added value from local food. First, there is increased willingness among tourists to pay for a locally identifiable product. Second, these products commonly attract a wealthier tourist segment. Third, and perhaps most important in a Norwegian setting where destinations have short and intensive tourism seasons, food products with a local identity might perhaps help to extend the season, because tourists in the shoulder seasons tend to be wealthier and more conscious. The key to developing a positive relationship between food and tourism is the backward linkages between the two sectors (Telfer and Wall 1996; Boyne *et al.* 2003). By making use of local food products, it is thus possible to ensure added value to the region. Moreover, employment of local people further strengthens these linkages (Telfer and Wall 1996).

Local food is also significant for giving tourism authenticity and uniqueness. Sims (2009) emphasises the potential for developing uniqueness and sense of place, while studying conceptualisations of the "authenticity" of local food from the viewpoint of producers and retailers. Everett and Aitchison (2008), on the other hand, take their approach from the tourists, focusing on the possibility in local food for reconnecting the consumer with the land. Such landscapes may have both a cultural and an economic effect through increasing the value of attractions (Telfer and Wall 1996). Furthermore, Sims (2010) and Everett and Aitchison (2008) emphasise that local food production embodies a potential value for the creation of a strengthened local or regional identity. The contents of these abstract notions all relate to the experienced quality of life of the local residents and the quality of the tourism product for the visitors.

Food tourism provides important links between authenticity, identity, and ownership (see Chapter 14 below). A prerequisite for an experienced improvement in the quality of the tourism product is that its authenticity is linked to the identity of the tourism entrepreneurs. There are several examples of the opposite situation, where the tourism product is staged (MacCannell 1973), offering an alternative authenticity often with a mediated version of the local identity. Such a mediated tourism product does not necessarily entail a quality improvement. However, introduction of local products, such as local food, may improve quality, because these products embed traditions and identity. Identity is also closely related to ownership. Hence, by ensuring ownership of more products, these can be introduced as part of a quality tourism product.

The question of ownership and identity leads us on to the issue of network formation. According to Jenkins (2008), tight networks are effective for the creation of ownership and identity. Hall *et al.* (2003) present several models for networking between local food producers and the tourism industry. In the highest level of integration in their typology, food producers and tourism industry representatives are included in the same network. In a study from Finland, Forsman and Paananen (2003) go further in their networking model, arguing that the lowest consumer level, i.e. the tourists, should also be integrated in order to increase achievements. Forsman and Paananen (2003) emphasise the role of networks for reciprocity and sharing of knowledge.

Networks have two important functions in this situation. First, they ensure social identity and ownership of products, and second, they play a significant role in promoting the integration of local food with tourism services. Networking and knowledge sharing are essential to overcome the perceived risks and sacrifices of using local food in tourism, and to make the perceived benefits higher (Forsman and Paananen 2003; Hall 2005; see also Chapter 2 above). This is a challenge, because the benefits are often of a qualitative and abstract character and therefore difficult to measure and evaluate, as the examples above demonstrate. The risks and sacrifices, on the other hand, are well known and easily measurable, such as higher prices, higher expenditure of time, lower reliability of delivery, small volumes, and seasonality (Telfer and Wall 1996). Hence, according to Forsman and Paananen (2003), networking can promote interdependent value creation, between actors at all levels in the value chain, from primary producers to tourism enterprises.

Before we move on to the next section, we would like to draw attention to the characteristics of different networks. Broadly, we may distinguish between two categories: formal and informal. The networks treated by Hall *et al.* (2003) and Forsman and Paananen (2003) are all formal, implying an establishment as well as some kind of commitment by those who are involved. Such commitments may take the form of fees, duties or benefits. On the other hand, informal, often personal, networks are more randomly constructed and do not involve formal commitment of any kind. There is, however, one important similarity between the different kinds of networks: both kinds promote knowledge sharing and reciprocity, and thus also ownership.

Discussion and conclusions

Rørosmat has been presented as a success story both by national media and academic studies (Gjelten 2001; Svendsen 2001; Stuen 2007). The tight networks and synergies between different strategies and stakeholder groups have been highlighted as reasons for this success. Consequently, we assumed that the Rørosmat organisation implied a formalisation of previous informal networks, and that the members thus identified other members of Rørosmat as their main network. However, this is generally not the case. When asked to identify their network, our respondents gave quite different answers. One, whose farm was situated on the outskirts of the defined region for Rørosmat, identified her network as situated far beyond the borders of the Rørosmat area. When defining her network, she focused on the importance of having members with similar production to hers, in order to discuss the historic production background and share experiences. In another interview, a farmer and tourist host perceived his network as focused on the small local community where he lived. For him, it was important to reduce as much as possible, the transport costs of the materials in the meals he served his tourists, and he therefore used his local contacts for all kinds of foodstuffs he did not produce himself. According to him, it was important to point out the origin of his products, and their quality. Only one farmer, who was also part of the Rørosmat board, emphasised the importance of making use of other Rørosmat producers in his network. Hence, we find a discrepancy between the formal Rørosmat network and the informal or personal network of the Rørosmat producers, in relation to both knowledge sharing and to the supply of products for use in on-farm tourism services.

Given that networking is an important factor in identity making, this situation with personal networks implies a threat to a common Rørosmat member identity. This was also confirmed by our respondents. Most of them do not particularly identify with being part of Rørosmat. Rather, their identity seems linked to the quality of their food and specific local history and traditions. As noted above, the brand name was changed from *Mat fra fjellregionen* to *Rørosmat* after five years of operation. One of the rationales for naming the brand *Mat fra fjellregionen* (Food from the Mountain Region) was that all producers could identify with being part of the mountain region. The name Røros was chosen later for easier branding of the products outside the region. However, Røros is the name of the town, and obscuring the rest of the mountain region by changing the name might have affected the position of the brand in the region. This is not to say that Rørosmat does not play an important role for producers. All our respondents express gratitude that they are a part of Rørosmat, because the corporation provides good services and better pay for its producers. However, service provision is only one of Rørosmat's potentials, and the corporation and the region as a whole could benefit from tighter networks.

Another implication from the lack of a shared network among the producers is that there is little exchange of products between the members. Many of the Rørosmat members are, like our respondents, both food producers and tourist hosts. In order to strengthen their tourism product, they might use other members' products to complement their own. However, there appears to be low awareness among the Rørosmat producers of the potential synergies of using a wider range of Rørosmat products for promotion of their own products and services. This is also related to a general low awareness of which other producers are incorporated in the brand and which are not. Only one producer from the interviews demonstrated high awareness of cooperation among the members of Rørosmat, and makes use of Rørosmat products other than his own. He has a special role as he has been part of Rørosmat from the early days, and has taken part in the development of its objectives.

Findings from our study of hotels and restaurants in the town of Røros also show that the level of distribution of local food in the hospitality industry is low. Local food forms a substantial part of the menu in one or two restaurants, but the general impression from our observations and interviews is that guests have to make an extra effort to obtain local food. This impression confirmed by Rørosmat members we interviewed. One producer said: 'The hotel promotes authentic and local food, but the commercial becomes the skeleton in their cupboard, because many who have been there do not recognise what has been promised.' Another shares his view: 'They do not follow up on a daily basis, do not make it part of their usual menu and stuff like that ... There is quite some distance between their expressed objectives, and what happens in practice.' It should be noted, however, that not all local food from this area is sold as part of the Rørosmat brand. When discussing distribution of local food in the tourism and hospitality industries, no differentiation is made between Rørosmat food products and other local products.

Our economic study revealed that only 10 per cent of Rørosmat products were sold locally. There is thus a large, unexploited potential for creating synergies between local food and tourism. This relates closely to the backward linkages noted by Telfer and Wall (1996), which are identified as essential for the creation of added value from food tourism (see also Forsman and Paananen 2003; Hall *et al.* 2003; Nummedal and Hall 2006; Hall and Sharples 2008). Our economic analysis of Rørosmat showed promising results with respect to the high survival rate of the enterprises combined with high capital inflow from external sources and low capital leakage from the region. However, despite these results, there are some challenges. In the case of Rørosmat, the initial consumer and producer networks were established separately. The consumer network ceased to exist after a few years, while the producer network developed into what has become the Rørosmat corporation. Since then, Rørosmat has included only producers among its members. The objective of Rørosmat corresponds with this:

We wish to contribute to the development of ... a brand known far beyond the mountain region. We will contribute to the development of the Røros area as a culinary region, where we are proud that delicious raw materials are produced, processed, sold and enjoyed.

(Rørosmat 2010)

Tourism and local sales have thus played only a small role in the strategy for Rørosmat, and this may have affected the distribution and use of Rørosmat goods in the local tourism industry.

As expressed in the interviews, it is intended that the interaction between Rørosmat and the tourism industry should be enhanced. Despite the weaknesses we identified there are positive developments in this area. First, since 2010, there has been a tourism representative on the board of Rørosmat. This does not imply any formal commitments from the hotels and restaurants as yet, but by introducing the tourism industry into the inner circles of Rørosmat it is possible to enhance networking and knowledge sharing between the two sectors, as well as to develop common goals. Second, the Rørosmat corporation is also tightening the commitments of its members. In an effort to strengthen the member network, all members must now attend at least one members' meeting annually. The rationale behind this is given by a board member in Rørosmat:

> We are together in the same place for several days. This is important for developing cooperation. One of the main reasons why we have come so far in Rørosmat is that we enable each other to obtain success. In order to do so, we must know each other and have full confidence in each other.... We have run some strategic processes around the awareness of that among our members.

By strengthening the ties with the tourism industry and among the producers, the Rørosmat corporation may achieve positive results by enhancing 'sense of place' and regional identity (Sims 2009, 2010), improving backward linkages (Telfer and Wall 1996; Boyne *et al.* 2003), and creating added value from the production of local food (Everett and Aitchison 2008). Hence, networking might be the most effective way to achieve the goal of value creation from food production and to establish the Røros area as a culinary region.

Future studies

In this chapter we have pointed out some of the weaknesses in the development of local food in the Røros area. These relate to networking and stakeholder involvement. Further studies are needed to identify immanent barriers to the use of local food in the tourism industry. These may for example be concentrated around perceived benefits, sacrifices and risks (Sims 2009) or structural barriers in hotel chains (Telfer and Wall 1996).

Finally, we would like to highlight a theoretical issue which has emerged during our work. The value of a local food brand like Rørosmat for regional identity is, as we have seen above, supported by many scholars. At the same time, the use of local food is promoted by environmentalists as a measure to reduce greenhouse gas emissions. However, we wonder if the values related to regional identity might still hold if the brand is not known or sold beyond the region. Hence, it might be worth posing the question as to whether the cultural and social benefits of such a brand are counterproductive to the environmental benefits of shorter food miles from local food.

References

Amilien, V., Schjøll, A. and Vramo, L.M. (2008) 'Forbrukernes forståelse av lokal mat', *Fagrapport nr. 1–2008*. Oslo: Statens institutt for forbruksforskning (SIFO).

Amilien, V., Torjusen, H. and Vittersø, G. (2005) 'From local food to *terroir* product? Some views about *Tjukkmjølk*, the traditional thick sour milk from Røros, Norway', *Anthropology of Food Reviews*, 4 (May). Online. Available: http://aof.revues. org/211?&id=211 (accessed 1 June 2012).

Boyne, S., Hall, D. and Williams, F. (2003) 'Policy, support and promotion for food-related tourism initiatives: a marketing approach to regional development', *Journal of Travel & Tourism Marketing*, 14(3): 131–54.

Destinasjon Røros (2010) Offisiell hjemmeside for Destinasjon Røros. Online. Available: www.roros.no/ (accessed 30 October 2010).

Enget, T. (2006) 'Spesialiteter gir fart på Røros', *Arbeidets Rett*, 19 May.

Everett, S. and Aitchison, C. (2008) 'The role of food tourism in sustaining regional identity: a case study of Cornwall, South West England', *Journal of Sustainable Tourism*, 16: 150–67.

Forsman, S. and Paananen, J. (2003) 'Local food systems: explorative findings from Finland', in Proceedings of the conference 'Local agri-food systems: products, enter-prises and local dynamics', 16–18 October, 2002, Montpellier, France. Online. Available: propuestasviables.com.ar (accessed 1 June 2012).

Gjelten, A. (2001) 'Matmangfold fra fjellet', *Bondebladet*, 2001: 20–1.

Hall, C.M. (2005) 'Rural wine and food tourism cluster and network development', in D. Hall, I. Kirkpatrick and M. Mitchell (eds) *Rural Tourism and Sustainable Business*, Clevedon: Channelview Press.

Hall, C.M. and Sharples, L. (2008) 'Food events and the local food system: marketing, management and planning issues', in C.M. Hall and L. Sharples (eds) *Food and Wine Festivals and Events Around the World: Development, Management and Markets*, Oxford: Butterworth-Heinemann.

Hall, C.M., Mitchell, R. and Sharples, L. (2003) 'Consuming places: the role of food, wine and tourism in regional development', in C.M. Hall, L. Sharples, R. Mitchell, N. Macionis and B. Cambourne (eds) *Food Tourism Around the World: Development, Management and Markets*, Oxford: Butterworth-Heinemann.

Idsø, J. (2009) Regionaløkonomisk utvikling og Rørosmat, paper presented at the confer-ence '*Balestrand Summit 2009*', 26 May 2009, Balestrand, Norway.

—— (2010) *Lokalmat i rørosregionen – en regionaløkonomisk analyse*, Vestlands-forsking-notat 1/2010, Sogndal: Vestlandsforsking.

Jenkins, R. (2008) *Social Identity*, 3rd edn, New York: Routledge.

Jortveit, G. (2007) 'Økologi og fjøskrakkfilosofi', *Arbeidets Rett*, 27 April.

KSL Matmerk (2010) 'Spesialitet', KSL Matmerk. Online. Available: http://kslmatmerk. no/merkeordningene/spesialitet (accessed 30 October 2010).

Kvale, S. (2009) *Interviews: Learning the Craft of Qualitative Research Interviewing*, 2nd edn, Los Angeles: Sage Publications.

Landbruks- og matdepartementet (LMD) (2001) *Verdiskapingsprogrammet for mat-produksjon. Et program for innovasjon og mangfold på matområdet*, Oslo: Land-bruksdepartementet.

LMD (2007) *Ta landet i bruk! Landbruks- og matdepartementets strategi for næringsut-vikling 2007–2009*, Oslo: Landbruks- og matdepartementet.

LMD (2008) *Smaken av Norge. En matpolitisk strategi 2008–2010*, Oslo: Landbruks- og matdepartementet.

Lovdata (2011) FOR 2004–02–10 nr 581: Forskrift om beskyttelse av produktbetegnelsen Økologisk Tjukkmjølk fra Røros som Beskyttet geografisk betegnelse. Online. Available: www.lovdata.no/for/sf/ld/xd-20040210–0581.html (accessed 30 May 2011).

MacCannell, D. (1973) 'Staged authenticity: arrangements of social space in visitor settings', *American Journal of Sociology* 79(3): 589–603.

Nærings- og handelsdepartementet (NHD) (2007) *Verdifulle opplevelser*, Oslo: Nærings- og handelsdepartementet.

Nummedal, M. and Hall, C.M. (2006) 'Local food in tourism: an investigation of the New Zealand South Island's bed and breakfast sector's use and perception of local food', *Tourism Review International*, 9(4): 365–78.

Riksantikvaren (2010) Utvidelse av verdensarvområdet Røros. Online. Available: www. riksantikvaren.no/Norsk/Tema/Verdensarv/Roros_bergstad/Utvidelse_av_verdensarvomradet_Roros/ (accessed 30 October 2010).

Roland, R. and Hanssen, E. (1999) 'Røkt sik og nordisk kefir', information folder, Røros: *Bærekraftige lokalsamfunn*.

Røe, K. (1995) 'Kjemper samme kamp', *Arbeidets Rett*, 13 March.

Rørosmat (2010) Rørosmat BA. Online. Available: www.rorosmat.no/ (accessed 30 October 2010).

Rørosmeieriet (2010) Rørosmeieriet as. Online. Available: www.rorosmeieriet.no/ (accessed 30 October 2010).

Sims, R. (2009) 'Food, place and authenticity: local food and the sustainable tourism experience', *Journal of Sustainable Tourism*, 17: 321–36.

Sims, R. (2010) 'Putting place on the menu: the negotiation of locality in UK food tourism, from production to consumption', *Journal of Rural Studies* 26(2): 105–15.

Stuen, M. (2007) Innovation among small-scale food producers in Fjellregionen – the case of Rørosmat. Master's thesis. Oslo: University of Oslo.

Svendsen, N.V. (2001) 'Smått, sært og smart', *Jordvett*, 2001(11): 10–11.

Telfer, D.J. and Wall, G. (1996) 'Linkages between tourism and food production', *Annals of Tourism Research*, 23: 635–53.

Verdensarven Røros (2010) Verdensarven Røros. En smakebit. Online. Available: www. verdensarvenroros.no/ (accessed 30 October 2010).

Vik, M. (2010) *Lokalmat i rørosregionen. Utvikling og samfunnsmessige rammevilkår.* Vestlandsforsking-notat 2/2010. Sogndal: Vestlandsforsking.

5 The local in farmers' markets in New Zealand

C. Michael Hall

Introduction

A significant proportion of consumers appear increasingly interested in more ethical or sustainable food and are seeking foods that may be variously categorised as healthy, spray-free, organic, non-genetically modified, ecological, with low food miles, ethically produced and/or fair trade, and traceable (e.g. Holloway and Kneafsey 2000; McEachern and Willock 2004; Groves 2005; Padel and Foster 2005; Seyfang 2006, 2008; Kneafsey *et al.* 2008; Thilmany *et al.* 2008; Middlemiss 2010; Morgan 2010). These constructs all require the consumer to be aware of the conditions under which food has been produced, who produced it and the trustworthiness of that producer. Although also very significant as tourist and community attractions (Hall and Sharples 2008), farmers' markets are a logical outcome of consumer interest in sustainable food systems as they represent the 'local' and allow the consumer to connect directly with the producer of the food as well as reduce the 'risks' that individuals perceive in contemporary food consumption (Holloway and Kneafsey 2000; Hall *et al.* 2008).

Although long established in more agrarian economies, where farmers' markets are a traditional retail outlet as well as being a source of 'embodied trust' (Sassatelli and Scott 2001), farmers' markets have only recently become widespread again in a number of developed countries. Farmers' markets have had substantial growth since they were (re)introduced in the USA, Canada, the UK, Australia and New Zealand (Brown 2001; Hall and Sharples 2008). In the United States there were 1,755 farmers markets operating nationwide by 1994, 2,863 by 2000, just under 4,500 by 2006 and 7,175 in 2012 (Hamilton 2002; United States Department of Agriculture 2006, 2012). However, the distribution of farmers' markets is very uneven as there are approximately 700 Certified Farmers' Markets in California alone, with just over half being seasonal (California Department of Food and Agriculture 2009; California Farmers' Market Association 2011). Similarly, the number of markets in Ontario, Canada, has increased from a low of 60 in the 1980s to 159 in early 2012 (Farmers' Markets Ontario (FMO) 2007a, 2012). However, it should be emphasised that while farmers' markets have continued to grow overall there have been numerous instances of farmers' market failure (Stephenson *et al.* 2006).

In the UK the first of the modern farmers' markets was (re-)established in 1997 as a pilot project in Bath, and followed many of the elements of the most successful US markets (Holloway and Kneafsey 2000). In 2002 there were 240 (Purvis 2002) and by 2006 the number had risen to more than 550 markets, with approximately half being certified, and there were estimates that up to 800 markets would be sustainable throughout the UK (FARMA 2006). Australian and New Zealand farmers' markets were similarly re-established in the late 1990s (Coster and Kennon 2005; Guthrie *et al.* 2006; New Zealand Farmers' Market Association 2007; Victorian Farmers' Market Association 2011). There were over 110 in Australia in 2009 and over 160 by early 2012 (Regional Food Australia 2007; Australian Farmers' Market Association 2009, 2012). There were 50 farmers' markets in New Zealand by October 2009 (Hall *et al.* 2008; Lawson *et al.* 2008; Mitchell and Scott 2008), although there were only 44 markets that were members of Farmers' Markets New Zealand in 2011 (Farmers' Markets New Zealand 2012a). However, the drop in the number of New Zealand markets is not necessarily a reflection of a decline in interest in farmers' markets, rather it is indicative of the difficulties in determining what exactly constitutes a farmers' market. This chapter seeks to examine these issues in more detail by examining the concept of authenticity in relation to farmers' markets. It does this primarily via the results of a survey of customers at farmers' markets in New Zealand, which discusses not only the consumer expectations and experiences at markets but also understandings of what constitutes local food. However, before looking at the New Zealand survey the chapter discusses overall issues associated with farmers' market definition and the importance of localism.

Defining farmers' markets

The local dimension of farmers' markets is reflected in definitions of several national and regional farmers' market organisations (Table 5.1), where terms such as 'local', 'fresh' (which implies that food has only travelled a short distance from its origin) and 'direct to consumer', or terms that imply that the goods are vendor-produced, are frequently used.

However, the definition of a farmers' market has long been regarded as problematic. As Pyle (1971: 167) recognised, 'everything that is called a farmers' market may not be one, and other names are given to meetings that have the form and function of a farmers' market'. Other names for similar types of markets in North America include swap meets, flea markets, tailgate markets and farm stands (Brown 2001). As Brown explained, this is a major problem in farmers' market studies as many markets will advertise that they are a farmers' market although they are technically not in the sense of direct purchase from the grower of the produce purchased. The different terms used for farmers' markets reflect retail change over time and different regional food supply and distribution channels. Nevertheless, the core of 'official' definitions of farmers' markets reflects the notion that farmers' markets are 'recurrent markets at fixed locations where farm products are sold by farmers themselves ... at a true farmers' market some, if not all, of the vendors must be producers who sell their own products' (Brown 2001: 658).

The issue of definition is not just academic but also reflects broader concerns of consumers and producers that the farmers' market and its produce be regarded as a space in which consumers can trust the 'authentic' and 'local' qualities of what is being offered. Indeed, the local dimension of farmers' markets remains a long-time recurring theme in international studies of consumers and visitors at farmers' markets (e.g. Connell *et al.* 1986; Balsam *et al.* 1994; Brown 2002; Govindasamy *et al.* 2002; United States Department of Agriculture 2002; Archer *et al.* 2003; Conrey *et al.* 2003; Griffin and Frongillo 2003; FARMA 2004; Feagan *et al.* 2004; Selfa and Qazi 2005; Suarez-Balcazar *et al.* 2006; Friends of the Greenbelt Foundation 2007; Conner *et al.* 2009; Farmers' Markets Ontario 2009; Feagan and Morris 2009; Carey *et al.* 2011).

The definition of 'farmers' market' is also affected by the regulatory environment that they operate in. For example, in California farmers' markets are certified under state legislation. According to the California Federation of Certified Farmers' Markets (2003), certified farmers' markets (CFMs) have operated in accordance with regulations established in 1977 by the California Department of Food and Agriculture and 'are "the real thing", places where genuine farmers sell their crops directly to the public', with multiple benefits accruing for small farmers, consumers and the community. Under Californian law, a CFM is a location approved by a county agricultural commissioner where certified farmers offer for sale only those agricultural products they grow themselves. Not only does such an approach reinforce the local nature of what is available at a farmers' market but it also provides a guarantee to customers that the food is direct from the producer rather than being repackaged. According to the California Department of Food and Agriculture (2012), there are approximately 700 certified farmers' markets and approximately 2,200 certified producers in the state. Of these markets, 51 per cent are year-round.

The province of Alberta in Canada has run an Alberta Approved Farmers' Market Program since 1973. As of early 2012 there were over 100 approved farmers' markets in the province. Under the programme, approved markets must maintain a minimum vendor split of 80/20 where 80 per cent of the vendors sell Alberta products which they, an immediate family member, a staff member or a member of a producer-owned cooperative or its staff have made, baked or grown. The remaining 20 per cent of the vendors can be made up of out-of-province sellers, resellers or vendors selling commercial products. If the annual average vendor calculation gives a result between a 70/30 split and an 80/20 split the market is given one year to improve to an 80/20 split. Below 70/30 there is an immediate loss of market approval status. Out-of-country products and franchises, distributorships and home-based businesses which vend products not made, baked or grown in Alberta are discouraged. Used, antique or flea market items are prohibited at any time (Government of Alberta 2012). With respect to who may sell, the programme guidelines state

Table 5.1 Definitions of farmers' market

Country	Organisation	Definition
Australia	Australian Farmers' Market Association	'a predominantly fresh food market that operates regularly within a community, at a focal public location that provides a suitable environment for farmers and food producers to sell farm-origin and associated value-added processed food products directly to customers.'
Australia – Victoria	Victorian Farmers' Market Association	'a predominantly local fresh food and produce market that operates regularly at a public location which provides a suitable environment for farmers and food producers to sell their farm origin product and their associated value added primary products directly to customers.'
Canada – British Columbia	BC Association of Farmers' Markets	'Only the farmer and/or the family are permitted to sell at a member market. Re-sellers are not permitted. At member markets, our focus is on selling locally grown or processed farm-fresh foods, so only a limited number of crafters can be found at our markets. You won't find any imported products. Most of our foods travel from less than 300 kilometres away'.
Canada – Ontario	Farmers' Markets Ontario	'is a seasonal, multi-vendor, community-driven (not private) organization selling agricultural, food, art and craft products including home-grown produce, home-made crafts and value-added products where the vendors are primary producers (including preserves, baked goods, meat, fish, dairy products, etc.)'
New Zealand	New Zealand Farmers' Market Association	'a food market where local growers, farmers and artisan food producers sell their wares directly to consumers. Vendors may only sell what they grow, farm, pickle, preserve, bake, smoke or catch themselves from within a defined local area. The market takes place at a public location on a regular basis.'
United Kingdom	National Farmers' Retail & Markets Association (FARMA)	'a market in which farmers, growers or producers from a defined local area are present in person to sell their own produce, direct to the public. All products sold should have been grown, reared, caught, brewed, pickled, baked, smoked or processed by the stallholder.'

United States	Farmers' Market Coalition	'A farmers' market operates multiple times per year and is organized for the purpose of facilitating personal connections that create mutual benefits for local farmers, shoppers and communities. To fulfill that objective farmers' markets define the term local, regularly communicate that definition to the public, and implement rules/guidelines of operation that ensure that the farmers' market consists principally of farms selling directly to the public products that the farms have produced.'
United States – California	California Farmers' Markets Association (CFMA)	'The Certified Farmers' Markets (CFM) are diversified markets offering both certifiable and non-certifiable goods for sale.
		The CFM provides producers with the opportunity to sell their fresh, local products directly to the consumers without the intervention of a middleman.
		Each CFM is operated in accordance with regulations established in the *California Administrative Code* (Title 3, Chapter 3, Group 4, Article 6.5, Section 1392) pertaining to Direct Marketing. Each market is certified by the County Agricultural Commissioner as a direct marketing outlet for producers to sell their crops directly to consumers without meeting the usual size, standard pack and container requirements for such products. However, all produce must meet minimum quality standards.
		The non-certifiable goods add variety and enhance the festive ambiance of the Farmers' Market. Although the State Direct Marketing regulations require the producers of fresh fruit, nuts, vegetables, flowers, honey, eggs, nursery stock, and plants to be certified, the same producer-to-consumer philosophy applies for all items sold at the Market. The resale of products is prohibited.'

Sources: Australian Farmers' Market Association (2009); BC Association of Farmers' Markets (2011); California Farmers' Markets Association (2006): 1; Farmers' Market Coalition (2008); Farmers' Markets Ontario (2007a); National Farmers' Retail & Markets Association (2009a); New Zealand Farmers' Market Association (2007a); Victorian Farmers' Market Association (2011).

Preference must be granted to Alberta producers who make, bake, or grow their products. Validated complaints will result in immediate loss of approval status.

Canadian producers who make, bake or grow their products supplement the market mix with those products not available in Alberta. These vendors fall into the 20% category.

Vendors reselling products that directly compete with products sold by Alberta producers are only allowed if the Alberta producers cannot meet customer demand.

Out-of-province products must be clearly labelled as to their province/country of origin.

(Government of Alberta 2012)

In the majority of legal jurisdictions there is no specific farmers' market legislation, as there is in the case of California. In these jurisdictions certification is usually undertaken via a self-regulatory process of membership organisations and relies on existing consumer rights legislation and trademarking. In Ontario a certification programme was developed by farmers in the Ontario Greenbelt and Greater Toronto area through the support of Farmers' Markets Ontario (FMO), Friends of the Greenbelt Foundation (FGF) and Weston Farmers' Market. It was introduced because many farmers' markets included non-farmers who resell produce bought at food terminals, and this was believed to be undermining consumer trust (Friends of the Greenbelt Foundation 2006). The Ontario certified farmers' market is dedicated to farmers selling locally grown products and excludes non-farmers reselling imports or produce bought from the Ontario Food Terminal (FGF 2007b). Based on the Greenmarket programme in New York City and the State of California certification programme, the Ontario certification process includes, but is not limited to, each farmer undergoing a third-party certification inspection, showing proof of a farm business registration number, and posting a sign at each market stall to identify the location of the farm and what it grows (FMO 2007b).

All Ontario bona-fide, conventional and organic growers and producers may apply for certification and, as part of the initial application, all prospective vendors are required to submit a full list of the produce/products to be sold and indicate when these items will be available for market. Table 5.2 outlines the various product categories of Ontario CFMs. The FMO reserves the right to choose market vendors based on their location as well as the overall product mix available at the market, and notes that not all applicants are necessarily accepted. The first Ontario CFM opened in May 2007 using the label of 'MyMarket Certified Local Farmers' Market' (MyMarket 2007). As of early 2012 five certified local farmers' markets had been established in Ontario (MyMarket 2012).

In the UK six core criteria have been developed with respect to farmers' markets. They have been enshrined in a certification scheme administered by the National Farmers' Retail and Markets Association (FARMA) and independently inspected (Table 5.3). As FARMA (2009b) sugested with respect to the adoption of the rules, the area that is defined 'as local is important for public perception of

Table 5.2 Product categories of the Ontario Certified Farmers' Markets

Primary products	Fresh/unprocessed fruit, vegetables, cut flowers, plants and nuts; honey and maple syrup; shell eggs; meat (fresh and frozen); fish (fresh and frozen); herbs; mushrooms
Secondary products must meet three conditions:	• The 'defining ingredient' must be from (produced on) the farmer's own farm • The value must be added from the farm (meat products may be an exception as the value might be added at an off-farm site) • The product must be in compliance with all regulations and there must be evidence of appropriate inspection (by health and/or other authorities)
Ready-to-eat 'Fast Food' permissible depending on agreement with host partners	• Coffee and tea sold by the market or a concession for community fund-raising obtained on a wholesale basis from an established business • Unique sandwiches such as venison on a bun provided that the principal ingredient (i.e. the venison) conforms to the requirements of secondary products

Source: derived from Farmers' Markets Ontario 2007b.

"local food" '. Where a market fulfils the criteria, FARMA recognises the market as a farmers' market although they note that 'more tightly defined criteria may be applied to fit local circumstances where this strengthens the philosophy behind Farmers' Markets' (FARMA 2009b).

The different sets of regulations illustrate the difficulties of making international comparisons between farmers' markets although the Alberta, California, Ontario and UK approaches towards certification highlight the significance of being able to ensure, from the perspective of consumer confidence, that a farmers' market is actually a market in which produce is made available by those who farmed it. Indeed, Hall *et al.* (2008) observed that if the UK approach was applied to many Australian or New Zealand farmers' markets, then many stallholders would not qualify.

In some locations, especially in higher-latitude countries, such as Canada, it can be extremely difficult for a stallholder to be able to provide farm-grown produce all year round as well as providing an environment that is comfortable for consumers. Therefore, many farmers' markets are seasonal, focusing on the harvest months of summer and autumn; this affects not only the range of available produce but also the number of stallholders. Although from some perspectives this may be appropriate with respect to the authenticity of seasonal local food, it can also pose significant business challenges for individual stallholders as well as a market as a whole with respect to retaining custom from competing food retailers (Hall *et al.* 2008).

Farmers' markets in New Zealand

The first modern farmers' market in New Zealand was established at Whangerei in 1998 (Guthrie *et al.* 2006). By October 2007 there were 36 farmers' markets

Table 5.3 Guidance criteria for UK FARMA Certified Farmers' Markets

Core criteria	Guidance to criteria
Locally produced. Only produce from the defined area shall be eligible for sale at a farmers' market. Producers from the area defined as local must be given preference.	To reach FARMA standards, markets must define an area as local from within which the majority of the producers will travel to sell at the market. There are two types of local definition that FARMA recognises: • Local as a radius: Local is a defined as a radius from the market. A definition of 30 miles is ideal, up to 50 miles is acceptable for larger cities and coastal or remote towns and villages. • Local as a county boundary: The definition of local may also be a county boundary or other geographic boundary such as a national park that is similar in size to the radius option. Producers from further afield may attend the market if there is no suitable local producer of a given product. Markets that accept producers from beyond their definition of local should include a clause that states 'preference will be given to the most local producer when a space becomes available at the market, without compromising quality'.
Principal producer. The principal producer, a representative directly involved in the production process or a close family member must attend the stall.	• The stall should be operated by someone directly involved in production, not just in other aspects of the producer's business. One of the key principles of a farmers' market is for the consumer to have a direct relationship with the producer. • Community associations such as local allotment societies or country market groups may be agreed as principal producers on a case-by-case basis by the local market. In all cases they must be bone fide producers.
Primary, own produce: All produce sold must be grown, reared, caught by the stall holder within the defined local area.	• Primary produce will have been grown or reared on the producer's land; for livestock and plants this means grown or finished (having spent at least 50 per cent to its life) on the producer's land. Preference should be given to the largest percentage of a product's life cycle spent on the producer's land. • Game shot or caught within the defined local area may be sold at farmers' markets by the person rearing or licensed to hunt the game. • Fish at a farmers' market, ideally, should be sold by the fisherman. A representative of a number of known local boats may attend the market so long as the fishing grounds are known local, inshore waters and a link to the fishing business/es can be proven.

Secondary, own produce: All produce must be brewed, pickled, baked, smoked or processed by the stall holder using at least one ingredient grown or reared within the defined local area. The base product should be substantially altered.

Policy and information: Information should be available to customers at each market about the rules of the market and the production methods of the goods on offer. The market should also publicise the availability of this information.

Other rules: Markets may establish other criteria in addition to the above provided they do not conflict with the core criteria.

Anyone processing produce or adding value is a secondary producer. For processed products the base product should be substantially altered and they must contain as much local ingredient as possible – this means grown or reared within the area the market defines as local. Receipts should be kept as proof of origin for inspection by the market manager and Trading Standards when requested; producers growing their own should be prepared to be visited by an appointed representative from the market management.

• Processors, who want to benefit from the success of farmers' markets, which is partly built on the localness of the food on offer, should be prepared to abide by similar principles.

• A Farmers' market should be clearly labelled as such and separate from any other retail operation, especially other market stalls that will confuse customers' perception of what a farmers' market is.
• Each farmers' market should be operated in accordance with Trading Standards, environmental health, alcohol licensing, market charters and other relevant legislation.
• The policy of each farmers' market in terms of sourcing locally produced food and encouraging sustainable methods of production should be available to customers.
• Producers must produce clear written information about production methods which shall be available to any consumer who requests it. The market must also publicise the availability of this information.
• Markets should, for the time being, include a policy that no genetically modified organisms are knowingly sold or included in products sold at the market.
• Markets may establish other standards which they feel are appropriate, e.g. restricting the use of ingredients perceived as undesirable by consumers, compliance with minimum animal welfare standards.
• Markets may set other rules which do not conflict with the main principles set out in the criteria.
• The prime aim of the market must be to develop a vibrant environment where consumers and producers are brought together and the farmers' markets principles are promoted and upheld.

Source: After FARMA (2009b).

listed by the Farmers' Market New Zealand Association (FMNZA), itself established in 2005, as being either open or about to open. By October 2009 this had
grown to 43 (Table 5.4). However, it is important to note that the 2009 figure
does not include all public food markets that are described as farmers' markets
as there are a number that operate that are not listed as members of the FMNZA.
If 'unofficial' farmers' markets were added, then it is likely that the total number
of markets operating could exceed 70.

The FMNZ (2007a) has the following aims:

- to facilitate the formation of a network of authentic farmers' markets
  throughout New Zealand;
- to clearly define the concept of an authentic farmers' market and facilitate
  the development of this model in the cities and provinces of New Zealand;
- to support the viable and self-sufficient operation of existing and future
  farmers' markets by sharing information and providing appropriate
  resources;
- to protect brand 'farmers' market', clearly distinguishing the concept of a
  farmers' market from other markets, both retail and wholesale;
- to advocate on behalf of members at a national level.

An authentic farmers' market was originally defined by the FMNZA (2007a) as
a market that has at least 80 per cent local produce stalls. In 2007 local meant
from within the regional boundaries established by individual farmers' markets
that also decided which stalls that sell food or farm-origin products, e.g. coffee
and bread, should be allowed a place in the market (Hall *et al.* 2008). By 2009
the focus on authenticity had become much greater, with the development of a

Table 5.4 Farmers' markets in New Zealand

Area	Total number October 2007	Members of FMNZA October 2007	FMNZA members October 2009	Farmers' Markets NZ Inc. April 2012
Northland	3	3	2	2
Greater Auckland	7	6	9	6
Waikato/Bay of Plenty	5	3	5	5
East Coast	4	3	4	4
Lower North Island	5	3	6	4
Marlborough/Nelson	2	1	3	3
Canterbury	7	5	10	10
Otago/Southland	3	2	4	6
Total	36	26	43	40*

Sources: FMNZ (2007b, 2009a, 2012b).

Note
* Does not include Belfast Farmers' Market (Canterbury) and Palmerston North Farmers' Market
(Lower North Island) which were listed as closed until further notice at time of analysis.

certification programme. According to FMNZA the reasons for this are 'We are now finding that some markets are only using the words "Farmers' Market" to attract more customers while not upholding the fundamental principles of what a real Farmers' Market is' (2009b: 1). Similarly, Angela Clifford, the Canterbury representative on the FMNZA board, stated,

> There needs to be some protection of that brand to make sure people aren't setting up a market using the term "farmers market" and then in some way duping the public into thinking that they are buying from the people who have grown or made the food.
>
> (The Press 2009: 12)

The FMNZA Authenticity programme was launched in June 2009 and identified an 'Authentic Farmers' Market', 'Certified Local Stall Holder' and 'Approved Local Stall Holder' categories. An Authentic Farmers' Market is defined as one

> which consists of at least 80% certified local stall holders and governed by accepted practices of farmers markets as per the FMNZ charter. That is, a Farmers' Market is full of locally grown and sourced food which is being sold by the producer, from a defined region.
>
> (FMNZ 2009b: 1)

The notion of what is local is defined by each market. 'Generally the catchment is 100 to 200 km radius and is not limited to the geographical boundaries of the [country's] regions' (FMNZ 2009b: 2). A certified local stallholder is defined as

> a stall from which a primary producer sells fresh, local produce they have grown or farmed themselves. In addition, a stallholder may sell value added products made from their own or other local produce sourced from the defined region of the market.
>
> (FMNZ 2009b: 1)

An approved stallholder 'is one that cannot become a certified local stall holder due to the nature of their wares, but makes every effort to be as local as possible' (FMNZ 2009: 1). A bread-maker who has to use New Zealand flour grown from outside a local region, or a coffee seller who uses imported beans that have been roasted locally would be an approved stallholder although the exact criteria for the category are determined by individual markets. In order to be certified by the FMNZ all existing farmers' markets were given a target of 12–36 months to achieve the authenticity standards, while all new farmers' markets were expected to achieve these standards from day one. However, as a result of opposition by some member markets, by 2012 the scheme had become optional for member markets. According to FMNZ (2012c),

Customers are demanding more transparency about where their food comes from, and should trust the integrity of their Farmers' Market.

The Authenticity Scheme aims to enhance the integrity and transparency of those markets that choose to undertake it by providing an operational framework within which they can manage their (Authentic) Farmers' Markets.

Joining the Authenticity Scheme clearly demonstrates that they are upholding Farmers' Markets values and beliefs.

It is up to each market to decide if and when they want to participate in the Authenticity scheme, but FMNZ hopes that in time most markets will join the scheme.

The requirements had also changed, with authentic markets needing to 'achieve a required percentage of Certified Local stallholders, currently 70%.... The remaining 30% of stallholders will be classified as Approved Local or in a small number of cases Permitted stallholders' (FMNZ 2012c).

The emphasis on localism and authenticity in farmers' market promotion as well as the different interpretations of what may constitute authenticity clearly raises issues of trust in the farmers' market for consumers. Therefore, research was undertaken into what factors and distances made a New Zealand farmers' market perceived as authentic and local by its customers, and it is to this that we now turn.

Method

A total of 361 surveys were conducted of local customers (from within 50 km of Christchurch) at two weekly Saturday morning farmers' markets at Lytellton and Riccarton in Christchurch, New Zealand, in 2007 and 2008. The surveys were almost equally divided between the two markets with 178 from Lytellton and 183 from the Riccarton market. Respondents were intercepted prior to entering the market areas and were asked to answer a series of survey questions with respect to regularity of farmers' market use, length of patronage of farmers' markets, what items selected from the literature on farmers' markets did they most associate with the authenticity of a farmers' market, how they understood the concept of local in relation to distance, and sources of knowledge with respect to understanding of the farmers' market concept. Following the survey questions, respondents were invited to make any other comments they liked with respect to the farmers' market experience. In addition, informal interviews were undertaken with customers and stallholders which helped to contextualise the survey results as well as the use of ethnographic study both to assist in the development of questions and to contextualise survey results. The ethnographic component began in mid-2006 and has continued to the time of writing. This chapter focuses on the survey component of the research.

Of the 361 surveys 191 were answered either solely or primarily by a female and 170 by a male. The word primarily is significant as just over 80 per cent of those surveyed had come to the market with someone else. This is in marked contrast to Ontario farmers' market shoppers where only 37 per cent of resondents to a survey stated that they visited as part of a group (FMO 2009). Respondents were also well educated (69 per cent had tertiary education) and were generally from well-off households with 73 per cent of respondents' households earning over NZ$50,000 per year (Table 5.5). The demographic profile of farmers' market customers is reasonably consistent with much of the American and British research on market attendees (Hall *et al.* 2003; United States Department of Agriculture 2006), although the proportion of females to males appears substantially lower than a profile of shoppers at farmers' markets in Ontario (FMO 2009).

Findings

The majority of respondents were regular visitors, with 68 per cent stating that they visited a farmers' market at least once a month (Table 5.6). This appears reasonably similar to profiles of market shoppers in Ontario (FMO 2009) and the UK (FARMA 2004). The majority of respondents (57 per cent) had been attending markets for at least a year (Table 5.7). Respondents were also asked if they had visited other farmers' markets outside Christchurch in the last five years (Table 5.8). Over 80 per cent of respondents stated that they had been to other

Table 5.5 Level of household income

Estimated respondent household income (NZ$)	%
Up to $10,000	6
$10,000–29,999	9
$30,000–49,999	12
$50,000–69,999	30
$70,000–99,999	27
>$100,000	26

Note
N = 344.

Table 5.6 Customer frequency of visit to a farmers' market

Frequency of visit	Visit markets (%)
Every week	37
At least once a month	31
Approximately once every six months	14
Approximately once a year	8
First time	10

Note
N = 361.

Table 5.7 Length of patronage of farmers' markets

Length of patronage	%
Less than one month	12
1–6 months	16
7–12 months	29
1–3 years	36
More than 3 years	7

Note
N=357.

Table 5.8 Visit to farmers' market outside Christchurch in last five years

Location	%
Elsewhere in New Zealand	45
Australia	21
United Kingdom and Ireland	35
Mainland Europe	41
Canada/United States	19
Other	12
None	18

Note
N=361.

markets, with 45 per cent saying that they had been to other New Zealand markets. However, a significant number of respondents had also been to markets in Europe and the United Kingdom. Indeed, it should be noted that this question often created substantial discussion following the formal part of the survey, with many respondents (approximately a third) stating how much they had enjoyed the farmers' market and market experience while travelling overseas.

Customers were asked to rate the relative importance of 33 items associated with farmers' markets that had been utilised in previous surveys of farmers' markets as well as identified in the relevant literature. A five-point Likert scale was used ranging from 1, no importance, to 5, very important. The four most highly ranked items in terms of importance with respect to the authenticity of a farmers' market were 'Fresh produce' (mean response of 4.34), 'Produce is sold by those that grow it' (4.31), 'Produce is sourced locally' (4.29), and 'Local' (4.16). The four lowest items were 'Educational' (2.20), 'Music' (2.60), 'Family oriented' (2.64) and 'Market is a public organisation' (3.12). The very low ranking of education as being a factor in authenticity was interesting given that education is noted as a benefit of certified farmers' markets in California. The fact that produce was cheap was not regarded as important (3.23), although value for money (4.07) was of importance. The overall results tend to reflect those of other surveys (e.g. Kezis *et al.* 1998; Payne 2002; FARMA 2004, 2006; Payet *et al.* 2005; Carey *et al.* 2011). For example, the results of the Ontario farmers' market shoppers survey reported that 57 per cent of respondents stated that fresh produce is their number one reason for visiting Ontario markets and 67 per cent stated that buying directly from a local farmer is extremely important (FMO 2009).

Shoppers were also asked about the distance that should be used in order for the produce at an 'authentic' farmers market to be classified as local (Table 5.10). Of respondents, 85 per cent stated that they felt that ≤30 km was local and 73 per cent ≤50 km (approximately similar to the UK rural farmers' market standard). Only 36 per cent felt that ≤75 km, similar to the UK farmers' market standard of local for an urban or coastal market, could be regarded as local. Interestingly, the standards proposed by Farmers' Markets New Zealand (2009b) had only limited perception as being local, while only 18 per cent of respondents felt that it should be up to each market to decide what is local.

Finally, given the relative newness of farmers' markets in New Zealand, respondents were asked which, if any, of a number of named factors influenced their understanding of what constitutes an authentic farmers' market. Respondents were then also given the opportunity to name any specific influence. The greatest influences on understanding were television cooking programmes (76 per cent), friends and family/word of mouth (61 per cent) and the food and lifestyle television channels (53 per cent) (Table 5.11). In what may be related to the timing of the surveys with respect to specific television programmes, a remarkable 34 per cent of respondents named Rick Stein's *Local Food Heroes* television series as an influence, while 16 per cent named *Market Kitchen*. Both of these programmes are British, the former focusing on local food champions in the UK and the latter featuring Borough Market in London where it is filmed, with frequent mentions of local food and farmers' markets. Interestingly, although television cooking had a significant impact on understanding, cookbooks had substantially less influence, as did food magazines.

Conclusions

The results of this research suggest possible gaps between customer understanding of what is local and authentic in a farmers' market and FNZMA policies as well as differences between New Zealand and international definitions of farmers' markets. Respondents perceived the identification of local produce in terms of far shorter distance than the FNZMA proposed for its certification programme. Although there may be differences in perceived and actual distances that may affect customer judgement the results clearly suggest that shoppers believe 'the shorter the better' with respect to ideas of the local. In addition, the results suggest that, at least in this relatively early stage of farmers' market development in New Zealand, customers' understanding of what a farmers' market is has been greatly influenced by their own international experiences when travelling as well as by food television programmes, which in the New Zealand context are primarily British and North American productions.

Table 5.9 Measures of the relative importance of various items to the concept of an authentic farmers' market (1 low to 5 high)

Attributes	No importance (%)				Very important (%)		
	1	2	3	4	5	Mean	Rank
Cheap	6.65	13.57	44.88	20.22	14.68	3.23	28=
Educational	33.52	37.95	11.91	8.59	8.03	2.20	33
Family oriented	13.02	33.52	36.57	9.97	6.93	2.64	31
Farmer grown	6.65	2.49	7.48	42.38	41.00	4.09	6=
Fresh produce	0.00	3.05	13.30	30.75	52.91	4.34	1
Friendly	5.54	10.53	44.32	31.30	8.31	3.26	25
Good customer service	6.37	10.80	27.98	43.21	11.63	3.43	23
Hard to obtain produce	11.91	7.76	36.57	31.30	12.47	3.25	26=
Healthy produce	11.36	13.02	22.44	37.40	15.79	3.33	23
High quality produce	3.88	8.59	21.61	44.88	21.05	3.71	14
Homemade	2.22	12.19	24.65	44.04	16.90	3.61	17
Homegrown	5.82	13.30	19.94	45.15	15.79	3.52	20=
Knowing where food comes from	7.20	6.93	28.53	33.52	23.82	3.60	18
Local	0.55	3.32	15.79	40.17	40.17	4.16	4
Market is a public organisation	9.97	13.57	44.04	18.84	13.57	3.12	30
Music	23.27	25.48	26.32	18.01	6.93	2.60	32
Nutritious	6.37	12.47	26.04	29.92	25.21	3.55	19

Open air	14.96	16.90	22.71	19.11	26.32	3.25	26=
Opportunity to meet the grower	3.05	7.48	11.91	29.64	47.92	4.12	5
Opportunity to sample	3.60	9.97	20.50	39.61	26.32	3.75	13
Organic produce	5.82	13.57	24.10	24.65	31.86	3.63	16
Produce is sold by those that grow it	0.83	3.88	11.36	31.02	52.91	4.31	2
Produce is sourced locally	2.22	6.93	12.47	16.34	62.05	4.29	3
Produce is grown sustainably	1.11	7.76	18.56	31.02	41.55	4.04	9
Reduces food miles	6.65	12.47	20.22	25.76	34.90	3.70	15
Reflects local community	3.32	9.42	27.15	26.04	34.07	3.78	12
Relaxed atmosphere to shop in	10.80	14.68	34.90	19.67	19.94	3.23	28=
Seasonal foods	5.26	9.70	18.84	25.76	40.44	3.86	11
Supporting farmers	11.36	10.80	24.38	27.42	26.04	3.46	22
Supporting local producers	2.49	10.53	15.79	17.73	53.46	4.09	6=
Taste	1.39	9.70	14.96	33.80	40.17	4.02	10
Value for money	1.66	8.03	20.22	21.33	48.75	4.07	8
Wide selection of produce	4.99	15.79	28.53	23.27	27.42	3.52	20=

Note
N=361.

However, while notions of the local may be different the importance that shoppers attach to the local and fresh food, as well as farmers' markets selling food produced by those who actually grow it, is very much in keeping with international studies of farmers' markets (e.g. Selfa and Qazi 2005; Kneafsey *et al.* 2008). Shoppers did appear more positive towards supporting local producers than farmers per se. The reason for this possibly lies in broader perceptions of the New Zealand farming community and the smaller lifestyle, alternative and organic focus of those selling at farmers' markets. This issue clearly presents an opportunity for further research with respect to consumer understandings of sellers at farmers' markets and alternative distribution channels in comparison with agribusiness and mainstream retail distribution. Indeed, Feagan and Morris', (2009) observation on different forms of embeddedness, and especially

Table 5.10 To be classified as a authentic farmers' market how far do you think the produce at the market travel should travel to be regarded as local?

Distance (km)	% agree
≤30 km	85
≤50 km	73
≤75 km	36
≤100 km	24
≤200 km	18
So long as it's from the South Island	19
So long as it's from New Zealand	15
It should be up to each market to decide what's local	18

Note
N=357.

Table 5.11 Which, if any, of the following have influenced your understanding of what constitutes an authentic farmers' market?

Factor	% Agree
Cookbooks	38
Television cooking programmes	76
• Rick Stein, *Local Food Heroes*	34
• *Market Kitchen*	16
Food and lifestyle TV channels	53
Food magazine	21
• *Cuisine*	12
• *Australian Gourmet Traveller*	11
Travel overseas	46
Friends and family/word-of-mouth	61

Note
N=357.

the difference between spatial and social rationales for farmers' market purchase, provides a useful pointer for further studies.

This chapter has also focused on ideas of authenticity with respect to perceptions and regulation of farmers' market space as opposed to the direct experience of it, although of course the two are related, with notions of territory and identity associated with the consumption and production of farmers' markets being explored by several authors (e.g. McGrath *et al.* 1993; Holloway and Kneafsey 2000; Hall and Sharples 2008). Holloway and Kneafsey (2000) suggest that farmers' markets can be conceived as both an 'alternative' space and a 'reactionary/nostalgic space' in which local place names and descriptors such as 'fresh' or 'natural' are used, implying something that has not travelled far and is derived directly from the countryside. They further argue that local farmers' markets result in a space that is constructed out of attempts 'to fix identity or build a sense of community' (Holloway and Kneafsey 2000: 295) and therefore have an inherent sense of lived authenticity which is highly desirable for consumers as well as stallholders (Hall 2007). Yet the experiential space of farmers' markets is also connected to the regulatory and institutional spaces of certification and health and safety. Although often self-regulatory, certification programmes help reinforce notions of trust between producers and consumers, particularly for those who have had relatively little previous experience or knowledge of producers or individual farmers' markets. However, it is important that certification programmes are relevant to consumer understandings and experiences in order for them to be accepted.

Undoubtedly farmers' markets can connect with the consumer in very personal ways (Tiemann 2004). According to Hall *et al.* (2008: 225), the farmers' market 'experience is one that is often dialogic, where the actors are in constant communication with each other, rather than monologic as is the case with other forms of retail experience'. In such a situation it would seem appropriate that not only should dialogue be part of the social construction of the farmers' market experience as 'local', but it also needs to become part of the process of negotiating the regulatory spaces of trust and risk reduction between producers and consumers in also certifying the local.

Acknowledgement

The assistance of Fiona Crawford in undertaking research on farmers' markets is gratefully acknowledged.

References

Archer, G.P., Sánchez, J.C., Vignali, G. and Chaillot, A. (2003) 'Latent consumers' attitude to farmers' markets in North West England', *British Food Journal.* 105(8): 487–97.

Australian Farmers' Market Association (2009) About. Online. Available: www.farmersmarkets.org.au/ (accessed 1 October 2009).

Australian Farmers' Market Association (2012) Australian Farmers' Market Directory. Online. Available: www.farmersmarkets.org.au/markets (accessed 27 March 2012).

Balsam, A., Webber, D. and Oehlke, B. (1994) 'The farmers' market coupon program for low-income elders', *Journal of Nutrition for the Elderly*, 13(4): 35–41.

BC Association of Farmers' Markets (2011) About us. Online. Available: www.bcfarmersmarket.org/about.htm (accessed 26 March 2012).

Brown, A. (2001) 'Counting farmers markets', *Geographical Review*, 91: 655–74.

Brown, A. (2002) 'Farmers' market research 1940–2000: an inventory and review', *American Journal of Alternative Agriculture*, 17(4): 167–76.

California Department of Food and Agriculture (2009) Verified Farmers Market Program. Online. Available: www.cdfa.ca.gov/is/i_&_c/cfm.html (accessed 2 October 2009).

California Department of Food and Agriculture (2012) Certified Farmers' Market Program. Online. Available: www.cdfa.ca.gov/is/i_&_c/cfm.html (accessed 26 March 2012).

California Farmers' Markets Association (2006) *California Farmers' Markets Association Rules and Regulations for Certified Farmers' Markets*. Walnut Creek: California Farmers' Markets Association.

California Farmers' Markets Association (2011) About CFMA. Online. Available: http://cafarmersmkts.com/about (accessed 27 March 2012).

California Federation of Certified Farmers' Markets (2003) What is a Certified, Farmers' Market? Available: www.cafarmersmarkets.com/about/ (accessed 25 January 2003).

Carey, L., Bell, P., Duff, A., Sheridan, M. and Shields, M. (2011) 'Farmers' market consumers: a Scottish perspective', *International Journal of Consumer Studies*, 35(3): 300–6.

Connell, C.M., Beierlein, J.G. and Vroomen, H.L. (1986) *Consumer Preferences and Attitudes Regarding Fruit and Vegetable Purchases from Direct Market Outlets*. Report 185. University Park: The Pennsylvania State University, Department of Agricultural Economics and Rural Sociology, Agricultural Experiment Station.

Conner, D.S., Montria, A.D., Montria, D.N. and Hamm, M.W. (2009) 'Consumer demand for local produce at extended season farmers' markets: guiding farmer marketing strategies', *Renewable Agriculture and Food Systems*, 24: 251–9.

Conrey, E.J., Frongillo, E.A., Dollahite, J.S. and Griffin, M.R. (2003) 'Integrated program enhancements increased utilization of farmers' market nutrition program', *The Journal of Nutrition*, 133(6): 1841–4.

Coster, M. and Kennon, N. (2005) *New Generation' Farmers' Markets in Rural Communities*, Barton: Rural Industries Research and Development Corporation.

Farmers' Market Coalition (2008) Welcome to the FMC. Online. Available: http://farmersmarketcoalition.org/ (accessed 26 March 2012).

Farmers' Markets New Zealand (2007a) Online. Available: www.farmersmarket.org.nz/home.htm (accessed 1 October 2007).

Farmers' Markets New Zealand (2007b) *Guide to Farmers' Markets in New Zealand and Australia*. Mosman: R.M. Williams Classic Publications.

Farmers' Markets New Zealand (2009a) Online. Available: www.marketground.co.nz/ClubSite.asp?SiteID=10563&PageTypeID=1&PageID=35251 (accessed 2 October 2009).

Farmers' Markets New Zealand (2009b) *Authentication of Farmers' Markets and Certification of Stall Holders in New Zealand June, 2009*. Hamilton: Farmers' Market NZ Inc.

Farmers' Markets New Zealand (2012a) History of the Farmers' Market Movement. Online. Available: www.farmersmarkets.org.nz/ (accessed 26 March 2012).

Farmers' Markets New Zealand (2012b) Markets' Locations. Online. Available: www. farmersmarkets.org.nz/ (accessed 1 April 2012).

Farmers' Markets New Zealand (2012c) Authenticity Scheme. Online. Available: www. farmersmarkets.org.nz/ (accessed 27 March 2012). FARMA: see National Farmers' Retail and Markets Association.

Farmers' Markets Ontario (FMO) (2007a) Membership Information. Online. Available: www.farmersmarketsontario.com/MembershipInfo.cfm (accessed 1 October 2007).

Farmers' Markets Ontario (FMO) (2007b) *'Real Farmers, Real Local' Certified Farmers' Market Rules & Regulations.* Brighton: Farmers' Markets Ontario.

Farmers' Markets Ontario (FMO) (2009) *Farmers' Markets Ontario Impact Study 2009 Report.* Brighton: Farmers' Markets Ontario.

Farmers' Markets Ontario (FMO) (2012) Member Markets. Online. Available: www.farmersmarketsontario.com/Markets.cfm?uSortOrder=Market (accessed 27 March 2012).

Feagan, R. and Morris, D. (2009) 'Consumer quest for embeddedness: a case study of the Brantford Farmers' Market', *International Journal of Consumer Studies*, 33(3): 235–43.

Feagan, R., Morris, D. and Krug, K. (2004) 'Niagara region farmers' markets: local food systems and sustainability considerations', *Local Environment*, 9(3): 235–54.

Friends of the Greenbelt Foundation (FGF) (2006) *Canada's First Certified Farmers' Market: Greenbelt Farmers and Toronto Residents to Benefit from the First Certified Farmers' Market in Canada.* Press Release, 22 November. Toronto: Friends of the Greenbelt Foundation & Farmers' Markets Ontario.

Friends of the Greenbelt Foundation (FGF) (2007) *Greenbelt Foundation 2007 Awareness Research. Summary prepared by Environics Research Group.* Toronto: Friends of the Greenbelt Foundation.

Government of Alberta, Department of Agriculture and Rural Development (2012) Alberta Approved Farmers' Market Program Guidelines. Online. Available: http://www1.agric. gov.ab.ca/$Department/deptdocs.nsf/all/apa2577 (accessed 26 March 2012).

Govindasamy, R., Italia, J. and Adelaja, A. (2002) 'Farmers' markets: consumer trends, preferences and characteristics', *Journal of Extension*, 40(1). Online. Available: http:// joe.org/joe/2002february/rb6.html (accessed 1 April 2008).

Griffin, M.R. and Frongillo, E.A. (2003) 'Experiences and perspectives of farmers from upstate New York farmers' markets', *Agriculture and Human Values*, 20: 189–203.

Groves, A. (2005) *The Local and Regional Food Opportunity.* Watford: Institute of Grocery Distribution.

Guthrie, J., Guthrie, A., Lawson, R. and Cameron, A. (2006) 'Farmers' markets: the small business counter-revolution in food production and retailing', *British Food Journal*, 108: 560–73.

Hall, C.M. (2007) 'Response to Yeoman et al: the fakery of "The authentic tourist"', *Tourism Management*, 28(4): 1139–40.

Hall, C.M. and Sharples, L. (eds) (2008) *Food and Wine Festivals and Events Around the World: Development, Management and Markets*, Oxford: Butterworth-Heinemann.

Hall, C.M., Mitchell, R. and Sharples, E. (2003) 'Consuming places: the role of food, wine and tourism in regional development', in C.M. Hall, E. Sharples, R. Mitchell, B. Cambourne and N. Macionis (eds) *Food Tourism Around the World: Development, Management and Markets.* Oxford: Butterworth-Heinemann.

Hall, C.M., Mitchell, R., Scott, D. and Sharples, L. (2008) 'The authentic market experiences of farmers' markets', in C.M. Hall and L. Sharples (eds) *Food and Wine Festivals and Events Around the World: Development, Management and Markets.* Oxford: Butterworth-Heinemann.

Hamilton, L.M. (2002) 'The American farmers market', *Gastronomica*, 2(3): 73–7.

Holloway, L. and Kneafsey, M. (2000) 'Reading the space of the farmers' market: a preliminary investigation from the UK', *Sociologia Ruralis*, 40: 285–99.

Kezis, A., Gwebu, T., Peavey, S. and Cheng, H. (1998) 'A study of consumers at a small farmers' market in Maine: results from a 1995 survey', *Journal of Food Distribution Research*, 29(1): 91–9.

Kneafsey, M., Holloway, L., Venn, L., Dowler, E., Cox, R. and Tuomainen, H. (2008). *Reconnecting Consumers, Food and Producers: Exploring Alternatives.* Oxford: Berg.

Lawson, R., Guthrie, J., Cameron, A. and Fischer, W. (2008) 'Creating value through cooperation? An investigation of farmers' markets in New Zealand', *British Food Journal*, 110(1): 11–25.

McEachern, M.G. and Willock, J. (2004) 'Producers and consumers of organic meat: a focus on attitudes and motivations', *British Food Journal*, 106(7): 534–62.

McGrath, M.A., Sherry, J.F. Jr and Heisley, D.D. (1993) 'An ethnographic study of an urban periodic marketplace: lessons from the Midville Farmers' Market', *Journal of Retailing*, 69(3): 280–319.

Middlemiss, L. (2010) 'Reframing individual responsibility for sustainable consumption: lessons from environmental justice and ecological citizenship', *Environmental Values*, 19(2): 147–67.

Mitchell, R. and Scott, D. (2008) 'Farmers' markets as events for local cultural consumption: the Otago Farmers' Market (Dunedin, New Zealand) explored', in C.M. Hall and L. Sharples (eds) *Food and Wine Festivals and Events Around the World: Development, Management and Markets.* Oxford: Butterworth-Heinemann.

Morgan, K. (2010) 'Local and green, global and fair: the ethical foodscape and the politics of care', *Environment and Planning A*, 42: 1852–67.

MyMarket (2007) Grand Opening in 2 New Locations. Online. Available: www.my-market.ca/ (accessed 1 October 2007).

MyMarket (2012) A New Season, MyMarket® Locations Are Back! Online. Available: www.my-market.ca/ (accessed 1 April 2012).

National Farmers' Retail and Markets Association (FARMA) (2004) *FARMA Consumer Survey June 2004: Nine out of Ten Households Would Buy from a Farmshopping Outlet if They Could.* Southampton: National Farmers' Retail and Markets Association.

National Farmers' Retail and Markets Association (2006) *Sector Briefing: Farmers Markets in the UK; Nine Years and Counting.* Southampton: Farmers' Retail and Markets Association.

National Farmers' Retail and Markets Association (2009a) Certified Farmers' Markets. Find a Farmers' Market. Online. Available: www.farmersmarkets.org.uk/findafmkt. htm (accessed 1 April 2012).

National Farmers' Retail and Markets Association (2009b) Certification – Abridged Rules. Online. Available: www.farmersmarkets.org.uk/findafmkt.htm (accessed 28 March 2012).

New Zealand Farmers' Market Association (2007) Fresh Market Locations. Online. Available: www.farmersmarket.org.nz/locations.htm (accessed 1 October 2007).

Padel, S. and Foster, C. (2005) 'Exploring the gap between attitudes and behaviour: understanding why consumers buy or do not buy organic food', *British Food Journal*, 107(8): 606–25.

Payet, J., Gilles, M. and Howat, P. (2005) 'Gascoyne growers market: a sustainable health promotion activity developed in partnership with the community', *Australian Journal of Rural Health*, 13(2): 309–14.

Payne, T. (2002) *U.S. Farmers Markets – 2000: A Study of Emerging Trends.* Washington, DC: Agricultural Marketing Service, USDA.

The Press (2009) 'Move to ensure markets genuine', *The Press*, Lifestyle Properties, 23 September: 12.

Purvis, A. (2002) 'So what's your beef?', *Observer*, 14 April. Online. Available: www.observer.co.uk/foodmonthly/story/0,9950,681828,00.html (accessed 25 January 2003).

Pyle, J. (1971) 'Farmers' markets in the United States: functional anachronisms?', *Geographical Review*, 61: 167–97.

Regional Food Australia (2007) Australian Farmers' Markets Listings. Online. Available: www.farmersmarkets.com.au/ (accessed 1 October 2007).

Sassatelli, R. and Scott, A. (2001) 'Novel food, new markets and trust regimes: responses to the erosion of consumers' confidence in Austria, Italy and the UK', *European Societies*, 3(2): 213–44.

Selfa, T. and Qazi, J. (2005) 'Place, taste, or face-to-face? Understanding producer–consumer networks in "local" food systems in Washington State', *Agriculture and Human Values*, 22: 451–64.

Seyfang, G. (2006) 'Ecological citizenship and sustainable consumption: examining local organic food networks', *Journal of Rural Studies*, 22(4): 383–95.

Seyfang, G. (2008) 'Avoiding Asda? Exploring consumer motivations in local organic food networks', *Local Environment*, 13(3): 187–201.

Stephenson, G., Lev, L. and Brewer, L. (2006) *When Things Don't Work: Some Insights into Why Farmers' Markets Close.* Special Report 1073. Oregon State University Extension Service.

Suarez-Balcazar, Y., Martinez, L.I., Cox, G. and Jayraj, A. (2006) 'African Americans' views on access to healthy foods: what a farmers' market provides', *Journal of Extension*, 44(2), 2FEA2. Online. Available: www.joe.org/joe/2006april/a2p.shtml.

Thilmany, D., Bond, C.A. and Bond, J.K. (2008) 'Going local: exploring consumer behavior and motivations for direct food purchases', *American Journal of Agricultural Economics*, 90(5): 1303–9.

Tiemann, T. (2004) 'American farmers' markets: two types of informality', *International Journal of Sociology and Social Policy*, 24(6): 44–57.

United States Department of Agriculture (2002) *Improving and Facilitating a Farmers' Market in a Low-Income Urban Neighborhood: A Washington, DC, Case Study.* Washington DC: Agricultural Marketing Service Transportation and Marketing Programs, Wholesale and Alternative Markets, United States Department of Agriculture.

United States Department of Agriculture (2006) Farmers' Market Growth. Online. Available: www.ams.usda.gov/farmersmarkets/FarmersMarketGrowth.htm (accessed 1 October 2007).

United States Department of Agriculture (2009) Farmers' Markets and Local Food Marketing. Online. Available: www.ams.usda.gov/AMSv1.0/FarmersMarkets (accessed 2 October 2009).

United States Department of Agriculture (2012) Farmers' Markets and Local Food Marketing. Online. Available: HTTP:www.ams.usda.gov/AMSv1.0/FARMERSMARKETS (accessed 27 March 2012).

Victorian Farmers' Market Association (2011) About the VFMA. Online. Available: www.vicfarmersmarkets.org.au/content/about-vfma (accessed 25 March 2012).

6   Is 'local' just a hot menu trend?

Exploring restaurant patrons' menu choices when encountering local food options

Carrie Herzog and Iain P. Murray

the importance of local comes from it being a 'delighter' once other needs have been met.

(Gooch *et al.* 2010)

Introduction

Local food has become a topic of great interest in recent years in many jurisdictions globally. Canada is no exception, and various provinces, including Ontario, have seriously promoted culinary tourism and local food to both domestic and foreign travellers. Public discourse has shown that Canada is experiencing its own movement around local food and this has translated into a marketing issue that is worth substantial amounts of money. Nonetheless, there is limited research on the intersection between local food and culinary tourism, especially in relation to consumer decision-making and motivations.

The intersection of local food and culinary tourism

Local food is a prominent topic in academic and industry circles. Numerous articles have been written addressing local food (see Weatherell *et al.* 2003; Born and Purcell 2006; Delind 2006; Feagan 2007) and local food has been declared by the Canadian Restaurant and Foodservice Association (CRFA) as the 'hottest menu trend in 2011' (CRFA 2011). In terms of consumer understanding of local food and its impact on purchase choice, studies have investigated local food in the context of grocery stores (Weatherell *et al.* 2003) and farmers' markets (Smithers *et al.* 2008). Local food has also received considerable attention regarding how it might relate to the identified tourism niche known as 'culinary' or 'food' tourism. It is argued that local food can help both to establish and to sell the uniqueness of an existing or potential tourism destination (Denault 2002; Cohen and Aveli 2003; Sims 2010).

There is currently a lot of excitement surrounding culinary tourism among tourism professionals. Many jurisdictions – from small regions to countries – are looking at ways to boost tourism revenues through developing culinary tourism products (Murray 2008). Consequently, it is common to come across reports that argue the benefits of culinary tourism and provide 'how to' guides to assist in the development of culinary tourism products (CTC 2003). The problem with some of these arguments in favour of culinary tourism is that the evidence presented is not specific enough and the research design has been seriously flawed (McKercher *et al.* 2008). One such example may be found in the following statement from an Ontario culinary tourism report: 'tourism accounts for 22% of all foodservice sales in Canada' (Ontario Culinary Tourism Advisory Council and Ministry of Tourism, Culture and Recreation, 2005). The statistic presented is problematic because '22%' includes all foodservice sales, including those from Quick-Service Restaurants (QSRs) and run-of-the-mill chain or independent restaurants that may hold little or no interest to true culinary aficionados. As University of Toronto sociology professors Josée Johnston and Shyon Baumann put it, 'one thing foodies flat-out refuse to eat is dinner at a mundane, generic chain restaurant' (quoted in Leung 2010).

Culinary tourism can generate economic development which may in turn help to preserve natural resources and improve the quality of life of communities (Hall and Sharples 2008). It may also help to ensure that indigenous foods and production methods are maintained over the long term (Buiatti 2011). If local or regional foods can be identified or even branded, this may provide differentiation and value-added aspects for tourists and tourism (Buiatti 2011). This notion has clearly been accepted by the provincial government in Ontario, Canada, where culinary tourism has been defined as 'travel that includes the appreciation and consumption of local/regional foods' (Ontario Culinary Tourism Advisory Council and Ministry of Tourism, Culture and Recreation 2005).

The word 'local' is commonly included in or alongside definitions of culinary tourism and descriptions of culinary tourism products. This is done despite the fact that consumers, marketers, government officials, and academics alike are at a loss to know exactly what 'local' means when used as a food label. An extensive search of Canadian sources produced only one official definition of 'local' (see also Chapter 5 above), and it is of little help in furthering our understanding of the word. The Canadian Food Inspection Agency (CFIA), a branch of the federal government, defines 'local' as follows:

> 'Local', 'locally grown', and any substantially similar term shall mean that the domestic goods being advertised originated within 50 km of the place where they are sold, measured directly, point to point, or meets the requirements of section B.01.012 of the *Food and Drug Regulations*, whichever condition is least restrictive.
>
> B.01.012 ... 'local food' means a food that is manufactured, processed, produced or packaged in a local government unit and sold only in
>
> a   the local government unit in which it is manufactured, processed or packaged,
> b   one or more local government units that are immediately adjacent to the one in which it is manufactured, processed, produced or packaged, or

c   the local government unit in which it is manufactured, processed, produced or packaged and in one or more local government units that are immediately adjacent to the one in which it is manufactured, processed, produced or packaged.

(Canadian Food Inspection Agency 2010)

Additionally, the search for an official Canadian definition of 'local government unit' failed to produce any result.

Despite the confusion over its meaning, 'local' has been declared the hottest menu trend in 2011 by chefs and restaurateurs in Canada (CRFA 2011). This declaration points to the need for more research on the benefits and challenges of using and promoting local food in restaurants. Smith and Hall (2003) investigate restaurateurs' opinions about and practices in using local food, but there exists a gap in the knowledge about restaurant patrons' perspectives of local. Murray's (2009) research on consumer opinions and meanings of 'local' has revealed considerable consumer interest in the meaning of the word as used to describe food on restaurant menus. The study utilized a paper-based, mail-back questionnaire and generated 117 usable questionnaires (61 per cent response rate). The findings revealed that restaurant patrons' expectations of the meaning of the word 'local' were quite diverse. At one extreme, it meant a food coming from anywhere in Canada. At the opposite extreme, it meant the food came from the individual's own community. In an open-ended question asking respondents to state what the phrase 'local beef short ribs' on a restaurant menu meant to them, answers included: 'safer than beef from another country, including U.S.A.', 'drug-free', 'sustainable', 'organic', 'fresh', 'animals raised humanely', 'raised within 50 km', and 'raised within 100 miles', among others. Murray's results highlight the multiple meanings of 'local' by consumers in several communities in south-central Ontario. As Gooch *et al.* (2010) suggest, consumers' meanings of local are apt to change in relation to 'the organization, the market in which it [the food product] is being sold, the commodity being discussed and the growing season'.

Adding to the complexity of the meanings of local food, Benaroia (2009) states that 'the term "locavore" proposes that people should only eat food grown or processed within a 100-mile radius of their homes'. In addition to 'locavore', this statement introduces the term 'produced', which further complicates the concept of local food. Murray (2009) asked respondents about the extent to which they would consider, for example, prepared mustard made in Halifax, Nova Scotia, using seed from the province of Saskatchewan, and served in a Halifax restaurant, to be local. (This would involve a distance in excess of 3,000 km. Respondents were split, with 42 per cent stating they would consider the mustard local, and 40 per cent saying they would not consider it to be local. Similar results were found with questions regarding wines, cheeses and sausages made (processed) in one geographic region using inputs from other geographic regions.

For many consumers, the concepts of sustainability, environmental impact, organic food, small-scale farms and fresh food are enveloped in the word 'local'.

Benaroia (2009) introduces more descriptors linked to local food when he states that 'we also know local food is fresh, nutritious, tasty and environmentally friendly. After all, it takes more energy to ship Peruvian asparagus to Canadian supermarkets, compared with Canadian spears'. Not surprisingly, there is little agreement on Benaroia's claims. Taylor (2009) cited long-time agricultural writer Jim Romahn who argued that local fruits and vegetables in southern Ontario were well below the quality of the same products shipped in from foreign countries and thousands of kilometres away. Responses from readers of Romahn's article demonstrated consumer outrage that anyone would dare question the quality of local produce.

Both Taylor (2009) and Leeder (2009a) cite University of Toronto Professor Pierre Desrochers who asserts that the 'food energy tab' is comprised of approximately 80 per cent for growing, 10 per cent for transport, and 10 per cent for cooking and disposal. Desrochers further suggests that 'productivity differentials' mean that some locations are better suited to producing certain types of food. 'A UK consumer driving 10 km to buy Kenyan green beans emits more carbon per bean than flying them from Kenya to the United Kingdom' (Desrochers quoted in Leeder 2009a; see also Desrochers and Shimizu 2010). Taylor concluded: 'Stop pretending [that buying local] provides any greater benefit to the environment. Local food helps local farmers. It does nothing for the rest of the world'. Similar arguments have been made about the larger carbon footprint for fresh local fish versus that caught commercially in waters far away (Leeder 2009b). Carlsson-Kanyama (2010) has conducted extensive research into the greenhouse gas (methane, nitrous oxide and carbon dioxide) emissions of numerous food items. She and her team have found, for example, that a tomato grown outdoors in Spain and shipped to Sweden generated fewer greenhouse gas emissions than a tomato grown in a greenhouse, warmed by fossil fuels, in Sweden (see also Carlsson-Kanyama and Lindén 2001).

While discussions of the value of local food in terms of quality, environmental sustainability and economic sustainability occur regularly, it is important to ask: how does the idea of local food impact consumers' behaviour and buying habits? Weatherell *et al.* (2003) note that the proportion of people in the United Kingdom who actively purchase local foods is much smaller than the proportion of those who express an interest in local foods. It is generally agreed that actual demand for local foods is weaker than expressed interest because consumers make tradeoffs between factors such as freshness, taste, and 'supporting local', and expediencies such as price, accessibility and convenience (Lappalainen *et al.* 1998). Weatherell *et al.*'s (2003) research confirmed these notions as they found that the first issues of importance when purchasing food were price, convenience and ease of preparation, although these varied between urban and rural residents. Further, they found that respondents generally agreed that they would try local foods, but would not continue to purchase them if the price and quality were not right.

The preceding discussion highlights the diversity, complexity and confusion over the meaning and importance of 'local' for consumers, marketers, government officials and academics. This context, in addition to the assertion that culinary tourism is built, at least in part, on local foods, leads to the study discussed in this chapter. The study builds on research that has examined local foods in grocery stores (Weatherell *et al.* 2003; Gooch *et al.* 2010) and farmers' markets (Smithers *et al.* 2008) as these are outlets where consumers show a willingness to purchase local food (see also Chapter 5 above; Nummedal and Hall 2006). Smith and Hall (2003) address local food in restaurants from the perspective of the restaurant. The purpose of this research was to take the perspective of restaurant patrons and determine the extent to which foods labelled as 'local' – or by a local brand name or a local geographic descriptor (e.g. the province in which the restaurant is located) – influenced their main course selection decision.

Methodology

In order to determine the influences of markers such as 'local', specific local brands and geographic descriptors, it was deemed important to obtain input from actual restaurant patrons in real restaurant settings. The research was conducted using a paper questionnaire and a postage-paid mail back procedure in order to minimize the impact of the researchers and foster more natural decision-making by consumers. Three restaurants in two cities and one town in southern Ontario were identified as having menus on which some, but not all, main course items were described with words such as 'local', described with a local brand, or described with a geographic descriptor (e.g. "Ontario lamb"). All three restaurants were personally contacted by the researchers and all three initially agreed to participate in the study. One restaurant, however, subsequently decided against participating. Restaurant A would best be described as fine dining, while Restaurant B offered both fine dining and pub options. In both restaurants, main course item prices ranged from C$10 to C$15 for lunch and C$12 to C$35 for dinner.

The contact persons at Restaurant A and B were the owner and general manager respectively. In both cases, these two individuals were responsible for encouraging waitstaff to actively distribute questionnaires to restaurant patrons. The suggested approach by the researchers was for the waitstaff simply to explain to the diners that the restaurant had agreed to assist the local university with a research project and then ask each guest who ordered a main course item from the menu if he or she would like to take home, complete and return a questionnaire in the postage-paid envelope provided.

To help achieve the best response rate possible, the questionnaires were kept short and did not ask respondents to identify themselves. Two separate questionnaires were prepared; the difference lay solely in the inclusion of one additional closed-ended question for Restaurant B to reflect the use of different words on the menu to describe main course items. The questionnaires were pilot-tested and this resulted in a few changes being made to clarify the wording.

For Restaurants A and B there were 10 and 11 closed-ended questions respectively that related specifically to the respondents' menu choice decision-making. Respondents were asked to rate the extent to which each statement 'had an influence on your decision to select the main course item that you ordered'. Each statement was to be rated using five possible responses of 'strong influence', 'medium influence', 'some influence', 'no influence' and 'not applicable'. In addition to these 10 or 11 closed-ended questions, there were four rows in which a respondent was given the opportunity to identify other issues that influenced his or her decision to select the item he or she did. Through an open-ended question, respondents were asked to indicate the primary reason why they chose this specific restaurant as opposed to any other for this particular meal. Finally, the diner was asked, through closed-ended questions, to indicate his or her frequency of dining at this restaurant and at restaurants of similar price range in the preceding 12 months, and to provide his or her gender, age range and the first three characters of his or her postal code.

During the months of July and August 2010, a total of 95 questionnaires were provided to Restaurant A and 105 to Restaurant B. Restaurant A distributed all 95 questionnaires and a total of 61 usable questionnaires were returned (64 per cent response rate). Restaurant B distributed only 32 of 105 questionnaires provided and a total of 15 usable questionnaires were returned (47 per cent response rate). No explanation was provided by Restaurant B for why most of the questionnaires were not distributed.

Part of the value of the research presented here is that it deals with the conundrum of 'theories of action' versus 'theories of use' – a problem that exists between what people say they will do and what they actually will do (Argyris 1995; see also Weatherell *et al.* 2003.) Alfnes and Sharma (2010) discuss this as 'hypothetical bias'; that is, responses derived from respondents who are answering inconsequential as opposed to consequential (real purchases using real money) decisions. Alfnes and Sharma (2010) also discuss 'social desirability bias' or the tendency to answer questions in a way that seems most 'correct' or socially desirable. Although these researchers go on to say that 'social desirability bias exists in virtually all types of self-reporting measures across nearly all social science literatures', they state that by having consumers make decisions with personal economic consequences, the social desirability bias is likely reduced. The research reported in this chapter gave respondents no reason to suspect that local food was in any way the topic of interest. This research design minimizes or eliminates both hypothetical bias and social desirability bias.

Results

The influence of local on main course item selection

Seventy-six usable questionnaires were returned and used for analysis. Sixty-one (80 per cent) of these came from Restaurant A. Respondents were evenly distributed between the age categories of 20–39, 40–59 and 60 plus years of age; more respondents, however, were female (61 per cent) than male (39 per cent) (Table 6.1). Sixty-one per cent had dined at restaurants of similar price range at least six times in the preceding 12 months, but 51 per cent stated that this was their first time visiting this particular restaurant in the preceding 12 months. Few respondents can be described as 'tourists' as 89 per cent lived within 50 km of the restaurant, and the remainder (eight respondents), except for one from the USA, lived within 100 km of the restaurant.

In the restaurants, local food was marketed solely on the menu. A total of 43 main course items were offered between Restaurants A and B. Of Restaurant A's 17 items, six were clearly presented on the menu as either 'Ontario', 'home-made' or branded with a small-scale local brand. Of Restaurant B's 26 items, 10 items were clearly presented as 'Ontario', 'local' or branded with one of four small-scale local brands. Between the two restaurants, 37 per cent of the menu items had some 'local' marker.

From this total of 43 main course items available, only 21 different items were selected by the 76 respondents. Of these 21 items ordered, eight (38 per cent) were identified as local in some way and these eight 'local' items were ordered by 39 of the 76 respondents (51 per cent). At first glance, this might suggest that the 'local' marker was influential in the respondents' main course item selection. However, of the 39 respondents who ordered one of the eight items identified as 'local' in some way, only nine (23 per cent) stated that the 'local' identifier had a strong influence on their decision, while 17 (44 per cent) said it had no influence at all. In contrast, 21 (54 per cent) of these same 39 respondents indicated that liking all components of the main course item was of strong influence.

An examination of the levels of influence of 10 different statements on all 76 respondents (Table 6.2) clearly reveals that 'Liked all components of the dish' was by far the single most influential issue when selecting their main course item. This was of 'Strong influence' to 42 respondents (55 per cent), and of

Table 6.1 Demographics of the respondents

		Gender				Total
		Male		Female		
		29		45		74[a]
Age						
20–9	30–9	40–9	50–9	60–9	70+	Total
9	13	11	15	19	7	74
Meal Period						
		Lunch		Dinner		
		7		68[b]		
Distance travelled from home[c]						
		<50 km		50–100 km		≥100 km
		65		7		1

Notes
N = 76.
a Two respondents did not provide their gender; two respondents did not provide their age.
b One respondent did not indicate the meal period (lunch or dinner).
c Three respondents did not provide a home location reference code (postal/zip code).

medium influence to an additional 21 respondents (28 per cent). Following as the second and third most influential issues were 'Would not make this item at home' and 'Liked the seasonings'. Respondents were not limited to selecting only one statement that was of 'Strong influence'.

Discussion

The importance of local to restaurant patrons when choosing a main course item

While not a key focus of this study, restaurant diners in both restaurants were asked to state the primary reason why they chose this restaurant over any other for the meal at which they received the questionnaire. All 76 respondents provided a reason and only three related in any way to local food ('advertised as local food'; 'local and seasonal items'; 'appreciate that they source food locally'). This finding suggests that local is probably not a key factor in choosing a restaurant at which to dine.

Contrary to the strong level of interest in 'local' on restaurant menus found by Murray (2009), results of the current study suggest that restaurant patrons are inclined to select their main course item based on what sounds as if it will taste good more than on any indication of the item being local in any way. Such a finding is consistent with that of Weatherell *et al.* (2003), who found that expressed interest is often not borne out in actual behaviour. Gooch *et al.* (2010) are quite emphatic as they declare: 'So complex are consumers' [food] purchasing decisions that anyone who believes local is THE driver of behaviour is either patently uninformed or ignorant of the facts.'

Table 6.2 Extent to which each statement influenced the choice of patron's main course item

Statement	Strong influence	Medium influence	Some influence	No influence
Liked all components of the dish	42	21	11	2
Would not make this at home	18	16	13	21
Liked the seasonings	12	19	17	14
Listed as an Ontario product[a]	9	12	9	18
Have ordered this item before	9	7	7	5
Listed as a local product	7	9	16	18
Listed as homemade	8	2	12	16
Identified by specific farm or supplier	6	2	12	19
Was a lower-priced item	3	6	8	33
Fit with my special diet	1	7	6	26

Notes
N=76.
a Responses here include those from the 11th question on Restaurant B's questionnaire 'This main course item uses Hallmark variety Ontario Wheat.'

The need for clarity and consistency in local food marketing in restaurants

Menus from the two restaurants used for the study revealed a range of terms and the potential for innuendo. Even within the menu of a single restaurant, inconsistencies and instances of questionable wording were common. For example, a single menu listed one pasta as 'homemade' and another as 'fresh'. Since these terms do not have the same meaning, there is the possibility of confusion in the mind of the average diner. It may be this sort of inconsistency in wording that prevents some consumers from fully engaging in the concept of local food in restaurants. Restaurant A, for example, clearly identified the lamb as being from Ontario on the dinner menu, but, despite it being the same cut of lamb from the same source, it was not given the 'Ontario' descriptor on the lunch menu. Restaurant B clearly stated on its menu that the '[brand] Beef' was 'locally sourced from … [brand] Packers'; given that this 'brand' is a 'packer', it is quite conceivable that the meat is not from the region and, in fact, could be imported from the USA.

Branding food as 'local' or 'Ontario'

The notion of whether or not 'Ontario' should be a term used to describe local food is interesting. Ontario is a province of just under 1.1 million square kilometres (158,654 km^2 of which is water) (Statistics Canada 2009: 190) and, as such, is almost twice the size of France. In spite of its size and diversity, the provincial government promotes the use of 'Ontario' as a food brand with its long-standing 'Foodland Ontario' marketing programme. In an American study, Darby *et al.* (2008) found that consumers placed a higher value on products produced 'in-state' and 'nearby' than products labelled as produced in the USA. It is unclear whether or not the 'Ontario' label might also be accorded the same value as found for a state-produced food in the USA. However, since about 90 per cent of Ontario's population of close to 13 million people (Statistics Canada 2009: 306, 308) live in the southern 10 per cent of the area of the province, it may well be that an Ontario food product does resonate as local in Ontario. More investigation into this issue is certainly warranted.

Restaurants need to 'sell the story' of local

Restaurants that truly want to carve out a reputation for serving local food would do well to tell more of the story about the sources of their food products, and be certain that they are crystal clear on issues such as where the foods were grown or raised versus where they might have been processed, produced or made. Clarity must be the order of the day. Perhaps the easiest and most effective way for a restaurant to convey its dedication to genuinely local foods is to present a clear statement of its philosophy. Fleshing this out with its own clear definition of local, as well as having both the philosophy and the definition widely available, would provide even more clarity to patrons. If, as some restaurateurs have indicated, sourcing local foods is more challenging and more costly, then menus should be written to clearly emphasize local food items and create a buzz that encourages a diner to select a well-described local food item.

The role of local food in culinary tourism

Results from this study were unable to provide information about culinary tourists in part because the number of respondents was lower than expected. One possible reason for the lack of responses from tourists (people living more than 100 km away) is that diners were asked if they would like to complete a questionnaire. Those from out of town may have declined, thinking that their views would not be valid. However, since roughly 75 per cent of all tourism in Canada involves Canadians travelling within Canada, culinary tourism involves marketing local food to Canadian residents. One particular city in southern Ontario, for example, sees culinary tourism as something that will occur in the city if top-of-mind awareness can be achieved in local residents regarding both local growers/producers and restaurants that serve local food. This way, when city residents have friends and relatives visiting, they will hopefully think of local food venues as places to take their guests (Vsetula 2010). This seems to be a very well-grounded approach to culinary tourism, especially in a city that does not have 'big draw' tourism attractions.

Restaurateurs as leaders of local food promotion

Given the current state of non-regulated use of the word 'local', the plethora of confusing terms and the lack of influence of 'things local' in restaurant patron decision-making when selecting main course items, it seems that there is substantial opportunity for restaurateurs to set the bar for truly local food. The key to promoting local foods in restaurant settings may well lie in some combination of menu engineering and clear messaging about the story of local food so that consumers feel connected with the food they are about to consume.

Conclusions

This study raises questions about the value of giving food a local brand, or describing it as 'local' or as being from 'Ontario', on restaurant menus. In turn, as argued in this chapter, these same questions may impact the value of 'local' food in culinary tourism. Although local has been identified as a hot menu trend, findings of this study suggest that restaurant patrons are only minimally influenced by menu offerings identified in any way as local. Nonetheless, it may be useful to elaborate on the way 'local' is marketed on restaurant menus (telling the story of local) and then investigate whether or not this elaboration has a more pronounced effect on patrons' menu item selection.

It is possible that restaurateurs have the potential to be leaders in the promotion of local food to consumers. What may be needed to realize the dream of increasing local food production and sales is greater understanding and collaboration between farmers and restaurateurs, and improved communication on menus to restaurant patrons. This potential for promotion of local foods notwithstanding, 'Quality in relation to price (which determines overall value) is the overriding factor driving consumers' [food] purchase decisions regardless of its source' (Gooch *et al.* 2010). If local food in restaurants is to be more than just a hot menu trend, consumer behaviour will have to become more closely aligned with expressed interest, and this will require a concerted, coordinated and sustained effort from producers, suppliers and restaurateurs.

References

Alfnes, F. and Sharma, A. (2010) 'Locally produced foods in restaurants: Are the customers willing to pay a premium and why?', *International Journal of Revenue Management*, 4(3/4): 238–58.

Argyris, C. (1995) 'Action science and organizational learning', *Journal of Managerial Psychology*, 10(6): 20–6.

Benaroia, I. (2009) 'On the terroir trail: Culinary tourism means big business for region's hotels and restaurants', *Foodservice and Hospitality*, 42(1): 33.

Born, B. and Purcell, M. (2006) 'Avoiding the local trap: Scale and food systems in planning research', *Journal of Planning Education and Research*, 26(2): 195–207.

Buiatti, S. (2011) 'Food and tourism: The role of the "Slow Food" association', in K. Sidali, A. Spiller and B. Schulze (eds) (2011) *Food, Agri-Culture and Tourism*, Heidelberg: Springer.

Canadian Food Inspection Agency (CFIA) (2010) Decisions: Claims – Composition, Quality, Quantity and Origin. Online. Available: www.inspection.gc.ca/english/fssa/labeti/decisions/compoe.shtml (accessed 11 July 2010).

Canadian Restaurant and Foodservices Association (CRFA) and BrandSpark International (2011) 2011 Canadian Chef Study. Online. Available: www.crfa.ca/aboutcrfa/newsroom/2011/the_chefs_have_spoken_local_is_the_hottest_menu_trend_in_2011.pdf (accessed 12 April 2011).

Canadian Tourism Commission (CTC) (2003) *How-to Guide: Develop a Culinary Tourism Product*, Ottawa: Canadian Tourism Commission.

Carlsson-Kanyama, A. (2010) Personal communication at Sustainable Food in Tourism Conference, Linnaeus University, Kalmar, Sweden, 30 September, 2010.

Carlsson-Kanyama, A. and Lindén, A. (2001) 'Trends in food production and consumption: Swedish experiences from environmental and cultural impacts', *International Journal of Sustainable Development*, 4(4): 392–406.

Cohen, E. and Aveli, N. (2003) 'Food in tourism: Attraction and impediment', *Annals of Tourism Research*, 31(4): 755–78.

Darby, K., Battle, M.T., Ernst, S. and Roe, B.E. (2008) 'Decomposing local: a conjoint analysis of locally produced foods', *American Journal of Agricultural Economics*, 90: 476–86.

Delind, L.B. (2006) 'Of bodies, place and culture: Re-situating local food', *Journal of Agricultural and Environmental Ethics*, 19(2): 121–46.

Denault, M. (2002) *Acquiring a Taste for Cuisine Tourism*, Ottawa: Canadian Tourism Commission.

Desrochers, P. and Shimizu, H. (2010) Food Miles: The Local Food Activists' Dilemma (a global warming inconvenient truth). Online. Available: www.masterresource. org/2010/10/food-miles-the-local-food-activists-dilemma-a-global-warming-inconvenient-truth/ (accessed 17 April 2011).

Feagan, R. (2007) 'The place of food: Mapping out the "local" in local food systems', *Progress in Human Geography*, 31(1): 23–42.

Gooch, M., Marenick, N. and Felfel, A. (2010) Local Food Opportunities: Focusing on the consumer, *Value Chain Management Centre*. Online. Available: www.georgemorris.org/GMC/Home.aspx (accessed 3 August 2010).

Hall, C.M. and Sharples, L. (eds) (2008) *Food and Wine Festivals and Events Around the World: Development, Management and Markets*, Oxford: Butterworth-Heinemann.

Lappaleinen, R., Kearney, J. and Gibney, M. (1998) 'A pan-European survey of consumers' attitude to food, nutrition and health: An overview, *Food Quality and Preference*, 9: 467–78.

Leeder, J. (2009a) 'U of T prof trumpets 10,000 mile diet', *The Globe and Mail* (Toronto), 5 December: M-3.

Leeder, J. (2009b) 'Debunking our fetish of the fresh', *The Globe and Mail* (Toronto), November 24, 2009: A-1. Online. Available: www.theglobeandmail.com/news/national/debunking-our-fetish-of-the-fresh/article1375159/ (accessed 12 June 2010).

Leung, W. (2010) 'Foodies: Culinary democrats or cultural snobs?', *The Globe and Mail* (Toronto), 27 April 2010. Online. Available: www.theglobeandmail.com/life/food-and-wine/foodies-culinary-democrats-or-cultural-snobs/article1548896/ (accessed 3 August 2010).

McKercher, B., Okumus, F. and Okumus, B. (2008) 'Food tourism as a viable market segment: It's all how you cook the numbers!', *Journal of Travel & Tourism Marketing*, 25: 137–48.

Murray, I.P. (2008) 'Culinary tourism: Segment or figment', paper presented at TTRA Canada Conference, Victoria, British Columbia.

Murray, I.P. (2009) '"Local": What restaurant diners say it means', unpublished paper presented at TTRA Canada Conference.

Nummedal, M. and Hall, C.M. (2006) 'Local food in tourism: An investigation of the New Zealand South Island's bed and breakfast sector's use and perception of local food', *Tourism Review International*, 9(4): 365–78.

Ontario Culinary Tourism Advisory Council and Ministry of Tourism, Culture and Recreation (2005) *Culinary Tourism in Ontario: Strategy and Action Plan 2005–2015*. Toronto: Ministry of Tourism, Culture and Recreation.

Sims, R. (2010) 'Putting place on the menu: The negotiation of locality in UK food tourism, from production too consumption', *Journal of Rural Studies*, 26: 105–15.

Smith, A. and Hall, C.M. (2003) 'Restaurants and local food in New Zealand', in C.M. Hall, L. Sharples, R. Mitchell, N. Macionis, and B. Cambourne (eds) *Food Tourism around the World: Development, Management and Markets*. Oxford: Butterworth-Heinemann.

Smithers, J., Lamarche, J. and Joseph, A. (2008) 'Unpacking the terms of engagement with local food at the farmers' market: Insights from Ontario', *Journal of Rural Studies*, 24: 337–50.

Statistics Canada (2009) *Canada Year Book 2009*. Ottawa: Ministry of Industry, Government of Canada.

Taylor, P. (2009) 'Save the planet – Buy California berries', *Waterloo Region Record*, 18 September 2009: A-15.

Vsetula, K. (2010) personal communication, 27 July 2010.

Weatherell, C., Tregear, A. and Allinson, J. (2003) 'In search of the concerned consumer: UK public perceptions of food, farming, and buying local', *Journal of Rural Studies*, 19: 223–44.

7 The links between local brand farm products and tourism
Evidence from Japan

Yasuo Ohe and Shinichi Kurihara

Introduction

Local food has attracted growing attention for its high potential to influence the sustainability of rural development (Vaz *et al.* 2009). In addition, local food is often discussed in connection with tourism in rural areas where resources for tourism are relatively limited (Bélisle 1983; Renko *et al.* 2010; Sims 2009, 2010). In this context, local food can play an important role in sustainable diversification of farm and rural economies. Policymakers also aim to reinforce this complementarity between local food and tourism (Telfer and Wall 1996; Sims 2010), generating a wide range of economic and social effects on the community (Everett and Aitchison 2008; Brandth and Haugen 2011). This chapter focuses on the economic effects that accrue to the local community and classifies these as either direct and indirect. The direct economic effects are sales and employment accrued from local food due to the development of production, processing and distribution systems. The indirect economic effects are generated as a result of diversification of the rural economy through taking advantage of the brand names of local food. Indirect economic effects are the sales and employment generated from visitor spending on accommodation and dining in local rural tourism facilities and restaurants. If the indirect effects increase, then sales of local products will also increase because visitors will buy local food on site or through the Internet. Thus, if these two effects are generated simultaneously, a large economic benefit will result for the local economy.

In this respect, the complementary relationship between local food and the tourism-related sector must work well. The rural cultural heritage has been recognized as closely connected with this complementarity (Szlanyinka 2009; Ohe and Ciani 2011). Types of tourism that are named after a crop, beverage or food-related activity are examples of complementarity between food and tourism; examples are food tourism (Hall *et al.* 2003; Hall and Sharples 2008), wine tourism (Hall *et al.* 2000; Hall and Sharples 2008; Kim *et al.* 2009b), culinary tourism (Montanari and Staniscia 2009; Horng and Tsai 2010), organic agriculture and agri-ecotourism (Kuo *et al.* 2006). Authenticity is a crucial issue in both local food production and food-related tourism (Sims 2009).

Previous studies of the economic effects on local food and tourism have focused on differentiation of tourism destinations (Haven-Tang and Jones 2005), effects of food consumption by tourists (Skuras *et al.* 2006; Kim *et al.* 2009a), backward economic linkages (Telfer and Wall 2000) and hedonic pricing evaluation (Ohe and Ciani 2011). However, there is a need to clarify under what conditions the relationship between food and tourism works most effectively, as this would allow suggestions to be made to rural communities on developing tourism by taking advantage of local food and heritage.

A programme for rural tourism, called 'Green Tourism', in Japan was inaugurated in 1994. The number of farmers who provide rural tourism activities has grown gradually, but many issues remain problematic such as lack of management skills and the ageing of the rural population (see Chapter 9 below). These obstacles involve issues that are commonly observed not only in rural Japan, but also in rural communities in other parts of the world.

This chapter focuses on the current supply-side situation of local brand farm products and sheds light on the direct and indirect economic effects of food-related tourism and how these two effects are connected. This is termed a complementarity hypothesis, and it is examined using the results of a survey of all agricultural cooperatives in Japan. Until the present report, this complementary relationship had not been fully tested statistically although descriptive case studies have been conducted. The reason why we focus on local brand farm products rather than local food in general is to control for issues of authenticity of local products. The term local food is too ambiguous for investigation. Finally, we present policy recommendations to strengthen the complementary relationship between local brand products and tourism development.

Complementarity between local brand products and tourism

A typical complementary relationship between products in economics is that of joint-products, in which one product technically accompanies another product or products. Sheep raising, in which wool and meat are both produced, is a familiar example. These joint-products are produced together because technically it is not possible to produce them separately. In the case of complementarity between local brand products and tourism, however, the relationship is not determined technically, but is formed intentionally by the efforts of local producers and concerned people in the rural community. Unless these efforts are made, the availability of local brands does not always create favourable conditions for the promotion of tourism activity in the local areas.

The economic factor that supports complementarity between local brand products and tourism is termed 'economies of scope', which is indicated by formula (1). This formula mathematically explains subadditivity (Panzar and Willig 1981; Baumol *et al.* 1988). This means that the production cost for producing both q_1 and q_2 together is less than the costs of producing q_1 and q_2 separately if economies of scope exist and justify diversification of activities by producing q_1 and q_2 together (Saloner *et al.* 2001; Besanko *et al.* 2000).

$$C(0, q_1) + C(q_2, 0) > C(q_1, q_2) \tag{1}$$

where

q_1 = product 1,
q_2 = product 2,
$C(0, q_1)$ = production cost when producing only q_1,
$C(q_2, 0)$ = production cost when producing only q_2,
$C(q_1, q_2)$ = production cost when producing q_1 and q_2.

Economies of scope can exist in the presence of indivisible input factors such as a facility and machinery that are available for multiple products. If an undivisible facility for production exists, the greater is the increase in the production level and the greater is the decrease in the facility's fixed costs. Other resources on farms that technically stipulate joint production are also reasons for economies of scope, as is exemplified by the case of sheep raising as mentioned above. Another cause of economies of scope is the existence of information goods such as a brand and trust in a product. The case in this study is a precise example of this. Once a brand is established, it exerts favourable conditions for products under the brand umbrella because consumers know what that brand is, which reduces their uncertainty regarding new related products. These reasons are theoretically conceived conditions, so that actual conditions faced by local brand-producing areas differ from one place to another. Therefore, we have to clarify empirically what conditions are necessary for a local community successfully to integrate tourism activity with local brand products below.

Legal framework of local brand products in Japan

Japan has a trademark system for local products that is similar to the geographical indications in the European Union designed to protect intellectual property rights for local brand products. That is the 'regional collective trademark', which is officially designated by the Japan Patent Office, Ministry of Economy, Trade and Industry (METI), which administers intellectual property rights. This system is an extended version of the conventional framework of trademarks and has been in place in this country since 2006. It was needed because within the conventional framework of trademarks, the use of names of local areas and products in trademarks is not allowed except in especially well-known cases. Thus, only areas with an already established reputation can have a conventional trademark, other areas being excluded under the conventional framework of trademarks. For this reason, the regional collective trademark supports attempts to brand local products at an early stage of local brand formation in order to overcome the problem in the conventional framework. In 2008, 402 out of 833 applications were officially approved and were allowed to use the regional collective trademark. Of the 402 designated cases, 211 (52.4 per cent) were for foods and liquor including one application each from Italy and Canada (Japan Patent Office

2008). The remaining accepted applications were for hot springs, traditional crafts such as lacquer ware, roof tiles, ceramics, textiles, timber and so on. The number of designated regional collective trademarks has gradually increased and continues to do so. Applicants are limited to local cooperatives that have legal status and are organized by cooperatives that represent the local producers. Applicants can apply for a regional collective trademark in combination with the name of the local area and of the product. Once designated, this trademark allows the holder to legally claim a violation of the holder's trademark if others use a similar or the same trademark representing a similar product or the same kind of product. This trademark is guaranteed for 10 years and can be renewed for another decade with no limitation on the number of renewals. In this sense, the regional collective trademark differs from a conventional trademark because the regional collective trademark focuses not on an individual producer, but on the collective action of producers that cover a particular producing area. In short, availability of the regional collective trademark provides a legal framework to promote local brand formation, which had not existed before.

Local brand products are not limited to recognition by a regional collective trademark only. In addition to regional collective trademarks administered by the central government, prefectural governments also provide their own local brand framework with their own official symbols. Despite the enthusiasm of prefectural governments, due to lack of publicity this framework does not gain much recognition even from local consumers. This is one reason why a national framework was required to establish nationwide standards for local brand products. An additional reason for a national framework was the need to protect local brands from the rising number of violations of trademarks by foreign companies, especially in Asia. However, neither of these policy frameworks provides supports measures for tourism-related activity.

Data

This study focuses on local brand farm products. The researchers define local brand farm products in a wide perspective, in that they are considered as locally connected farm products, which includes those having regional collective trademarks, a trademark and/or a designation at the prefectural level, and a reputation as a local product despite having no official designation. Data were obtained from a questionnaire of all agricultural cooperatives in Japan conducted from January to February 2009. The survey was conducted jointly by the Organization for Urban–Rural Interchange Revitalization and the authors in consultation with the Ministry of Agriculture, Forestry and Fisheries (MAFF), which provided the funding for this survey project. Survey sheets were distributed to each agricultural cooperative and returned by surface mail. The response rate was 225 out of 757 cooperatives (29.7 per cent). That response rate is about normal for this kind of survey, with about 30 per cent being the usual rate of response in this country. The questions asked concerned various aspects of local brand products and the cooperatives, such as what they produce, size of production, history of production and branding, positioning of the local brand, and quality standards. Information was also elicited on the effects of local brand products such as direct and indirect economic effects and non-economic effects and issues including tourism development and necessary support measures for the future. This survey was the first comprehensive one in terms of local brand farm products in this country, as far as we know.

Survey results: profiles of cooperatives producing local brand farm products

First, we examined profiles of local brand farm products from the survey results. The average number of producers in each cooperative was 406.4. The average sales per cooperative were worth 1,165 million yen (€9.87 million when €1 = 118 yen), with the average sales per producer being 2.9 million yen. The composition of local brand farm products is shown in Table 7.1. Vegetables and other field products are dominant (45.8 per cent) followed by fruit (19.1 per cent) and rice (15.6 per cent). Examples of vegetables are potatoes, melons, strawberries and green onions. Beef, which includes 'Matsuzaka beef', a world-renowned quality beef, and 'Wagyu' Japanese beef, was not a major local brand product in terms of share, i.e. less than 10 per cent of total local brand farm products. This relative scarcity supports evidence showing how precious Wagyu beef is.

Table 7.1 Profiles of local brand products

Composition of local brand products	Sample size	%
Vegetables and other field products	103	45.8
Fruit	43	19.1
Rice	35	15.6
Beef	19	8.4
Others: tea, mushrooms, flowers and fish	11	4.9
No answer	14	6.2
Total	225	100.0
Area range of local brand products		
Prefecture	21	9.3
Multiple municipalities	87	38.7
Single municipality	65	28.9
Part of single municipality	39	17.3
No answer	13	5.8
Total	225	100.0
Position of local brand products		
Extra high-end	17	7.6
High-end	72	32.0
Slightly high-end	59	26.2
Ordinary	64	28.4
No answer	13	5.8
Total	225	100.0

As to the range of areas producing local brand farm products, multiple municipalities were dominant, accounting for nearly 40 per cent of the respondents, followed by single municipalities, with about 30 per cent of respondents. Prefectures accounted for less than 10 per cent of respondents. Therefore, the municipality is the basic unit for production of local brand farm products. As to the positioning of local brand farm products, about 40 per cent of the respondents positioned their goods as extra high-end and high-end and about one-quarter indicated their goods were slightly high-end (Table 7.1).

Table 7.2 shows that, in general, the history of production within an area or cooperative is long. Cooperatives having a greater than 50-year history accounted for nearly 30 per cent of responding cooperatives, with nearly one-quarter of respondents having a history of more than 30 years but less than 50 years. In summary, production of more than half of the local brand farm products began at least 30 years ago. On the other hand, those with over 10 years to less than 30 years accounted for about 30 per cent of responses.

Regarding the history of brand formation (Table 7.2), those cooperatives that have a history of brand formation of more than five years but less than 15 years accounted for nearly 40 per cent of the cooperatives and those with a history of brand formation of more than 15 years but less than 30 years accounted for nearly 30 per cent. Only 14.7 per cent of cooperatives had a history of brand formation of less than five years. Among products, the brand formation period for rice was significantly shorter. The reason was that the percentage of cooperatives with more than 15 years of brand formation for rice was only 8.5 per cent but it was 20.6 per cent for non-rice products. This is because of the more recent emergence of better-tasting varieties of rice that resulted from competition in breeding among major rice-producing prefectures. Thus, there is role sharing between the cooperatives and prefectures, with the prefectures responsible for the

Table 7.2 Histories of production and local brand formation

History of production	Sample size	%
Less than 10 years	31	13.8
Over 10 years but less than 30 years	64	28.4
Over 30 years but less than 50 years	53	23.6
Over 50 years	64	28.4
No answer	13	5.8
Total	225	100.0
History of local brand formation		
Less than 5 years	33	14.7
Over 5 years but less than 15 years	85	37.8
Over 15 years but less than 30 years	62	27.6
Over 30 years	32	14.2
No answer	13	5.8
Total	225	100.0

development of new varieties and cooperatives responsible for production and marketing. This point demonstrates that the definition of a local brand farm product in Japan differs from the geographical indications of the European Union, which especially emphasizes traditional production methods and local heritage while its Japanese counterpart permits producing areas to explore brand formation with new products.

With regard to name recognition of local brand farm products, only 2.2 per cent of the sample reported recognition of local brand products from abroad, indicating that cooperatives were oriented towards domestic recognition (Table 7.3). Of the cooperatives, 35.6 per cent indicated that their local brand farm products were recognized nationwide and more than 50 per cent indicated that their products were recognized within neighbouring prefectures or only in the area of production. These findings are in sharp contrast with the European geographical indications that are oriented towards international recognition and intellectual property protection and marketing abroad. Existence of a unified criterion is essential for quality control to secure authenticity in local brand farm products. Of the responding cooperatives, 62.2 per cent had a unified criterion and 20.9 per cent had a rough standardization for quality but no explicit criteria (Table 7.3).

Effects of local brand products

With respect to the direct economic effects of local brand products, about half of the respondents expressed satisfaction in that the effects were greater or almost the same as expected (10.7 per cent and 40.4 per cent respectively). The remaining respondents felt that the effects were less than expected (21.3 per cent) or that they could not judge the effects yet (21.8 per cent) (Table 7.4). As to the

Table 7.3 Name recognition and quality standards

Degree of brand name recognition	Sample size	%
Only recognized in the producing area	44	19.6
Recognized in neighbouring prefectures	83	36.9
Recognized nationwide	80	35.6
Recognized abroad as well	5	2.2
No answer	13	5.8
Total	225	100.0
Existence of quality/certification standard		
Unified standard	140	62.2
Roughly standardized	47	20.9
Certified case by case	6	2.7
Nothing	17	7.6
No answer	15	6.7
Total	225	100.0

indirect economic effects, i.e. mainly tourism aspects, less satisfaction was expressed than for the direct effects. Effects were reported as less than expected by 32.4 per cent of respondents, and 35.6 per cent indicated that they did not know yet whether the effects were favourable or unfavourable (Table 7.4). About one-quarter of respondents stated that the effects were greater than expected or almost the same as expected. Reasons for this low level of satisfaction as to indirect economic effects are the difficulty in attaining indirect effects and also difficulty in measuring these effects.

The non-economic effects on the local communities, which can be generalized as social effects, are indicated in Table 7.5. One of the expected social effects of local brand products is increased name recognition of the local community. This is an effect on society outside the local community. Over half of respondents indicated that this effect was greater or almost the same as expected. Other social effects were related to the impact on the community by local brand farm products. As to the revitalization of the local community, expressions were divided almost equally between indications of meeting expectations and not meeting expectations. A similar pattern was revealed regarding increasing local residents' interest in their community. The effect on the understating of local food and culinary heritage inside and outside the local community was evaluated a little more favourably than the other two effects. In short, about half of the respondents were satisfied with social effects on the local community.

Well-coordinated cooperation with local governments is a significant factor for the development of local brand farm products. Table 7.5 shows that in evaluating the state of cooperation with local governments, respondents were divided between satisfaction and dissatisfaction with the current state of cooperation: 43.1 per cent of respondents were satisfied, 31.1 per cent were neither satisfied nor dissatisfied, while 20.5 per cent were dissatisfied.

Table 7.4 Direct and indirect economic effects

Direct economic effects	Sample size	%
Greater than expected	24	10.7
Almost the same as expected	91	40.4
Less than expected	48	21.3
Do not know yet	49	21.8
No answer	13	5.8
Total	225	100.0
Indirect economic effects		
Greater than expected	7	3.1
Almost the same as expected	49	21.8
Less than expected	73	32.4
Do not know yet	80	35.6
No answer	16	7.1
Total	225	100.0

Statistical tests on direct and indirect economic effects of local brand farm products in connection with various factors

Here, we focus on direct and indirect economic effects and conduct statistical tests to examine the complementary relationship between these two main effects of local brand farm products and various other factors surveyed. To avoid the complexity of statistical tests on the direct and indirect effects, we classified the

Table 7.5 Non-economic effects on local communities

Improvement of name recognition of local community	Sample size	%
Greater than expected	26	11.6
Almost the same as expected	98	43.6
Less than expected	50	22.2
Do not know yet	37	16.4
No answer	14	6.2
Total	225	100.0
Revitalization of local community		
Greater than expected	12	5.3
Almost the same as expected	100	44.4
Less than expected	56	24.9
Do not know yet	43	19.1
No answer	14	6.2
Total	225	100.0
Rising interest towards own community among local residents		
Greater than expected	20	8.9
Almost the same as expected	104	46.2
Less than expected	57	25.3
Do not know yet	31	13.8
No answer	13	5.8
Total	225	100.0
Rising understanding of local food culture		
Greater than expected	17	7.6
Almost the same as expected	108	48.0
Less than expected	46	20.4
Do not know yet	40	17.8
No answer	14	6.2
Total	225	100.0
Partnership with municipality		
Satisfied	21	9.3
A little satisfied	76	33.8
Neither satisfied nor dissatisfied	70	31.1
A little dissatisfied	29	12.9
Dissatisfied	17	7.6
No answer	12	5.3
Total	225	100.0

answers into two categories, positive and negative. Responses such as 'Greater than expected' or 'Almost the same as expected' were classified as 'Yes', while responses such as 'Less than expected' or 'Do not know yet' were classified as 'No'. The authors used this classification for the direct and indirect effects.

From the results of the statistical test shown in Table 7.6, nearly 90 per cent of those who recognized the direct economic effects also acknowledged the presence of indirect economic effects. In contrast, only about 40 per cent of those who did not acknowledge direct economic effects acknowledged the indirect effects. From these results, we confirmed the complementarity hypothesis between the direct and indirect economic effects. Since indirect economic effects represent effects on the local tourism business as mentioned, it is safe to say that there is a positive relationship between local brand products and tourism. We can also observe the complementary relationship between the two economic effects and social effects on the local community.

Product-wise, complementarities were also confirmed between the two economic effects and between the two economic effects and social effects although there were several cases for which there was no significance or slight significance, such as for rice, vegetables and upland farm products, fruit and beef (Table 7.7). Interestingly, the percentage of those who acknowledged indirect economic effects was relatively low in both rice- and vegetable-producing areas. This is because the paddy and vegetable fields constitute the most common agrarian landscape, and it is often difficult to differentiate one own local community from that of rivals.

Local brand products exerted not only economic effects but also effects on local residents in terms of raising interest in their local community, which leads to enhanced confidence among local residents in the long term. However, as may be expected, not all local brand-producing areas enjoyed all these effects. Table 7.8 shows the results of how the profiles of producing areas are connected with the two economic effects. Profiles that had a connection with direct and indirect economic effects with statistical significance were those that had high-end products, a history of over 15 years of brand formation and their own quality standards. This indicates that it takes time to form a brand that exerts complementary direct and indirect economic effects and that quality management is crucial. A good partnership with local government is also an important factor in nurturing branding of farm products, especially for the establishment of direct economic effects because of the higher significant connection that was observed than for indirect economic effects.

Table 7.9 indicates what sort of intellectual property rights work on the generation of economic effects. The researchers tested two cases: the case of local brand farm products and the case of non-brand products. Among various intellectual property rights, the results of statistical tests revealed that only specific intellectual property rights actually work. Interestingly, in the case of local brand farm products the regional collective trademark worked effectively on the indirect economic effect, while it had no significant effect on the direct economic effect. On the other hand, the local certification framework was effective in generating both

Table 7.6 Connection of direct and indirect economic effects of local brand farm products with various factors (%)

Effects (greater than expected or as expected = 1, others = 0)	Direct economic effects			Indirect economic effects		
	Yes	No	Test result	Yes	No	Test result
Direct economic effects	–	–	–	87.5	39.1	***
Indirect economic effects	42.6	6.4	***	–	–	–
Improvement in name recognition of local community	72.2	37.3	***	94.6	42.0	***
Revitalization of local community	72.2	26.4	***	87.5	37.3	***
Increasing interest towards own community among local residents	77.4	31.8	***	89.3	43.8	***
Increasing understanding of local food culture	74.8	35.5	***	85.7	45.6	***

Notes
Statistical method was chi-square test and ***, **, *, +, + (reference), ns are 1%, 5%, 10% and 20% significance level and not significant, respectively. Sample size was 225.

Table 7.7 Product-wise connection among effects (%)

Effects (greater than expected or as expected = 1, others = 0)	Local brand farm products				
	Rice	Vegetables	Fruit	Beef
Direct economic effects (Yes)				
Indirect economic effects	87.5**	88.0***	86.7**	100.0**
Improvement in name recognition of local community	66.7**	71.2***	66.7^{ns}	61.5$^+$
Revitalization of local community	66.7*	75.9***	77.3**	81.8***
Increasing interest towards own community among local residents	73.7***	73.3***	74.1**	63.4$^+$
Increasing understanding of local food culture	66.7**	71.7***	76.0**	61.5$^+$
Indirect economic effects				
Direct economic effects	41.2**	39.3***	50.0**	55.6**
Improvement in name recognition of local community	44.4***	44.2***	46.7**	38.5$^+$
Revitalization of local community	53.3***	38.9***	59.1***	45.5**
Increasing interest towards own community among local residents	36.8**	36.7***	51.9***	45.5**
Increasing understanding of local food culture	44.4***	33.3**	52.0***	38.5$^+$

Notes
Statistical method and signs of statistical significance and sample size are the same as in Table 7.6. Sample sizes for each product are 35 (rice), 103 (vegetables), 43 (fruit) and beef (19).

Table 7.8 Connection between economic effects and profiles of local brand products (%)

Profiles	Direct economic effects			Indirect economic effects		
	Yes	No	Test result	Yes	No	Test result
Area range of local brand product: multiple municipalities (multiple municipalities or wider = 1, others = 0)	50.4	45.5	ns	46.4	48.5	ns
Position of local brand (extra high-end or high-end product = 1, others = 0)	46.1	32.7	**	53.6	34.9	**
History of production (30 years or more = 1, others = 0)	54.8	49.1	ns	60.7	49.1	+
History of local brand formation (15 years or more = 1, others = 0)	49.6	33.6	**	58.9	36.1	***
Degree of brand name recognition (nationwide or abroad = 1, others = 0)	48.7	26.4	***	42.9	36.1	ns
Existence of quality/certification standard (yes = 1, others = 0)	76.5	47.3	***	83.9	55.0	***
Partnership with municipality (a little satisfied or satisfied = 1, others = 0)	49.6	36.4	**	53.6	39.6	*

Notes
Statistical method and signs of statistical significance and sample size are the same as in Table 7.6.
ns = not significant.

Table 7.9 Connection between economic effects and employed intellectual property rights (%)

Employed intellectual property rights (yes = 1, no = 0)	Direct economic effects			Indirect economic effects		
	Yes	No	Test result	Yes	No	Test result
Local brand farm products						
Regional collective trademark	27.0	23.6	ns	37.5	21.3	**
Trademark in general	38.3	31.8	ns	35.7	34.9	ns
Patent	2.6	1.8	ns	5.4	1.2	+
Design right	2.6	0.9	ns	1.8	1.8	ns
Breeder's right	0.9	0.9	ns	0.0	1.2	ns
Local certification framework	24.4	15.5	*	28.6	17.2	*
Nothing	16.5	22.7	ns	10.7	22.5	*
Non-local brand farm products						
Regional collective trademark	11.3	10.9	ns	17.9	8.9	*
Trademark in general	28.7	17.3	**	23.2	23.1	ns
Patent	0.9	1.8	ns	3.6	0.6	+
Design right	1.7	0.0	ns	1.8	0.6	ns
Breeder's right	0.9	0.0	ns	0.0	0.6	ns
Local certification framework	23.5	12.7	**	37.5	11.8	***
Nothing	33.0	34.6	ns	23.2	37.3	*

Notes
Statistical method and signs of statistical significance and sample size are the same as in Table 7.6.

direct and indirect economic effects (although the statistical significance was at the 10 per cent level). This is probably because local certification frameworks were established earlier than regional collective trademarks. Thus, there is a need to monitor the effect of the national framework on the regional collective trademark over the long term. In the case of non-brand products, results were similar to those for local brand products with higher statistical significance on the local certification framework for both direct and indirect economic effects. This result shows that the local certification framework is particularly effective for a non-brand product that has the potential to become a brand product in the future. From this perspective, the local certification framework is compatible and complementary with the national framework in sharing a role.

Table 7.10 shows the results of statistical tests on the connection between the two economic effects and various specific effects. Acknowledgement of the achievement of indirect economic effects was significantly associated with the expectation of wider effects than was the acknowledgement of direct economic effects. On the other hand, acknowledgement of direct economic effects was significantly associated with expectations of raising the recognition of local community and pride compared with not acknowledging direct economic effects. However, there was no statistically significant difference in this expectation between those who did and did not acknowledge an indirect economic effect.

There are many issues to be overcome in the development of local brand farm products (Table 7.11). Advertisement and promotion activity was a common issue among those who acknowledged direct and indirect economic effects. In contrast, increases in acknowledgement of indirect economic effects were noted in relation to issues such as quality management and securing marketing-capable human resources.

Table 7.12 shows the responses of the cooperatives with respect to the various efforts undertaken for the development and maintenance of local brand products. Most of these efforts were made by those respondents who had acknowledged both direct and indirect economic effects. Activities included making a plan for branding local products, establishing a system for branding such products, defining a linkage between the locality and the product, and developing new products. Other actions were management of quality and quantity of goods, advertisements, and forming partnerships with the local tourism and restaurant sectors. Thus, it is reasonable to argue that these are the necessary common conditions to generate the direct and indirect economic effects of local brand products. A higher percentage of those who acknowledged direct economic effects responded positively with regard to actions in defining the value of the local products, naming the products and creating a logo and securing funds for activity than those who did not. With respect to those who acknowledged an indirect effect, on the other hand, higher percentages responded that they established a system to prevent illegal use of production technology or seed varieties and took action for the continuation of the local heritage than those who did not acknowledge an indirect effect. Developing human resources to implement brand management was a common issue in acknowledgement of both direct and indirect economic efforts.

Table 7.10 Connection between expected economic effects and actual evaluation (%)

Expected effects (expected or a little expected = 1, others = 0)	Direct economic effects			Indirect economic effects		
	Yes	No	Test result	Yes	No	Test result
Increase in producer income and employment	90.4	81.8	*	94.6	83.4	**
Revitalization of related industry	67.0	55.5	*	73.2	57.4	**
Increase in exports	28.7	24.6	ns	32.1	24.9	ns
Increase in no. of tourists	46.1	30.9	**	66.1	29.6	***
Protection of brand (prevention of plagiarism)	56.5	52.7	ns	64.3	51.5	*
Increase in recognition of brand among consumers	81.7	69.1	**	83.9	72.8	*
Increase in recognition of local community and pride	93.0	84.6	**	94.6	87.0	+
Revitalization of local community	79.1	63.6	**	92.9	64.5	***
Succession of local cultural heritage including culinary aspects	75.7	68.2	ns	87.5	66.9	***
Rediscovery of local resources	63.5	55.5	ns	69.6	56.2	*
Creation of new business	53.9	43.6	+	64.3	43.8	***

Notes
Statistical method and signs of statistical significance and sample size are the same as in Table 7.6.

Table 7.11 Connection between economic effects and various issues (%)

Issues (yes = 1, no = 0)	Direct economic effects			Indirect economic effects		
	Yes	No	Test result	Yes	No	Test result
Making plan of action for branding of local product	42.6	50.9	ns	37.5	49.7	+
Forming system for branding local product	44.4	50.0	ns	41.1	49.1	ns
Defining linkage between locality and product	33.0	28.2	ns	37.5	28.4	ns
Defining product value such as taste, nutrition, etc.	45.2	34.6	+	48.2	37.3	+
Marketing/needs survey	40.9	40.9	ns	42.9	40.2	ns
New product development including processing	47.0	50.0	ns	57.1	45.6	+
Maintenance and improvement of quality	50.4	48.2	ns	62.5	45.0	**
System of securing production amount	60.0	53.6	ns	62.5	55.0	ns
System to prevent illegal use of production technology and seed varieties	15.7	16.4	ns	19.6	14.8	ns
Naming, creation of logo or package design	24.4	18.2	ns	26.8	19.5	ns
Advertisement and promotion activity	38.3	52.7	**	28.6	50.9	***
Development of human resources capable of brand management and marketing	47.0	39.1	ns	57.1	38.5	**
Securing funds for activity	27.0	29.1	ns	26.8	28.4	ns
Promotion of exports	13.0	15.5	ns	12.5	14.8	ns
Succession of local heritage including culinary aspects	13.9	15.5	+	14.3	14.8	ns
Partnership with tourism and restaurant sectors	34.8	25.5	+	30.4	30.2	ns
Decision-making and coordination of people concerned	21.7	21.8	ns	16.1	23.7	ns
Gaining regional collective trademark or trademark	15.7	10.9	ns	17.9	11.8	ns

Notes
Statistical method and signs of statistical significance and sample size are the same as in Table 7.6.

Table 7.12 Connection between economic effects and actions actually taken (%)

Actions (intensively taken or taken = 1, others = 0)	Direct economic effects			Indirect economic effects		
	Yes	No	Test result	Yes	No	Test result
Making plan of action for branding of local product	55.7	28.2	***	58.9	36.7	***
Forming system for branding of local product	53.0	24.6	***	60.7	32.0	***
Defining linkage between locality and product	38.3	22.7	***	46.4	25.4	***
Defining product value such as taste, nutrition, etc.	48.7	28.2	***	48.2	35.5	*
Marketing/needs survey	33.9	26.4	ns	39.3	27.2	*
New product development including processing	31.3	15.5	***	41.1	17.8	***
Maintenance and improvement of quality	75.7	47.3	***	76.8	56.8	***
System of securing production amount	67.8	45.5	***	75.0	50.9	***
System to prevent illegal use of production technology and seed varieties	32.2	24.6	ns	41.1	24.3	**
Naming, creation of logo or package design	62.6	36.4	***	60.7	46.2	*
Advertisement and promotion activity	73.0	44.6	***	76.8	53.3	***
Developing human resources capable of brand management and marketing	23.5	13.6	*	26.8	16.0	*
Securing funds for activity	37.4	16.4	***	30.4	26.0	ns
Promotion of exports	9.6	5.5	ns	8.9	7.1	ns
Succession of local heritage including culinary aspects	27.0	16.4	*	39.3	16.0	***
Partnership with tourism and restaurant sectors	31.3	18.2	**	48.2	17.2	***

Notes
Statistical method and signs of statistical significance and sample size are the same as in Table 7.6.

To summarize, the results in this study indicate that a large part of the efforts were made by utilizing common managerial resources with a long-term perspective for the generation of direct and indirect economic effects in the producing areas. In this context, it is safe to say that these areas have ample opportunity to take advantage of the economies of scope between local brand products and tourism-related business. At the same time, the results also showed that there are differences in terms of necessary conditions between the direct and indirect effects. The indirect economic effects require local producers to look more carefully at issues of cultural heritage and the local community, which suggests the importance of a wider perspective.

Conclusion

This chapter investigated empirically the relationship between local brand farm products and tourism activity, based on the results of a questionnaire survey on effects and issues related to local brand farm products that was targeted at agricultural cooperatives in Japan. The main points revealed from the study are as follows. First, the complementary connection between local brand farm products and tourism is understood as an issue of economies of scope. If producing areas have a good connection between the local brand farm products and tourism, then we can say that the economies of scope work and vice versa. Second, local brand products are not officially defined, but are a 'regional collective trademark' established to designate local brand products and to stimulate local economies in 2008. Food accounted for about half the products that obtained a regional collective trademark. A local certification framework promoted by prefectural governments also exists in Japan. The survey covered all these types of local brand farm products with a wider connotation. Third, the result of statistical tests on the relationship between the direct economic effects from the local brand farm products and the indirect economic effects, mainly tourism, empirically clarified that there was a complementary relationship between the two economic effects. We can say that economies of scale reflected this complementarity. Those producing areas that acknowledged the two economic effects have a relatively long history of branding formation of products, systems of quality control and preserving the local heritage.

To strengthen the complementary relationship, concerned people in the producing areas need to have wider and longer perspectives in local resource management than that of solely promoting local brand products. Thus, these points should be considered when support measures are designed for diversification of farm and rural economies.

Acknowledgement

This study was funded by the Grants-in-Aid for Scientific Research, No. 20248024, Japan Society for the Promotion of Science (JSPS).

References

Baumol, W.J., Panzar, J.C. and Willig, R.D. (1988) *Contestable Markets and the Theory of Industry Structure,* revised edn, New York: Harcourt Brace Jovanovich.

Belisle, F.J. (1983) 'Tourism and food production in the Caribbean', *Annals of Tourism Research*, 10: 497–513.

Besanko, D., Dranove, D. and Shanley, M. (2000) *Economics of Strategy*, 2nd edn, New York: John Wiley & Sons.

Brandth, B. and Haugen, M.S. (2011) 'Farm diversification into tourism – Implications for social identity?', *Journal of Rural Studies*, 27: 35–44.

Everett, S. and Aitchison, C. (2008) 'The role of food tourism in sustaining regional iden-tity: A case study of Cornwall, South West England', *Journal of Sustainable Tourism*, 16: 150–67.

Hall, C.M. and Sharples, L. (eds) (2008) *Food and Wine Festivals and Events Around the World: Development, Management and Markets*, Oxford: Butterworth-Heinemann.

Hall, C.M., Sharples, L., Cambourne, B. and Macionis, N. (2000) *Wine Tourism around the World: Development, Management and Markets*, Oxford: Butterworth-Heinemann.

Hall, C.M., Sharples, L., Mitchell, R., Macionis, N. and Cambourne, B. (2003) *Food Tourism around the World: Development, Management and Markets*, Oxford: Butterworth-Heinemann.

Haven-Tang, C. and Jones, E. (2005) 'Using local food and drink to differentiate tourism destinations through a sense of place: A story from Wales–dining at Monmouthshire's Great Table', *Journal of Culinary Science & Technology*, 4(4): 69–86.

Horng, J.-S. and Tsai, C.-T.S. (2010) 'Government websites for promoting East Asian culinary tourism: A cross-national analysis', *Tourism Management*, 31: 74–85.

Japan Patent Office (2008) *Designated Regional Collective Trademark* (in Japanese), issued in August 2008, Tokyo: Japan Patent Office.

Kim, Y.G., Eves, A. and Scarles, C. (2009a) 'Building a model of local food consumption on trips and holidays: A grounded theory approach', *International Journal of Hospital-ity Management*, 28: 423–31.

Kim, Y.H., Yuan, J.J., Goh, B.K. and Antun, J.M. (2009b) 'Web marketing in food tourism: A content analysis of web sites in West Texas', *Journal of Culinary Science & Technology*, 7: 52–64.

Kuo, N.-W., Chen, Y.-J. and Huang, C.-L. (2006) 'Linkages between organic agriculture and agro-ecotourism', *Renewable Agriculture and Food Systems*, 21(4): 238–44.

Montanari, A. and Staniscia, B. (2009) 'Culinary tourism as a tool for regional re-equilibrium', *European Planning Studies*, 17(10): 1463–83.

Ohe, Y. and Ciani, A. (2011) 'Evaluation of agritourism activity in Italy: Facility-based or local culture-based?', *Tourism Economics*, 17(3): 581–601.

Panzar, J.C. and Willig, R.D. (1981) 'Economies of scope', *The American Economic Review*, 71 (2): 268–72.

Renko, S., Renko, N. and Polonijo, T. (2010) 'Understanding the role of food in rural tourism development in a recovering economy', *Journal of Food Products Marketing*, 16: 309–24.

Saloner, G., Shepard, A. and Podolny, J. (2001) *Strategic Management*, New York: John Wiley & Sons.

Sims, R. (2009) 'Food, place and authenticity: Local food and the sustainable tourism experience', *Journal of Sustainable Tourism*, 17(3): 321–36.

Sims, R. (2010) 'Putting place on the menu: The negotiation of locality in UK food tourism, from production to consumption', *Journal of Rural Studies*, 26: 105–15.

Skuras, D., Dimara, E. and Petrou, A. (2006) 'Rural tourism and visitors' expenditures for local food products', *Regional Studies*, 40: 769–79.

Szlanyinka, E. (2009) 'Role of cultural values in rural development', in T. Vaz, P. Nijkamp and J.L. Rastoin (eds) *Traditional Food Production and Rural Sustainable Development: A European Challenge*, Farnham: Ashgate.

Telfer, D.J. and Wall, G. (1996) 'Linkages between tourism and food production', *Annals of Tourism Research*, 23(3): 635–53.

Telfer, D.J. and Wall, G. (2000) 'Strengthening backward economic linkages: Local food purchasing by three Indonesian hotels', *Tourism Geographies*, 2(4): 421–47.

Vaz, T., Nijkamp, P. and Rastoin, J.L. (eds) (2009) *Traditional Food Production and Rural Sustainable Development: A European Challenge*, Farnham: Ashgate.

8 The evolving relationship between food and tourism

A case study of Devon in the twentieth century

Paul Cleave

Introduction

This chapter investigates aspects of the relationship that tourists develop with food over time. Devon, a county in the south-west of England, is used as a case study and geographical focus. It aims to show how using a specific location and a twentieth century timescale enables the researcher to find out how and why the relationship between place and food evolves. The chapter draws on the experience of domestic tourism during the interwar period from the end of the First World War to the outbreak of the Second World War in 1939.

Tourists and food

Tourism necessitates eating away from home, and for some tourists this may be an incentive to visit particular destinations. The appeal of local food is considered an important part of the attraction of the holiday and the burgeoning interest in food and wine tourism. This has attracted international interest with, for example, Hall *et al.* (2003), Boniface (2003), Hall and Sharples (2008) and subsequently Vitterso and Amilien (2011) associating food and tourism with food heritage (see also Chapter 15 below). This interest is at times gastronomic, for example in the quest for high-quality dining, and at others ethnographic, when traditional foods and dishes are sought. Tourists' interests in food are complex, a dimension of tourism, a quest for the authentic, the traditional and heritage in the context of food. These interests embrace the experience of eating out and commercial hospitality, food as an experiential activity whether visiting a vineyard or a fishery and the emergence of food tourism. Everett (2008) defines food tourism as a desire to experience a particular type of food or the produce of a specific region and distinguishes between those who visit specific food and tourism sites and those who utilise the generic hospitality sector. Cole (2007) indicates that hospitality becomes commoditised and proposes that tourists' perceptions of authenticity vary according to their point of view. From the perspective of food, this may be interpreted as what is perceived as local, traditional and *Devonshire*.

Mintz and Du Bois (2002: 104–7) affirm the interest in food and eating patterns as being of growing interest to ethnographers as food reflects changes in societies; both food and humans travel, thus contributing to changes in food consumption. Food and eating are suggested as a way of studying how humans connect food to rituals, symbols and belief systems. In the circumstances of tourism, food and eating on holiday often represent a search for local, authentic and traditional food experiences and the eating rituals of the tourist's hosts.

The attraction of food in tourism is complex and often associated with a search for the real, the true and the authentic. Taylor (2001) equates authenticity with tradition, suggesting that in tourism the production of authenticity sometimes pays a homage to the past in terms of food. This may be illustrated using particular food products, their production and processing, where elements of the past contribute to an authentic foodstuff and reproduction of the original, for example cheese, cider and clotted cream. Quan and Wang (2004) advocate that the experience of food consumption in tourism can be analysed from either its relationship to the peak or daily touristic experience and that food is an extension of that consumed at home. However, it is proposed that the 'quest for various foods is one of appealing experiences' and a change in routine. This can be described as novelty seeking where tourists look for new foods and consumption experiences, for example Michelin star dining, food festivals and field kitchens.

Food is frequently associated with place, whether ingredients, local produce, speciality dishes or restaurants, but this association evolves over time and is subject to external influences. In the case study of Devon it is found to be associated with landscape, health and agriculture. Food also offers pleasure and entertainment and serves a social purpose, often providing an opportunity for tourists to engage with local cultures and customs (Henderson 2009). However, Mead (1997) discusses the significance of food in global terms, suggesting that its meaning may be interpreted as a need for nourishment and a search for pleasure. In the framework of tourism food contributes to the enjoyment and sustenance of the tourist experience. Barthes (1997) advises that food frequently carries the notion of representing the flavourful survival of culinary traditions, extending Mead's nourishment and pleasure proposal.

The current interest in food tourism as a genre emerged through the twentieth century under the influence of changes in food production, diet and consumer trends. The investigation of one region to identify the association of food with place will be presented, using one of England's major tourist destinations. Studying one era may inform the development of another; thus, the past is a key to understanding the future.

The historical dimension of food and tourism

Devon has a long history whereby tourists to the region relate and record their experiences of the food there as part of their overall tourist experience. This chapter focuses on the relationships between food and tourism. It utilises personal holiday records such as the postcard to show that food has interested and attracted tourists to the county. These were supported by the use of qualitative data derived from interviews with tourists and those involved in the production of food for tourist consumption.

The background and context of the research

The background and context of the research is derived from an apparent gap in the historiography of tourism on the changing relationships between food and tourism. Bessiere (1998) presents detailed research but this tends to be limited to one point in time and does not explore development in an individual location over an extended timescale. The twentieth century provides numerous opportunities from which the relationships between food and tourism can be studied. These include diet, health, technology, leisure and culture. The study of food is not restricted to eating out in the commercial domain but includes the domestic domain – food in the home and food as a tourist activity. Slattery (2002) affirms a third social domain of hospitality as the social settings in which acts of hospitableness take place. This expands the scope of the research to include what appear to be routine and mundane activities in tourism that Towner (1995) suggests have been overlooked. The case study of Devon provides an example of a location that has successfully combined tourism and food production since travellers such as Celia Fiennes (1685), Daniel Defoe (1724–7) and Mavor (1798) visited the region and subsequently wrote about the food they enjoyed on their travels.

The twentieth-century timescale of the research shown in Table 8.1 is presented as five eras. These span the era of Veblen's (1961) conspicuous consumption of the *belle époque* to the experience economy of the late twentieth century.

These divisions relate to significant stages in the development of tourism and leisure in the United Kingdom. Pimlot (1976) identifies key dates in tourism, indicating that events such as the 1938 Holidays With Pay Act stimulated the annual summer holiday and subsequently the provision of accommodation and amenities at resorts. The timescale begins with the *belle époque* an era of polarised leisure, a time of leisured classes rather than a leisured society. It is during this period that an interest in nutrition and diet, and a scientific connection between health and diet, were first identified (Drummond and Wilbraham 1957). The interwar period is typified by a growth in mass consumption including leisure and an interest in tourism and health. The expansion of modern mass tourism, the Development of Tourism Act (DTA) 1969, and package tours is represented in era 3. Towards the end of the twentieth century, in eras 4 and 5,

Table 8.1 Twentieth century tourism timescale eras

1	1914	The *belle époque* leading to the First World War
2	1939	Inter-war depression leading to World War Two
3	1969	Development of Tourism Act
4	1989	Review of the Development of Tourism Act
5	2000+	Environmental context

tourism appears to be characterised in terms of globalisation, its sustainability and environmental impacts and a return in food production to local produce, production, and traceability.

As the aim of the chapter is to show how tourists' relationships with food have developed it is necessary to demonstrate how the timescale is linked to the tourists' food journey. These range from periods in the first half of the twentieth century identified by leisured classes and an interest in the rustic and rural, to a time of Michelin stars, food tourism and the experience economy by the end of the century.

The evolution of food and tourism in the twentieth century

Table 8.2 presents the eras in Table 8.1 in the context of food and tourism. These are significant in their relationship to health, tourism and leisure and show how the interests in food have changed through the period of a century. The table demonstrates how food is linked to the consumption of tourism and that throughout the timescale of the research interest in food can be examined in a broader context including health and leisure. During each stage in the timescale food is subject to trends and fashions often linked to health. For example, in era 2 prevailing medical research advised that good food and a balanced diet contributed to good health. This recommendation is often conveyed in tourism literature of the period. *Holiday Haunts 1939* (Fraser 1939) includes numerous advertisements for hotels in Devon such as the Osborne Hotel, Torquay, which boasted 'Clotted cream and rich milk from tuberculin tested herd and garden produce sent in daily from our own 300 acre farm' (Fraser 1939: 482–3). In Devon it is the variety, abundance and production of food that appear to be important dimensions of its attraction.

Table 8.2 Twentieth-century tourism eras, food, health and leisure influences

Era	Food	Food and leisure
1>1914 *Belle époque*	• Culinary imperialism • The farm economy and its food	• Leisured classes • Awareness of the dietary value of food
2>1939 Inter-war	• Tea shops, eating out as an occasional treat	• Keeping fit • National Dietary Survey
3>1969 DTA	• Austerity and affluence	• Rationing • Post-war overseas travel
4>1989 Review of DTA	• Nouvelle cuisine and fast food culture	• Global tourism • Fusion cuisine
5>2000+ Environment	• Culinary 'celebrification' • Sustainable food production	• Sustainable tourism • Food tourism • Experience economy

The five eras presented in Table 8.2 show how food and diet are linked to leisure. For example, era 2 the interwar period, indicates that the relationship between food and tourism is connected to a healthy lifestyle. The benefits of fresh air, holidays and good food were regarded as essential for the health of the nation. The foreword to the British Health Resorts Associations *Official Handbook* (Fortescue-Fox 1938) by the Minister of Health Sir H. Kingsley Wood, MP, promoted the benefits of resorts linking environment to health. Advertisements in the section for Devon included the Torbay Hotel where 'Diets ordered by Doctors arranged on request' (Fortescue-Fox 1938: 275) were available. The Association had reported on 'food at the health resort' at its 1936 conference and this was recorded in the *British Medical Journal* (1936). The idiosyncratic Torquay Chamber of Commerce (1937) guide, *A Few Pictures of Torquay Other Places in Glorious Devon*, also promoted the health aspects of the resort, suggesting in the introductory letter from the publicity committee that 'Torquay has no industry apart from the manufacture of health'.

The tourists' experience of food

This was investigated through 30 in-depth semi-structured interviews of individuals who had stayed in Devon as tourists in the interwar period. The aims of the interviews were to find out how the interests in food and tourism had evolved, and to identify trends in the provision of food for tourists. Of the 30 interviews, 10 identified the interwar period as important, recounting memories of a time of economic adversity and social change. Respondents in an age range from 80 to 90+ were able to recall the period with great clarity. This demonstrated the presence of a reminiscence bump, Wing Sun Tung and Ritchie (2011) suggesting that many experiences (including leisure and tourism) between the ages of 20 and 30 are frequently recalled as important, influential and enjoyable. It was interesting to note that the respondents were happy to share these, relive the past and recall the holidays of their youth. The cohort represents a valuable but diminishing generational resource in tourism research.

Using snapshots, postcards and personal records conjointly with the interviews allowed the researcher to discover more about the role of food, tourism and leisure in the interwar period. Ephemera associated with the era evoked many memories, one respondent noting the use of language in Cattell's (1937) account of a sailing holiday in *Under Sail through Red Devon* as 'just how they spoke at that time'. Although some respondents had visited Europe for winter sports and summer holidays it was the time spent in Devon that had been regarded as influential, perhaps as early and powerful childhood memories were prompted. Some had written of these in the form of life histories or autobiographies for their families.

The interwar era is significant in tourism and leisure research. A time of depression and economic hardship for many, it was one in which the link between health and food was keenly investigated. (Crawford 1938; Drummond and Wilbraham 1957). Graves and Hodge (1941) suggest that the era was in some ways characterised by new forms of leisure consumption which included the holiday camp and an interest in keeping fit. At this time Devon was frequently promoted with references to its food. GWR's *Holiday Haunts, 1939* (Fraser 1939) describes the county thus: 'no one could possibly mistake Devon for any other county. It is not only that its yellow clotted cream is different ... in Devon loveliness reaches its zenith.'

Snapshots and personal records in the form of postcards and journals provide an important record of tourists' involvement and relationships with food. Numerous snapshots, described in the Kodak handbook (Kodak Limited 1920: 21–2) as 'instantaneous exposures popular with amateurs', record tourists consuming food. These are usually taken during a picnic or other shared meal and show some detail of the food but often lack any detail or description beyond place and time. For example, a photograph from a family album (Figure 8.1) shows the ubiquitous seaside picnic and emphasises the fresh air dining and holiday experience popular at the time, and later encouraged by bodies such as the British Health Resorts Association (Fortescue Fox 1938).

However, it is the postcard that often depicted local foods and these are perhaps an under-used resource in tourism and leisure research. Postcards showing food in Devon are a widely used form of holiday communication and were often retained as souvenirs and mementoes. Ballengee-Morris (2003) states that souvenirs include multiple forms ranging from the everyday to historical and cultural items. Souvenirs are significant in tourism research as their semiotic

Figure 8.1 Picnic, Paignton, South Devon, *c.*1930 (source: author's collection).

and symbolic values indicate communication between consumer and place, people and cultures. In terms of food, snapshots and postcards are a versatile and enduring medium and souvenir. Their interest is derived not only from the visual image which frequently records events and places at a particular time but also from messages or comments referring to food. The postcard often provides an evolving record of tourism over a period of time, for example at a resort or particular attraction.

Examples of food production have been regarded as an attraction throughout the twentieth century. Some of these are identified in Table 8.3. During the first half of the timescale fishing, game hunting and agriculture were fashionable tourist activities. Table 8.3 shows how through the timescale the attraction of food has evolved and that the agricultural landscape remains crucial in the food and tourism relationship, whether as an attraction, activity or consumption as a souvenir. These change over time – for example, the decline and revival of Devon's orchards and its emerging vineyards.

Postcards as a tourism research resource

Postcards provide the researcher with much information regarding the evolution of tourism and its relationship with food. The postcard as a mass-produced resource is associated with the rise of mass tourism from the late nineteenth century. Stevens (1995) states that individually and collectively postcards not only contain visual images but the messages reveal a great deal about individual

Table 8.3 The evolution of food production as an attraction

Agriculture/landscape	Food examples	Tourism examples
Fishing	Sea and fresh water fish	Holiday activity, sport
Mariculture	Shellfish, branded oysters, mussels, cockles	Oyster beds
Horticulture, viticulture	Fruit and wines	Vineyard tours, tastings
Cider orchards	Ciders, perry	Tastings, tours and festivals
Arable	Fruit, vegetables, cereals	Farmers' markets, farm shops and tours
Dairy	Milk, butter, clotted cream and cheese	Cream teas, souvenirs
Livestock	Cattle, sheep, pigs and poultry	Restaurants, shops, markets and festivals
Game, wood, field and river	Furred, feathered and fish	Sport
Experiences represent an existing but previously unarticulated genre of economic output.	The Experience Economy	

or societal values. Ephemeral items made to be used and often discarded, they 'offer a window into the world as viewed by the society of its time' (Stevens 1995: 1–3) and are subsequently viewed as historical records by researchers. Kneafsey (2000) supports the use of postcards as an important form of supplementary secondary data.

Photographic postcards are important visual records of place and time. Batchen (1999: 212) asserts that photography and the photographic image are often held to be 'a proof of that thing's being'. This may contribute to the popularity of the photographic postcard and is demonstrated in the sample used for this research.

The postcard is also an important visual component of the 'retroscape' described by Brown and Sherry (2003: 12) where a sense of place is evoked through images of the past. The postcards depicting food in Devon display a strong interest in the culinary heritage and traditions of the region. Three postcards have been identified to reflect domestic and commercial interests in food during the interwar period. Analysis may be conducted on various levels of interest: the picture, the sender's message and references to food, or a combination of these. The appearances of such representations are ambiguous and subject to interpretation. Images that seem sentimental, stereotyped or contrived now in the twenty-first century may have appeared to represent a true and authentic image at the time of circulation. Corky and Bailey (1994) state that the postcard provides an excellent window onto the process of commodification. In the case of Devon it is through food and tourism that this can be detected. During the period under focus commodification is observed through postcard imagery of food and landscape subjects. The value of the image is greatly enhanced by the narratives (in the form of senders' messages or captions) that refer to the research topic, food in the context of tourism.

Many postcards used local dialect in the depiction of stereotypical foods associated with rural life. These are frequently shown in a domestic setting, not a staged commercialised presentation. Cards were produced showing some of the county's heritage foods: Devonshire dumplings (apples baked in a pastry case) and clotted cream (thick cream with a minimum 55 per cent butterfat content) made from the rich Devonshire milk; junket (a sweet dish made from milk, sugar and rennet – a coagulant); raspberries and clotted cream. As there are few traditional dishes associated with the county, these are important records, rare examples of domestic hospitality and authenticity. These are in sharp contrast to the commercial versions represented in the images of hotels, restaurants and cafés. Messages sometimes refer to establishments visited or clotted cream being sent by post as a gift, a delicacy and welcome adjunct to fruit, puddings and scones.

Three contrasting examples of postcards were used to identify food in the context of one era and area. One showed the domestic hospitality domain, the second a commercial outlet and the third the traditional production of clotted cream. They show the researcher details of the era as presented to the tourist. During the interviews respondents frequently evoked such images, for example in describing farmhouse accommodation and eating out in a café.

The 'Real Devonshire cream' postcard (*c.*1920) (Figure 8.2) shows the traditional farmhouse production of clotted cream, a practice that has virtually disappeared. Thus the card has a historic value as a record of the rural economy for which Devon was famed. The sender's message reads: 'most of the cottagers only have the open hearth and burn peat and send all they want roasted to the bakers. I can't say I like it smells smoky'. Such a detailed and concise ethnographic observation of the rural lifestyle is invaluable in tourism research. It exemplifies the value of the narrative, in this example a combination of image, title and sender's message.

The second postcard (Figure 8.3) shows the elaborate galleried interior of Deller's Café Exeter. The sender's message recounts the details of a 1932 touring holiday in the West Country, noting: 'we have just had tea at the celebrated café'. The café was described by Hoskins (1960: 128) as: 'well known to citizens and holiday makers all over England. There was nowhere else quite like it anywhere'. At this time the café was a significant public space, providing an opportunity for eating out at an affordable price. Shaw *et al.* (2006) attribute the trend in early twentieth century dining out in part to the popularity of cafés and tea shops such as Deller's. They were especially well liked by holidaymakers; Deller's also operated a summer café on the sea front at Paignton, a popular south Devon resort where patrons could eat *al fresco*. During the interviews several respondents recalled visiting the café and clearly described its ambience, elegance and delicious food.

The third postcard (Figure 8.4), of Devonshire dumplings, *c.*1920 (one of a series by local photographer Chapman of Dawlish), combines colloquial dialect with stereotypical foods associated with the county and rural life. Devonshire

Figure 8.2 Real Devonshire Cream, postcard, *c.*1920 (source: author's collection).

Figure 8.3 Deller's Café, Exeter, postcard, *c*.1930 (source: author's collection).

dumplings and clotted cream, one of the county's heritage foods, are shown in a domestic setting, as they would have been presented at home. Lashley (2007) identifies hospitality as a human phenomenon which involves the relationship between host communities and guests – tourists whether in a domestic or commercial setting. This is depicted in each of the postcard images. Similar cards were produced showing junket and raspberries and clotted cream. As there are few traditional dishes associated with the county these are important records, rare examples of domestic hospitality and authenticity in contrast to the commercial versions represented in the images of hotels, restaurants and cafés.

Postcards indicate that tourists' interests in food were varied. The items depicted on the cards show that it was regarded as a memento or souvenir and sometimes connected to folklore, health and the landscape. Collectively these provide an important narrative of tourism in this period. The value of the personal narrative is significant in tourism research. Hendry (2007) endorses its use, stating that it can provide a more complex and complete picture of social life. Prochaska (2000) emphasises the significance of postcard messages in that the message puts the card into circulation, appropriating it from the producer, and that it often does not refer to the postcard image.

The cards indicate a strong tradition of dairy produce, rural authentic dishes and the popularity of the commercial food outlet. There is too a nostalgic representation in the cards evoking the pastoral and picturesque and a past that has attracted visitors to the county for generations.

What do these images tell us about the evolution of a relationship between food and tourism? The interests in food can be linked to the local and traditional,

Figure 8.4 Devonshire Dumplings, postcard, *c.*1925 (source: author's collection).

and the attraction of commercial outlets evolves over time. Postcards of cafés, restaurants and tea rooms confirm the prevalent fashion for afternoon teas in the interwar era.

What do they tell us about leisure, tourism and food? Food is significant in leisure as an attraction, motivation and interest, and in addition food has social and cultural implications for both the tourist and the destination. The images show how the experience of leisure and the experience economy have evolved and how food has played an important part in this evolution.

The resources used in this research indicate the interests in health and leisure of the era, and show that these were topical, for example in the benefits of sunshine and fresh air. Period archive sources demonstrate that a destination such as Devon was able to appeal to a wide spectrum of tourists, from exclusive to mass market, to those who visited the Hydro Hotels or who spent a working holiday on a fruit farm. The advantages of geography, climate and wholesome food appear to have contributed to the attraction of the county as a tourist destination.

Conclusions

The evolution of tourism presents researchers with many opportunities to discover how the phenomenon developed. It provides a framework in which to explore tourism in a broader context, for example the ways in which food has emerged as an attraction (Hall *et al.* 2003; Kivela and Crotts 2009). The focus on one era shows its significance and relationship to the preceding decades and provides a context for examination of later twentieth-century tourist activities.

The example of the interwar era illustrates an important stage in the evolution of food tourism. A preoccupation with disease demonstrated that health and food in combination with sunshine and fresh air were important in the context of tourism and the destination.

Using a case study, timescale and topic such as food provides many opportunities for the tourism researcher to discover more about the evolution of an industry and the relationships that consumers form with it. This chapter has focused on the interwar period, a time of change and adversity, but one that provides a structure for further research and evaluation. It could be utilised as a framework for a temporal investigation, the evolution of food tourism over an extended timescale.

References

Ballengee-Morris, C. (2003) 'Tourist souvenirs', *Visual Arts Research*, 28(2): 102–8.

Barthes, R. (1997) 'Towards a psychosociology of contemporary food consumption', in C. Counihan and P. Van Esterik (eds) *Food and Culture: A Reader*, New York: Routledge.

Batchen, G. (1999) *Burning with Desire: The Conception of Photography*, Cambridge, Mass.: Massachusetts Institute of Technology.

Bessière, J. (1998) 'Local development and heritage: traditional food and cuisine as tourist attractions in rural areas', *Sociologica Ruralis*, 38(1): 21–34.

Boniface, P. (2003) *Tasting Tourism: Travelling for Food and Drink*, Aldershot: Ashgate.

British Medical Journal (1936) 'Woodhall Spa rehabilitated: visit of Health Resorts Association', *British Medical Journal*, 1(3932): 1010–12.

Brown, S. and Sherry Jr, J. (2003) *Time Space and the Market: Retroscapes Rising*, New York: M.E. Sharpe.

Cattell, R.B. (1937) *Under Sail Through Red Devon – Being the log of the voyage of 'Sandpiper'*, London: Maclehose.

Cole, S. (2007) 'Beyond authenticity and commodification', *Annals of Tourism Research*, 34: 945–60.

Corky, C. and Bailey, A. (1994) 'Lobster is big in Boston: postcards place commodification in tourism', *Geojournal*, 34: 491–8.

Crawford, W. (1938) *The People's Food*, London: Heinemann.

Croce, E and Perri, G. (2010) *Food and Wine Tourism*, Wallingford: CABI.

Defoe, D. (1962) *Tour Through the Whole of Great Britain (1724–1727)*, London: Dent.

Drummond, J.C. and Wilbraham, A. (1957) *The Englishman's Food: Five Centuries of British Diet*, London: Jonathan Cape.

Everett, S. (2008) 'Beyond the visual gaze? the pursuit of an embodied experience through food tourism', *Tourist Studies*, 8(3): 337–58.

Fortescue-Fox, R. (1938) *British Health Resorts, Spa, Seaside and Inland, including the British Dominions and Colonies: Official Handbook*, London: J. & A. Churchill.

Fraser, M. (1939) *Holiday Haunts, 1939*, Great Western Railway, Official Guide, London.

Graves, R. and Hodge, A. (1941) *The Long Weekend. A Social History of Great Britain: 1918–39*, London: Reader's Union and Faber and Faber.

Hall, C.M. and Sharples, L. (eds) (2008) *Food and Wine Festivals and Events Around the World: Development, Management and Markets*, Oxford: Butterworth-Heinemann.

Hall, C.M., Sharples, L., Mitchell, R., Cambourne, B. and Macionis, N. (eds) (2003) *Food Tourism Around the World: Development, Management and Markets*, Oxford: Butterworth-Heinemann.

Henderson, J.C. (2009) 'Food tourism reviewed', *British Food Journal*, 111(4): 317–26.

Hendry, P.M. (2007) 'The future of narrative', *Qualitative Inquiry*, 13(4): 487–98.

Hoskins, W.G. (1960) *Two Thousand Years in Exeter*, Exeter: James Townsend and Sons.

Kivela, J.J. and Crotts, J.C. (2009) 'Understanding travellers' experiences of gastronomy through etymology and narration', *Journal of Hospitality and Tourism Research*, 33(2): 161–92.

Kneafsey, M. (2000) 'Tourism and place identities and social relations in the European rural periphery', *European Urban and Rural Studies*, 1(7): 35–50.

Kodak Limited (1920) *How to Make Good Pictures*, London: Kodak Limited.

Lashley, C. (2007) 'Discovering hospitality: observations from recent research', *International Journal of Culture, Tourism and Hospitality Research*, 1(3): 214–26.

Mavor, W. (1798) *The British Tourists' or Travellers' Pocket Companion through England, Wales, Scotland and Ireland*, London: E. Newberry.

Mead, M. (1997) 'The changing significance of food', in C. Counihan and P. Van Esterik (eds) *Food and Culture: A Reader*, New York: Routledge.

Mintz, S.W, and Du Bois, C.M. (2002) 'The anthropology of food and eating', *Annual Review of Anthropology*, 31: 99–119.

Pimlot, J.A.R. (1976) *The Englishman's Holiday*, 2nd edn, Hassocks: Harvester Press.

Pine, B.J. and Gilmore, J.H. (1999) *The Experience Economy: Work is Theatre and Every Business a Stage*, Harvard, Mass.: Harvard Business School Publishing.

Prochaska, D. (2000) 'Exhibiting the museum', *Journal of Historical Sociology*, 13(4): 391–438.

Quan, S. and Wang, N. (2004) 'Towards a structural model of the tourist experience: an illustration from food experiences in tourism', *Tourism Management*, 25: 297–305.

Shaw, G., Curth, L.H. and Alexander, A. (2006) 'Creating new spaces of food consumption: the rise of mass catering and the activities of the Aerated Bread Company', in J. Benson and L. Ugolini (eds) *Cultures of Selling: Perspectives on Consumption and Society since 1700*, Aldershot: Ashgate.

Slattery, P. (2002) 'Finding the hospitality industry', *Journal of Hospitality, Leisure, Sport & Tourism Education*, 1(1): 19–28.

Stevens, J. (1995) *Postcards in the Library, Invaluable Visual Resources*, New York: Haworth Press.

Taylor, J. (2001) 'Authenticity and sincerity in tourism', *Annals of Tourism Research*, 28(1): 7–26.

Torquay Chamber of Commerce (1937) *A Few Pictures of Torquay and Other Places in Glorious Devon*, Torquay: Alan Austin.

Towner, J. (1995) 'What is tourism's history?', *Tourism Management*, 16(5): 339–43.

Veblen, T. (1961) *The Theory of the Leisure Class. An Economic Study of Institutions*, New York: Random House.

Vitterso, G. and Amilien, V. (2011) 'From tourist product to ordinary food?', *Anthropology of Food*, 8/2011. Online. Available: http://aof.revues.org/6833

Wing Sun Tung, V. and Ritchie, J.R. (2011) 'Investigating the memorable experiences of the senior travel market: an examination of the reminiscence bump', *Journal of Travel and Tourism Marketing*, 28: 331–43.

9 Raising awareness of local food through tourism as sustainable development

Lessons from Japan and Canada

David J. Telfer and Atsuko Hashimoto

Introduction

With growing interest in farm-to-table cuisine and local food as place branding identifiers in many destinations, this chapter examines how the culinary tourism industry has the opportunity to be a leader in promoting the use of local food not only to tourists but also to local clientele, contributing towards sustainable development. The chapter is based on research from two destinations that in many ways are very different. However there are a number of common lessons to be learned in the development and promotion of local food for the culinary tourism industry. In Japan research was conducted in Oita prefecture on the island of Kyushu where initiatives to promote local food in tourism include One Village One Product, road stations (farmers' markets), Green Tourism, *ekiben/soraben/ hayaben* (packed lunches for travellers), and food and drink festivals. In Niagara, Canada known for Niagara Falls, efforts are under way to rebrand the region around local food. Initiatives such as the Niagara Culinary Trail, Niagara Wine Route, Niagara Agritourism circuit, the Greenbelt and various festivals and events featuring local food all highlight the link between local food and tourism. These research sites were selected because both locations are utilising culinary tourism and agritourism as economic rejuvenation tools and both are close to major cities. The findings from these two sites illustrate how tourism can be an effective mechanism for branding and promoting local food and thereby promoting sustainable development. After exploring the relationship between local food and sustainable development, the chapter will examine the common themes which emerged from both destinations. The chapter will conclude with a discussion of some of the common challenges that face both destinations.

Local food, tourism and sustainable development

There is an emergent, politically orientated set of food movements and practices that is relocalizing food system production and consumption (Feagan 2007). In reviewing the literature, Feagan (2007) identifies some of these movements as including alternative food initiatives and agri-food networks, community food security, civic and democratic agriculture, post-productivism, alternative or shortened food chains and the quality turn. He groups these under the umbrella of local food systems (LFS) (Feagan 2007). This shift towards a relocalisation has become a selling point for destinations as they are marketed and even rebranded around culinary tourism. A key feature of new local supply networks is their capacity to resocialise or respatialise food that comes to be defined by its locale 'i.e. either the locality or even the specific farm where it is produced' (Sonnino and Marsden 2006: 183). The 100-mile diet concept, which focuses on only eating food grown in an area of 100 miles from where one lives, was pioneered in British Columbia, Canada, and is indicative of the new shift to re-emphasise the locality (Smith and MacKinnon 2007). The use of local food in the tourism industry takes many forms, ranging from the use of local products on menus to visitors exploring rural farms, vineyards and markets and attending food and wine festivals. Visitors are encouraged to 'taste the view' and experience local culinary treasures (Everett and Aitchison 2008; Produced in Norfolk n.d.). In examining Canadian culinary tourists, Ignatov and Smith (2006) found the food tourism segment to be six times larger than the wine tourism segment. The shift towards local food is in part a reaction to the trends in major food markets over the past few decades as highlighted below:

- standardisation of production techniques;
- shift of value added along the production chain from producer to processor;
- growing internationalisation of markets;
- increasingly anonymous sources of food supply; and
- consumers' search for more convenience and time saving (Stagl 2002: 150).

Some consumers have become more concerned over how and where their food is produced, with a new emphasis on local food and agriculture although there can be challenges for consumers in consuming more local food (see Brown 2003; Weatherell *et al.* 2003). In a review of local food initiatives in Canada, the Canadian Co-operative Association (2008) cites studies indicating a rise in local farmers' market income. In Vancouver sales grew from C$1.2 million in 2005 and were projected to rise to C$3 million in 2008. Stagl (2002) argues that community-supported agriculture (CSA) re-establishes spatial, social and value connections that have been lost in conventional food markets. The shift back to the local has also been linked to sustainable development. Feagan (2007) suggests that the relocalisation of LFS is partly a derivative of early sustainability directives that called for 'decentralisation, democratisation, self-sufficiency and subsidiarity which are all spatially referenced concepts'. In tourism the importance of experiencing and consuming the 'place' is increasingly becoming more important for destinations as they compete for tourists. In fact Seyfang (2006: 383) argues that *sustainable consumption* 'has become a core policy objective of the millennium in national and international arenas'. Stagl (2002: 152) highlights a number of potential contributions local food markets can make towards sustainable development which include:

- requiring less transport;
- addressing an array of consumer demands;
- offering proximity of producers to consumers which leads to a possibility for consumers to learn about sustainability which generates trust;
- offering a variety of products; and
- extending to new consumer groups.

For tourism, the focus on the 'local' represents an opportunity to promote a region's sense of identity as well as to endorse the concept of sustainable development. Places are becoming known for their regional products and cuisine, and this is stimulating demand in the local agricultural sector, thereby possibly contributing towards sustainable development, as suggested above by Stagl (2002). When there are established links between tourism and agriculture, there is the potential to increase the backward linkages between tourism and local food production but there are substantial challenges in institutionalising these linkages (Telfer and Wall 1996).

It must be noted that there are debates over the link between local food and sustainability. Watts *et al.* (2005) suggest that more detailed scrutiny of the social, economic and environmental consequences of alternative systems of food provision is required. Kneafsey (2010) draws on the work of Born and Purcell (2006), who identify the existence of a 'local trap'. The local trap refers to the tendency by food activists, researchers and policy makers and planners to assume something inherent about the local scale. 'The local is assumed to be desirable; it is preferred a priori to larger scales. What is desired varies and can include ecological sustainability, social justice, democracy, better nutrition, and food security, freshness and quality' (Born and Purcell 2006: 195). According to Kneafsey (2010), Born and Purcell (2006) maintain that scale is socially constructed and the local food systems are equally likely to be just or unjust or sustainable or unsustainable. Sonnino (2010: 24) explores the criticisms of the local food movement and indicates that what was seen a few years ago to be a form of resistance to the 'destructive neo-liberal logics of globalisation is now increasingly seen as so embedded in these logics as to become an obstacle in the pursuit of sustainable development'. Sonnino (2010) states that 'the local trap' approach has dismantled the assumption that local food systems contribute unequivocally to sustainable development. The criticisms of food relocalisation are based on a new awareness of the complexity of 'local' in terms not only of scale but also the concept itself, thereby questioning the assumption that food relocalisation is a key to sustainability (Sonnino 2010). In response to the 'local trap' critique, Sonnino (2010) focuses on the relocalisation of school food in the UK and the commitment towards sustainable development by the local governments involved. The success of these projects, he argues, illustrates the fallacy of thinking about devolution and localisation in monolithic and abstract terms. Drawing on the work of Morgan (2004), Sonnino (2010) suggests that the benefits, or the lack of benefits, of both localism and devolution should be examined concretely for their capacity and ability to create or enhance intrinsically significant things such as deeper democratic structures, social and spatial solidarity and sustainable development. Hinrichs (2000) also makes the important point that social inequalities can exist in direct agricultural markets just as they can in sustainable agriculture. 'Some farmers' markets and CSAs in the US have targeted or ended up serving largely educated, middle class consumers' (Hinrichs 2000: 301).

Within the framework of these sustainability debates, the tourism industry is focusing on culinary tourism as a way of promoting place. Place is being commoditised through specific values such as historic, cultural or economic values and in the highly competitive tourism industry not all places have an established culture of *terroir* (Watts *et al.* 2005) and as such are less likely to benefit from this type of branding (Feagan 2007). However, if there is no traditional *terroir*, then it is being constructed in many destinations through the assistance of tourism. The chapter now turns to examine two cases where tourism is promoting local food and thus helping to stimulate the agricultural sector. However, as noted above, caution must be used in making claims that the production, processing, distribution and consumption of local food products leads to sustainable development.

Background to the research sites and study approach

In both Canada and Japan emerging environmental and social trends, including environmental concern, 'Slow Food' and 'Locally Grown – Locally Consumed' movements, are growing. Furthermore, these high-consumption societies have also begun to see the emergence of those who are very food-conscious – 'foodies' who prefer high-quality food. In Ontario, Canada, for example, the website of the Ontario Culinary Tourism Alliance (2012) has links to a growing number of local food initiatives such as farm to table, farm gate, markets and food festivals at 14 different regions in the province that cater to both tourists and locals. Tourism destinations in these countries are trying to capitalise on these social and environmental movements. Given this background, this research focuses on how tourism can generate awareness of local food and contribute to sustainable development. Two sites were selected as comparative case studies. Both include rural areas and are trying to rejuvenate the local economy and livelihoods through agriculturally based tourism, as there has been a decline in agriculture.

The Niagara Peninsula region is located in southern Ontario and is known for its temperate climate and soft fruit production such as peaches, plums, cherries, grapes, apples, apricots, nectarines and northern kiwi and a wide range of vegetables. The Niagara Peninsula has been known as a fruit belt with fertile agricultural land. Fruit farmers have, however, been facing competition from developing countries which can offer similar produce at much lower prices and some agri-businesses have been forced either to relocate or to close (e.g. E.D. Smith and Sons, Ltd: see Harling 2000). For economic diversification purposes and to compensate for a fluctuating international tourist market to Niagara Falls, the Niagara region has been working to develop wine and culinary tourism, setting the destination up as a rural getaway. With an emphasis on locally grown foods and local wine, local food producers, processors, distributors, hotels, wineries, restaurants and chefs have formed various strategic alliances for wine and culinary tourism to increase awareness and experiences for both local residents and travellers. A very successful wine route has developed with over 80 wineries in the region.

The Kunisaki Peninsula in Oita prefecture, Japan, is located on the southern island of Kyushu, which was formed by volcanic eruption (Umeki 2008). The peninsula has been known as a Shinto and Buddhism centre but has never been a major tourist area. Since religious institutions owned vast areas of rice paddies, historically agriculture was the major industry until recent times. The ageing and depopulation of farming villages have become a threat to the area in the past few decades. The Ministry of Agriculture, Forestry and Fisheries along with other ministries launched agriculturally based Green Tourism projects in order to revitalise declining rural communities where 50 per cent of the population is 65 years of age or older. In Japan, the concept of consuming local food has a long tradition. The Buddhist concept of *Shindo Huni* (身土不二) was widespread in the early fourteenth century, which in simple terms means that the body's present condition is a result of its environment. In 1907, the *Shokuyoukai* (食養会) organisation was established with the full support of the Home Ministry to advocate nurturing the body through a balanced diet. *Shokuyoukai*'s philosophy that 'local (regional) food is good for the body and imported food has adverse effects' was derived from Buddhist teaching; however, the organisation called it '*Shindo Huji*' and it encourages the consumption of seasonal local food. In the late 1980s, this Shindo Huji movement was introduced into South Korea and was widely accepted. In 1981, the Japanese government started the *Chisan Chisho* (地産地消, meaning locally grown, locally consumed) movement to encourage peripheral primary industries and to empower the female population in local areas by teaching them how to preserve local/regional cuisine while learning to reduce sodium content and adding more vitamin-rich food ingredients (MAFF(a) n.d.; Kinki Agri High-tech n.d.; Nippon Shokuyou no Kai n.d.; Sakurai and Shimoura 2007; Wikipedia 2011a, 2011b, 2011c).

In order to investigate culinary tourism in Kunisaki and Niagara, the study method taken was based on a phenomenological approach (site visits, participatory observation, conversational interviews and key informant interviews) in order to collect the primary data. Secondary data were collected through an examination of government documents, related literature and industry-related websites. Study visits to Japan occurred in 2003–4, 2005, 2007, 2008 and 2010 while the Niagara Region is the location of both authors' home university. The sections that follow represent the common lessons learned in developing agriculturally based tourism in both locations. Table 9.1 contains a list of selected initiatives from both countries in terms of how they are trying to raise awareness of local food. Important steps have been taken in all three areas of government initiatives, partnerships and promotion and some of these examples are covered below.

Table 9.1 Raising awareness of local food: selected initiatives

	Oita, Japan	*Niagara, Canada*
Government initiatives	• Basic Law on Food Education • Basic Plan for Food, Agriculture & Rural Areas • Locally Grown, Locally Consumed project • One Village One Product (tourism/product promotion) • Green Tourism funding (farmers' markets, B&Bs) • Oita Prefecture, Agriculture, Forestry and Fisheries Research Centre (Agricultural Research Division)	• Canadian Tourism Commission: Culinary Tourism Product Development Strategies/Guides • Provincial wine and culinary strategies • Greenbelt protection • Agricultural Research Station • Foodland Ontario local food promotion
Culinary Tourism Partnerships	• Government-determined partnerships for Green Tourism • Oita Agricultural Park • Vertical and horizontal business collaboration often focuses around in-group communities	• Wine Council of Ontario (Niagara Wine Route) • Niagara Culinary Trail • Discover Niagara's Bounty • Vertical and horizontal business collaboration
Promoting Local Food	• Historical connection of local consumption and health • Government food safety and traceability initiatives • Food festivals • *Ekiben/Soraben* (packed lunches) • Green Tourism farmers' markets	• Wine and food festivals • Farmers' markets • Local produce/farmers highlighted in grocery stores and restaurant menus • Niagara brand

Government initiatives

Government involvement and agricultural policy are crucial, as revealed in Hjalager and Corigliano (2000), who compared Denmark and Italy their food image. They found that 'national economic, agricultural and food policies, rather than tourism policies, determine the standards and development of food for tourists' (2000: 291). In Japan and Canada, government participation at various levels has been instrumental in a variety of ways ranging from financing, promotion and passing legislation which have contributing either directly or indirectly to the development of local food initiatives including culinary tourism. A few examples of governmental initiatives from both countries are presented below.

In Japan, these initiatives stem from governmental policies on food security, food education, alternatives to conventional agriculture and tourism and holidays. Japan has a long history of authoritarianism, and it is through this style of government that initiatives and directives have been executed at the grassroots level (Sugimoto 2010; Iokibe 1999). Japanese government projects on the improvement of diet started with a focus on the poor (imbalanced) diet of farmers and fishermen in the 1970s. Led by Oita prefecture, the One Village One Product movement began in the late 1970s in order to stimulate each village's production by designating unique agricultural/fishing produce (e.g. water melon, shrimp) to each village. Each village became known for specific products. This project resulted in place branding for tourism around specific products (Oita OVOP 2009). One Village One Product signs were put up at railway stations and along main roads leading into villages in the Kunisaki Peninsula highlighting the designated products of each village.

Changes in demographics, consumer preferences and concerns over food safety have also led to government action in Japan. The ageing and depopulation of Japanese rural areas, along with the increasing number of seniors living in urban areas, have become serious issues over the past 20 years or so. This, along with rapid industrialisation and westernisation of the nation, and a shift in citizens' preferences towards non-native foodstuffs, is directly related to the conservation of Japanese food culture and self-sufficiency. The shift in food preferences has raised the issue of national health, especially in the increasing number of cases of obesity and obesity-related illness, and the recognition of people's lack of knowledge of food and food sources. In recent years the safety of imported food has also triggered a series of food traceability and food safety initiatives (MHLW 2011; MAFF 2011).

Against this background, the Japanese government has issued numerous directives, guidelines and new laws. A few of those since 2005 include: Locally Grown, Local Consumed (2005 Memorandum); Basic Law on Food Education (2005); Basic Plan for Food, Agriculture and Rural Areas (2010). These laws and directives are designed to: (1) entice younger generations to work in agriculture and agri-businesses; (2) diversify the agricultural economy in rural areas; (3) improve food awareness and knowledge; (4) enforce food traceability and safety; (5) improve diet and health; (6) bridge the rift between urban life and rural life; and (7) conserve of culture and tradition.

Green Tourism is a government initiative and it focuses on rural rejuvenation projects based on rural characteristics, i.e. agriculture and rural lifestyle, to address the issues mentioned above (MAFF(b) n.d.). The government provides start-up funding and technical support for communities which choose to participate in Green Tourism. Examples in Kunisaki include the development of farmers' markets as well as the establishment of an outdoor eco-museum that focuses on historic rice cultivation. The government also encourages schools in urban areas to bring children to rural communities to enjoy learning experiences in the natural environment. Many prefectural governments provide incentives to offset the cost of student field trips and offer training programmes to those developing rural B&Bs. Some B&B operators in the Kunisaki Peninsula indicated a growth in the number of the student visitors they have been receiving.

Similarly in Canada, there have been a variety of government initiatives at different levels developed to promote local agriculture and culinary tourism. At a national level the Canadian Tourism Commission (CTC) supports the development of culinary tourism, wine tourism and rural tourism as well as enhancing tourism activities across the country. The CTC's support has focused on encouraging new tourism products and providing technical support or workshops. Buckingham (2004) and Fuller and Buckingham (1999) differentiate between agricultural law and food law in Canada. Agricultural law relates to the public and private aspects of legal regulations surrounding the production and marketing of agricultural products. Food law has a much wider focus, including, for example, processors, retailers, consumers, packagers and labellers of food. Stewart *et al.* (2008) argue that changes in laws and vinifera plantings have allowed Niagara to flourish into a wine and culinary tourism destination. More specifically, they highlight the changes in Ontario wine and liquor laws in the 1990s allowing wineries to have on-premise restaurants as a key factor in the development of culinary tourism in Niagara (Stewart *et al.* 2008). The province of Ontario now has wine/culinary strategies including 'Poised for Greatness' (a strategic framework for Ontario's wine industry); *Wine of Ontario* (Sales and Marketing Plan) and the Wine and Culinary Tourism in Ontario Strategy, which specifically recommended a culinary strategy for the Niagara Region (Telfer and Hashimoto 2003). The continued prominence of Niagara is highlighted in the more recent Ontario's Four-Year Culinary Tourism Strategy and Action Plan 2011–2015 (Ministry of Tourism, Government of Ontario 2011). In developing this plan the Ministry of Tourism, Government of Ontario developed ten success criteria to identify potential culinary regions in Ontario as listed below:

- Leadership
- Market-ready or near-market-ready culinary products and resources
- Integrated strategy
- Partnership and community based collaboration
- Financial support and performance measures
- Destinations with good access from key origin markets
- Sufficient market intelligence
- Culinary tourism resources distinctive to the region
- Destination with multiple culinary tourism experiences
- An effective destination marketing organization (DMO)
  (Ministry of Tourism, Government of Ontario 2011: 11)

The Greenbelt of Ontario is the largest greenbelt in the world, located in the Golden Horseshoe area of Ontario, and the Niagara Peninsula is part of it. The Greenbelt's primary purpose is to protect agricultural land. The Friends of the Greenbelt Foundation is an independent organisation which was entrusted with C\$25 million from the Ontario government (Green Belt 2011). This fund is given to local food programmes which support agriculture and viticulture activities within the Greenbelt and has included projects related to agritourism. The

Ontario Ministry of Agriculture, Food and Rural Affairs is directly involved with Foodland Ontario, which includes a consumer promotion programme to promote Ontario-produced fresh and processed products. The programme aims to maintain consumer intent to purchase over 80 per cent local produce by promoting the Ontario brand (Foodland Ontario 2011). There are a few grocery stores in the Niagara Peninsula called Foodland, but other retail shops also sell Ontario produce with the Foodland logo. The Pick Ontario Freshness Strategy 2007 is designed to expand the Foodland marketing programme to include deli products, meats, dairy and baked goods and to boost the 'Savour Ontario' dining programme (Foodland Ontario 2011). This programme is developed in partnership with the Ministry of Agriculture, Food and Rural Affairs, the Ministry of Tourism and the Ontario Tourism Marketing Partnership Corporation, and is designed to promote and encourage consumers to choose Ontario foods on menus in restaurants and other establishments.

The few examples listed above illustrate that the involvement of government at various levels in both countries has been important although in different ways (laws, policies, plans and funding initiatives). In Japan the strategies of Green Tourism, education and increasing awareness of sustainable food consumption have been implemented through a more top-down approach. On the other hand, the Ontario government has tended to follow very specific strategies to increase an awareness of agricultural products in Ontario and to promote culinary tourism. These initiatives have promoted local food to both locals and tourists.

Partnerships in culinary tourism

Linked to governmental initiatives has also been the support for grassroots-level initiatives or industry developments and partnerships. Partnerships in developing culinary tourism have proved very important in both locations. Collaboration between tourism and agriculture can take many forms. Horizontal integration between homogenous types of businesses (e.g. wineries) has been implemented, and vertical integration of heterogeneous types of businesses at different levels (e.g. wineries and tour operators) has also been organised (Telfer 2001). Partnerships and collaboration may produce more powerful and effective marketing and business management systems, but individual participants have to cope with the loss of a certain amount of control, which can also be an obstacle to collaboration (Plummer *et al.* 2006). In the area of partnership, collaboration and strategic alliances, this study illustrates socio-cultural differences, demonstrating a clear contrast between the two research sites.

In the Canadian case, as noted above, there have been cases of successful strategic alliances at the grassroots level and the government has then responded to the needs of the industry by developing policy documents and providing funding for product development. In the Niagara Peninsula, the needs of economic diversification using available resources, i.e. agriculture, led to the formation of strategic alliances between the wineries in the region. The Wine Council of Ontario (WCO 2011), a non-profit organisation, has been involved in developing the wine route from an early stage. With remodelled wineries to accommodate tourists the wine route is now linked with tour operators and bus companies. Today there are nearly 80 wineries in the region and many of them are participating in this initiative. The town of Niagara-on-the-Lake (NOTL), for example, has its own collaboration among NOTL wineries and other tourism attractions and operators (Telfer 2001).

The success of wine tourism in Niagara has motivated other sectors in the area to expand partnership potentials. The Niagara Culinary Trail has over 70 agricultural destinations including farmers' markets and visits to on-farm markets. Restaurants, cafés and eateries that feature local food products and ingredients are also part of this scheme. The website for the organisation launched in 2008 states 'The Niagara Culinary Trail works to link agriculture, tourism and the food community to promote sustainable cuisine by celebrating the joys of local, seasonal and artisanal cooking' (Niagara Culinary Trail 2011). In a similar concept, the Niagara Agritourism Circuit (2011), originally conceived and implemented by the Francophone association Niagara 2000 in order to attract more Francophone tourists to the Niagara region, envisages cyclists visiting fruit and vegetable farms, dairy farms, livestock farms, bakeries, cafés, wineries and retail shops. Participating farms and establishments all celebrate Niagara's agriculture and food culture.

There are numerous public agencies involved in developing culinary tourism partnerships. Discover Niagara's Bounty is a partnership between the regional government of Niagara, the Niagara Culinary Trail, the Niagara Economic Development Corporation, Foodland Ontario and the Niagara North Federation of Agriculture. This website-based collaboration directs customers to local farms and retail shops to purchase food direct from farmers.

Of course some businesses prefer to work more on their own and do not participate in partnerships or alliances. Yet, in the case of Niagara, the business traditions and cultural foundations permit various stakeholders to form partnerships and reap the harvest of working together. Often significant individuals or companies have led the way in developing partnerships which are evident at various food and wine festivals in the region. These grassroots-level initiatives have been a driving force for further government support. In developing Ontario's Four-Year Culinary Tourism Strategy and Action Plan 2011–2015, the Ministry of Tourism, Government of Ontario (2011) identified some of the highlights of Niagara's culinary tourism and many of these reflect the opportunities and challenges of developing partnerships as seen below:

- There are more farm events such as elaborate dinners in orchards and vineyards.
- More and more chefs want to use local foods, however access is still a challenge.
- The Niagara Culinary Trail links consumers with sources of local food. They have a new local food culinary guide that promotes local food destinations though 5 distinctly different areas of the region.

- The number of farmers' markets in the region are growing as attendance increases.
- Work continues to bring a stronger relationship between the wine industry and local food partners.
- Niagara is hopeful that the new tourism association will see a role for local food in their tourism plans.
- The Niagara Region under the Agricultural Task Force and the Niagara Culinary Trail has formed a strong relationship and has engaged in a number of initiatives.

(Ministry of Tourism, Government of Ontario 2011: 12)

In Japan, on the other hand, partnership and collaboration are strongly influenced by historical in-group/out-group relationships of stakeholders, especially in remote rural areas. Geographically, the communities in the Kunisaki Peninsula have experienced segregation on account of mountainous terrain, waterways and religious institutions. Even today, when the national road and railway systems have removed these barriers, and the religious institutions' landowner system has been removed, people remain aware of who belongs to which group. These cultural and historical connections determine many decisions. Green Tourism encourages the expansion of social and business networks. Linked to this is the empowerment of women as it is often women who take on key roles in Green Tourism. However, within the boundary of in-group communities, business and social networks have long been established. Findings from the interviews conducted in Oita illustrate that it does not even occur to the decision makers to suggest collaboration or to develop alliances with out-group communities unless there is a direct order to do so from the authorities. This is perceived as a forced partnership and it receives minimal attention and never really flourishes.

Historical and cultural ties tend to create complexity in other areas. The authorities and outside agents do attempt to collaborate with Green Tourism communities. Government involvement in an overseer capacity tends to be the norm in Green Tourism. In order to receive resource allocation for tourism promotion and funding, involved municipalities need to demonstrate collaboration among municipalities by producing joint marketing materials (brochures, websites and tourist maps) and holding joint events. Yet no true business partnership has been established which could subsequently benefit stakeholders at an operational level. As part of government directives, links between tour operators and auxiliary service sectors are often predetermined in this top-down system. Green Tourism stakeholders who believe they lack sufficient knowledge and experience in such endeavours do not question these kinds of partnerships, which are perceived as being forced if out-group members are involved.

At the grassroots level, vertical integration of in-group communities is much easier than simple horizontal integration with out-group communities. Partnerships and collaboration are based strongly on human networks. Therefore, local farmers and fishermen have agreements with markets, restaurants, food processing firms and other retail shops for supply; the transport of produce is arranged by local businesses; and the accommodation sector (farm stay establishments, B&Bs or inns) has its own referral network for surplus guests. All participants in Green Tourism are involved in farming in one way or another, and this close-knit support system also comes into play in the case of emergencies.

The challenges of this type of network-based partnership and collaboration are obvious. Those stakeholders who want to expand their partnerships with out-group stakeholders may go through tremendous difficulties and it is possible that they may be shunned by in-group stakeholders. In rural areas where the traditional social system is still intact, maintaining the harmony of the in-group is considered more important than business opportunities. Interviews indicated that external entrepreneurs who are interested in collaborating with Green Tourism stakeholders are unlikely to be welcomed. The situation may be different in agricultural communities closer to larger cities; nevertheless, the rural areas of the Kunisaki Peninsula in Oita remain very traditional and conservative even though Green Tourism is something new.

Promoting local food to tourists and locals as sustainable development

Raising awareness of local food through place branding has the potential to educate tourists and locals about what is available and the benefits of consuming locally. In Japan historically there has been a strong cultural tradition of consuming locally produced food that comes from the natural environment in which a person lives. There is also a growing recognition of programmes that emphasise consuming local food (like the 100-mile diet) in Canada which support local agriculture including a national product development strategy for cuisine tourism (Deneault 2002). Worldwide environmental concerns are pressuring agriculture to be more natural and organic and to rely less on fossil fuels for production and transport. If local farmers grow produce for local consumption rather than for export, increased self-sufficiency will clearly be one of the benefits to the regional economy. Recent initiatives in food safety and food traceability have the potential to increase environmental protection. However, globalisation has already changed consumers' understanding of 'food' and 'food sources' and eating habits. Furthermore, local production of a variety of food cannot always satisfy consumers' needs. For instance, neither in Niagara nor in Kunisaki can coffee beans or sugar cane be produced in the natural environment nor is the use of hydroponics and technology without controversy.

Yet promoting local food to both tourists and locals can contribute to sustainable development. Even without 100 per cent self-sufficiency, if more food is produced and consumed locally some of the environmental pressure associated with food miles may be reduced. It also serves an educational purpose. As in the case of Japan, the government is concerned about people's knowledge about food, nutrients and eating habits in order to maintain a healthy life. Celebrating local agriculture/ aquaculture can reintroduce nearly lost common knowledge. It can also make tourists and local residents aware that there are regional and seasonal differences in food sources and consumption. Carefully planned projects and events for tourists and local residents may strengthen local identity and pride.

The Niagara Food Festival is a showcase of local restaurants/cafés, wineries, catering companies and cooking schools that demonstrate their signature dishes with local ingredients. The Niagara Wine and Grape Festival in late summer/early autumn and the Ice Wine Festival in the winter focus on Niagara wines and unique food pairings. Throughout the summer months, Niagara is host to various local food-related events to attract tourists as well as increasing awareness among residents of what products are available locally. Some restaurants includw the names of farmers on menus. In a similar manner, there are numerous local food-related events in Kunisaki Peninsula. The community of Tashibunosho's rice planting festival and harvest festival draw large numbers of tourists as it is performed in centuries-old fashion. The Soba noodle festival signifies that Bungotakada city's unique One Village One Product is soba (buckwheat). In fact, Japan boasts hundreds of festivals that focus on regional and traditional delicacies all over the country throughout the year and these are major domestic tour products (Hashimoto and Telfer 2008). *Ekiben/soraben/hayaben* (packed lunches for train/domestic flight/road travellers) have recently been developed and elaborated to entice tourists with 'exclusively' regional cuisine. Local markets developed through Green Tourism initiatives are becoming tourist attractions and local hotels and spas often feature a small farmers' market in the lobby of the hotel. Such promotion of regional cuisine has successfully re-established regional identity through food. With such projects, some communities have started to grow old-fashioned native food ingredients instead of more profitable non-native varieties. Even in the Kunisaki Peninsula, a few communities are focusing on reviving old-fashioned native vegetables and rice varieties. At the Oita Agriculture and Culture Park, visitors learn about agricultural production and nature, eat at the restaurant based on local food.

Challenges

In conducting the study, several common as well as some unique challenges were observed in both locations as to how tourism can play a role in raising awareness of local food and thereby contributing to sustainable development. The challenges relate to (1) the production, distribution and consumption of agricultural products and (2) the interface between agriculture and tourism.

On the production/distribution/consumption side globalisation of the international food system has resulted in large grocery stores and food wholesalers stocking food from around the world at relatively affordable rates. If local peak crop availability does not coincide with the peak tourism season, or if non-local products are cheaper, then food products may be imported. This has put pressure on local producers, especially as demand in the tourism sector can be variable. As a result there are significant challenges of getting the local people, the tourism industry and tourists to consume more local food. It is known that Niagara local residents are hesitant to buy local produce due to higher prices and seasonality. Price is important, raising questions in Niagara such as 'Why would I drive to a local farm to buy one box of strawberries for $5.00 when I can get two boxes for the same price at the grocery store?' The boxes of strawberries in the grocery store come from California. It cannot be denied that a considerable proportion of local residents can only afford cheaper imported food products. A report by the Niagara Community Observatory at Brock University in Niagara, titled *Niagara Food: It's Nutritious, Delicious, and Available But We're Not Buying It … Why Not*, illustrates the challenges in increasing local consumption. However, even larger grocery stores are starting to promote local food. Restaurants featuring local food can also have higher price points and therefore may only be attracting customers who are already interested in this type of product. Globalisation has also impacted the wine industry in Niagara. VQA (Vintners Quality Alliance) wine is made from locally available grapes, signifying specific local appellations. Some wineries are blending inexpensive imported grape juice with local grape juice, which allows them to offer affordable wines labelled Cellared in Canada (CIC) to local consumers. Using imported grapes has left some farmers in Niagara struggling to sell their grapes at a good price to the Niagara wine industry. Globalisation is also linked to the movement of farm workers and farm labourers from countries such as Mexico come to the Niagara region every year to work in the fruit orchards. In Japan the ageing population in rural areas poses the question of who will take over agriculture and rural tourism development in the future. In terms of consumption, in Japan there is a tendency for consumers to prefer larger, better-shaped vegetables, which are often treated with chemicals, over the less attractive-looking and more costly organic products. After a number of food safety scares in the past few years, the Japanese prefer to purchase produce 'made in Japan', or 'produced by local farmers'; however, the price of the products is a hurdle that has to be overcome.

The second area of challenges relates to the interface between agriculture and tourism. As suggested by Telfer and Wall (1996), the relationship between tourism and agriculture can range from conflict to symbiosis. In the cases examined here there can be challenges with respect to acquiring sufficient funds from the government to maintain existing products or to promote new culinary tourism products. Those who have been primarily in the agricultural sector are now having to adjust to tourists and so need further training with respect to marketing, staffing and financing, as well as technology including Internet-based marketing and accommodation booking. Tensions are also present along the continuum from collaboration to competition. While firms and communities are working together to help promote the location as a culinary tourism destination, these firms and communities also compete with each other for customers. The necessary elements for successful collaboration between tourism and agriculture can be difficult to maintain, especially in the case of rural Japan where in-group preferences inhibit more broad-based collaboration with those who could be considered outsiders.

Conclusion

Environmental and social concerns have helped position local food as a new place-based marketing tool for destinations. The use of local food can help foster stronger backward linkages from tourism to the agricultural sector and promote sustainable development. Although both destinations share some common rural characteristics, there are differences in how several of the rural tourism projects investigated function. In the Japanese case more traditional elements of a top-down approach can be found in terms of government direction and the importance of community-based ties and group cohesion was evident. Historical and cultural differences need to be taken into consideration when developing new products. While there are differences between the countries in how partnerships have developed and operate, both destinations have benefited from having partners in promoting culinary tourism and highlighting local cuisine. The importance of government support has been found to be very important in passing legislation and funding and developing strategic marketing plans related to culinary or Green Tourism. Tourism is just one avenue of promoting local food. If visitors and locals become aware of what is available and purchase more locally grown products, we have argued that steps can be taken towards sustainability. Through place branding and the consumption of local products and agriculture-related experiences, the tourism industry has a role in raising awareness of local food and promoting sustainability to tourists and locals.

References

Born, B. and Purcell, M. (2006) 'Avoiding the local trap', *Journal of Planning Education and Research*, 26(2): 195–207.

Brown, C. (2003) 'Consumers' preferences for locally produced food: A study in southeast Missouri', *American Journal of Alternative Agriculture*, 2003: 213–24.

Buckingham, D. (2004) *Canadian Agriculture and Food Law*. Online. Available: www.canadianlawsite.ca/agriculture.htm (accessed 27 February 2012).

Canadian Co-operative Association (2008) *Local Food Initiatives in Canada – An Overview and Policy Recommendations*. Online. Available: www.coopscanada.coop/assets/firefly/files/files/pdfs/GovSubmissions/LocalFoodInitiatives_in_Canada_Brief-Final_18jun08.pdf (accessed 2 March 2012).

Deneault, M. (2002) *Acquiring a Taste for Cuisine Tourism: A Product Development Strategy*, Canadian Tourism Commission Online. Available: http://publications.gc.ca/collections/collection_2008/ic/Iu86–24–2002E.pdf (accessed 2 March 2012).

Everett, S. and Aitchison, C. (2008) 'The role of food tourism in sustaining regional identity: A case study of Cornwall, South England', *Journal of Sustainable Tourism*, 16: 150–67.

Feagan, R. (2007) 'The place of food: Mapping out the "local" in local food systems', *Progress in Human Geography*, 31(1): 23–42.

Foodland Ontario (2011) *Foodland Ontario*, Online. Available: www.foodland.gov.on.ca/english/index.html (accessed 23 January 2011).

Fuller, S. and Buckingham, D. (1999) *Agriculture Law in Canada*, Toronto: Butterworth.

Green Belt (2011) *Green Belt*. Online. Available: www.greenbelt.ca/ (accessed 23 January 2011).

Harling, K. (2000) 'E.D. Smith and Sons, Ltd', *International Food and Agribuisness Management Review*, 3(2000): 381–402.

Hashimoto, A. and Telfer, D.J. (2008) 'From sake to sea urchin: Food and drink festivals and regional identity in Japan', in C.M. Hall and L. Sharples (eds) *Food and Wine*

Festivals and Events Around the World: Development, Management and Markets, Boston: Elsevier/Butterworth-Heinemann.

Hinrichs, C. (2000) 'Embeddedness and local food systems: notes on two types of direct agricultural markets', *Journal of Rural Studies*, 16(3): 295–303.

Hjalager, A. and Corigliano, A. (2000) 'Food for tourists – determinants of and image', *International Journal of Tourism Research*, 2: 281–93.

Ignatov, E. and Smith, S. (2006) 'Segmenting Canadian culinary tourists', *Current Issues in Tourism*, 9(3): 235–55.

Iokibe, M. (1999) 'Japan's civil society: An historical overview', in T. Yamamoto (ed.) *Deciding the Public Good: Governance and Civil Society in Japan*, Tokyo: Japan Center for International Exchange.

Kinki Agri High-tech (n.d.) *Macrobiotic*. Online. Available: http://kinkiagri.or.jp/library/foods/macrobiotic.htm (accessed 23 January 2011).

Kneafsey, M. (2010) 'The region in food – important or irrelevant?', *Cambridge Journal of Regions, Economy and Society*, 2010 (3): 177–90.

MAFF (2011) *Ministry of Agriculture, Forestry and Fishery Food Traceability Homepage*. Online. Available: www.maff.go.jp/j/syouan/seisaku/trace/index.html (accessed 18 January 2012).

MAFF(a) (n.d) *Ministry of Agriculture, Forestry and Fishery Chisan Chisho Home Page*. Online. Available: www.maff.go.jp/j/seisan/gizyutu/tisan_tisyo/index.html (accessed 23 Jaunary 2011).

MAFF(b) (n.d) *Ministry of Agriculture, Forestry and Fishery Green Tourism Homepage*. Online. Available: www.maff.go.jp/j/nousin/kouryu/kyose_tairyu/k_gt/ (accessed 23 Jaunary 2011).

MHLW (2011) *Ministry of Health, Labour and Welfare Food Homepage*. Online. Available: www.mhlw.go.jp/seisakunitsuite/bunya/kenkou_iryou/shokuhin/index.html (accessed 18 January 2012).

Ministry of Tourism, Government of Ontario (2011) *Ontario's Four-Year Culinary Tourism Strategy and Action Plan 2011–2015*. Online. Available: www.mtc.gov.on.ca/en/publications/Culinary_web.pdf (accessed 18 January 2012).

Morgan, K.J. (2004) 'Sustainable regions: governance, innovation and scale', *European Planning Studies*, 12(6): 871–9.

Niagara Agritourism Circuit (2011) *Niagara Agrotourisme*. Online. Available: www.bon-journiagara.com/agrotourisme/locator.php?user_origin=L0S%201M0 (accessed 23 January 2011).

Niagara Community Observatory at Brock University (n.d.) *Niagara Food: It's Nutritious, Delicious, and Available But We're Not Buying It ... Why Not.* Online. Available: www.brocku.ca/webfm_send/7493 (accessed 23 January 2011).

Niagara Culinary Trail (2011) *Niagara Culinary Trail*. Online. Available: http://niagaraculinarytrail.com/ (accessed 23 January 2011).

Nippon Shokuyou no Kai (n.d.) *Nippon Shokuyou no Kai Home Page*. Online. Available: www.nihon-syokuyounokai.com/ (accessed 23 January 2011).

Oita OVOP Exchange Promotion Committee (2009) *One Village One Product Home Page* [English]. Online. Available: www.ovop.jp/en/ison_p/haikei.html (accessed 23 Jaunary 2011).

Ontario Culinary Tourism Alliance (2012) *About the Ontario Culinary Tourism Alliance*. Online. Available: HYPERLINK http://ontarioculinary.com/ontario-regions/huron-county (accessed 2 March 2012).

Plummer, R., Telfer, D. and Hashimoto, A. (2006) 'The rise and fall of the Waterloo Ale

Trail: A study of collaboration within the tourism industry', *Current Issues in Tourism*, 9: 191–205.

Produced in Norfolk (n.d.) *Taste the View*. Online. Available: www.producedinnorfolk. com/news_473.php (accessed 29 February 2012).

Sakurai, S. and Shimoura, M. (2007) *Development of Local Food Market in Korea, Agriculture & Livestock Industries Corporation (ALIC)*. Online. Available: http://vegetable. alic.go.jp/yasaijoho/kaigai/0806/kaigai1.html (accessed 23 January 2011).

Seyfang, G. (2006) 'Ecological citizenship and sustainable consumption: Examining local organic food networks', *Journal of Rural Studies*, 22(4): 383–95.

Smith, A. and MacKinnon (2007) *The 100-Mile Diet: A Year of Local Eating*, New York: Random House.

Sonnino, R. (2010) 'Escaping the local trap: Insights in re-localization from school food reform', *Journal of Environmental Policy & Planning*, 12(1): 23–40.

Sonnino, R. and Marsden, T. (2006) 'Beyond the divide: Rethinking relationships between alternative and conventional food networks in Europe', *Journal of Economic Geography*, 6(2): 181–99.

Stagl, S. (2002) 'Local organic food markets: Potentials and limitations for contributing to sustainable development', *Empirica*, 29(2): 145–62.

Stewart, J., Bramble, L. and Ziraldo, D. (2008) 'Key challenges in wine and culinary tourism with practical recommendations', *International Journal of Contemporary Hospitality Management*, 20(3): 302–13.

Sugimoto, Y. (2010) *An Introduction to Japanese Society*, 3rd edn., Cambridge: Cambridg University Press.

Telfer, D.J. (2001) 'Strategic alliances along the Niagara wine route'. *Tourism Management*, 22(1): 21–30.

Telfer, D.J. and Wall, G. (1996) 'Linkages between tourism and food production', *Annals of Tourism Research*, 23(3): 635–53.

Telfer, D.J. and Hashimoto, A. (2003) 'Food tourism in the Niagara region: The development of nouvelle cuisine', in C.M. Hall and L. Sharples (eds) *Food Tourism Around the World: Development Management and Markets*, Oxford: Butterworth-Heinemann.

Umeki, H. (2008) Kunisaki Hantou no Yama no Rekishi to Keikan [History and Landscape of Mountains of Kunisaki Peninsula], *Oita Press*, 1 April. Online. Available: www.oita-press.co.jp/featureNews/120894237407/2008_1208944332.html (accessed 20 September 2008).

Watts, D., Ilbery, B. and Maye, D. (2005) 'Making reconnections in agro-food geography: Alternative systems of food provision', *Progress in Human Geography*, 29(1): 22–40.

Weatherell, C., Tregear, A. and Allinson, J. (2003) 'In search of the concerned consumer: UK public perceptions of food, farming and buying local', *Journal of Rural Studies*, 19: 233–44.

WCO (2011) *Wines of Ontario*. Online. Available: http://winesofontario.org/ (accessed 23 January 2011).

Wikipedia (2011a) *Chisan Chisho*. Online. Available: http://ja.wikipedia.org/wiki/地産地消 (accessed 23 January 2011).

Wikipedia (2011b) *Shindo Huni.* Online. Available: http://ja.wikipedia.org/wiki/身土不二 (accessed 23 January 2011).

Wikipedia (2011c) *Shokuyoukai.* Online. Available: http://ja.wikipedia.org/wiki/食養会 (accessed 23 January 2011).

Part III

Slow and sustainable food and tourism

10 Nordic eco-gastronomy

The Slow Food concept in relation to Nordic gastronomy

Jan Henrik Nilsson

Introduction

What we eat and how we eat have become major issues in the public debate of the last decades. On one level, the debates are concerned with medical and health-related issues, such as diets, nutrition, eating disorders and weight problems. But there is also an interest in food from a lifestyle perspective. Eating has gone from being a matter of food supply to being an identity and lifestyle marker. The public interest in food manifests itself, for instance, in numerous gastronomic magazines, cookery books, TV shows, websites and food blogs. Food has also become a major issue in tourism; it is no longer only part of the travel experience in general, it has become an important factor in the choice of destination for a substantial part of the travelling public.

Food has also emerged as an important topic in relation to the environment. Environmental degradation owing to pesticides and artificial manure that cause pollution of soils and waters has made people aware of the relationship between the environment and the quality and safety of food. There is also an increasing concern about what modern agriculture does to our landscape and about ethical questions related to animal breeding. From a sustainability perspective, there is a close relationship between food production and climate change. Agriculture is in itself a major source of CO_2 emissions (IPCC 2007), and food is increasingly transported over long distances, causing growing food miles. The Scandinavian countries, for instance, have become extremely dependent on food transported over long distances. Some countries like Sweden have abolished earlier policies aimed at sustaining at least a certain level of self-sufficiency for security reasons. Decreasing relative transport costs and deregulation of international trade have been other important factors behind this development.

Since food is an essential part of tourism and hospitality, the debates around food and the environment have important implications for tourism development. Food tourism is seen as a component in the development of rural tourism, for instance in wine tourism, food paths and agri-tourism (Hjalager and Richards 2002; Hall *et al.* 2003; Hall 2006; Miele 2006). In many regions, the gastronomic heritage has become an important part of regional marketing profiles (Bessière 1998; Woods and Deegan 2003; Hagström 2006; Everett and Aitchison

2008; Croce and Perri 2010; Nilsson *et al.* 2011). The increasing interest in gastronomy and gastronomic heritage, in combination with environmental awareness and concern, are important reasons for the development of eco-gastronomy. Gastronomy could be defined as 'reflective cooking and eating' (Scarpato 2002: 52). Following that, eco-gastronomy is here defined as *reflective cooking and eating in which environmental concern becomes a major factor in the choice of ingredients, in preparation and in marketing.* In a tourism perspective, the concept would also mean that eco-gastronomy is a culturally and geographically embedded activity, in which the symbolic meanings of eating become significant (cf. Bessière 1998).

In the field of eco-gastronomy, the Slow Food movement has over the last 20 years become an increasingly important actor and source of inspiration (see Hall 2012). In the beginning its ideas and policies were very much based on Italian socio-political circumstances. This gastronomic and ecological movement has, however, become almost worldwide in scope. Still, Slow Food is very much associated with Italian food traditions and the Italian way of eating; Slow Food cookery books are for instance normally full of Italian dishes. Following the widespread interest in Slow Food, it seems interesting to study to what extent the fundamental ideas and philosophies behind Slow Food have been adopted in other culinary traditions and what that adaptation looks like, how it changes. This is especially interesting in a region where gastronomic traditions differ significantly from the Italian, such as in the Nordic countries. The purpose of this chapter is to investigate the influence of Slow Food on Swedish gastronomy, and to discuss how the programmatic values of Slow Food could be reinterpreted in a Baltic Sea context.

In this chapter, first, the Slow Food movement, its fields of action and its policies are presented. This is followed by a section in which Nordic and Swedish gastronomy is discussed from the perspective of eco-gastronomy. The chapter will discuss how Swedish Slow Food could be defined and described, based on the relationship between basic Slow Food principles and Nordic traditions. Following a section on method, an empirical survey based on the menus of a number of distinguished Swedish East Coast restaurants is presented in order to trace influences of Slow Food philosophy or otherwise of eco-gastronomic thinking. Based on the survey, the chapter will end with a discussion of the Swedish gastronomic heritage in relation to eco-gastronomy and Slow Food.

Slow Food

The Italian Slow Food movement started in the late 1980s as a protest against the establishment of fast food restaurants, and to present a pleasurable alternative to mass-produced globalized food. Today the Slow Food movement numbers about 100,000 individual members in more than 100 countries. The name 'Slow Food', a playful antithesis to fast food, is well known today among people interested in gastronomy (Petrini 2001; Slow Food 2010). The Slow Food movement calls itself an ecological and gastronomic movement, born out of the pleasure of eating and concern for good food. It is also a cultural movement trying to counteract the contemporary trend towards an increasingly 'fast' way of life. Its aim is to unite food and pleasure with social and ecological consciousness and responsibility, which, in the movement's vision, is translated into the three concepts, good, fair and clean (Petrini 2001; Malatesta *et al.* 2005):

> [T]here came into being a worldwide movement aimed at gaining and spreading knowledge about material culture; preserving our agricultural and alimentary heritage from environmental degradation; protecting the consumer and the honest producer; and researching and promoting the pleasures of gastronomy and conviviality.
>
> (Petrini 2001: 8)

The Slow Food movement has, simply speaking, three main fields of action. The first is preservation of gastronomic traditions and biological diversity. In a project called 'the Ark of Taste', species, breeds and products endangered by large-scale production, industrial standardization and environmental change are listed. In order to save these species and products the movement organizes so-called *presidia* projects, locally based projects where restaurants and shops are encouraged to buy endangered products and where the producers are helped to promote their goods. There are in all 250 such projects in the world today (Petrini 2001; Malatesta *et al.* 2005). The second field of action is to promote network building among small-scale producers and between producers and consumers. Most of these activities are organized on the local level, in tastings and seminars and around to local events and projects. The movement also organizes larger events. The Turin-based Salone del Gusto, a biannual food fair aimed at people in business and consumers, is the best known. The international conference Terra Madre more specifically targets small-scale producers. They can engage in network building and take part in seminars concerning sustainability, biological diversity and local development (Petrini and Padovani 2005). The third field is education, to enhance consumers' knowledge of food, taste, nutrition and the environment. This line of work is mainly conducted at the local level. Children, the future consumers, are an important target group; the movement thus tries to become involved in schools. It also publishes a multilingual magazine and a wide range of books. It runs a university in two campuses in northern Italy, focused on theoretical gastronomy (Malatesta *et al.* 2005; Petrini and Padovani 2005).

Slow Food has attracted considerable attention, not least from academics interested in the sociologies and geographies of consumption. Burstedt (2004), Frykman (2000) and Parkins (2004) discuss the relationship between time and eating. They share a relatively individualistic perspective, i.e. Slow Food is seen as part of a possible strategy to organize one's daily life so as to counteract the fast pace of contemporary society. Slow Food is also discussed as a new set of practices in which the consumption of food becomes a matter of culture, identity and aesthetic distinction (Miele and Murdoch 2002; Jones *et al.* 2003; Miele

2006; Wilk 2006; Hayes-Conroy and Martin 2010). Lotti (2010) makes a critical analysis of the effects of Slow Food activities on commoditization of agricultural products and on local biodiversity in the Basque Country. In some of the anthropological as well as the business-related literature, there is a special interest in 'authentic' gastronomic products and the meanings and importance of local production and marketing, including tourism (Leith 2003; Mattiacci and Vignali 2004; Nosi and Zanni 2004; Nilsson *et al.* 2011; Hall 2012). Nosi and Zanni (2004) also emphasize the vital role of Slow Food in many local production and consumption networks, in which the movement acts almost as an intermediary. Pietrykowski (2004) interprets the movement's activities as a means of creating social economies, based on conscious ideas of individual choice, consumption, social life and heritage. 'The movement attempts to create a social economy around the preservation of food as both a bearer of cultural heritage and an embodiment of material pleasure' (Pietrykowski 2004: 315).

These different perspectives on Slow Food are all somehow concerned with sustainability. The perspective on networks and social economy highlights issues related to social and economic sustainability, not the least in peripheral regions. Environmental sustainability is a less developed subject; biodiversity and environmental issues are more or less taken for granted; ecology, food safety, food miles and so on are often mentioned but seldom developed at any length. In relation to tourism, most texts emphasize local processes. Slow Food is viewed in relation to the qualitative development of culinary tourism, as a way of strengthening the position of authentic gastronomic heritage (cf. Hall 2006). However, a lot of eco-gastronomic businesses and activities have nothing to do with Slow Food; Slow Food is in the end a movement with specific aims and policies, dependent on local organizations and activists. But it is reasonable to use Slow Food policies as a way of conceptualizing general eco-gastronomic thinking, not the least because they are actually put into writing.

Nordic eco-gastronomy

While Slow Food was growing and becoming an international movement, it adapted itself to national and regional differences. At the same time, it seems that the fundamental policies are more or less unchanged, summarized in the three concepts:

> [t]hat inform the Slow Food philosophy. The food we eat should taste *good*; it should be produced in a *clean* way that does not harm the environment, animal welfare or human health; and its producers should receive *fair* compensation for their work.
>
> (Malatesta *et al.* 2005: 3, original emphasis)

To be able to discuss the internationalization process, we need to develop and expand on these policies in order to understand their meaning. In this section the concepts of good, clean and fair will be discussed and adapted to a context other than that in which they were developed in the first place. Sweden, which will be the focus of this chapter, has culinary traditions that differ quite significantly from those in Mediterranean Europe. It is, however, very difficult to speak of one Swedish gastronomy in general terms. On the one hand, the regional differences between various parts of the country are considerable (it is more than 1,500 km from north to south). On the other hand, there are large similarities with the other Nordic countries but also with other countries around the Baltic Sea, such as Estonia, Poland and Germany. It would thus be more accurate to speak about a Nordic gastronomic tradition which could be divided into several regional varieties, not necessarily following present political borders. This said, what I will try to do here is to perform a translation, focusing on what the three central Slow Food concepts might mean when discussed in relation to Nordic landscapes and culinary traditions. First, however, a few words should be said about food and culinary traditions around the Baltic Sea.

Preconditions for Nordic culinary traditions

Despite the fact that large-scale trade in food has very long historical roots, only 100 years ago the majority of the population were dependent on food produced in their vicinity. Foreign culinary innovations were thus adapted to local environmental preconditions. Two factors have been essential in determining agricultural production: climate and physical geography.

In Northern Europe the growing season is generally shorter than in other parts of Europe, although with considerable differences within the region (Wallén 1968). Limited growing seasons also entail the risk of having the harvest destroyed by frost, an important factor in determining the choice of methods and crops. For instance, resistant plants like rye, roots and cabbage have been more common than wheat and more vulnerable types of grain and vegetables. The long winters make food storage and preservation a major issue. Dried, smoked and fermented dishes have become essential parts of the culinary heritage, the (in)famous Baltic fermented herring probably being the best-known example. The Nordic countries mainly lies within the northern temperate climate zone, strong Atlantic influences meaning that precipitation is evenly distributed over the year. Together with the predominance of relatively bad soils except in Denmark and parts of southern Sweden (Sømme 1968; Rudberg 1968), this has resulted in a mainly cattle-dependent agriculture. Grass, for grazing and hay production, is transformed into milk protein and animal fats. Northern Europe also has the advantage of long coastlines and many lakes and rivers. As a result, fishing has been an important source of food and income, not the least in agriculturally marginal regions. The coasts and rivers of Northern Europe have historically been the most important trading routes as well as links for innovation and the spread of traditions, not the least culinary ones (Hellström 2005). In this part of the world, water has generally been the connecting element.

Good: the culinary heritage

Earlier in this chapter gastronomy was defined as 'reflective cooking and eating'. According to that definition, gastronomy ought to be something more than eating, as reflectivity suggests that a certain level of knowledge and effort is needed. To be a reflective eater means that you are able to appreciate the unusual, the specific. In Slow Food thinking the specialities are the good things to eat. Specialities are the dishes that have their roots in regional traditions and in the natural variation in species, breeds and culinary products. As shown by Leith (2003), in an article discussing the political complexities related to the Italian pork speciality *lardo di Colonnata*, traditions are broadly speaking to do with ingredients, preservation and cooking methods. Traditions should, however, not be interpreted as something static; they change with time and context. Culinary traditions are also invented or reinvented based on some assumption of authenticity, often in a tourist context. Although not in a Slow Food context, Mykletun and Gyimothy (2010) describe this type of phenomenon in an article about the staged consumption of sheep's head in Voss, Norway. In relation to culinary heritage, Slow Food thinking suggests that traditions and place-specific qualities ought to be considered, rather than simply conserved. Slow Food in a Nordic context would mean that an eco-gastronomic cuisine is largely built on indigenous ingredients and that traditional preservation and cooking methods are used and developed.

Clean: ecology

In Slow Food thinking, the relation between authenticity in food (Sims 2009) and ecology is more or less taken for granted (Petrini 2001). In this context, eco-logical cooking is related to environmental aspects; it takes health, ecology and natural conservation into consideration. Food thus ought to be produced accord-ing to ecological methods, free from pesticides and artificial fertilizer. In many countries, there are organizations that certify food and other products according to ecological guidelines, for instance the Swedish KRAV system (cf. KRAV 2011). Clean is an essential quality in the food people eat, but the concept is also concerned with the landscape where our food is produced. Small-scale farming is seen as having formed the traditional rural landscape, whereas large-scale agribusinesses tend to harm both people and the environment. Biodiversity is another important issue in the relationship between food and landscape. when a large variety of plants and breeds are used in the regional gastronomy, local vari-eties have a better chance of surviving or even being re-established. In a study of pig farming in the Basque Country Lotti (2010) describes how the Slow Food movement, in a *presidia* project, supports the breeding of endangered varieties and helps to promote products by offering links to the market, thereby support-ing sustainable rural lifestyles. In Sweden, two endangered food products, a cheese and *suovas* (smoked reindeer), have become objects of *presidia* projects (Slow Food Jämtland 2011). Eco-gastronomy could in this context be regarded as a strategy for landscape and biodiversity conservation. Large-scale production is a serious threat to biodiversity. There are also ethical problems in relation to animal production; protection of animal rights is thus another important issue in relation to eco-gastronomy. Fishing is another line of food production with serious harmful effects, mainly overfishing and the possible extinction of fish stocks. In eco-gastronomy, small-scale fishing ought to be promoted.

Fair: global concern

The concept of clean has an emphasis on food and nature, while the concept of fair is mainly concerned with relations to fellow humans. In Slow Food thinking the local perspective is always prevalent, both in relation to production (producer-landscape) and consumption (cook–guest or retailer–customer). Building social relations between producers, restaurants, retailers and consumers is one of the organization's primary objects, thereby trying to help invigorate the local social economy (Pietrykowski 2004). To help create fair conditions for local small-scale farmers and artisans was also very much in focus for the various projects related to eco-gastronomy discussed in Nilsson *et al.* (2011). As in the Basque case, the emphasis is on improving economic and ecological sustainable production facilities and promoting links to regional markets. The local network perspective has a direct link to ecology since locally produced food reduces the number of food miles and hence has wider ecological implications. In this perspective, fair becomes a signifier for global concern. In Slow Food, fair, however, means valuing fair and equal relations not only in the local networks but also in business partnerships and relations with producers in other parts of the world. Fair trade thus becomes a natural consequence of Slow Food thinking. To sum up, the last three paragraphs have been an attempt, in general terms, to clarify how the three main Slow Food concepts may be interpreted in relation to food production and consumption. For the sake of this chapter, however, there is a need to clarify their use in relation to the empirical investigation.

Method

Investigating the influences of Slow Food on Nordic gastronomy requires a field in which these influences take place. In this perspective, it is reasonable to think of restaurants as the arena where gastronomy develops and where innovation takes place, i.e. where influences are most likely to be seen. Nordic gastronomy refers to the gastronomy of the Nordic countries. In this study Swedish gastronomy is in focus, but for a limited study like the one presented here only a small part of the country can be considered. As the south-east of the country represents different regional traditions, this makes it a suitable area to study. It does not represent the whole country, but it contains a large degree of diversity, in terms of both culinary traditions and contemporary influences. It also contains a variety of large cities, small towns, peripheries and tourist destinations. Among the provinces in south-east Sweden, Skåne is recognized as *the* food region, with a long history as the richest agricultural region in Sweden. Today the mainly rural culinary traditions are mixed with cosmopolitan influences in the major cities where immigrants make up a significant part of the population. The two Baltic islands, Öland and Gotland, are mainly summer destinations, where culinary tourism is an important part of the economy, though highly seasonal. The other provinces have generally a lower profile in their use of gastronomy in tourism marketing.

The restaurants of south-east Sweden are the objects of this particular investigation. The empirical study is based on *Sveriges bästa restauranger* [The best restaurants in Sweden] White Guide 2010. The editorial office is independent, but the guide is owned by a partnership consisting of the Union of Swedish Hotels and Restaurants (SHR), the Swedish railways, private companies and other stakeholders in the Swedish hospitality sector. The 405 restaurants listed in the guide are ranked in five categories, from 'international master class' (only 13 restaurants) to 'a good place'. In a sixth non-ranked category, restaurants and cafés of particular tourist interest are listed. Interestingly, the White Guide emphasizes the ecological perspective by using a symbol measuring 'high ecological ambitions'. For this study, the 119 ranked restaurants in the provinces of Skåne, Blekinge, Småland, Öland, Gotland, Östergötland and Södermanland were chosen. The study is based on the information available in the White Guide and on the restaurants' homepages. Menus are an essential part of the study, but statements on policy, general descriptions, links and references to partners are also important sources of information. The author has personal experience of around 25 of the restaurants. This might have influenced the evaluation in some specific cases, but is unlikely to be a problem for the general analysis. The homepages of all 119 were studied. In nine cases the information on the web was inadequate, containing merely contact information. One restaurant had burned down. In the end, information about 110 restaurants was gathered and analysed.

In the analysis of the restaurants the three basic Slow Food concepts, good, fair and clean, were used to structure the material. In the study good refers to regional profiling, choice of ingredients and cooking methods; clean refers to ecological certification and/or use of ecological food, vegetarian alternatives and references to animal protection and/or biodiversity; fair refers to the use of local suppliers and network connections, food miles or other transport-related issues and fair trade. These issues will be developed further in the following paragraph. Every restaurant got a score from 1 to 3 in the three categories mentioned, i.e. a total score of 3 to 9. The mark 1 means that there are no signs on the menu or elsewhere that the restaurant was making an effort in the category. Mark 2 indicates clear and significant signs of effort. In the category clean this could mean that a restaurant has more than just a few dishes with ecological ingredients, a selection of ecological wines or has been certified. Mark 3 is a sign of excellence in the particular category. This means that the restaurant has a significant strategy involving several subfields, for instance food, wine, bread, certification and marketing. In the empirical analysis most restaurants generally got low marks.

To qualify this, an extra level of 1+ was introduced as a subcategory to mark 1 to signify a single observation in a particular field. A typical example in the category good is when a restaurant has a single dish which is significantly influenced by traditional Nordic cuisine, typically an SOS (*smör, ost och sill*; butter, cheese and herring) served as a first course. Or there could be one ecological wine on the wine list or one local cheese on the menu. This kind of categorization is of course far from objective or scientifically correct in an absolute sense. And it will not be used to evaluate any specific item, but it might be of value for the sake of generalization.

Results

Overview

As could be expected, only a few restaurants got high scores in all three categories. The largest number of restaurants got relatively low marks. It has to be remembered that low marks do not mean that these are bad restaurants in any way. The White Guide is a selection of good restaurants. It does not include any fast food places, roadside diners or combined pizzeria and Thai restaurants, the latter being a popular innovation in the Swedish countryside. The number of ethnic restaurants is also rather small in the material investigated. Two out of 119 restaurants are Asian, one Chinese and one Vietnamese; five have a clear Italian profile. This small percentage is interesting because Asian (mainly Thai and Chinese) and Italian restaurants have a very strong presence in most Swedish towns. All seven ethnic restaurants fell into the category that received 3 as their total mark. It is interesting to see that Slow Food thinking does not seem to appeal to these Italian restaurants. Restaurants that specialize in one particular kind of food, such as fish or grill restaurants, are common in this category. But, the largest number could be described as traditional 'fine' dining places which serve international or continental cooking, i.e. food without any specific profile. This would normally be the kind of cooking one would find in the better hotel restaurants. There is also a small selection of exclusive places that make a point of providing exotic food from around the world at high prices with champagne; these obviously cater for the rich and stupid.

There are two main types of category 4 restaurants. The first contains restaurants that are focused on regional traditions but lack reference to ecology or local production. Many of these seem to be a bit old fashioned, like some country inns. The other category 4 type are places were continental cooking, e.g. French bistros, is combined with a deliberate use of locally produced ingredients such as meat, vegetables or cheese. It is very rare (one case) to find restaurants with an ecological profile without reference to locally produced food. Category 5 restaurants could often be seen as a combination of the two above-mentioned types, a kind of restaurant geared towards regional or traditional cooking which uses local products. The restaurants that manage to get a mark of 6 tend to be a bit more ambitious in selecting those local producers or delivery chains that have an

Table 10.1 Distribution of restaurants in categories based on total marks

Marks	Frequencies
no data	10
3	38
4	25
5	22
6	14
7	7
8	3
9	1

Note
N = 119.

ecological certification (KRAV). Many of these are also serve ecologically produced wines. There is one type that is very common among the ecologically conscious restaurants. They serve food that is mix of regional and European gastronomy, such as Skånsk–Mediterranean or Gotland–French. Many of these seem to create something rather innovative in the process. One entrée from a Gotland restaurant may illustrate this: 'truffle omelette with hot smoked Baltic salmon, mustard brandade and dried Gotland bread'.

Only one restaurant reached the level excellent in innovative regional cooking using locally produced food but totally lacked any reference to ecology. Another had a clear focus on local networks but had no reference to tradition or ecology. These could be considered as exceptions to the rule. Most of the restaurants reaching mark 6 and above (21 per cent of the sample) did well on all counts. Those that reached the highest levels, 7 and over, are typically very innovative in cooking and in their choice of deliveries, covering a wide spectrum of aspects. The old country inn of a small Skåne town managed to score top marks in all three categories. They had a menu mixing innovation and tradition based on regional food products with reference to farmers and breeders; they had a wide selection of ecological wines and served ecological breakfast. And, very importantly, the restaurants that received high marks were all clever enough to use this profile in their marketing material. During the empirical analysis, several cases emerged where restaurants seemed to be very ecologically conscious but information was rudimentary.

Geographically, the restaurants with the highest scores fall into two categories: country restaurants situated near the coast with a clear tourist profile, and top restaurants in Malmö, the only large city in the area of survey. Fine dining is generally unevenly distributed in Sweden. Top restaurants are mainly concentrated in Stockholm, Malmö and Göteborg. The province of Skåne in the south also stands out favourably. Apart from that there is a considerable concentration in tourist regions, mountain resorts in the north as well as coastal regions such as Bohuslän, Öland and Gotland. Medium-size towns in the interior and in the north are rather badly supplied. It is also in these towns that we find a

Table 10.2 Distribution of scores, in categories

Marks	Good	Clean	Fair
3	9	8	6
2	39	34	41
1+	34	5	15
1	28	63	48
Total	110	110	110

Note
N = 110.

disproportionate number of restaurants with low scores in this study. Unsurprisingly, there seems to be a connection between the general level of gastronomy and the prevalence of eco-gastronomic establishments.

Good

This category is supposed to reflect influences of traditional cooking on the restaurants' menus. More than half of them display only limited ambitions in this direction. They focus on serving good food, and sometimes a traditional dish enters the menu. Mark 2 normally suggests that a restaurant has a substantial part of its menu influenced by traditional regional cooking. This can be shown in different ways. Either they offer a range of traditional dishes or concepts or they use traditional ingredients in non-traditional ways. The highest mark in this category stands for a combination of tradition and innovation. In many cases old styles of preparation and cooking are renewed and combined in new ways.

The survey shows that almost half the restaurants promote some kind of attachment to their regional culinary heritage. Among them, three different sub-categories are visible: the traditional, the eclectic and the (re-)innovative. The traditional ones have a focus on traditional courses based on steak, pork and fish, together with a lot of duck and goose in the south. These restaurants mainly develop their quality through increased use of local deliveries and by developing the seasonal dishes on their menus. The eclectic restaurants develop traditional courses to new levels with new recipes and new methods. They use less fat, together with more roots and vegetables, and these are slightly undercooked instead of overcooked, which used to be normal. The ambition is often to let the raw ingredients speak for themselves, giving a different impression from the traditional. Their cooking is often influenced by continental, mainly French and Italian, gastronomy. These two sub-categories have a similar approach to first courses (entrées): these are often based on traditional smorgasbord dishes, such as smoked or marinated fish, smoked meat or salads. The smorgasbord itself is becoming more and more unusual in quality restaurants – nowadays they are only for Christmas. The (re-)innovative restaurants take up influences from the past, from the old, forgotten cuisine. In the White Guide this tendency is called 'rich poverty', meaning that it is based on food that used to be poor people's staples such as cabbage, roots, beans and grain. These are now combined with herbs, wild mushrooms, leaves and other things found in the countryside but which no one used to eat in the past. Some coastal restaurants use local seaweed and algae as ingredients of dishes, at times combined with a shot called 'stroll on the beach', vodka flavoured with herbs from the beach outside the restaurant. These restaurants also use cuts of meat and fish species that used to be considered inferior. Old ways of preservation are also often found on these restaurants' menus, giving tastes that tend to come close to the traditional Nordic mix of sweet, sour and salty.

Clean

Most restaurants that received a 1 in the clean category made no mention of ecology at all; it was not visible on the menu or elsewhere in the material except for in a few cases that received 1+. Mark 2 in this category indicates that a significant part of food on the menu was ecological. This was often seen in combination with a selection of ecological wines or other drinks. Based on the expertise of the White Guide, restaurants receiving the 'high ecological ambitions' symbol were generally given at least mark 2 in the clean category. Nine restaurants were selected this way, i.e. visitors using the White Guide were able to notice a clear ecological profile during their visit, but the restaurants neglected to use it in their information, or used very vague indicators. Mark 3 was given to restaurants with a significant ecological profile, meaning ecological cooking for both food and drinks.

A problem regarding ecological restaurants is that there is no established method to certify the restaurant as such, although there is an organization promoting ecological restaurants. It is, however, possible to certify hotels (through *Svanen*); a couple of the restaurants covered in this study are thus indirectly certified through the hotels. Otherwise the level of ecological concern has to be discerned through other methods. Some restaurants make clear statements on their homepages about their ecological policy. It has, for instance, become increasingly common not to sell bottled mineral water, thereby reducing food miles. They may also use ecological products such as ecological chicken or beef (though not acknowledging its climate change effects); the certification may then be visible on the menu. In some cases the certification is only indirectly visible, through partners. Another step in the process of becoming an ecologically concerned restaurant is to introduce eco products such as wine, other drinks or bread. To have a reasonable selection of vegetarian alternatives is also seen as a sign of ambition in this field. To serve fish that is threatened (eel) or environmentally harmful (scampi) is a sign of the opposite. Ecological ambitions are generally less developed as regards fish than agricultural products. 'Green fish' and 'KRAV fish' were mentioned in only a handful cases. The choice of fish is of course very important in relation to ecology. In general, Swedish fresh-water fish are less endangered than sea fish. Some of the high-score restaurants are consciously use for instance pike-perch from nearby lakes.

Fair

Those with the lowest mark in the category fair hardly mention the origin of their ingredients. They receive a plus if there is some mention of a local product or producer on the menu. The most common note in this category is 'not mentioned'. On the other hand, 46 restaurants have locally produced food (or in a few cases drinks) as part of their profile. The highest mark was given to those that provide the fullest information for this category, including, mentioning food miles The mark was raised if fair trade products, mainly chocolates and coffee, are mentioned. This happened only rarely. The most common ways of advertising local products was to mention the geographical origin on the menu, e.g. strawberries from Österlen. It is also fairly common to use the producer's name on the menu or elsewhere in the marketing material, e.g. chicken from Bosarp or cheese from Vilhelmsdal. There may also be links to the most important partners on the homepages. A final way of promoting local production is through different forms of storytelling, for example pictures or small texts. Normally these illustrations portray a beautiful landscape, children with lambs or a smiling farmer. They are very similar to the kind of material provided by regional destination marketing organizations. A few restaurants take storytelling a bit further. A restaurant in the province of Småland has been very successful in developing its menu based on local suppliers. One such local supplier is a cow named Pärla; she delivers the milk used for the restaurant's 'single cow's milk cheese'; it could hardly be more authentic than that.

Concluding discussion

There are a few, but not many, examples of restaurants in the empirical material that directly state that they are inspired by Slow Food. On the other hand, about half of the restaurants studied turn out to have been influenced by eco-gastronomic thinking in different ways. It is possible to see some interesting patterns in these influences. In many cases the best-known restaurants, those with high ratings, have taken the lead in eco-gastronomy. A real impact on sustainable development would result, however, if these restaurants could influence the ordinary ones, the diners and pizzerias. It is also the top restaurants that are getting attention in media.

Eco-gastronomic restaurants tend to be localized in urban centres; Malmö is a case in point. It is also reasonable to believe that the chefs in Malmö are influenced by gastronomic developments in the Copenhagen area, only 30 minutes away. Some of the most influential chefs and restaurants in Scandinavia are now based in Copenhagen. For instance, the famous chef Claus Meyer has been a very important promoter of ecologic cooking and the use of local products, whereas the two-star restaurant NOMA (abbreviation for Nordic food) has become famous for its inventive Nordic and North Atlantic cuisine. Closeness to centres of innovation thus seems to be important in gastronomy. The concentration of eco-gastronomic restaurants in tourist areas could mainly be viewed as a seasonal extension of urbanness. So far there are few eco-gastronomic restaurants in other peripheral areas. On the other hand, the kind of marketing visible in restaurant menus, homepages and material from regional destination marketing organizations is generally rural in character. Association is made with rural landscapes and traditional farming, although very little such farming remains, much less than in southern Europe. There seems to be a contradiction here that would be interesting to explore further but is outside the scope of this study.

Then, what would contemporary Nordic eco-gastronomy look like? The traditional cuisine could certainly be developed further, although it has a strong position, particularly in the province of Skåne. Based on this material, it seems that modern eco-gastronomy is mainly influenced from three directions. The first is ecological, where the quality of ingredients is an important issue. The second is the ambition to take advantage of regional and historical specificities, exemplified by 'rich poverty'. The third important influence comes from Mediterranean cuisine, which adds a lighter touch to the food and changes the balance towards more vegetables and vegetarian ingredients. Another vital continental contribution is of course wine. Nordic gastronomy without wine is unthinkable today, although hardly any is produced in the area. Thus, traditions are always changing, even in contexts where the promotion of place-specific qualities is in focus, as in many cases discussed in this chapter. This is, however, quite in line with Slow Food principles; there need not be a contradiction between innovation and tradition.

References

Bessière, J. (1998) 'Local development and heritage: traditional food and cuisine as tourist attractions in rural areas', *Sociologia Ruralis*, 38(1): 21–34.

Burstedt, A. (2004) 'What "time" do we eat? Some examples of the relationship between time and food', in P. Lysaght (ed.) *Changing Tastes. Food Culture and the Processes of Industrialization*. Basel.

Croce, E. and Perri, G. (2010) *Food and Wine Tourism. Integrating Food, Travel and Territory*. Wallingford: CABI.

Everett, S. and Aitchison, C. (2008) 'The role of food tourism in sustaining regional identity: a case study of Cornwall, South West England', *Journal of Sustainable Tourism*, 16(2): 150–67.

Frykman, J. (2000) 'Slow Cities – med snigeln som signum', *00-tal*, 4: 34–9.

Hagström, B. (2006) *Solens mat. En matreseguide till Italien*. Malmö: Damm förlag.

Hall, C.M. (2006) 'Introduction: culinary tourism and regional development: from Slow Food to slow tourism', *Tourism Review International*, 9(4): 303–6.

Hall, C.M. (2012) 'The contradictions and paradoxes of slow food: environmental change, sustainability and the conservation of taste', in S. Fullagar, K. Markwell and E. Wilson (eds) *Slow Tourism: Experiences and Mobilities*. Bristol: Channel View.

Hall, C.M., Sharples, L., Mitchell, R., Macionis, N. and Cambourne B. (eds) (2003) *Food Tourism Around the World. Development, Management and Markets*. Oxford: Butterworth-Heinemann.

Hayes-Conroy, A. and Martin, D.G. (2010) 'Mobilising bodies: visceral identification in the Slow Food movement', *Transactions from the Institute of British Geographers*, 35: 269–81.

Hellström, M. (ed.) (2005) *Östersjömat. Traditioner, recept och matkultur.* Stockholm: Carlssons.

Hjalager, A.-M. and Richards, G. (eds) (2002) *Tourism and Gastronomy.* London: Routledge.

IPCC (2007) *Summary for Policymakers: Intergovernmental Panel on Climate Change: Fourth Assessment Report Climate Change 2007: Synthesis Report.* Cambridge: University Press.

Jones, P., Shears, P., Hillier, D, Comfort, D. and Lowell, J. (2003) 'Return to traditional values? A case study of Slow Food', *British Food Journal*, 105(4/5): 297–304.

KRAV (2011) Krav Homepage. Online. Available: www.krav.se (accessed 5 April 2011).

Leith, A. (2003) 'Slow Food and the politics of pork fat: Italian food and European identity', *Ethnos*, 68(4): 437–62.

Lotti, A. (2010) 'The commoditization of products and taste: Slow Food and the conservation of agrodiversity', *Agriculture and Human Values*, 27(1): 71–83.

Malatesta, S., Weiner, S. and Yang, W. (2005) *The Slow Food Companion.* Bra: Slow Food.

Mattiacci, A. and Vignali, C. (2004) 'Introduction. The typical products within food "glocalisation". The makings of a twenty-first-century industry', *British Food Journal* 104(10/11): 703–13.

Miele, M. (2006) 'Consumption culture: the case of food', in P. Cloke, T. Marsden and P. Mooney (eds) *Handbook of Rural Studies.* London: Sage.

Miele, M. and Murdoch, J. (2002) 'The practical aesthetics of traditional cuisines: Slow Food in Tuscany', *Sociologia Ruralis*, 42(4): 312–28.

Mykletun, R.J. and Gyimothy, S. (2010) 'Beyond the renaissance of the traditional Voss sheep's-head meal: tradition, culinary art, scariness and entrepreneurship', *Tourism Management* 31: 434–46.

Nilsson, J.H., Svärd, A-C., Widarsson, Å. and Wirell, T. (2010) '"Cittáslow" Sustainable destination management through the pleasures of food and ecological concern', *Current Issues in Tourism*, 14(4): 373–86.

Nosi, C. and Zanni, L. (2004) 'Moving from "typical products" to "food related services". The Slow Food case as a new business paradigm', *British Food Journal* 104(10/11): 779–92.

Parkins, W. (2004) 'Out of time – fast subjects and slow living', *Time and Society* 13(2/3): 363–82.

Petrini, C. (2001) *Slow Food: The Case for Taste.* New York: Columbia University Press.

Petrini, C. in conversation with Padovani, G. (2005) *Slow Food Revolution. A New Culture for Eating and Drinking.* New York: Rizzoli.

Pietrykowski, B. (2004) 'You are what you eat: the social economy of the Slow Food Movement', *Review of Social Economy*, 62(3): 307–21.

Rudberg, S. (1968) 'Geology and Morphology', in A. Sømme (ed.) *A Geography of Norden*, 3rd edn. Oslo: J. W. Cappelens Forlag.

Scarpato, R. (2002) 'Gastronomy as tourist products: the perspective of gastronomy studies', in A-M. Hjalager and G. Richards (eds) *Tourism and Gastronomy.* London: Routledge.

Sims, R. (2009) 'Food, place and authenticity: local food and the sustainable tourism experience', *Journal of Sustainable Tourism*, 17: 321–36.

Slow Food (2010) Slow Food. Online. Available: www.slowfood.com (accessed 28 June 2010).

Slow Food Jämtland (2011) Homepage. Online. Available: www.slowfoodjamtland.se (accessed 5 April 2011).

Sømme, A. (1968) 'Resources and industries', in: A. Sømme, (ed.) *A Geography of Norden*, 3rd edn. Oslo: J.W. Cappelens Forlag.

Wallén, C.C. (1968) 'Climate', in: A. Sømme, (ed.) (1968) *A Geography of Norden*, 3rd edn. Oslo: J.W. Cappelens Forlag.

White Guide (2010) *Sveriges bästa restauranger.* Stockholm: Millhouse Förlag.

Wilk, R. (ed.) (2006) *Fast Food/Slow Food. The Cultural Economy of the Global Food System.* Lanham, Md.: Altamira Press.

Woods, M. and Deegan, J. (2003) 'A warm welcome for destination quality brands: the example of the Pays Cathare Region', *International Journal of Tourism Research.* 5: 269–82.

11 Collaboration in food tourism

Developing cross-industry partnerships

Sally Everett and Susan L. Slocum

Introduction

Food tourism is a concept that has gained significant attention in recent tourism literature. It is recognised as a vehicle that can enhance a destination's tourism offering and create backward linkages that generate additional economic opportunities for local residents in tourism destinations (Telfer and Wall 1996). Especially in areas where farming and food production constitute a large economic sector in a region, food tourism provides an avenue to promote and distribute local produce while simultaneously offering the tourist a means by which cultural experimentation can occur (Everett 2009). Governments have also realised the potential of food tourism to enhance the sustainability of tourism development (Du Rand *et al.* 2003) and have created a culturally aware and critically orientated policy research agenda that supports agriculture and tourism partnerships (DEFRA 2002) and has provided an avenue to enhance the provision of tourism product offerings across the country. The result is that food is increasingly becoming part of the sustainability agenda for many communities around the UK and emphasis has been placed on food tourism to supplement the agricultural sector and broaden the scope of regional development schemes in rural areas (Sharples 2003).

Food tourism is important in strengthening a region's identity, sustaining cultural heritage, easing fears of global food homogenisation, and supporting a region's economic and socio-cultural foundation (Everett and Aitchison 2008). Therefore, community identity and cultural distinctiveness can be expressed through food tourism while providing an avenue for economic development (Rusher 2003). The ultimate policy agenda of uniting food production and tourism is twofold: to fulfil utility goals that involve the contribution of the farming sector in the overall health of the economy; and to enhance equity goals that focus on the provision of satisfactory incomes for rural populations (Pretty 2002). However, how these policy agendas are realised on the ground remains obscure and under-investigated in academic literature. Because of the inherent differences in how business is conducted in tourism and in agriculture, and the different attributes of each economic sector, the UK has struggled to provide coherent, methodical best practices that can be easily accessible to small and medium-sized businesses in each sector. Moreover, the dissemination of information across regions and countries within the UK has proved to be problematic (Slocum and Everett 2010). Therefore, this chapter sets out to investigate the ways in which organisations react to globalisation pressures through food tourism initiatives and the need for these organisations to negotiate this emerging field of food tourism provision.

Following consultation with food tourism providers and an analysis of recent initiatives relating to food and tourism, a need for systematic research was identified to develop a vehicle of practical support to facilitate and encourage closer producer and consumer engagement and to raise the profile of food initiatives and networks within the UK tourism sector. The result was a research-informed project which bolstered an online resource to support food tourism development, thereby providing a promotion tool and a centralised database of information for food producers and consumers. The key objectives for this project were: to facilitate communication between public and private sector food and tourism consumers/providers; to build understandings of visitor behaviour in order to enhance the enjoyment and experience of food tourism; to make practical recommendations on how to make local food more widely accessible and affordable; to develop a powerful online web portal to promote, share and disseminate good practice; and to help rural communities build sustainable food tourism networks, thereby maintaining livelihoods, skills and cultures. In preparing to develop this online web-based portal, extensive research was conducted to advise on and ensure the practicality and longevity of the website's usage and substance. Therefore, the methodology in the preparation for this project comprised a literature review of previous studies, current practice and policy; 20 stakeholder interviews (food tourism providers); a survey of over 250 consumers/tourists; and four national food seminars.

Food tourism

Food tourism research is on the rise, both in academic circles and in government discussion papers. Food tourism is defined as 'the desire to experience a particular type of food or the produce of a specific region' (Hall and Sharples 2003: 10) and encompasses food-related attractions, food-centred holidays, gourmet festivals, farmers' markets, the promotion of regional gastro-specialties, taste trails and food-based souvenirs (Boniface 2003; Okumus *et al.* 2007). Previous food tourism research has tended to focus on economic linkages and food as an economic commodity (Telfer and Wall 1996), destination marketing strategies (Okumus *et al.* 2007; Hashimoto and Telfer 2008) and consumer behavioural/motivational analysis (Du Rand and Heath 2006; Ignatov and Smith 2006). Other work has recognised food as a material object and as a communicator of contemporary socio-cultural meaning (Oakes 1999; Van Westering 1999), making it a valuable asset to a region's tourism offering (Hall and Sharples 2003, 2008). It has also been argued that in order to identify synergies across the various academic disciplines that engage in food tourism studies and simultaneously inform policy initiatives, multiple disciplinary approaches must be embraced (Scarpato 2002; Everett 2009).

Although there are studies that elicit data from food producers, such as Kneafsey and Ilbery's (2001) West Country survey, it is difficult to locate a study that simultaneously engages producers and consumers and examines the relationships between the impact of food tourism on producers as well as the growing demand and changing needs of new culinary tourists. A few studies have addressed the impact of food-related tourism on producers in the regions, such as Long (2004), whose contributors generally concentrate on tourists and their experiences, with little discussion of the impact on the destination's culture and community, and Boniface (2003), which focuses on the tourist, rather than the host culture. Hjalager and Richards (2002) address this split and remind researchers of the need to develop an approach in the study of food from different perspectives through the pursuit of creative and innovative lines of enquiry which will, in turn, uncover new avenues of food research.

Given that food and beverages constitute up to one-third of total tourist expenditure (Meler and Cerović 2003), and is worth nearly £6 billion each year in the United Kingdom (ICTA 2007), it is not surprising that there has been rising awareness of food tourism as a growing area in tourism studies. Food tourism is increasingly being recognised as a powerful vehicle for behaviour and attitudinal change, specifically in regard to sustaining rural businesses and communities (Everett and Aitchison 2008; Sims 2009). As part of a rise in new consumption patterns, food-motivated travel is becoming a significant 'pull' factor in management and marketing strategies (Okumus *et al.* 2007) and the UK has witnessed a significant rise in food tourism destinations, trails and festivals. Many places are now internationally renowned and have transformed previously deprived rural regions with high levels of food tourism-induced prosperity (Sharples 2003). However, practice has been found to be generally fragmented and poorly supported. Therefore, knowledge and food offers from across the country are being centrally collated to bolster food initiatives and support future food tourism development.

Globalisation, diversification and resistance

Globalisation is a concept closely associated with the destruction of local cultural identities and the encroachment of homogenising westernised consumer culture. Tregear (2003) has suggested that global processes have been ongoing since early industrialisation and have led to a rural exodus, delocalisation and loss of inherited knowledge and skills. The concept of resistance has frequently been linked with research examining alternative systems that resist this apparent process of globalisation, excessive regulation, standardisation and uniformity (Watson 1997; Murdoch and Miele 1999). It has been suggested that if food production processes erase much of the material substance of traditional life in rural areas, the food distribution process erodes the culinary heritage of regions. The drive to rationalise and standardise, combined with the global sourcing of ingredients, has muted the effects of climate and seasonality and international-ised the cuisine of western societies. There is a strong sense that aggressive food firms and the increased standardisation of food threaten the inherent cultural and environmental qualities of local foods (Bessière 1998) and that a revalorisation of (rural) regional cuisines is needed (Ilbery and Kneafsey 1998). Boniface (2003) suggests active 'disenchantment' has occurred as a result of the perceived rationalisation of society and homogenisation of foodstuffs. It is suggested that food and drink tourism provides a means through which distinctiveness can be reasserted and offers a mechanism with which individuals can consciously resist gastronomic blandness. Likewise, Fernandez-Armesto (2001: 252) concludes by expressing his belief that, 'Fussiness and "foodism" are methods of self-protection for society against the deleterious effects of the industrial era: the glut of the cheap, the degradation of the environment, the wreckage of taste.'

Traditional industries such as farming are facing new challenges with increas-ingly globalised supply chains and price-competitive marketing strategies employed by food service providers. However, consumer fears of farming crises and animal diseases, in combination with concerns over food mileage, homoge-nising global food powers and perceived loss of distinguishable food identities, have resulted in widespread disillusionment with the food chain (Goodman and Du Puis 2002). In this climate, not only are consumers turning to regionally identified foods, but local food producers are rapidly becoming a significant industry group (Lockie and Kitto 2000; Sage 2003; Holloway *et al.* 2007). This rise in food tourism interest is reflected in the establishment of government policy commissions which have sought to regenerate the British countryside by promoting sustainable tourism, diversification and the reconnection of consum-ers with the land (DEFRA 2002; Eastham 2003). These developments marked a significant move towards greater convergence between production and consump-tion and between policy development and academic research. The creation of the Policy Commission on the Future of Farming and Food in 2001 represented a particularly important British policy attempt at discovering how to 'create a sus-tainable, competitive and diverse farming and food sector which contributes to a thriving and sustainable rural economy' (FCFFF 2002). It recognised that true sustainable farming is only achieved through the reconnection of consumers with the environment in which food is produced.

The Policy Commission on the Future of Farming and Food (PCFFF 2002: 13) report states that 'it is our strong view that the farming and food industry is on a path that cannot be sustained in the long term'. One of its key recommended strategies to improve this situation is diversification and the report specifically highlights tourism as the most common form of farm diversification. As previ-ously discussed in the academic literature review, rural and farm tourism is increasingly regarded as a significant means of boosting a struggling agricultural industry and sustaining a rich and diverse rural heritage and landscape: 'tourism is a key earner in rural areas, and a healthy, attractive and diverse farmed land-scape is the foundation for its future' (PCFFF 2002: 53). This sentiment is re-emphasised within the government's official response to the Commission's findings (DEFRA 2002: 49). Although clearly concerned with other areas of the farming industry such as Common Agricultural Policy reform, European Union involvement and the overall health of the nation, DEFRA (2002) acknowledges the need to diversify outside the traditional boundaries of farming and use the wider resources of individual farms.

For example, the South West region's response to the PCFFF report and Government Strategy was *Making a Difference – the Delivery Plan for a Sustainable Farming and Food Industry in South West England*. It is a comprehensive and region-focused document which offers a clear and organised response to the government's recommendations, and its thematic approach represents a potentially influential systematic delivery plan for the South West. Its structure outlines clear aims, objectives, outcomes and even time frames while sensitively recognising the specific needs and character of this 'region of regions' (South West Strategy of Sustainable Farming and Food Steering Group 2004: 5). Rather than offering a traditional economic appraisal and profit-based plan, it acknowledges that 'true sustainability requires much more than that' (South West Strategy of Sustainable Farming and Food Steering Group 2004: 3) and addresses numerous social, cultural and environmental dimensions. An obvious priority in this plan is strengthening the regional food and drink industry and bolstering its relationship with tourism.

It is suggested here that the pressure to diversify and embrace new externally driven agricultural policy directions is not always welcomed, or feasible at ground level. It is this 'resistance on the ground' which has become a particular area of interest for those examining relationships between food producers, consumer demand and top-down agricultural development. Studies have certainly focused on the apparent link between identity loss and the blurring of global/ local boundaries through the impact of external influences. They draw attention to 'how spatially bounded and diasporic communities in an increasingly globalised world seek to reaffirm their identity through the reappropriation of their cultural heritage' (Harvey *et al.* 2002: 17). For example, Kneafsey (2002: 123) succinctly summarises the context for this destabilisation of centre/periphery in an analysis of Ireland and Brittany:

> broader tourism-related processes are simultaneously contributing to the destabilisation of these centre–periphery relations and to the multiplication of sites of the construction of Celticity. It is suggested that the production of Celticity is becoming more geographically diffused as a result of increased commodification and globalisation.

Research has identified that self-removal and escape to less rationalised settings may not be direct 'resistance' in the traditional sense, but it has been argued that producers can then express a dissatisfaction with commercial pressures, finding solace in the small scale and personal. It is the ability to momentarily discard and resist the social structures which regulate lives in order to pursue the extraordinary in a kind of alternative world (Graburn 1983).

The employment of 'resistance' as a theoretical concept in tourism research is often more implied than explicit. Jamal *et al.* (2003) claim it is fragmentary and piecemeal in the tourism literature, displaying a significant lack of empirical testing. Before the cultural turn in tourism and reconceptualisation of consumption structures in society, a study of 'resistance' in a tourism context would certainly have presented a case for the way local people were contesting tourism development and opposing the destruction of their culture and land by powerful external forces (e.g. De Kadt 1979; Turner and Ash 1975). A plethora of studies reflect this kind of resistance between the tourist and the local. Selwyn (1996: 9) suggests that 'tourism is one of the engines which manufactures and structures relationships between centres and peripheries'. As tourism research continues to embrace the fluid and disrupting forces of critical theories in relation to spatialisations and centres of power, it is unsurprising that the subject of resistance in relation to centre/periphery and top/down has begun to attract particular attention and has become a richly contested tourism conceptualisation.

For example, social networking is part of a 'new economic dynamic' in West Cork (Sage 2003). In placing a focus on taste, quality and culture, artisans are actively seeking to displace the iron law of price. In placing themselves in spaces that fall between sites of resistance and exploitation, individual/community pride is fostered while ensuring that businesses remains viable. Individuals who are able to achieve a balance between 'formal–informal processes, strategies–tactics and exploitation–resistance' have been found to be in the strongest position to draw on sources of both formal and informal power (Round *et al.* 2008: 182). Alternative food networks have been extensively examined and theorised in agri-food research (Lockie and Kitto 2000; Sage 2003; Holloway *et al.* 2007). The relevance here is how such formations act as vehicles of social resistance, particularly at an informal level. Although the scope and relative development of these networks varied across the study's locations, Pile (1997) points out that it is no coincidence that 'communities of resistance' are termed 'movements' in much political analysis. Social networking is vital in helping producers find avenues of influence and obtain the power to retain local food identities, yet taking this a step further to respond to wider policy initiatives that seek to assist the development of their business may be rejected as being both excessively complex, unattractively bureaucratic and compromising the small-scale nature of their business which they wish to retain.

As a result of the political and economic environments facing tourism and food-producing organisations, it was determined that a national programme designed to reduce barriers to communication and facilitate knowledge exchange was needed across the UK. This collaborative project responded to the need for social research to inform practice and policies that recognise that food-related tourism must be a priority if Britain is to sustain its rich agricultural heritage and diverse regional identities (DEFRA 2010). If livelihoods are to prove sustainable, rural businesses must be encouraged to embrace integrated development and diversification into the tourism sector in order to survive. However, there has been limited research into how the consumer can work with the producer and the most effective mechanisms for engaging consumers with food and its original producer. One example is Kneafsey and Ilbery's (2001) West Country study, but it remains difficult to locate work that simultaneously engages producer and consumer with a view to offering tangible ways of practically harnessing this growing demand for new culinary experiences.

Collaboration and knowledge networks

Collaboration and knowledge networks are vital elements of successful diversification for small and medium-sized businesses facing rapid change within the economic environment (Gartner and Lime 2000). Elements such as the deregulation of national economies, internationalisation and globalisation, changing expectations and increasing consumer disloyalty reduce economies of scope and displace an organisation's market position and autonomy (Pechlaner *et al.* 2002). These trends have been increasingly recognised within not only the tourism sector (Pechlaner and Tschurtschenthaler 2002) but also the agricultural sector worldwide (McGehee 2007). Collaboration and knowledge networks increase competitive advantage through cooperative, yet independent, relationships (Pechlaner *et al.* 2002) that typically encompass vertical integration, new information and communication systems and a reduction in redundancy (Miles and Snow 1986). Successful partnerships usually require a broker, or hub firm, responsible for network design and maintenance (Jarillo 1988). Tourism literature has presented frameworks that investigate community- or region-based collaboration (Boyne *et al.* 2001), within industry collaboration (Porter 1991), and destination marketing partnerships (Kotler *et al.* 2002), but a thorough investigation of collaboration between differing industries, especially the food and tourism sectors, at the national level is all too scarce (Gal *et al.* 2010).

Recent research has shown that sustainability involves a transition and a learning process that incorporates elements of adaptive management, such as collective learning, stakeholder engagement and environmental adaptation (Holling 1978). Knowledge generation, use and transfer allow organisations within the partnership an opportunity to formulate strategy and influence dynamic environments (Nonaka and Takeuchi 1995). Due to the policy environment in the UK, regional development agencies in England and the food and drink sector in Wales and Scotland have been tasked with the responsibility to grow the food tourism offering (Slocum and Everett 2010). This regionalisation has created partnerships and networks at the local level; however, knowledge sharing between countries and regions is virtually non-existent. Organisations such as Tastes of Anglia and Tastes of Arran have geographically widened these networks, but still provide businesses with limited information from across the entire UK. On the other hand, extensive transport networks and the relatively small size of the UK allow tourists to combine regions in close proximity during a single travel experience. Rather than heading directly to a predetermined destination, many leisure tourists meander across a somewhat preplanned route, heedless of regional political boundaries (Tideswell and Faulkner 2002).

In particular, UK food tourism policy and strategies involve diverse industries and distinctly different business models in an effort to utilise tourism supply chains as a means to revitalise a troubled agricultural industry. Matching hoteliers with farmers, and food sector distributors with tour operators, combines dissimilar marketing strategies, value chain management and communication challenges (Slocum and Everett 2010). Further complexity surrounds managers' approach to business, such as lifestyle entrepreneurs, family-run businesses and complex corporate enterprises, as well as the level of domestic and international experience (Weiermair 2001). Definitions of food tourism itself, such as food-based attractions, the exploration of locally sourced produce, the sampling of traditional recipes, regional food-based souvenirs and farm-based accommodations and experiences imply that understanding niche markets within food tourism and accessing information of tourist motivations within each niche becomes a complex, time-consuming task. Developing partnerships and disseminating large amounts of food and tourism information is often cumbersome and repetitive as different organisations continually reinvent the wheel. Simultaneously communities in the south are facing similar challenges to communities in the north, but there is no means through which information and best practices can be shared between these two geographically and politically distinct areas.

A group of local authorities, regional agencies, food networks, private sector consultants and tourism marketing associations met to discuss the development of a new food tourism website that would help form partnerships, while at the same time providing a marketing tool for food tourism and information dissemination. Having organised the gathering of 60 professionals at the Big Food Debate at the Abergavenny Food Festival to discuss issues around the subject of food tourism, several areas of work were identified as necessary to drive and promote food tourism across the UK. These included the need to adopt an evidence-based approach with research and statistics to inform food tourism development at a national level which prompted the initial creation of a not-for-profit website framework and interactive forum: ukfoodtourism.com.

Findings and discussion

The purpose of this research was to examine how food-related tourism can deliver socially, culturally and environmentally sustainable development in rural regions and communities, and then to develop tangible and practical solutions to achieve this. This research involved a two-step process of data collection. First, a series of tourist surveys were conducted at three of the UK's leading food festivals during the summer and autumn of 2009: the Abergavenny Food Festival (Wales), the Stratford Festival (England) and the East Midlands Food Festival (England) (Table 11.1). While it is acknowledged that survey response rates were relatively low, the results support the concerns and challenges addressed in the interview data and provide insight into the issues facing the food tourism industry. Participants were asked to choose only one answer to the questions listed in Table 11.2 and only the top responses are discussed in this chapter.

Table 11.1 Festival attendance and surveys collected

Festival	Approximate attendance	Surveys collected
Abergavenny Food Festival	37,000	143
Stratford Food Festival	13,000	65
East Midlands Food Festival	15,000	59

Seventy-four per cent of the respondents expressed an interest in local food as a motivator to attend the festival. Participants were equally interested in learning about all types of food tourism activities such as food festivals and events (26 per cent), local food markets (25 per cent), new restaurants using local food (20 per cent), visits to local producers (17 per cent) and food trails (12 per cent). It was noted that tourists seek specific details such as better information on where to go to buy local food (32 per cent), better publicity of foodie events (31 per cent), making foodie events easier to find (23 per cent), and more information

Table 11.2 Key findings from tourist survey

Question	%
Why did you decide to visit this food festival?	
Interests in food	74
How did you hear about this festival?	
Been before	47
Friends and family	22
What would make you attend more food festivals?	
Better publicity	31
If they were closer to home	21
Free entry	15
More information about the food	15
What food-related activities do you engage in on a regular basis?	
Eating out in restaurants	36
Food markets	31
Food festivals and events	23
What makes you buy local food when you are on holiday?	
Better information about where to go	32
More accessible and easier to find	23
More information about the food	15
How do you prefer to find out about food-related events?	
Interactive website	52
What things would you find helpful on a food tourism website	
Interact UK map	28
Interactive events diary	25

Note
N=267.

about the food itself (15 per cent). Most respondents had heard about the food festival event because they had attended in the past (47 per cent) or had heard about the event from family and friends (22 per cent). Tourists were most interested in utilising an interactive website as a means to gather food tourism information (52 per cent). Tourists preferred interactive features within the website, such as interactive maps (28 per cent) and interactive event diaries (25 per cent). The overall findings from the tourism survey data (Table 11.2) suggest that there is a lack of food tourism information available to tourists planning their holiday.

The second phase in the data collection process included a series of stakeholder interviews via telephone to a variety of organisations exploring or participating in food tourism initiatives. Participants included tourism consultants, food festival organisers, local government organisations, food-based non-profit groups, agricultural producers and tour operators. In total, 16 interviews were conducted during the spring of 2010 (Table 11.3). Some of the common challenges facing the interview participants include a need to identify and access tourists and to gain knowledge about tourism markets, as data are fragmented and not well maintained. Additionally, food tourism providers need information on building a destination brand based on local food production to collaborate and network between regions and groups and to access best practices from across the country. The communication barrier is twofold: producers acknowledged that information about tourism is often confusing while hospitality organisations lack information about locally produced food options. All groups expressed a lack of time and resources to further investigate food tourism options and a belief that a consolidated information source would be extremely helpful. The most important attribute of a national website is a series of UK-based case studies, links to

Table 11.3 Interview participants

Organizational type	Location
1 Consultant	British Isles
2 Consultant	Scotland
3 Consultant	Scotland
4 Food Festival	England
5 Food Festival	England
6 Local Government	Wales
7 Local Government	Wales
8 Local Government	England
9 Local Government	Wales
10 Non-profit Organisation	Scotland
11 Non-profit Organisation	England
12 Producer	Wales
13 Producer	Scotland
14 Producer	Scotland
15 Tour operator	Scotland
16 Tour operator/farmers' market	England

funding schemes, and a forum for communication between different organisations and different regions.

In order to facilitate a networking and collaboration system between the tourism sector, the agricultural sector and the tourist, it is vital to understand the convergences and tensions facing each entity in the attempt to bring together diverse industries. The participants in this study achieved a number of common insights in negotiating the complex relationship between tourism and agriculture. All those involved in the study consider local food production a valuable expression of cultural and regional identity that preserves local heritage and reflects a unique lifestyle and value set. As one food tourism consultant from the Isle of Wight said, 'We need to express the cultural value in food, to show that food is really fun.' It was widely agreed that food tourism can cumulatively expand economic opportunities for food producers and food service providers, encouraging economic growth through job creation and increases in earnings. A local government official stated that, 'Supermarkets have bankrupted our agriculture, which affects jobs. Local farmers have had to diversify in order to stay viable.'

However, the implementation challenges facing this collaborative effort include a lack of understanding and available knowledge on food tourism, in particular: information regarding the role food plays in destination branding; access to food tourists and an understanding of their motivations; and innovative partnerships that incorporate food into the tourism offering. Consumers have also recognised these constraints and have had difficulty understanding the convoluted and contradictory messages the food tourism sector is expounding. 'We need to keep aware about what's happening in the sector and who's doing what. From the producer end, being aware of new products, new packaging and new approaches and also being aware from a destination marketing perspective. There is a massive vacuum as far as any knowledge is concerned', said a tourism consultant from Scotland. Building a regional destination brand based on local food production requires best practice knowledge that encourages a wider use and better promotion of locally sourced food. Often restaurants have no knowledge of the source of their food, and if it is produced locally, they fail to capitalise on the marketing potential given that they lack comprehension on the tourist's food choice motivations. Consumers are frustrated by the inability to find locally produced food once on holiday.

Participants feel that producer and food service complacency limits the establishment of networks and the sharing of information which could potentially enhance the tourism distribution system and establish a viable local supply chain. Farmers have established a traditional means of distribution and often are unaware of what happens to their produce once it leaves the farm. Food service providers rely on industry distribution systems that provide low-cost and well-rounded inventories, facilitating a one-stop shopping experience. Networking between these two links in the value chain has proved complex because channels of communication are non-existent. The perception is that producers want to acquire the highest price for their commodities, whereas food service providers want to negotiate the lowest cost for their food staples.

Outside the hospitality industry, there is limited evidence of alternate food tourism collaborations. The regionalisation of agriculture, and more specifically tourism, has limited the transference of information regarding successful food-based attractions, farm-based travel experiences, and other innovative food tourism partnership ideas. Each sector posseses limited understanding of the other, and they often work dichotomously, rather than congruently, when promoting programmes and agendas. One local producer from northern England explains:

> The agricultural industry is still very traditional ... taking lamb to market and never know what happens to them. They have been doing it that way for centuries. Some farmers are aware that they want to do more, like how do they brand their product and look at the added value there, but the barrier is knowledge on how to do that. Also there is an attitude that 'I am a farmer, that's what I do. I don't market or brand'. There is a handful that has really gone to town and sells their cheeses directly to the consumer, but mostly in our area, you find the former, those that don't want to change or are aware they need to change but don't know how.

Local agricultural producers face numerous options and pressures to diversify their offerings which have led to resistance against the newly formed food tourism policy agenda. Previous diversification strategies encouraged at the policy level, including equine services, animal food production, farm structure letting and the export of surplus produce, were investigated by the study participants. Many producers feel that food tourism is the latest trend promoted by rural development agencies. In the current policy environment, fears of reduced funding and political changes suggest food tourism may be a transitory trend. On the other hand, producers face many tangible constraints that pose challenges to food tourism. Producers tend to be widely dispersed geographically, decreasing visibility to tourism consumers. Many local producers view their trade as a lifestyle business, maintaining hostility to commercial pressures and preferring to engage in small-scale operations. Tourism consumers require a high level of engagement, a practice not currently familiar to agricultural producers. Growth of an agricultural business forces farmers to adopt new administration skills, such as personnel management. A local government official in Wales informs that,

> These are lifestyle businesses and [they] don't want to grow. They don't want to hire employees. Hotels do source locally, but distribution is difficult because the producers are widely dispersed. It's hard to get produce to the hotels. The hotels struggle with getting enough local food, higher prices, and good quality because of the distribution problems.

Resources needed to navigate food tourism markets vary according to firm size, isolating small-scale producers with fewer resources. Small producers lack economies of scale and unique selling points and frequently cannot compete in the fragmented tourism sector.

This research shows that information exchange and collaboration are highly valuable and seriously lacking in contemporary food tourism initiatives nation-wide in the UK. While numerous organisations are engaged in network develop-ment and knowledge exchange, their focus appears to be with either the food producers or the hospitality industries and not between the two. Furthermore, neighbouring regions have no knowledge of what initiatives are being applied or the constraints and challenges facing other organisations tasked with the same development objectives. In general, the responses from all stakeholders and tour-ists support the development of an interactive website designed to forge partner-ships and disseminate information relating to food and tourism provision, best practices and general marketing channels.

The online food tourism initiative

The ukfoodtourism.com website seeks to share and disseminate best practices; encourage and provide a tangible means for people to access and enjoy locally produced food while encouraging enhanced tourist spending. It not only promotes local food purchasing as economically beneficial but, by offering an enhanced experience while on holiday, it has begun to support local community development and provision. This multi-agency work is now directly influencing practice across a range of food-related areas, providing a valuable online data-base of food producers with shared resources on attracting tourists, understand-ing tourist interests, providing food-inspired attractions, developing food festivals, creating food initiatives and undertaking effective marketing.

Small local food businesses and tourists have expressed an overwhelming inter-est in developing sustainable food tourism, but an approach was required to ensure development was conducted in the most appropriate way and to secure the wider benefits of food tourism. As people have become more aware of food origins, increased interest and research are required to identify how best to develop schemes and make local food more widely accessible. The website offers an innovative way of encouraging consumers to intimately connect with places of production – bringing consumers directly to the 'point of sale'; encouraging people to seek out and enjoy local specialities, producers and places, thereby raising their enjoyment of an area while simultaneously supporting rural businesses dependent on selling local food and drink. In seeking to demonstrate the positive role of food in a social context, or how food can contribute to community cohesion, this project has directly benefited small community projects such as the Scottish Borders Network. Another example, The Hebridean Kitchen, is a cooperative that brings local people together in a small community building where locally produced food is sold to tourists; however, they lack the funds to publicise the centre. By devel-oping an online vehicle that raises the profile of such initiatives while gaining insights from other projects, this website has been able to bolster and encourage these kinds of community projects to grow and attract tourists.

A number of 'champions' of food tourism have been identified who have a wealth of experience and can offer assistance to embryonic food tourism projects. Cognisant of the need for tourism research to have a practical application, the proposed work ultimately aimed to scale up these successful regional projects and practices. By sharing effective practices in localised areas, this ongoing project is creating a wider platform from which other food projects can learn and develop. Until now, there has been no national structure in place to facilitate this and limited research exists about how best to achieve it. Rural initiatives lack the resources to fully engage with the general public, so this project offers a solution and encourages successful regions to work with embryonic and struggling projects to achieve national coverage and raise awareness of the benefits of food tourism.

The knowledge gained is generating usable and relevant content for a website that offers the first clickable and downloadable food map of its kind – specifically focused on bringing national food outlets, producers and consumers together. Ukfoodtourism.com is dedicated to promoting food and sharing best practice across the country and literally 'putting food tourism on the map'. It is providing a forum for the pooling of resources, offering a support network for small and local producers. This site includes a clickable UK map listing regional food initiatives, case studies to inform policy and practice, user-authored discussions, food tourism guides, an extensive resource of contacts and initiatives, case studies, event listings, best practice models and links.

The interactive map forms the largest food tourism resource in the country (accessible by producers and consumers) and is the first time multi-region food producers involved in national projects have been able to access and share information online. Without such externally funded and implemented projects, food tourism initiatives lack the resources to fully develop and engage the general public on a large scale. This project is ongoing and will be monitored and is designed to become self-supporting through subscription. However, at this time, resources to effectively promote the website and recruit membership are scarce. Further government budgetary constraints have resulted in the widespread restructuring of local government organisations, further separating the tourism and agricultural sectors and resulting in the reshuffling of regional economic development agencies. Many not-for-profit food organisations are facing serious financial constraints and reduced staffing as a result of the current economic climate. While this project focused on initiating significant growth in the sector and driving the development of food tourism in a sustainable and supported direction, changes in the political climate across the UK have delayed the arrival of significant long-term benefits for both producer and consumer.

Conclusions

This research was undertaken as a means to develop a powerful online web portal to promote, share and disseminate good practice related to food and tourism collaborative partnerships in the UK. Through consumer surveys and industry interviews, it was discovered that facilitating communication between public and private sector food and tourism consumers/providers was a key factor in current food tourism initiatives. By allowing user-defined content and access to best practice information, this project enables users to build understandings of visitor behaviour in order to enhance the enjoyment and experience of food tourism and makes practical recommendations on how to make local food more widely available and affordable. The website also brings together information from two distinctly different industries, those of food production and tourism, as a means to find common ground through which to develop cross-industry partnerships. As food tourism is currently a key economic development policy focus in the UK, ukfoodtourism.com is a step forward in the mission to help rural communities build sustainable food tourism networks, thereby sustaining livelihoods, skills and cultures.

The infrastructure of the website is now in place and underpinned by a database that is self-evolving and self-managed by its users, allowing it to be regularly updated with user-generated material. Having established the initial content and design of the site, the team has begun to embark on its long-term business plan to introduce a membership fee system as businesses sign up and use the facility, thereby making it self-supporting after the initial start-up grant from the Esmée Fairbairn Foundation. Furthermore, once the website is fully established, food tourism partners and initiatives will be better informed and with be able to work more closely together in order to secure future development grants from bodies such as regional development agencies and through the LEADER + European Development Funding streams, and provide an effective example of multi-agency collaboration between academia, the third sector and industry to deliver practical solutions. Moreover, the site provides a vehicle through which producers are channelling resistance and developing networks to strengthen the local and distinctive offering in the face of increased homogenisation and this responds to the call for these kinds of initiatives. Despite the fact that regional and local agencies are facing new challenges in a turbulent economic climate, the team is optimistic that the underpinning research has provided a solid sustainable foundation that has helped this initiative to address the most pressing needs within the food and tourism partnership.

References

Bessière, J. (1998) 'Local development and heritage: traditional food and cuisine as tourist attractions in rural areas', *Sociologia Ruralis*, 38(1): 21–34.

Boniface, P. (2003) *Tasting Tourism: Travelling for Food and Drink*. Aldershot: Ashgate.

Boyne, S., Williams, F. and Hall, D.R. (2001) 'Innovation in rural tourism and regional development: tourism and food production on the Isle of Arran', in J. Ruddy and S. Flanagan (eds) *ATLAS 10th Anniversary International Conference on Tourism Innovation and Regional Development*. Dublin Institute of Technology, Ireland, 4–6 October.

Boyne, S., Williams, F. and Hall, D.R. (2010) 'Policy, support and promotion for food-related tourism initiatives: a marketing approach to regional development', *Journal of Travel and Tourism Marketing*, 14: 131–54.

De Kadt, E. (1979) *Tourism: Passport to Development? Perspectives on the Social and Cultural Effects of Tourism in Developing Countries.* Oxford: Oxford University Press.

DEFRA (Department for Environment, Food and Rural Affairs) (2002) *Our Countryside: The Future – A Fair Deal for Rural England.* Government White Paper.

DEFRA (2010) *Food 2030.* Online. Available: www.defra.gov.uk/foodfarm/food/pdf/food2030strategy.pdf. (accessed 1 April 2012).

Du Rand, G.E. and Heath, E. (2006) 'Towards a framework for food tourism as an element of destination marketing', *Current Issues in Tourism*, 9(3): 206–34.

Du Rand, G., Heath, E. and Alberts, N. (2003) 'The role of local and regional food in destination marketing', *Journal of Travel and Tourism Marketing*, 14(3): 97–112.

Eastham, J.F. (2003) Valorising through tourism in rural areas, moving towards regional partnerships', in C.M. Hall, E. Sharples, R. Mitchell, B. Cambourne and N. Macionis (eds) *Food Tourism around the World: Development, Management and Markets.* Oxford: Butterworth-Heinemann.

Everett, S. (2009) 'Beyond the visual gaze? The pursuit of an embodied experience through food tourism', *Tourist Studies*, 8(3): 337–58.

Everett, S. and Aitchison, C. (2008) 'The role of food tourism in sustaining regional identity: a case study of Cornwall, South West England', *Journal of Sustainable Tourism*, 16(2): 150–67.

Fernandez-Armesto, A. (2001) *Food: A History.* London: Macmillan.

Frochot, I. (2005) 'A benefit segmentation of tourist in rural areas: a Scottish perspective', *Tourism Management*, 26(3): 335–46.

Gal, Y., Galb, A. and Hadasc, E. (2010) 'Coupling tourism development and agricultural processes in a dynamic environment', *Current Issues in Tourism*, 13(3): 279–95.

Gartner, W.C. and Lime, D.W. (eds) (2000) *Trends in Outdoor, Recreation, Leisure and Tourism.* Oxford: CAB International.

Goodman, D. and Du Puis, E.M. (2002) 'Knowing food and growing food: beyond the production–consumption debate in the sociology of agriculture', *Sociologia Ruralis*, 42(1): 5–22.

Graburn, N. (1983) 'The anthropology of tourism', *Annals of Tourism Research*, 10(1): 9–33.

Hall, C.M. and Sharples, E. (2003) 'The consumption of experiences or the experience of consumption?' An introduction to the tourism of taste', in C.M. Hall, E. Sharples, R. Mitchell, B. Cambourne and N. Macionis (eds) *Food Tourism Around the World: Development, Management and Markets.* Oxford: Butterworth-Heinemann.

Hall, C.M. and Sharples, L. (2008) *Food and Wine Festivals and Events around the World: Development Management and Markets.* Boston: Elsevier/Butterworth-Heinemann.

Harvey, D., Jones, R., McInroy, N. and Milligan, C. (eds) (2002) *Celtic Geographies: Old Culture, New Times.* London: Routledge.

Hashimoto, A. and Telfer, D.J. (2008) 'From sake to sea urchin: food and drink festivals and regional identity in Japan', in C.M. Hall and L. Sharples (eds) *Food and Wine Festivals and Events Around the World: Development, Management and Markets.* Oxford: Elsevier/Butterworth-Heinemann.

Hjalager, A. and Richards, G. (eds) (2002) *Tourism and Gastronomy.* London: Routledge.

Holling, C.S. (ed.) (1978) *Adaptive Environmental Assessment and Management.* Chichester: Wiley.

Holloway, L., Kneafsey, M., Venn, L., Cox, R., Dowler, E. and Tuomainen, H. (2007)

'Possible food economies: a methodological framework for exploring food production–consumption relationships', *Sociologia Ruralis*, 47(1): 1–18.

Ignatov, E. and Smith, S. (2006) 'Segmenting Canadian culinary tourists', *Current Issues in Tourism*, 9(3): 235–55.

Ilbery, B. and Kneafsey, M. (1998) 'Product and place: promoting quality products and services in the lagging rural regions of the European Union', *European Urban and Regional Studies*, 5(4): 329–41.

International Culinary Tourism Association (ICTA) (2007) *Culinary Tourism*. Online. Available: www.culinarytourism.org (accessed 1 April 2010).

Jamal, T., Everett, J. and Dann, G.M.S. (2003) 'Ecological rationalisation and performative resistance in natural area destinations', *Tourist Studies*, 3(2): 143–69.

Jarillo, J.C. (1988) 'On strategic networks', *Strategic Management Journal*, 9: 31–41.

Kneafsey, M. (2002) 'Tourism images and the construction of Celticity in Ireland and Brittany', in D.C. Harvey, R. Jones, N. McInroy and C. Milligan (eds) *Celtic Geographies: Old Culture, New Times.* London: Routledge: 123–38.

Kneafsey, M. and Ilbery, B. (2001) 'Regional images and the promotion of speciality food and drink products: initial explorations from the "West Country"', *Geography*, 86: 131–40.

Kotler, P., Hamlin, M.A., Rein, I. and Haider, D.H. (2002) *Marketing Asian Places.* Singapore: John Wiley & Sons.

Lee, K., Lee, T. and Lin, C. (2008) 'Channel strategy for food tourism industry', *Tourism and Hospitality Planning & Development*, 5(3): 247–56.

Lockie, S. and Kitto, S. (2000) 'Beyond the farm gate: production–consumption networks and agri-food research', *Sociologia Ruralis*, 40(1): 3–19.

Long, L. (2004) *Culinary Tourism.* Lexington, Ky: The University Press of Kentucky.

McGehee, N. (2007) 'An agritourism systems model: a Weberian perspective', *Journal of Sustainable Tourism*, 15(2): 111–24.

Meler, M. and Cerovi´c, Z. (2003) 'Food marketing in the function of tourist product development', *British Food Journal*, 105(3): 175–92.

Miles, R.E. and Snow, C.C. (1986) 'Organizations: new concepts for new forms', *California Management Review*, 28: 62–73.

Montanari, A. (2009) 'Culinary tourism as a tool for regional re-equilibrium', *European Planning Studies*, 17(10): 1463–83.

Murdoch, J. and Miele, M. (1999) 'Back to nature: changing worlds of production in the food sector', *Sociologia Ruralis*, 39(4): 465–83.

Nonaka, I., and Takeuchi, H. (1995) *The Knowledge Creating Company: How Japanese Companies Create the Dynamics of Innovation.* New York and Oxford: Oxford University Press.

Oakes, T. (1999) 'Eating the food of the ancestors: place, tradition, and tourism in a Chinese frontier river town', *Ecumene*, 6(2): 123–45.

Okumus, B., Okumus, F. and McKercher, B. (2007) 'Incorporating local and international cuisines in the marketing of tourism destinations: the cases of Hong Kong and Turkey', *Tourism Management*, 28(1): 253–61.

Pechlaner, H. and Tschurtschenthaler, P. (2002) 'Tourism policy, tourism organizations and change management in Alpine regions and destinations – a European perspective', *Current Issues in Tourism*, 6: 508–39.

Pechlaner, H., Abfalter, D. and Raich, F. (2002) 'Cross-border destination management systems in the Alpine region: the role of knowledge networks on the example of Alpnet', *Journal of Quality Assurance in Hospitality*, 3(3–4): 89–107.

Pile, S. (1997) 'Introduction: opposition, political identities and spaces of resistance', in S. Pile and M. Keith (eds) *Geographies of Resistance*. London: Routledge.

Policy Commission on the Future of Farming and Food (PCFFF) (2002) *Farming and Food: A Sustainable Future*. Online. Available: http://archive.cabinetoffice.gov.uk/farming/pdf/PC%20Report2.pdf. (accessed 28 October 2006).

Porter, M.E. (1991) *Competitive Advantage: Creating and Sustaining Superior Performance*. New York: The Free Press.

Pretty, J.N. (2002) *Agri-Culture: Reconnecting People, Land and Nature*. London: Earthscan.

Round, J., Williams, C.C. and Rodgers, P. (2008) 'Everyday tactics and spaces of power: the role of informal economies in post-Soviet Ukraine', *Social and Cultural Geography*, 9(2): 171–85.

Rusher, K. (2003) 'The Bluff Oyster festival and regional economic development: festivals as culture commodified', In C.M. Hall, E. Sharples, R. Mitchell, N. Macionis and B. Cambourne (eds) *Food Tourism Around the World: Development, Management and Markets*. Oxford: Butterworth-Heinemann.

Sage, C. (2003) 'Social embeddedness and relations of regard: alternative "good food" networks in South West Ireland', *Journal of Rural Studies*, 19(1): 47–60.

Scarpato, R. (2002) 'Sustainable gastronomy as a tourist product', in G. Richards and A.-M. Hjalager (eds) *Tourism and Gastronomy*. London: Routledge.

Selwyn, T. (ed.) (1996) *The Tourist Image: Myths and Myth Making in Tourism*. London: Wiley.

Sharples, L. (2003) 'Food tourism in the Peak District National Park, England', in C.M. Hall, L. Sharples, R. Mitchell, N. Macionis and B. Cambourne (eds) *Food Tourism Around the World: Development, Management and Markets*. Oxford: Butterworth-Heinemann.

Sims, R. (2009) 'Food, place and authenticity: local food and the sustainable tourism experience', *Journal of Sustainable Tourism*, 17(3): 321–36.

Slocum, S. and Everett, S. (2010) 'Food tourism initiatives: resistance on the ground', in *Conference Proceedings of the Fourth International Conference on Sustainable Tourism*, July 2010. Southampton: WIT Press.

South West Strategy of Sustainable Farming and Food Steering Group (South West SSFFSG) (2004) *Making a Difference: The South West Delivery Plan for Sustainable Farming and Food*. Online. Available: www.gos.gov.uk/gosw/docs/246139/165816/2004_making_difference_delivery (accessed 15 September 2006).

Telfer, D. and Wall, G. (1996) 'Linkages between tourism and food production', *Annals of Tourism Research*, 23(3): 635–53.

Telfer, D. and Wall, G. (2000) 'Strengthening backward economic linkages: local food purchasing by three Indonesian hotels', *Tourism Geographies*, 2(4): 421–47.

Tideswell, C. and Faulkner, B. (2002) 'Multi-destination tourist travel: some preliminary findings on international visitors' exploration of Australia', *Tourism*, 50(2): 115–30.

Tregear, A. (2003) 'From Stilton to Vimto: using food history to re-think typical products in rural development', *Sociologia Ruralis*, 43(2): 91–107.

Turner, L. and Ash, J. (1975) *The Golden Hordes: International Tourism and Pleasure Periphery*. London: Constable.

van Westering, J. (1999) 'Heritage and gastronomy: the pursuits of the "new tourist."', *International Journal of Heritage Studies*, 5(2): 75–81.

Watson, J. (ed.) (1997) *Golden Arches East: McDonald's in East Asia*. Stanford, Calif.: Stanford University Press.

Weiermair, K. (2001) 'The growth of tourism enterprises', *Tourism Review*, 56(3/4): 17–25.

12 Sustainable winegrowing in New Zealand

Tim Baird and C. Michael Hall

Introduction

Although wine, like wine regions and businesses, is often promoted in terms of its environmental attributes, the reality is that winegrowing is an industrial process. In many cases winegrowing requires substantial chemical inputs, such as biocides and fertilisers, and is also responsible for emissions, including during the transport of wine from the vineyard to the retailers – what is sometimes referred to as 'wine miles' (Hall and Mitchell 2008). As a result, many wineries and wine regions are not only seeking to make their wine production more sustainable but are also looking to use sustainable practices as a point of differentiation in an otherwise congested and highly competitive market.

Following a review of some of the key issues associated with sustainable winegrowing, this chapter provides an overview of sustainable winegrowing in New Zealand at three different levels: first, the way in which New Zealand wine is positioned within the clean and green New Zealand brand and the reality of that positioning; second, the adoption of the sustainable winegrowing strategy within the New Zealand wine industry; third, the results of a survey of New Zealand wineries with respect to wine tourism and the nexus of sustainability, biosecurity, innovation, marketing, networks and cooperation. This chapter also notes the significance of sustainable winegrowing as part of the positioning of New Zealand wine in the international marketplace but suggests that substantial issues loom with respect to the broader adoption of sustainable practices.

Key issues within sustainable winegrowing

The concept of sustainability in viticulture and oenology, which are jointly described here as winegrowing, has been defined as 'growing and winemaking practices that are sensitive to the environment (environmentally sound), responsive to the needs and interests of society-at-large (socially equitable), and are economically feasible to implement and maintain' (California Sustainable Winegrowing Alliance 2001, as cited in Zucca *et al.* 2009: 190). Although Ohmart (2008a) writes of a synchronicity that can be achieved when the goals of sustainable winemaking practices are in tandem with both the local community and the natural environment, the development of sustainable winegrowing presents a number of challenges to existing practices within wine production and marketing (Hall and Mitchell 2008; Alonso and Liu 2012). Not only have there been changes made to production methods, but also the move towards sustainable practices within the wine industry has created several significant issues: first, the adoption, implementation and governance of these practices; second, how these sustainable practices are promoted in terms of brand positioning and competitive advantage; and, finally, whether sustainable winegrowing represents a pathway towards long-term economic viability for wineries.

Although designed to promote a unified industry-wide benchmark for vineyards, wineries and other wine businesses to strive to achieve in terms of sustainable practices, the adoption of initiatives such as industry-wide sustainability schemes are important as they can be used in the promotion not only of wine products but also of tourism-related ventures such as wine regions and wine trails (Kennedy 2009) that are of major marketing and retail importance for many wineries and wine brands. Yet the development of such ventures is dependent not only on the size and economics of individual wineries, but also on the ability of wineries to deal with the inherent risks born from engagement in tourism, including problems in terms of biosecurity (Hall 2003, 2005). As a number of vineyards and wine regions have experienced, the introduction and spread of diseases and vectors harmful to viticulture such as phylloxera and Pierce's disease can potentially destroy a vineyard, financially if not biologically.

The recognition of the importance of sustainability issues occurs on multiple levels both internal and external to the winery concerned (Marshall *et al.* 2005; Gabzdylova *et al.* 2009; Alonso and Lin 2012). First, stakeholders perceive sustainability as an important source of competitive advantage which can be translated into a positive, environmentally conscious image in the mind of the consumer (Kennedy 2009), resulting in increased sales and brand loyalty (Sen *et al.* 2006). Second, wine producers face an extremely competitive business environment given a decline in per capita wine consumption, the increased internationalisation of wine sales, and shifts in consumer taste (Hall and Mitchell 2008). For example, in a domestic market of around 4 million people the New Zealand wine industry has become increasingly crowded with 511 wineries registered in *The Australian and New Zealand Wine Directory* in 2009 (Winetitles 2009) as compared to 193 in 1995 (Hall 1996).

The adoption of sustainable practices as a point of differentiation among wineries appears to be a growing trend (Flint and Golicic 2009; Atkin *et al.* 2011; Carmichael and Senese 2012). The way in which the end product reaches consumers has become important, given environmental issues such as carbon emissions and food miles created in the journey from the vineyard to final consumption (Kennedy 2009). Attracting wine tourism via the promotion of sustainable methods of onsite viticultural production is another path which is being used to pursue competitive advantage. However, this pursuit, although undertaken in the interests of protecting the immediate environment, does not always marry with the political and ecological realities of sustainability on a global scale

(Hall 2010b). Therefore, to be truly sustainable, winegrowing needs to understand the environmental, social and economic effects of both its supply chain and its distribution channels as well as the perceptions of the value of sustainable approaches within the wine industry.

In their study of sustainable viticulture practices in California, Zucca *et al.* (2009) contend that it appeared to be the larger wineries that had the resources and financial means to pursue their locally based sustainability programme. Their study indicated that there appeared to be a slower rate of adoption by smaller vineyards that were less financially empowered (Zucca *et al.* 2009). Carmichael and Senese (2012) point out in their study of two contrasting Canadian wine regions (the Niagara Peninsula of Ontario and the Okanagan Valley of British Columbia) that adoption of sustainable practices is also dictated by the stage of business development of each individual winery. This scenario suggests what Wall (1997) described as a delicate balancing act: a balance that creates synergy between the supply and demand forces at work in order to maintain both a competitive and viable market position while addressing both political and ecological concerns (Zucca *et al.* 2009; Hall 2010b; Carmichael and Senese 2012). Indeed, Sinha and Akoorie (2010) argue that New Zealand wineries that are committed to an export orientation are more likely to adopt environmental practices, and it is not institutional pressure that forces these organisations to do so.

The positioning of New Zealand wine within the national brand

The somewhat idealistic personification of the New Zealand national brand with emphasis placed on the three traits of clean, green and pure (Hall 2010a; Marshall *et al.* 2010) has been criticised as being at odds with the overseas perception of New Zealand, including its wine exports (Beverland and Lindgreen 2002; Clayton and Stevens 2007; Cumming 2010). Criticism has been levelled particularly in terms of the food miles involved in such exports (Gabzdylova *et al.* 2009; Kennedy 2009; Kemp *et al.* 2010). As an early adopter of the Brand New Zealand strategy (Spratt 2010), New Zealand wine has been marketed internationally as being born of an industry that is both sustainable and innovative (Kennedy 2009). On the surface the image portrayed is one where industry-wide sustainability initiatives are readily accepted and incorporated into wine production, with New Zealand Winegrowers (2011: 21) claiming in their 2011 annual report that 'over 95% of our vineyard area and wine production is now participating in this Sustainable Winegrowing programme'. New Zealand Winegrowers (2011: 21) also state:

> Over the last year we have conducted research in our main markets, and have had conversations throughout the value chain. We have asked them what their concerns are with respect to sustainability, how we rate, and how they would like to learn more about what we do. They tell us we need to provide a layered message; building simple awareness with consumers,

providing assurance to our customers that we won't let their brand down, and that it must be backed up with evidence.

These claims raise important issues as to where the current position of New Zealand wine in the context of sustainability really lies; if such assertions were taken at face value, then it would appear to suggest that the introduction of sustainable practices within the New Zealand wine industry has been without problems. However, a second glance at this image appears to reveal significant problems in measuring up to the reality that this brand position dictates.

Sustainable winegrowing initiatives in New Zealand

The evolution of industry-focused initiatives to promote sustainable winegrowing within the New Zealand wine industry on a systematic basis began in 1995 with the development of the Sustainable Winegrowing New Zealand (SWNZ) organisation (SWNZ 2010). The SWNZ scheme was first introduced commercially in 1997 with the expectation that it would be adopted by winegrowers from all grape-growing regions (SWNZ 2010), and, coupled with the introduction of winery standards in 2002 (NZ Wine 2010), aimed to underline an industry-wide commitment to sustainable production practices and techniques. The goal of this initiative was to have full participation in the scheme by all New Zealand winegrowers by 2012, and steps to ensure this have been taken by making SWNZ membership mandatory for all wineries if they wish to take part in trade shows and export their products under the Wine New Zealand banner (SWNZ 2010). Enforcement is also undertaken through external auditing of sustainable practices by SWNZ-appointed agents (NZ Wine 2010).

The adoption of sustainable winegrowing strategies within the New Zealand wine industry

SWNZ seeks to provide a best-practice model which wineries can utilise to benchmark their environmental practices (SWNZ 2010). This should provide a greater degree of quality during all stages of production and, by recognising that sustainability is also an important issue to the end consumer, it should positively influence decisions to buy wine produced in New Zealand (SWNZ 2010). The SWNZ manifesto (NZ Wine 2010) encompasses five core strategies which are designed to provide benefits to all members of the scheme:

1   provide a framework for viticultural and winemaking practices that protect the environment while efficiently and economically producing premium wine grapes and wine;
2   implement a programme of continual improvement to ensure companies operate with the goal of improving their operational practices;
3   provide a platform for technology transfer so that companies are kept up to date regarding any new technology and its application;

4   create an external audit structure that has integrity and rigour to comply with market expectations;

5   give winegrowers the opportunity to be a part of a positive future and meet the New Zealand wine industry goal of 100 per cent of grape growers and winemakers operating under approved, independently audited, sustainability programmes.

As membership of the SWNZ scheme is mandatory for all New Zealand wineries (SWNZ 2010), then applying such a framework to the New Zealand wine industry creates the potential for division should wineries choose to reject the aims of the scheme altogether. Although as of 2011 the number of sustainable winegrowing vineyards exceeds the number of grape growers (New Zealand Winegrowers) by the year ending June 2009 only 135 wineries, representing 21 per cent of New Zealand wineries (Table 12.1), had actually become members of the sustainable winegrowing scheme. Commitment to carbon-neutral wine exports remained the focus of only a few, high-profile wineries (NZ Wine 2010), so based on this evidence alone it would appear that there are some significant issues at play in the adoption of a sustainable winegrowing approach. Furthermore, SWNZ is limited to physical wine production elements; other issues such as the brand positioning of wine products, the implications of wine tourism and biosecurity, and wine miles are not included.

The relationship between biosecurity and sustainability in the New Zealand wine industry

The need to incorporate biosecurity elements into the framework of sustainability programmes in New Zealand has been suggested by Renton *et al.* (2009) who argue that accessible biosecurity information needs to be provided to winegrowers in order to protect vineyards from disease and pests. Exploration of the relationship between biosecurity and sustainable wine tourism in New Zealand was first undertaken by Hall (2003). Key themes that have emerged within the area of wine tourism in relation to biosecurity and invasive species concern the level of awareness of potential biosecurity risks, what strategies are in place to deal with any such occurrences, and where wineries are able to turn in order to gain the information required to deal with and contain any problems that could

Table 12.1 Membership of SWNZ

	2004	2005	2006	2007	2008	2009
Vineyards	403	431	432	457	683	1,244
Total wineries	463	516	530	543	585	643
Member wineries	30	51	53	59	77	135
% membership	6.5	9.9	10	10.9	13.2	21

Source: derived from New Zealand Winegrowers (2009).

potentially arise as a result of a breach of biosecurity protocols. It has been noted that there is a limited awareness of biosecurity risks at the level of the wine tourist who comes into the country from a foreign destination (Hall 2003), while an awareness of the same risks has been recognised as being important by those who are at the stakeholder level within the wine industry (Wilkins and Hall 2001; Hall 2005). However, this has tended to be perceived as a national level issue rather than one to be dealt with at the vineyard scale.

Christensen *et al.* (2004) found that only 6 per cent of respondents to the New Zealand National Wineries' Survey conducted in 2003 had an active biosecurity strategy in place; this in itself provides a cause for alarm. International recognition of the importance of strict biosecurity protocols and the importance of a high degree of information sharing regarding potential biosecurity risks within wine production was noted by Poitras and Getz (2006) in their study of wine tourism in Oliver, British Columbia. Protection of the natural environment from biosecurity risks that could be introduced by visitor traffic onsite was seen by stakeholders as paramount to any long-term strategies to promote sustainability initiatives (Poitras and Getz 2006).

Innovation in the context of the New Zealand wine industry sustainability initiatives

A further important element of sustainability is the capacity for businesses and organisations to innovate with respect to the mitigation of and adaptation to environmental change (Gössling *et al.* 2009). Innovation is defined as being 'the development or introduction of any new or significantly improved activity' (OECD and Statistical Office of European Communities 2005) undertaken by participants, and encompasses any products, processes and methods that may first have been developed by a particular organisation and since been adopted by others (OECD and Statistical Office of European Communities 2005). Innovation is increasingly seen as an important element of sustainability, including with respect to the adaptation to and mitigation of climate change. The OECD and Statistical Office of European Communities (2005) definition of innovation suggests a potential dilemma for the New Zealand wine industry. On one hand, you have the approach taken within the SWNZ scheme whereby the sustainable processes methods and products produced must meet a predetermined criterion dictated by this organisation (SWNZ 2010), while on the other hand there are many wineries which predate the introduction of SWNZ in 1995 (SWNZ 2010), and arguably have already created their own innovations within the context of this definition without external intervention. Pickersgill and Edwards (2005: 8) remark that 'innovation is a complex, multiple dimensional process that involves scientific and technical expertise, technical and educational infrastructure, integrated product and supplier networks and effective management and marketing strategies and government support'. Treatment of this complexity needs to be addressed at all levels of governance (Curtain 2004) within the myriad of sectors that constitute the New Zealand wine industry in order to ensure the successful implementation of innovative processes and techniques.

Extant literature in the field of innovation has pointed towards four main categories that exist: product and process innovations with the addition of organisational and marketing innovations (OECD and Statistical Office of European Communities 2005). Product innovations include significantly improved good and services, and have been noted as also encompassing the activities that tourists may experience and participate in when visiting destinations (Sørenson 2001; Stamboulis and Skayannis 2003; Hall 2009). In the context of sustainable winemaking, this notion applies to two dimensions: first, wine tourists who are attracted to wineries because the process and production methods used on site fit within their political ideology; second, the end consumer who purchases a particular brand of wine because it is manufactured using sustainable methods.

Process innovations are the new or improved methods of production or delivery within an organisation that aim to improve efficiency and flow (OECD and Statistical Office of European Communities 2005; Hjalager 2009). These are associated primarily with the implementation of new technologies designed to achieve specific managerial objectives (Yuan *et al.* 2006; Ohmart 2008b; Bessant *et al.* 2009; Giuliani *et al.* 2011). Organisational innovations are deemed to be those which improve existing business practices, workplace organisation or relations external to the firm (OECD and Statistical Office of European Communities 2005). Innovations at the organisational level can signal significant changes to existing strategies, structures and routines (Statistics New Zealand 2007), and as such serve to develop the existing knowledge base within an organisation (Hall and Williams 2008; Hall 2009). Finally, marketing innovations are any new or significantly improved marketing methods that may have been adopted by the organisation (OECD and Statistical Office of European Communities 2005) in order either to increase market share or to facilitate entry into new markets.

Method

The 2010 New Zealand National Wineries' Survey was designed to facilitate the collection of information about wine tourism in New Zealand from the wineries' perspective. The sample population was derived from all New Zealand wineries registered in *The 2009 Australian and New Zealand Wine Industry Directory* (Winetitles 2009) and it was the third survey of its type to be undertaken as part of a longitudinal study.

Survey design

Based on the template provided by the two previous New Zealand National Wineries' Surveys (Hall and Johnson 1998; Christensen *et al.* 2004), survey questions included those created by the researchers involved, those posed by previous New Zealand studies (Reid 1990), and international studies (Golledge and Maddern 1994; Dodd and Bigotte 1995; Maddern and Golledge 1996; Macionis

1997). A question regarding biosecurity was added to the second New Zealand National Wineries' Survey (Christensen *et al.* 2004), and this was expanded into a series of questions that make up a section dedicated solely to biosecurity issues in the 2010 New Zealand National Wineries' Survey. The current New Zealand wine industry stance towards sustainable practices as a form of innovation was introduced as a new section in the 2010 New Zealand National Wineries' Survey which utilised the OECD and Statistical Office of European Communities (2005) framework as a basis for the questions. In addition, questions based on those in the *Innovation in New Zealand* survey (Statistics New Zealand 2007) were used in order to provide a joint benchmark between the wine industry and other agricultural-based industries and the tourism sector.

The 2010 New Zealand National Wineries' Survey was divided into seven main sections. The first two sections focused on the winery and visitor profiles. This was then followed by sections dedicated to biosecurity and sustainability, before innovation in the New Zealand wine tourism industry was examined. The final section which focused on tourism and marketing led into a set of questions that were designed to gather respondent contact information. Questions in the 2010 survey were similar to those asked in the 1997 and 2003 surveys with some modifications designed to gather updated information regarding biosecurity issues. Further adaptations were made based on the results of previous New Zealand wine tourism research (Hall and Johnson 1998; Hall *et al.* 2000; Mitchell and Hall 2001a, 2001b; Christensen *et al.* 2004).

Source data

The 2010 survey utilised primary data obtained from participants who represent each of the 511 vineyards located within New Zealand as per publicly available winery listings published in *The 2009 Australian and New Zealand Wine Industry Directory* (Winetitles 2009) who initially received the survey via email (491 wineries) or by post (20 wineries). It was originally envisaged that conducting the survey by email for a majority of the participants would yield a greater response rate than previous New Zealand national wineries' surveys had been able to obtain. This particular approach to data collection yielded an unsatisfactory response rate initially (with only 43 responses) as respondents appeared unwilling to provide industry-sensitive information via an online survey. To counter this, a further postal mail to all wineries which had not yet responded to the online survey was conducted, and this yielded a far more successful response rate: a further 82 wineries responded, raising the response rate to 125 wineries (25 per cent) in total. Of these 125 wineries, 22 responded that they had in fact gone out of business since the publication of *The 2009 Australian and New Zealand Wine Industry Directory* (Winetitles 2009) but as these were still judged as valid responses, these surveys were included in the overall response rate. The remaining 103 wineries which responded then provided the data that this study was based upon. Prior response rates to the 1997 survey obtained 111 responses out of 270 producers, giving a response rate of 41.1 per cent (Hall and Johnson

1998), while the second survey conducted in 2003 achieved a response rate of 121 usable responses out of the 419 wineries surveyed, resulting in a response rate of 28.9 per cent. This compares favourably with other business surveys conducted within the New Zealand wine industry (Christensen *et al.* 2004). For example, in the 2009 New Zealand wine industry benchmarking survey by Deloitte (2010) survey questionnaires were sent to over 580 members of New Zealand Winegrowers; they had 32 respondents, a response rate of less than 6 per cent (although Deloitte (2010) did note that survey participants accounted for approximately 19 per cent of the New Zealand wine industry by litres of case wine produced and 31 per cent by export sales revenue generated for the year 2009).

In the 2010 New Zealand Wineries survey, participants were asked a series of questions related to sustainability practices. The first set of questions employed a five-point Likert scale (1 = Strongly disagree, 5 = Strongly agree) and asked how important participants believed sustainability practices were for the New Zealand wine industry, and whether any sustainability practices utilised on site provided their winery with an important source of competitive advantage. Participants were then asked what the reasons were for the sustainability practices that they had chosen to employ. Nine options were presented: to increase revenue, to reduce costs, to increase market share, to reduce energy consumption or to reduce environmental impact. Also included in the options listed were to establish and/or exploit market opportunities, to improve productivity or to attract visitors to their particular winery. A final option was provided where participants could list any other reasons which fell outside these options. Further questions were added to determine what type of relationship winegrowers had with SWNZ, and also asked whether participants thought that biosecurity should be part of the overall SWNZ scheme.

A set of environmentally based questions regarding innovation in terms of changes to operational methods through the adoption of sustainable practices were adapted from the *Innovation in New Zealand* study (Statistics New Zealand 2007) which contained questions based on innovation measures set by the OECD and Statistical Office of European Communities (2005). Participants were asked the reasons for the sustainability practices that they had chosen to employ. Nine options were presented in the same fashion as in the previous section regarding sustainability. Applying these innovation measures as set out by the OECD and Statistical Office of European Communities (2005) framework to the New Zealand wine industry provided an opportunity to benchmark attitudes towards innovation and provided the basis for comparison with past innovation studies conducted within the New Zealand agricultural sector towards sustainable practices.

Sustainability

Over half of respondents either agreed or strongly agreed that sustainability practices are important for the New Zealand wine industry. Of respondents, 19.4

Table 12.2 Belief in importance of sustainability practices (%)

Statement	Strongly disagree	Disagree	Unsure	Agree	Strongly agree
Sustainability practices are important for the New Zealand wine industry	7.5	18.4	19.4	33.0	21.4
Sustainability provides an important source of competitive advantage	16.5	38.8	16.5	17.5	10.7

per cent were unsure about the importance of such practices, while over a quarter of respondents either disagreed or strongly disagreed that sustainability practices were important (Table 12.2). In contrast to the position of Wine New Zealand, over half of respondents did not believe that sustainability practices provided wineries with a source of competitive advantage.

Over half (56.3 per cent) of respondents reported that their winery was an accredited member of Sustainable Wineries New Zealand, while the remainder did not have accredited membership of the SWNZ scheme. In terms of the SWNZ scheme, 75 respondents (62.1 per cent) were already members. Eighteen respondents (15.5 per cent) had contact as required with SWNZ, while a further 18 (15.5 per cent) had no relationship at all with SWNZ. Seven respondents (5.8 per cent) used cooperative marketing or promotion instead of the SWNZ scheme.

An overwhelming majority of 88.3 per cent of respondents stated that they did not choose to employ sustainability practices to increase revenue, while 70.9 per cent responded that they did not choose to employ sustainability practices to reduce costs. Instead, the focus was on the reduction of environmental impact (60.2 per cent) and, to a lesser extent, the reduction of energy consumption (32 per cent) (Table 12.3). Other reasons that were given by respondents for the adoption of sustainable practices included soil health, 'company conscience', the fact that SWNZ membership was compulsory, and also that it was mandatory to

Table 12.3 Reasons for winery choosing to employ sustainability practices (%)

Reason	Yes	No
To increase revenue	11.7	88.3
To reduce costs	29.1	70.9
To increase market share	16.5	83.5
To reduce energy consumption	32.0	68.0
To reduce environmental impact	60.2	39.8
To establish/or exploit new market opportunities	19.4	80.6
To improve productivity	21.4	78.6
To attract visitors to my winery	12.6	87.4
Other	29.1	70.9

be a member of SWNZ if wineries wanted to enter wine shows. Respondents also stated that they felt that SWNZ membership had no real benefit to them, and one respondent even went as far as to refer to sustainability as 'paper pushing B.S.'.

Discussion

Sustainable practices in the New Zealand wine industry

Based on the findings from the 2010 New Zealand National Wineries Survey, it appears that there is some disagreement within the New Zealand wine industry as to whether there is any real value to be gained from the adoption of the SWNZ scheme, and this is underlined by the indifferent attitude shown towards sustainable methods of production. There is a distinct division in terms of agreement over the importance of sustainability practices, which runs counter to one of the main aims of SWNZ: that is, to implement a model of best practice for all wineries to use as a benchmark (SWNZ 2010). If there is little or no perceived advantage to be gained when viewed from the supply-side perspective in terms of competitive advantage (38.8 per cent disagreed that sustainable methods provided this in this survey), then in order to achieve a high rate of adoption of the scheme SWNZ must address this gap.

Institutional pressures are not the sole significant force at play here. Sinha and Akoorie (2010) suggest that other factors such as the export orientation of wineries are also important, as the end consumer places value on how many food miles a product that is supposedly sustainable has clocked up in reality, while Zucca *et al.* (2009) cite winery size, financial means and resource availability as critical factors in the adoption of sustainable practices. This would suggest that adoption of sustainable practices by New Zealand wineries is inhibited by SWNZ's approach where wineries are treated in a somewhat homogenous manner regardless of size, financial means and stage of business development (see also Carmichael and Senese 2012); as it disregards the individualistic nature of those wineries which SWNZ is aiming to attract, it would seem that full industry adoption of the SWNZ scheme in 2012 could be asking for the impossible.

Leading reasons for the employment of sustainable methods were found to be the reduction of environmental impacts, the reduction of costs and the improvement of productivity. Attracting wine tourists, and in turn also seeking to increase revenue through openly advocating sustainability, were not viewed by wineries as motivating factors to adopt these methods, which disputes the notion that innovative practices are an important dimension to the tourist destination experience (Sørenson 2001; Stamboulis and Skayannis 2003).

Only 56.3 per cent of wineries surveyed in the 2010 New Zealand National Wineries Survey stated that they were accredited members of SWNZ; this figure itself speaks volumes about the seeming disparity between the vision of SWNZ where all wineries were to be participants of this scheme by 2012, and the reality that some wineries either simply appear not to see any true value being gained through accreditation or appear to mistrust the ability of SWNZ to be able to follow through on delivering the strategic intent on which this scheme is based. This disparity is further increased by the fact that 15.5 per cent of wineries state that their only relationship with SWNZ is when it is required; this does not bode well in the context of attracting more wineries to adopt the aims of the scheme; this lack of confidence is also reflected by only 5.8 per cent of respondents considering it beneficial to have SWNZ involved in terms of cooperative marketing or promotion; this is embarrassing to say the least when the promotion of sustainable methods of production is noted as being attractive to the success of wineries with a strong export orientation (Sen *et al.* 2006; Sinha and Akoorie 2010). With several respondents highlighting the fact that membership of the SWNZ scheme is now mandatory if wineries wish to participate in events such as trade shows or engage in exporting their products, it appears that there exists resistance towards the motives of SWNZ within some sectors of the New Zealand wine industry.

Biosecurity and sustainable winemaking in New Zealand

Significant issues with respect to sustainability are also seen in terms of biosecurity in New Zealand wineries. Almost a third of respondents (31.1 per cent) allowed visitors to wander at their leisure through the vines at their winery. When asked whether their vineyard had biosecurity measures in place for wine tourists, 22.3 per cent of respondents believed that the current measures that they employed were adequate. Measures cited by respondents were the exclusion of cars, control of visitor access, and warning notices. Some areas that were vulnerable to phylloxera were fenced off while other wineries refuse to allow visitors who have visited other vineyards onto their vineyard. Footwear checks, education, good management and visual or verbal warnings were also utilised.

When asked whether the current level of information received from government agencies was adequate, over half of the respondents (51.5 per cent) replied that they felt unsure that the current level of information available was adequate. Another 25.2 per cent believed that the information currently received regarding biosecurity threats was inadequate, while only 9.7 per cent of respondents agreed that government agencies were providing an adequate level of information to their winery. Almost half of the respondents surveyed (48.5 per cent) were unsure as to whether they had effective strategies in place at their vineyards to deal with biosecurity threats and only 24.3 per cent felt that the current strategies that they were employing would be effective. Nevertheless, the majority of respondents (58.3 per cent) felt that there was no need to include a biosecurity component as part of the SWNZ scheme.

The remnant of good news here with respect to sustainability is that the 23 per cent of wineries which have measures in place has grown substantially from only 6 per cent found in the previous 2003 New Zealand National Wineries Survey (Christensen *et al.* 2004). These figures highlight a gap in the knowledge of wineries of the potential dangers due to lack of adequate information sharing by those responsible for the governance of biosecurity protocols (Hall 2003; Renton *et al.* 2009). Information accessibility needs to be improved and biosecurity protocols standardised, otherwise the New Zealand wine industry will run the risk of being seriously affected by potential disease outbreaks. With almost a third of wineries reporting that visitors were able to wander freely among the vines, it appears that the attitude of wineries towards risk mitigation requires more caution. As Poitras and Getz (2006) point out, lack of protection of the natural environment can effectively shatter any long-term strategies that wineries have in place with regard to sustainability initiatives, no matter how honourable the motivations behind such strategies may be.

The area of greatest concern appears to be the high level of uncertainty (48.5 per cent) among respondents as to whether they currently had an effective strategy in place to deal with potential biosecurity threats. Of respondents, 19.4 per cent deem current strategies in this area to be ineffective and 31.1 per cent stated that they received no information at all from any organisation charged with the governance of sustainable practices. Clearly this shows a significant gap in information sharing that needs to be addressed. Nevertheless, this situation is only likely to continue given that 58.3 per cent of the wineries surveyed believed that there was no need for a biosecurity component in the SWNZ scheme. Clearly, encouraging adoption of the SWNZ scheme by New Zealand wineries could in fact present a prime opportunity to improve the poor levels of information sharing with regard to biosecurity threats (Hall 2003). Promoting SWNZ as a quality source of information regarding biosecurity protocols could give the scheme added value, and in turn attract a greater rate of adoption of the scheme.

Sustainable innovation

Resistance towards innovation through the improvement of operational processes was also found within the New Zealand wine industry, with only 22.3 per cent of respondents actively stating that they had introduced new or significantly improved operational processes which include sustainable production methods. Of those who had changed their methods of production, 17.5 per cent had developed their own innovative methods, while 5.8 per cent had done so in partnership with other businesses. This negative attitude towards innovative practices in sectors of the New Zealand wine industry could also be found in figures given for the percentage of sales that came as a result of new or significantly improved goods or services, with 37.9 per cent of respondents stating that innovative practices, if adopted, had actually had no effect on sales whatsoever. Only 13.6 per cent of wineries surveyed believed that innovations introduced had actually been responsible for 10 per cent or less of their overall sales.

The underlying theme regarding innovation which this survey revealed was that unless there was a proven track record for an innovative process which could enhance the managerial and organisational objectives of the wineries involved (OECD and Statistical Office of European Communities 2005; Yuan *et al.* 2006), or provide more efficient organisational and marketing objectives through product innovations (OECD and Statistical Office of European Communities 2005; Hjalager 2009), then New Zealand wineries tended to avoid innovation to a degree. This could serve to explain why there appears to be such a cautious approach in the industry towards the adoption of sustainable methods of wine production. This could be combated through SWNZ-introduced agent assistance (Bessant *et al.* 2009) programmes relating to sustainable methods. Such an initiative could address this gap in innovation capability in the New Zealand wine industry where 'firms may have a general awareness of the potential of the innovation on offer but do not see its relevance or applicability to them' (Bessant *et al.* 2009: 7).

Conclusion

From the evidence presented in this chapter it is apparent that there are some significant issues at play in the New Zealand wine industry in terms of the adoption of sustainable winegrowing methods. There appears to be a very real risk that even with the full implementation of the SWNZ scheme in 2012 there will be a considerable backlash from some wineries towards the scheme. This could serve to create a division within the industry itself as the policies advocated by SWNZ are implemented by some but rejected by others. This also runs counter to one of the strategic aims of SWNZ – to have all New Zealand wineries participating in this scheme. It appears from the findings presented here that the implementation of SWNZ has actually alienated sections of the New Zealand wine industry, and this appears to place a question mark over whether this scheme is in keeping with the political, financial and ecological context that the New Zealand wine industry currently inhabits.

The New Zealand wine industry is not immune from problems experienced by other international wine regions, and the relative isolation of New Zealand is not enough to offer barriers against disease. This is especially important given that the success and future growth of the New Zealand wine industry in terms of exports and attracting visitor traffic appear strongly dependent on the position of New Zealand wine as a sustainable product. Such brand positioning not only relies on the overall national branding strategy (Hall 2010a) organisations which govern the New Zealand wine industry. The need for a unified approach in terms of sustainable winegrowing has also been noted by Alonso and Liu (2012) in a longitudinal study into similar sustainable winegrowing arrangements in the Spanish Canary Islands. In a statement that could equally be applicable to the situation that New Zealand winegrowers currently face, Alonso and Liu (2012: 13) warn that 'in times of fierce competition from different tourist destinations, different countries/regions producing quality (and affordable) wines ... the importance for tourist and wine regions [is] to make concerted efforts and work towards sustainability (economic, environmental, and social)'. This statement suggests that initiative and innovation not only need to intersect in a unified fashion in order to produce success, but must do so in a way that is also realistic for the very constituents (in the case of this chapter the New Zealand wine industry) to which sustainable winegrowing programmes are aimed.

Acknowledgement

The assistance of the University of Canterbury Summer Scholarship Scheme in the initiation of the third national wine tourism survey research project is gratefully acknowledged.

References

Alonso, A.D. (2010) 'How "green" are the small wineries? Western Australia's case', *British Food Journal*, 112(2): 155–70.

Alonso, A.D. and Liu, Y. (2012) 'Old wine region, new concept and sustainable development: winery entrepreneurs' perceived benefits from wine tourism on Spain's Canary Islands', *Journal of Sustainable Tourism*, 20: 1–19.

Atkin, T., Gilinsky Jr., A. and Newton, S.K. (2011) 'Sustainability in the wine industry: altering the competitive landscape?', paper presented at the 6th AWBR International Conference, Bordeaux Management School, France, 9–10 June.

Bessant, J., Tsekouras, G. and Rush, H. (2009) 'Getting the tail to wag: developing innovations capability in SMEs', paper presented at CI Net 2009, Brisbane, Australia, 6–8 September.

Beverland, M. and Lindgreen, A. (2002) 'Using country of origin in strategy: the importance of context and strategic action', *Journal of Brand Management*, 10(2): 147–67.

Carmichael, B.A. and Senese, D.M. (2012) 'Competitiveness and sustainability in wine tourism regions: the application of a stage model of destination development to two Canadian wine regions', in P.H. Dougherty (ed.), *The Geography of Wine: Regions, Terroir and Techniques*, New York: Springer.

Christensen, D., Hall, C.M. and Mitchell, R. (2004) 'The 2003 New Zealand wineries' survey', in C. Cooper, C. Arcodia, D. Soinet and M. Whitford (eds), *Creating Tourism Knowledge, 14th International Research Conference of Australian University Tourism and Hospitality Education, Book of Abstracts*, Brisbane: University of Queensland.

Clayton, G. and Stevens, N. (2007) '"False idol" economy: the New Zealand wine industry', *International Journal of Systems Applications, Engineering and Development*, 3(1): 69–73.

Cumming, G. (2010) New Zealand: 100 per cent pure hype. *The New Zealand Herald*. 6 January. Online. Available: www.nzherald.co.nz/nz/news/article.cfm?c_id=1&objectid=10618678 (accessed 20 January 2012).

Curtain, R. (2004) *Vocational Education and Training, Innovation and Globalisation*, Adelaide: NCVER.

Deloitte (2010) *Vintage 2009 New Zealand Wine Industry Benchmarking Survey*. Auckland: Deloitte and New Zealand Winegrowers.

Dodd, T.H. and Bigotte, V. (1995) *Visitors to Texas Wineries: Their Demographic Characteristics and Purchasing Behaviour*, Lubbock, Tex.: Texas Wine Marketing Research Institute.

Flint, D.J. and Golicic, S.L. (2009) 'Searching for competitive advantage through sustainability: a qualitative study in the New Zealand wine industry', *International Journal of Physical Distribution and Logistics Management*, 39(10): 841–60.

Gabzdylova, B., Raffensperger, J.F. and Castka, P. (2009) 'Sustainability in the New Zealand wine industry: drivers, stakeholders and practices', *Journal of Cleaner Production*, 17: 992–8.

Giuliani, E., Morrison, A. and Rabellotti, R. (eds) (2011) *Innovation and Technological Catch-Up: The Changing Geography of Wine Production*, Aldershot: Edward Elgar.

Golledge, S. and Maddern, C. (1994) *A Survey of Tourism Activity at Victorian Wineries*, Melbourne: Victorian Wineries Tourism Council.

Gössling, S., Hall, C.M. and Weaver, D. (eds) (2009) *Sustainable Tourism Futures: Perspectives on Systems, Restructuring and Innovations*, New York: Routledge.

Hall, C.M. (1996) 'Wine tourism in New Zealand', in J. Higham (ed.), *Proceedings of Tourism Down Under II: A Tourism Research Conference*, Dunedin: University of Otago.

Hall, C.M. (2003) 'Biosecurity and wine tourism: is a vineyard a farm?', *Journal of Wine Research*, 14(2–3): 121–6.

Hall, C.M. (2005) 'Biosecurity and wine tourism', *Tourism Management*, 26(6): 931–8.

Hall, C.M. (2009) 'Innovation and tourism policy in Australia and New Zealand: never the twain shall meet?', *Journal of Policy Research in Tourism, Leisure and Events*, 1(1): 2–18.

Hall, C.M. (2010a) 'Tourism destination branding and its effects on national branding strategies: brand New Zealand, clean and green but is it smart?', *European Journal of Tourism, Hospitality and Recreation*, 1(1): 68–89.

Hall, C.M. (2010b) 'Changing paradigms and global change: from sustainable to steady-state tourism', *Tourism Recreation Research*, 35(2): 131–43.

Hall, C.M. and Johnson, G. (1998) 'Wine and food tourism in New Zealand: difficulties in the creation of sustainable tourism business networks', in D. Hall and L. O'Hanlon (eds), *Rural Tourism Management: Sustainable Options, Conference Proceedings*, Ayr: Scottish Agricultural College.

Hall, C.M. and Mitchell, R. (2008) *Wine Marketing*, Oxford: Butterworth-Heinemann.

Hall, C.M. and Williams, A.M. (2008) *Tourism and Innovation*, London: Routledge.

Hall, C.M., Johnson, G., Cambourne, B., Macionis, N., Mitchell, R.D. and Sharples, E. (2000) 'Wine tourism: an introduction', in C.M. Hall, E. Sharples, B. Cambourne and N. Macionis (eds), *Wine Tourism Around the World*, Oxford: Butterworth-Heinemann.

Hjalager, A.M. (2009) 'A review of innovation research in tourism', *Tourism Management*, 31(1): 1–12.

Kemp, K., Insch, A., Holdsworth, D.K. and Knight, J.G. (2010) 'Food miles: do UK consumers actually care?', *Food Policy*, 35(6): 504–13.

Kennedy, C. (2009) The greenest grape: New Zealand's commitment to sustainable winegrowing. Online. Available: http://lehigh.edu/~incntr/publications/documents/GreeGrape.pdf (accessed 20 January 2012).

Macionis, N. (1997) 'Wine tourism in Australia: emergence, development and critical issues', unpublished Master's thesis, University of Canberra.

Maddern, C. and Golledge, S. (1996) *Victorian Wineries Tourism Council Cellar Door Survey, Final Report May 1996*, Melbourne: Victorian Wineries Tourism Council.

Marshall, R.S., Cordano, M. and Silverman, M. (2005) 'Exploring individual and institutional drivers of proactive environmentalism in the US wine industry', *Business Strategy and the Environment*, 14: 1–20.

Marshall, R.S., Akoorie, M.E., Hamann, R. and Sinha, P. (2010) 'Environmental practices in the wine industry: an empirical application of the theory of reasoned action and stakeholder theory in the United States and New Zealand', *Journal of World Business*, 45(4): 405–14.

Mitchell, R.D. and Hall, C.M. (2001a) 'Wine at home: self ascribed wine knowledge and the wine behaviour of New Zealand winery visitors', *Australian and New Zealand Wine Industry Journal*, 16(6): 115–22.

Mitchell, R.D. and Hall, C.M. (2001b) 'Lifestyle behaviours of New Zealand winery visitors: wine club activities, wine cellars and place of purchase', *International Journal of Wine Marketing*, 13(3): 82–93.

New Zealand Winegrowers (2009) New Zealand wine industry announces 2009 vintage results. Online. Available: http://www.nzwine.com/assets/Vintage_Press_Release_15_June_09.pdf (accessed 29 April 2012).

New Zealand Winegrowers (2011) Annual Report. Online. Available: www.nzwine.com/assets/sm/upload/i1/24/wa/w9/NZ%20Winegrowers%20Annual%20Report%202011%20for%20web.pdf (accessed 20 February 2012).

NZ Wine (2010) Annual report 201. Online. Available: www.nzwine.com/assets/sm/upload/hp/ds/41/cq/NZW_Annual_Report_2010_media.pdf (accessed 20 January 2012).

OECD and Statistical Office of European Communities (2005) *Oslo Manual: Guidelines for Collecting and Interpreting Innovation Data*, 3rd edn, Paris: OECD.

Ohmart, C. (2008a) 'Green wine without green washing?', *Wines & Vines*, 89(7): 77–9.

Ohmart, C. (2008b) 'Innovative outreach increases adoption of sustainable winegrowing practices in Lodi region', *California Agriculture*, 62(4): 142–7.

Pickersgill, R. and Edwards, D. (2005) The contribution of VET to innovation in regional industry. Online. Available: http://avetra.org.au/documents/PA035Edwards.PDF (accessed 20 January 2012).

Poitras, L. and Getz, D. (2006) 'Sustainable wine tourism: the host community perspective', *Journal of Sustainable Tourism*, 14(5): 425–48.

Reid, A.L. (1990) 'Grape expectations? An exploratory evaluation of the tourist potential of the New Zealand wine industry', unpublished Dip. Tour. dissertation, Dunedin: University of Otago.

Renton, T., Manktelow, D. and Kingston, C. (2009) Sustainable winegrowing: New Zealand's place in the world. Online. Available: http://nzwine.com/swnz/articles.html (accessed 20 April 2010).

Sen, S., Bhattacharya, C.B. and Korschun, D. (2006) 'The role of corporate social responsibility in strengthening multiple stakeholder relationships: a field experiment', *Journal of the Academy of Marketing Science*, 34(2): 158–66.

Sinha, P. and Akoorie, M.E. (2010) 'Sustainable environmental practices in the New Zealand wine industry: an analysis of perceived institutional pressures and the role of exports', *Journal of Asia-Pacific Business*, 11(1): 50–74.

Sørensen, F. (2001) *Tourism Experience Innovation Networks*, Roskilde: Roskilde University, Centre of Service Studies.

Spratt, M.F. (2010) Is the New Zealand wine industry destroying its brand in the global wine market? Online. Available: www.destinybaywine.com/documents/IstheNewZealandwineindustrydestroyingitsbrandintheglobalwinemarket.pdf (accessed 20 January 2012).

Stamboulis, Y. and Skayannis, P. (2003) 'Innovation strategies and technology for experience-based tourism', *Tourism Management*, 24(1): 35–43.

Statistics New Zealand (2007) Innovation in New Zealand 2007. Online. Available: http//:www.stats.govt.nz/.../innovation-in-new-zealand-2007.aspx (accessed 20 January 2012).

SWNZ (2010) About Sustainable Winegrowing New Zealand: what we do. Online. Available: http://wineinf.nzwine.com/swnzabout.asp (accessed 20 January 2012).

Wall, G. (1997) 'Sustainable tourism – unsustainable development', in S. Wahab and J. Pilgrim (eds), *Tourism Development and Growth*, London: Routledge.

Wilkins, M. and Hall, C.M. (2001) 'An industry stakeholder SWOT analysis of wine tourism in the Okanagan Valley, British Columbia', *International Journal of Wine Marketing*, 13(3): 77–81.

Winetitles (2009) *The Australian and New Zealand Wine Industry Directory*, Adelaide: Hartley-Higgins.

Yuan, Y.L., Gretzel, U. and Fesenmaier, D.R. (2006) 'The role of information technology use in American convention and visitor bureaus', *Tourism Management*, 27(3): 326–41.

Zucca, G., Smith, D.E. and Mitry, D.J. (2009) 'Sustainable viticulture and winery practices in California: what is it, and do customers care?', *International Journal of Wine Research*, 2: 189–94.

13 Regulatory and institutional barriers to new business development

The case of Swedish wine tourism

Karin Malm, Stefan Gössling and C. Michael Hall

Introduction

Wine tourism is widely regarded as a significant contributor to regional tourism development in those countries where winegrowing occurs. Wine tourists are often seen to be higher yielding than non-wine tourists, while wine tourism is also often associated with other cultural and heritage attractions. From a regional perspective, in addition to its direct employment effects, wine tourism is important for the differentiation of regional brands while the association with a quality wine product can help to create a 'halo effect' for other similarly positioned regional agricultural and food products. Wine tourism has also been associated with the development of new visitor attractions related to food and culinary heritage and products, including agricultural and industrial tourism activities, as well as potentially extending the length of stay of visitors (Hall and Sharples 2008). Importantly, wine tourism appears very significant for creating long-term relationships for visitors not only with individual wineries but also with a region's products after they return home. In an increasingly competitive environment for rural producers such relationships may prove crucial for maintaining or increasing sales levels.

Wine tourism, in terms of visits to wineries and the 'cellar door', also provides opportunities for winegrowing businesses to establish direct relationships to consumers and enjoy greater returns than if they were selling through intermediaries and retailers. The manner in which wine tourism is used as a component of the business mix depends on the stage of business development, overall business goals, location, target markets and regulatory structures. The advantages of wine tourism at the level of the individual business that is able to sell wine to tourists on site are (Hall *et al.* 2000; Hall and Sharples 2003, 2008):

- *increased consumer exposure* to product and increased opportunities to sample product;
- *building brand awareness and loyalty* through establishing links between producer and consumer including the purchase of wine and other products;
- *creating relationships with customers*: the opportunity to meet staff and to see 'behind the scenes' can lead to positive relationships with consumers

which may lead to both direct and indirect sales through positive 'word of mouth' advertising.

* *increased margins* through direct sale to consumers, to whom the absence of distributor costs is not carried over entirely;
* an additional *sales outlet*, or for smaller producers who cannot guarantee volume or constancy of supply, perhaps the only feasible sales outlet;
* *marketing intelligence*: producers can gain instant and valuable feedback on the consumer reaction to their existing products, and are able to trial new additions to their product range;
* *marketing intelligence on customers*: visitors can be added to a mailing list which can be developed as a customer database to both target and inform customers;
* *educational opportunities*: visits can help create awareness and appreciation of specific types of wine and wine and food as a whole, and the knowledge and interest generated by this can be expected to result in increased consumption and/or quality of what is consumed.

However, it is important to note that wine tourism may not be appropriate for some businesses because of the extra investment of scarce capital that may be required, time and opportunity costs, seasonality, and health and safety requirements (Mitchell and Hall 2006). Nevertheless, despite such issues, many regions and individual businesses are seeking to develop wine tourism as a means to promote rural tourism and encourage appropriate regional development. However, in addition to the 'usual' range of barriers to business development that face rural food producers, wine tourism faces an additional barrier in that it is often regarded as a 'sin product', meaning that it faces significant regulation in trade and, at times, prohibition (Brook 2000; Charters 2006; Hanson 2007; Hall and Mitchell 2008). Prohibition is often associated with countries and regions that have an active religious base. Although alcohol is strictly forbidden in some religions such as Islam, it is also the subject of temperance movements in some Christian denominations, especially Protestant churches. As Hall and Mitchell (2008: 63) commented,

> The influence of the prohibition movement on the business of wine is substantial because the social movement of temperance has a lasting legacy in the institutional arrangements that were established to satisfy the demands of the movement ... and therefore on viticultural and winery production, regulation of sales and shipping, taxation and ... trade in wine.

In some countries wine sales, including with respect to wine tourism, have come to be strictly controlled by legislation and regulation that may affect not only how much can be served and tasted at the winery, but also the nature of sales outlets, including direct marketing and sales. Such regulation is often especially strict where there are state alcohol monopolies. In such cases, in Ontario and British Columbia in Canada for example, regulatory exemptions are usually made to enable winegrowers to sell their wine on site as a way of encouraging business as well as tourism and regional development. However, this chapter examines the extent to which institutional structures associated with the state alcohol monopoly in Sweden serve to substantially restrict wine tourism and prevent the expansion of rural food and wine tourism in a new wine region. Indeed, it could be argued that the regulatory environment is such that it may make winegrowing unsustainable in many cases.

Regulatory and institutional structures surrounding alcohol in Sweden

Swedish alcohol politics are primarily concerned with public health, partly as a result of the impact alcohol consumption had on workers in the nineteenth century, the influence of the temperance movement and the government's ambition to control any substances harming the individual (Nycander 1998). To control consumption, a state monopoly on alcohol was implemented in the mid-1800s, and sales were restricted to government-controlled stores, since 1955 called Systembolaget (literal translation: 'The system's company'). Even today, the government still considers its main purpose to be control of alcohol consumption, as outlined on its website: 'Systembolaget exists for one reason: to minimize alcohol-related problems by selling alcohol in a responsible way, without profit motive' (Systembolaget 2012). After Sweden entered the European Union in 1995, the Swedish alcohol monopoly had to be adjusted due to conflicts with EU legislation. For instance, the monopoly on imports and exports of alcohol had to be given up, with the consequence that individual imports could now comprise far larger purchases for personal consumption, while commercial imports also became possible. The monopoly on alcohol retail remained in place, however (Holder *et al.* 1995; Holder 2000).

Changes in alcohol legislation had positive effects on the development of Swedish alcoholic products, as markets opened up and it became easier to obtain licences (Holder 2000). Another important legislative change took place in May 2008, when it became possible for alcohol producers to sell their products in the nearest local retail outlet of Systembolaget, a concession made because of an increasing demand for local products (Systembolaget 2008, 2010). As a consequence, many new alcoholic beverages entered the market, even though these highly localized products remained very expensive as they could only be sold, and hence be produced, in very small quantities. By 2010, alcohol producers were allowed to deliver their beverages to the three geographically closest Systembolaget stores, but this did not greatly increase demand. In 2009, a government investigation (Statens Offentliga Utredningar (SOU) 2009: 22) concluded that the attraction of alcoholic beverages lay in particular in the possibility of their being bought at the place of production, i.e. at the 'cellar door', and another, parallel investigation emphasized that legislation implied a lost opportunity in particular for farm-based wineries (SOU 2009).

Pressure to liberalize alcohol policy has increased ever since. In 2009, the Minister of Rural Affairs, Eskil Erlandsson, emphasized that food, beverages and tourism have a strong development potential for rural economies, and that vineyard sales can contribute to employment in rural areas (Centerpartiet 2009). The Swedish Association of Wine Growers (Föreningen Svenska Vinodlare) argued on similar lines, suggesting that such vineyard sales should be seen as a precondition for developing Sweden's commercial vineyards for tourism (Svenska Vinodlare 2010). At the same time, commentators suggested in the national media that if vineyard sales went ahead, Sweden might be forced to abolish Systembolaget altogether, because the argument for maintaining a state retail monopoly on alcohol on public health grounds would collapse (*Dagens Nyheter* 2010; Sveriges Radio 2010; Szyber 2010). The longer-term consequence, it was argued, would be a less regulated market for alcohol, with grocery stores taking over sales, and an expected increase in alcohol consumption of 30 per cent (Holder 2008). This argument was also given particular weight in a study by the Ministry of Health and Social Affairs (Socialdepartementet), which concluded that vineyard sales should not be allowed and that the retail monopoly as one of the key pillars of Swedish alcohol policy should be maintained (SOU 2009).

Since then, several influential bodies, such as the Swedish Competition Authority (Konkurrensverket), the National Board of Trade (Kommerskollegium) and the Swedish Board of Agriculture (Jordbruksverket), have argued that the issue deserves further study. In April 2010, the Ministry of Health and Social Affairs initiated another investigation to clarify whether vineyard sales are in conflict with EU competition laws (Riksdag och Departement 2010). Results presented in December 2010 indicated that vineyard sales could go ahead without breaching EU law (SOU 2010). Nevertheless, no political consensus on the issue has been reached. While the Ministry of Rural Affairs continues to argue that vineyard sales will be beneficial for rural areas (Jordbruksdepartementet Regeringskansliet 2010), there is continued debate as to whether such changes will undermine the government's alcohol policy (*Dagens Nyheter* 2010; Szyber 2010). The current situation is an impasse, with direct sales still being prohibited. As of the time of writing this affects a total of 33 commercial vineyards in Sweden, all of them small-scale producers (SOU 2010: 98). In the light of this situation, the following sections present the findings of a study of the viewpoints of winemakers in order to derive new insights regarding the changes that may be expected in the event of the legalization of direct sales of locally produced alcoholic beverages at the farm.

Industry perceptions on winegrowing

Open interviews were carried out with representatives of six Swedish vineyards in November 2010 in the island of Öland in the Baltic Sea (two interviews), and in the southern Swedish region of Scania (four interviews). Interview topics included perspectives on motivations for alcohol sales, entrepreneurship, quality and alcohol policy. Interviews were recorded and transcribed, evaluated based on content analysis, and subsequently structured into categories. The following sections present winemakers' perspectives on various issues, including customer motivations for wine purchases, the state monopoly on alcohol, the perceptions of visitors, entrepreneurship, commercialization, quality, sustainability, and the potential for the future development of wine tourism in Sweden.

Results – winemakers' perspectives

Motivations for wine purchases

As outlined above, the major government concern about allowing vineyard sales is public health, with concerns having been raised that these will make alcohol more accessible, and consequently have negative impacts on levels of alcohol consumption. Winemakers provide a number of reasons for why they do not think this is a valid argument, in particular outlining the motivations of farm visitors, prices and visitor types. In particular, winemakers emphasize that farm visitors are not typically seeking to get drunk on alcohol, as the cost of locally produced alcohol would make this prohibitive. Farm sales, in their opinion, also serve a different purpose from a consumer perspective, i.e. the experience of a locally produced, unique beverage.

> It won't make a difference [to sell alcohol on the farm], because they [the visitors] are not that type of clientele. Those who drink to get drunk, they are not our customers.
>
> (Winemaker I)

> It's not the same people we are talking about here, those with an alcohol problem. It is not them we are talking about when we are talking about vineyard sales.
>
> (Winemaker II)

> There is a fear that there will be some sort of drunkenness out in the bushes. I really can't see why, because these wines are pretty expensive. There are very few people who would go and buy them just to get drunk. I find that hard to believe. ... You don't go out to a vineyard to shop for Friday. No, it's about the whole experience. You visit the vineyard and then you would like to buy a bottle just like any other souvenir. So it's not at all about going there just to buy wine to get drunk.
>
> (Winemaker III)

State monopoly and vineyard sales

Although from the winemakers' perspective, the risk of increased alcohol consumption appears to be less relevant as an argument for the continuation of a state monopoly on sales, compatibility with EU law is another issue to be considered. Winemakers are generally comfortable with Systembolaget. There are, however, different perspectives on the lifting of restrictions, with some wine-makers welcoming the idea of selling their own products and those of their partners to attract wine tourists, while other winemakers wish to focus entirely on their own wines. Systembolaget, from this perspective, would continue with mass-market sales, while vineyards would take over niches. Current obstacles to sales of locally produced alcoholic beverages, such as opening hours – Systembolaget closes at 3 p.m. on Saturdays and is closed on Sundays – would be overcome through direct sales.

> We are not in any way against Systembolaget. We don't want to jeopardize Systembolaget, that's not our goal.
>
> (Winemaker II)

> Systembolaget, with their bulk wine, can be one player on the market. We can instead represent small wine houses in Europe and also attract tourism. Then you can be a European tourist and come to Sweden and experience Swedish wine tourism.
>
> (Winemaker IV)

> Foreign guests come here on Saturdays at half past two. Systembolaget has closed by then and the guests are leaving the next day. Consequently, they have no opportunity to buy our products.
>
> (Winemaker III)

Alcohol policy and visitors

When tourists understand that they cannot buy local alcohol products, in contrast to the international norm at wine tourism attractions, reactions are mixed. Swedish visitors are generally aware of the fact that alcohol can be bought only at Systembolaget, while foreign visitors react to this with surprise. This can create conflict at the farm.

> It's weird, a lot of people think they are allowed to buy. They're almost totally sure that they can buy. And everybody thinks it's crazy [that they cannot].
>
> (Winemaker III)

> A lot of visitors, well they are Swedish and they understand when you explain to them ... foreign visitors, they just don't understand. They think we're pulling their leg!
>
> (Winemaker II)

> Our foreign guests especially don't understand what I'm saying. If I say they can't buy, they take it as an insult, that *they* specifically cannot buy it. They say: 'But I have money, I have Swedish money.'
>
> (Winemaker I)

Entrepreneurial obstacles and adaptation

As alcohol products can only be sold through Systembolaget, farms have developed different strategies to deal with the situation. One option at least to partially bypass legislation is to open a restaurant, where it is possible to sell wine to customers by the glass or by the bottle, as long as it is consumed in the restaurant. Other farms have focused on developing vineyards and the winery into an attraction, as it is still relatively unusual to grow grapes in Sweden. In this case, guided tours and subsequent sales in farm shops make up for lost direct sales opportunities. Regulation, in both cases, has led to adaptive responses.

> If you have an alcohol permit you can let your guests taste and drink the wine. That is the only reason why I have a restaurant.
>
> (Winemaker III)

> In Sweden we really have a unique position regarding how we should handle our vineyards. If you start a vineyard in Europe you can start selling immediately. We haven't been given that chance. We have been forced to find other ways to survive, for example tourism. We have learned to charge for it and make it into a product. ... When [vineyard sales] are allowed, it will be a lot easier for us to manage. We have diversified, and I'm not sure that would be the if vineyard sales had been allowed from the beginning.
>
> (Winemaker IV)

Winemakers also point out, however, that they are not currently dependent on vineyard sales, as their adaptive process has included distribution through Systembolaget, farm-based restaurants, and guided tours of vineyards and wineries. Diversification into other sales options, such as direct sales, may become yet another opportunity, although none of the interviewed winemakers are currently dependent on such future liberalization. However, winemakers believe that it would be economically impossible to survive on direct sales alone.

> We grow such small quantities [that] we must use what we have around us to make people interested in visiting a Swedish vineyard. The sale of the actual wine is just one part of it all.
>
> (Winemaker III)

> [If there was a change in policy] you wouldn't be allowed to sell more than 10,000 litres per year. And you just can't live on that. You can't build a company on just that. Besides, there is another limitation: each visitor can't buy more than one litre of spirits, three litres of wine or five litres of beer. ... Then we will have to limit them and say that they can only buy four bottles. Otherwise, we'll kill the business because we will have no bottles left for the last visitors. And it is a fact that we can't just live on the wine. No, we should live on the wine *and* the tourism business.
>
> (Winemaker II)

Commercialization

At the time of writing there were 33 commercial wineries in Sweden that produced a total of 16,600 litres of wine or fruit wine per year (SOU 2010: 98).
However, potentially more could operate commercially: the Swedish Association of Wine Growers (*Föreningen Svenska Vinodlare*) has 250 members, even
though most are amateur wine growers (Svenska Vinodlare 2010). Of the existing wineries, several have possibly chosen not to become commercial because
the market is seen as too regulated. However, winemakers suggest that in the
Swedish wine community many actors may be waiting for legislative changes, in
the event of which the number of vineyards could double. At the same time, they
caution that obstacles, involving costs, viticultural knowledge and administrative
work should not be underestimated. An important rural development perspective
is that direct sales opportunities might increase visitor numbers, and hence
provide new opportunities for restaurants, accommodation or other products.
Winemakers also point out that such changes would require adjustments in hospitality and services, leading to more working time and entailing a need for more
corporate business and niche marketing approaches, including potentially a
trade-off in the type of visitors they attract.

> There will probably be up to 60–70 [wineries] in the near future if the law
> changes.
>
> (Winemaker V)

> I don't think that this change will be that easy. I think it will be associated
> with a lot of rules and paperwork. I don't think the average person can grow
> a bit and then make a bottle and sell at the farm, I think there will be fairly
> stringent controls.
>
> (Winemaker III)

> There won't be any profits anyway, because machinery, equipment, permits
> and facilities cost a fortune. Furthermore, the tax is high.
>
> (Winemaker I)

> I could expand as I will be able to contact groups myself. I can have guided
> tours, I can have wine tasting and visitors can buy a bottle and take it home.
> … Then perhaps we wouldn't invest as much in the tourism business as we
> could do otherwise by building up a nice site where it will be easy to invite
> people and arrange wine tastings.
>
> (Winemaker III)

> The business would change quite considerably. It requires us to be available
> and be open in a completely different way. There will probably be more of
> those spontaneous visits. Now, we have no special opening hours.
>
> (Winemaker VI)

Quality and sustainability

Winemakers stress the importance of quality. It is understood that the wine business will lose prestige if wineries cannot maintain high quality. For this purpose, international collaboration has already been initiated to strategically learn from other regions. Winemakers are convinced that the slow development of wine tourism is helping to ensure the quality of the products and that high quality will be a precondition for the continued development of southern Sweden as a wine region. In this context, climate change is seen as a factor that will increasingly facilitate viticulture because of a warmer climate.

> We don't release anything if we feel uncertain about the quality. ... Right now it's good that it hasn't gone too fast, because the industry needs to mature and we need to improve. We need time to develop quality and our experience. ... things are happening with the climate that are making our climate increasingly interesting.
>
> (Winemaker VI)

> We are planning to turn Öland into a quality region. We have gained a lot through cooperation with Señor [Joseph] Perez because he was involved in building up Priorat [Catalonia, Spain] into a quality wine region. He is determined that if you want to do something, you should do it with a focus on quality, starting already in the vineyard and then *continuing. That's what we're aiming for now.*
>
> (Winemaker III)

The future: classification of Swedish wines

In traditional wine-producing countries, wines are judged by different criteria and then classified. Classifications represent quality levels, displayed on the bottle. France, for instance, has two quality labels which include regional restrictions regarding grape varieties or maximum harvest per hectare. In New World wine-producing countries, other mechanisms are often used to indicate wine quality including cooperative accreditation and classification schemes, labelling requirements and wine competitions (Hall and Mitchell 2008). In the perception of winemakers, classification programmes are needed in Sweden to build up trust and, ultimately, 'to be taken seriously', i.e. to have an objective quality measurement system in place:

> It's difficult to build up trust. We need some type of evaluation. So far, there's no such classification of wines in Sweden.
>
> (Winemaker I)

> Not only for wines, but for all products. We need to start having quality labels. ... It [the certification] is a step that we have to work on so that we are taken seriously.
>
> (Winemaker IV)

Today we are only allowed to produce table wine. That is the lowest grade in Europe. But this wine, even if it is called table wine, could be in a class with, for example, the German quality wines. But we aren't allowed to produce quality wines or regional wines here in Sweden, only table wine. And we want to change that.

(Winemaker V)

Regulatory and institutional barriers to new business development

As outlined above, the Swedish Systembolaget's mandate is 'to help limit the medical and social harm caused by alcohol and thereby improve public health', with a vision of a 'society in which everyone can enjoy alcoholic drinks with due regard for health considerations and without harming either themselves or other people' (Systembolaget 2012). To achieve this, access to alcohol is restricted through limitation on the number of retail stores, specific opening hours, non-maximization of profit, avoidance of sales promotions, brand neutrality and a high standard of customer service.

The view that public health is an issue to be managed by government has a long tradition in Sweden. Sandberg (1999) even suggests that without strict government control of public health in Sweden, it might not have been possible for the country to industrialize and grow economically. Today, the situation may be different, in the sense that alcohol sales have become an economic system in their own right. With over 400 stores, Systembolaget is a significant employer (Systembolaget 2012). Yet the health issue continues to dominate public discussions (e.g. *Dagens Nyheter* 2010; Szyber 2010). From the winemakers' viewpoint, however problems related to public health are being overemphasized, given that with production of 16,600 litres per year, or 0.002 litres per capita of the population, Sweden is hardly a country where considerable amounts of wine are produced.

While it consequently appears less relevant how much wine is produced in Sweden, direct farm sales might have an impact on overall consumption, given wider availability and potentially greater access – in time and space – to alcohol. Winemakers believe that their customers have no ambition to get drunk, as wines are costly and will only be purchased by consumers with a genuine interest in local products and quality wine. Rather than increasing consumption, direct farm sales might consequently serve to replace some imports. In Sweden, a 2010 report to the government in this regard (SOU 2010: 98) acknowledged that:

It is legally possible to introduce vineyard sales ... but it must be done using a model that does not prevent foreign manufacturers from selling their products through vineyards or to establish themselves in Sweden to engage in vineyard sales and as long as the model for vineyard sales is consistent with Swedish alcohol policy.

However, political progress on the issue is difficult as there is no consensus among the political parties.

Internationally, there has been considerable growth in wine production and global competition for wine tourism although global per capita wine consumption is actually falling and there is increased competition between producers (Hall and Mitchell 2008). Interest in vineyards and wine production has increased in line with this phenomenon, and direct vineyard sales now present a significant share of the wine trade in many countries, but especially in new and emerging regions (Charters and Ali-Knight 2002; Niel and van Westering 2003; Mitchell and Hall 2006; Getz *et al.* 2007; Hall and Mitchell 2008). Due to the unique situation in Sweden, customers from outside the country in particular react with surprise to the fact that direct farm sales are not possible. According to winemakers, this encounter with Swedish wine policy is sometimes perceived as outlandish: where different ethical frameworks for dealing with alcohol consumption meet (Kurzer 2001), images of Sweden as a country with a very 'different' alcohol policy may be reinforced.

Even though regulation is perceived as an obstacle to the development of vineyards, interviews have also shown that this has forced wine entrepreneurs to adapt and develop other dimensions of the wine experience. Measures have included the opening of restaurants to allow 'at-the-vineyard' consumption and guided tours of vineyards and wineries, and have potentially facilitated other tourism-related developments such as increased sales in farm shops or farm accommodation. Through the latter, economic linkages have been reinforced, and turnover has increased. However, wine tourism experiences around the world show that such developments are often the norm: the ability to taste and then purchase wine made on site remains the core of wine tourism businesses (Hall and Sharples 2003, 2008). Direct sales of alcohol would undoubtedly make another contribution to farm-related spending, though they would potentially require some additional investments.

Wine tourism could have considerable potential in Sweden, given the growing international interest in Nordic cuisine (see Chapter 10). The existence of vineyards often includes an element of surprise for international and even domestic visitors, who do not expect to find either vineyards or wineries in Sweden. Respondents outlined three major barriers to entry into the wine market and wine tourism, including the current climate which may make viticulture marginal in some districts; high investment costs, as wine production is capital-intensive; and legal difficulties, i.e. licences to sell wine through Systembolaget or at the farm (Hall and Mitchell 2008). But in a situation of liberalization, the number of vineyards could grow considerably, with some winemakers predicting that numbers will double.

Wine tourism, if further developed, would support the development of Sweden as a food nation, a key objective in the government's strategic plans for rural development (SOU 2009/10). A focus on quality wines may also serve this purpose, with the added option of strengthening the culinary reputation of regions (e.g. Pike and Melewar 2006; Menival and Charters 2008; see also

Chapter 10 above). Even though the number of vineyards is limited in southern Sweden, their contribution to the diversification of tourism products could be considerable. As Hashimoto and Telfer (2003) have argued, regional brands are important for destination differentiation, adding value to rural areas.

Conclusion

This chapter has provided some new insights with regard to regulation and policy making, focusing on the perspectives of winemakers in the emerging wine region of Sweden. Results indicate that there is a complex legislative situation, due to the government's continued control of alcohol sales in the otherwise liberalized markets of the European Union. The government's main concern is public health, and the development of direct sales in vineyards have so far been prevented based on arguments about increased consumption and the potential loss of the government's retail monopoly. There is clear evidence that consumption is unlikely to increase, due to the limited number of vineyards in Sweden, the type of wine purchases, prohibitive costs, and the reasons for purchases which may be more focused on the experience of vineyards, wineries and new alcoholic products. With regard to the government's retail monopoly, evidence presented by the government would suggest that the continuation of the monopoly under EU law is not endangered. Yet, while there is support for direct vineyard sales from the Minister of Rural Affairs, Eskil Erlandsson (Centerpartiet 2009), and in investigations on behalf of the government (SOU 2010: 98), political parties have not reached any consensus on the issue.

While regulation currently prevents winemakers from making additional sales on the farm, the regulated market for alcohol in Sweden has also had positive effects in that it has forced entrepreneurs to adapt, for example by opening restaurants for wine sales or organizing guided tours of vineyards and wineries. If regulation is eased, more vineyards may become interested in commercialization of their products, however, while turnover on already established vineyards is likely to increase. This could also have secondary benefits for sales in farm shops or vineyard-based accommodation. Overall, Sweden as an emerging wine region and wine tourism destination provides important insights into the complex interrelationships of wine business development, governance and rural economies.

References

Brook, S. (2000) 'Wine, food, style and pleasure', in S. Brook (ed.) *A Century of Wine: The Story of a Wine Revolution*, London: Mitchell Beazley.

Carlsen, J. (2004) 'A review of global wine tourism research', *Journal of Wine Research*, 15: 5–13.

Centerpartiet (2009) Eskil Erlandsson vill tillåta gårdsförsäljning [Eskil Erlandsson wants to allow vineyard sales]. Online. Available: www.centerpartiet.se/Nyheter/Arkiv-2009/ Eskil-Erlandsson-vill-gora-gardar-till-systembolag/ (accessed 28 October 2010).

Charters, S. (2006) *Wine and Society: The Social and Cultural Context of a Drink*, Oxford: Elsevier Butterworth-Heinemann.

Charters, S. and Ali-Knight, J. (2002) 'Who is the wine tourist?', *Tourism Management*, 23: 311–19.

Dagens Nyheter (2010) 'Utredning vill tillåta spritbutiker' [Investigation wants to allow liquor stores], *Dagens Nyheter*, 17 November. Online. Available: www.dn.se/nyheter/sverige/utredning-vill-tillata-spritbutiker (accessed 1 April 2012).

Dagens Nyheter Ekonomi (2010) 'Svårt att införa Gårdsförsäljning' [Difficult to introduce farm sales], *Dagens Nyheter Ekonomi*, 18 November. Online. Available: www.dn.se/ekonomi (accessed 18 November 2010).

Furnham, A. and Bochner, S. (1986) *Culture Shock: Psychological Reactions to Unfamiliar Environments*, Cambridge: Cambridge University Press.

Getz, D., Carlsen, J., Brown, G. and Havitz, M. (2007) 'Wine tourism and consumers', in A. Woodside and D. Martin (eds) *Tourism Management: Analysis, Behaviour, and Strategy*, Wallingford: CABI Publishing.

Granlund, A. and Lindberg, E. (2005) Vad händer efter en avreglering? – En studie av den svenska detaljhandelsmarknaden för alkohol, Magister thesis, Linköpings Universitet, Sweden.

Göteborgsposten (2010) 'Gårdsförsäljning ett hot mot folkhälsan', *Göteborgsposten*, 30 November 2010. Online. Available: www.gp.se/nyheter/debatt/1.498950-gardsforsaljning-ett-hot-mot-folkhalsan (accessed 1 April 2012).

Hall, C.M. and Mitchell, R. (2008) *Wine Marketing – A Practical Guide*, Oxford: Elsevier.

Hall, C.M. and Sharples, E. (2003) 'The consumption of experiences or the experience of consumption? An introduction to the tourism of taste', in C.M. Hall, E. Sharples, R. Mitchell, B. Cambourne and N. Macionis (eds) *Food Tourism Around the World: Development, Management and Markets*, Oxford: Butterworth-Heinemann.

Hall, C.M. and Sharples, L. (eds) (2008) *Food and Wine Festivals and Events Around the World: Development, Management and Markets*, Oxford: Butterworth-Heinemann.

Hall, C.M., Johnson, G., Cambourne, B., Macionis, N., Mitchell, R. and Sharples, L. (2000) 'Wine tourism: an introduction', in C.M. Hall, L. Sharples, B. Cambourne and N. Macionis (eds) *Wine and Tourism Around the World: Development, Management and Markets*, Oxford: Elsevier.

Hanson, D. (2007) *National Prohibition of Alcohol in the US*, Potsdam: Sociology Department, State University of New York.

Hashimoto, A. and Telfer, D.J. (2003) 'Positioning an emerging wine route in the Niagara region: understanding the wine tourism market and its implications for marketing', in C.M. Hall (ed.) *Wine, Food and Tourism Marketing*, Binghamton, NY: The Haworth Hospitality Press.

Holder, H. (2000) *Sweden and the European Union: Changes in National Alcohol Policy and their Consequences*, Stockholm: Almqvist & Wiksell International.

Holder, H. (2008) *Alkoholmonopol och folkhälsa: Vilka skulle effekterna bli om Systembolagets detaljhandelsmonopol avskaffades?* [Alcohol monopoly and public health: what would the impacts be if Systembolaget's monopoly was abolished?], Statens Folkhälsoinstitut, Östersund, Vällingby: Elanders.

Holder, H.D., Giesbrecht, N., Horverak, O., Nordlund, S., Norstroem, T., Olsson, O., Oesterberg, E. and Skog, O.-J. (1995) 'Potential consequences from possible changes to Nordic retail alcohol monopolies resulting from European Union membership', *Addiction*, 90: 1603–18.

Howley, M. and van Westering, J. (2008) 'Developing wine tourism: a case study of the attitude of English wine producers to wine tourism', *Journal of Vacation Marketing*, 14(1): 87–95.

Jordbruksdepartementet, Regeringskansliet (2010) *Sverige – Det nya matlandet*, [Sweden – the new food country], Uppdaterad handlingsplan, Nya jobb genom god mat och upplevelser, Davidsons tryckeri, Sweden.

Kurzer, P. (2001) *Markets and Moral Regulation: Cultural Change in the European Union*, Cambridge: Cambridge University Press.

Malmberg, B., Andersson, E., Johansson, M. and Hermansson, K. (2007) *Hälsans betydelse för individens och samhällets ekonomiska utveckling*, Östervåla: Statens Folkhälsoinstitut, Elanders.

Menival, D. and Charters, S. (2008) 'The impact of tourism on the willingness to pay for a bottle of standard quality champagne', *Enometrica*, 1(1): 9–20.

Mitchell, R. and Hall, C.M. (2006) 'Wine tourism research: the state of play', *Tourism Review International*, 9(4): 307–32.

Niel, E. and van Westering, J. (2003) 'The organization of wine tourism in France: the involvement of the French public sector', *Journal of Travel & Tourism Marketing*, 14: 35–47.

Nycander, S. (1998) 'Addiction history. Ivan Bratt: the man who saved Sweden from prohibition', *Addiction*, 93: 17–25.

Pike, W. and Melewar, T.C. (2006) 'The demise of independent wine production in France: a marketing challenge', *International Journal of Wine Marketing*, 18(3): 183–203.

Riksdag och Department (2010) *Alkoholpolitik* [Alcohol politics]. Online. Available: www.rod.se (accessed 28 October 2010).

Sandberg, H. (1999) *Hälsokommunikation i ett historiskt perspektiv*, Medie- och Kommunikationsvetenskap, Lunds Universitet.

Socialdepartementet (2010) *Gårdsförsäljning av alkoholdrycker och alkoholservering på särskilda boenden*, Statens offentliga utredningar, Kommittédirektiv 2010:21. Stockholm: Socialdepartementet.

SOU (Statens Offentliga Utredningar) (2009) Socialdepartementet Alkohollagsutredningen, *En ny Alkohollag – Slutbetänkande av alkohollagsutredningen*, Stockholm: Edita Sverige AB.

SOU (2009/10) Regeringens Proposition, *En Ny Alkohollag – Frågan om Gårdsförsäljning*, Stockholm.

SOU (2010) *Gårdsförsäljning*, Stockholm: Elanders Sverige AB.

Svenska Vinodlare (2010) *Syftet med Föreningen Svenska Vinodlare* (The purpose of the Swedish winegrowers association). Online. Available: Svenskavinodlare.se (accessed 11 November 2010).

Sveriges Radio, Gotlandsnytt (2010) *Oenighet om gårds-försäljning*, Sveriges Radio, Gotlandsnytt, 25 October. Online. Available: www.sr.se/gotlandsnytt (accessed 28 October 2010).

Systembolaget (2008) *Bättre tillgänglighet för lokala producenter* [Better access for local producers], press release 27 May. Online. Available: Systembolaget.se (accessed 11 November 2010).

Systembolaget (2010) *Lokalproducerat nu I de tre närmaste Systembutikerna* [Local products now in the three closest Systembolaget stores], press release 17 May. Online. Available: Systembolaget.se (accessed 19 November 2010).

Systembolaget (2012) *Om Systembolaget* [About Systembolaget]. Online. Available: Systembolaget.se (accessed 1 April 2012).

Szyber, C. (2010) 'Gårdsförsäljning – bara ett svepskäl' [Vineyard sales – only an excuse], *Svenska Dagbladet Opinion*, Online posting. Available: www.svd.se/opinion (18 November 2010).

Wargenau, A. and Che, D. (2006) 'Wine tourism development and marketing strategies in Southwest Michigan', *International Journal of Wine Marketing*, 18(1): 45–60.

14 Sustaining *halal* certification at restaurants in Malaysia

Sharifah Zannierah Syed Marzuki, C. Michael Hall and Paul W. Ballantine

Introduction

Food is the most basic of human needs and some people have dietary restrictions in accordance with their religion and beliefs. Religious foodways can have profound implications for the economic sustainability of the hospitality and tourism businesses but just as importantly being able to satisfy such foodways also acts to further the cultural sustainability of different communities and ways of being. Although there is clear recognition of the regulatory and institutional issues surrounding the role of certification for organics, Genetic Engineering (GE) free and food miles in food supply chains for the tourism and hospitality industries (see Chapter 1 above), there is much less awareness of the significance of religious food certification.

This chapter examines *halal* food and certification in the context of the Malaysian restaurant sector. *Halal* food is not mainly to do with slaughtering animals or *halal* meat, which is often how it is primarily understood in many Western countries. It entails more than that. It relates to issues of production, handling, distribution, storage, display, packaging, labelling, preparation and serving. In fact the whole food supply chain must be *halal*. *Halal* means permitted, lawful or fit for consumption under Islamic dietary laws. The realm of *halal* affects all dimensions of human life including protection of the environment, humane treatment of animals, ethical investment, decent service and the provision of wholesome food. This chapter discusses the nature of Islamic dietary laws and the concepts of *halal* and *haram* before going on to examine the regulatory structures surrounding *halal* food in Malaysia. The chapter then presents the results of a survey on the expectations of restaurant managers toward *halal* certification in Malaysia.

Islamic dietary laws

The word 'Islam' means total submission and refers to the basic teaching of absolute submission to the will of God (Kocturk 2002). In Islam the Prophet Muhammad received the first revelation affirming the oneness of God, Allah, from the archangel Gabriel (see Surah 96, Al-Alaq [The Clot, Read!]) at Mount

Hira near the city of Mecca on the Arabian Peninsula around AD 610 during the lunar month of Ramadhan. The Prophet Muhammad is considered the last of God's messengers after Adam, Abraham, Moses and Jesus. Islam has dietary restrictions which are very clear and are concerned not only with the prescription of permissible food and drink but also with the practice of consuming (Mohamed Nasir and Pereira 2008). Like many commentators, Riaz and Chaudry (2004) observe that Islam is a way of life; it is not merely a religion of rituals but one of rules and manners that govern the life of the individual Muslim. Hence, one of the important aspects of a Muslim life is the food and dietary code.

According to the Islamic dietary laws, there are three main categories of food for Muslims: *halal*, *haram* and *syubha*. Following the Islamic dietary laws is a Muslim symbol of faith. In addition, the life of a Muslim revolves around the concept of *halal* and *haram* (Riaz and Chaudry 2004). *Halal* is a term describing foods that are lawful for Muslims to consume, according to Islamic dietary laws found in the Quran, *hadith* (books that recorded the sayings and practices of the Prophet Muhammad) and in the *fiqh* (jurisprudence) of Muslim jurists. *Haram* foods are unlawful and prohibited for Muslims, while *syubha* foods are questionable and therefore should be avoided.

In a *hadith* reported by al-Bukhārī and Muslim (two of the canonical *hadith* collections), the Prophet Muhammad said:

> *halal* (lawful) is clear and *haram* (prohibited) is clear; in between these two are certain things which are suspect or *syubha*. Hence, many people may not know whether those items are *halal* or *haram* (but) whosoever leaves them, is innocent towards his religion and his conscience.

The *hadith* further explains anyone who gets involved in any of these suspected items, may fall into the unlawful and prohibited. *Halal* and *haram* foods must be kept separate so that the purity of the *halal* foods can be maintained (Mohamed Nasir and Pereira 2008). They emphasized that when a Muslim takes only those that are *halal* and good, it means that he is showing his gratitude towards Allah for all the blessings that He has given.

In Islam the sphere of prohibited things is very small, while that of permissible things is extremely vast (Al-Qaradawi 1980). In fact, only a small number of sound and explicit texts discuss prohibitions, while whatever is not mentioned in a *nas* (a verse of the *Al-Quran*) or a clear, authentic and explicit *sunah* (sayings and practices of the Prophet Muhammad) as being lawful or prohibited falls under the general principle of permissibility and is within the domain of Allah's favour. In the *sunah*, the Prophet Muhammad also said:

> Allah has prescribed certain obligations for you, so do not neglect them; He has defined certain limits, so do not transgress them; He has prohibited certain things, so do not do them; and He has kept silent concerning other things out of mercy for you and not because of forgetfulness, so do not ask questions concerning them.

In essence, all pure and clean foods are permitted for consumption by Muslims except for the following categories, including any products derived from them or contaminated with them (Riaz and Chaudry 2004: 9):

- carrion or dead animals;
- flowing or congealed blood;
- swine (all variants), including all byproducts;
- animals slaughtered without the name of God being pronounced;
- animals slaughtered while a name other than God was pronounced;
- animals killed in a manner that prevents their blood from being fully drained from their bodies;
- intoxicants of all types, including alcohol and drugs;
- carnivorous animals with fangs, such as lions, dogs, wolves or tigers;
- birds with sharp claws (birds of prey) such as falcons, eagles, owls or vultures;
- land animals such as frogs or snakes.

With respect to terrestrial animals, from a Muslim perspective Allah has prohibited the eating of pork, the flesh of any animal which dies of itself or is sacrificed to anyone other than Allah, and the drinking of blood. In relation to other prohibited animals, Al-Qaradawi (1980) defined wild animals as those which prey on other animals and devour them by tearing them apart, for instance the lion, leopard and wolf, and birds with talons such as the hawk, eagle and falcon, to name a few. Additionally, blood that pours forth from permitted and non-permitted animals alike is prohibited from being consumed (Regenstein *et al.* 2003; Riaz and Chaudry 2004). Therefore, Muslim scholars have generally agreed that anything made from blood is unacceptable. A *hadith* which was reported by al-Bukhārī and Muslim states that the Prophet 'forbade the eating of any wild animals with a canine tooth and of any bird with talons'.

Muslims are supposed to make an effort to maintain the intake of *halal* food of good quality (Riaz and Chaudry 2004). Importantly, the entire food supply chain must follow the *halal* standard, including the slaughtering of animals, storage, display and preparation. The standard therefore makes compulsory the requirement to physically separate *halal* from non-*halal* food and products in order to maintain the wholesomeness (*Halalan Toyyiban*) of *halal* food that covers the requirements of Islamic law and the requirements for hygiene, sanitation and safety. Mohamed Nasir and Pereira (2008) emphasized that it is important to note that under Islamic law, not only are there rules and prohibitions on food and drink, but the slaughtering, processing and serving of any food and drink must also conform to Islamic law. The animals that are to be slaughtered must be of *halal* species as well.

The halal *slaughter*

Although *halal* applies to much more than meat, the focus and indeed level of understanding of *halal* by many non-Muslims is on the provision of *halal* meat

(Wan Hassan and Hall 2003). Islam considers all animals to be as important as humans and this is clearly stated in the Holy Quran (Aidaros 2005). The Islamic method of slaughter (*halal* method) is regarded by Muslims as the least painful method if the correct measures are undertaken. This is to ensure the highest benefit to both animals and consumers. The slaughter of animals must be performed by a Muslim of sound mind and maturity, who fully understands the fundamentals and conditions related to this activity (Riaz and Chaudry 2004; Bonne and Verbeke 2008). For example, the Department of Standards Malaysia (2004) details that the act of slaughtering shall be done with *niyyah* (intention) and the slaughterman must be well aware of his action. The purpose of slaughtering is only for Allah and not for other purposes. Furthermore, the animal must be one that is *halal* and must be alive or deemed to be alive at the time of the slaughter. The animals to be slaughtered must be healthy and have been approved by the competent authority.

The Department of Standards Malaysia (2004) further explains that the act of *halal* slaughter shall begin with an incision on the neck at some point just below the glottis (Adam's apple) and after the glottis for long-necked animals. In addition, the slaughter shall severe the trachea (*halqūm*), oesophagus (*mari'*) and both the carotid arteries and jugular veins (*wadajain*) to hasten the bleeding and death of the animal. According to Riaz and Chaudry (2004), the traditional method of slaughter in Islam is to slit the throat, cutting the carotid arteries, jugular veins, trachea and the oesophagus, without severing the head. As a result, the bleeding shall be spontaneous and complete. In order for the meat to become *halal*, a trained Muslim inspector who is responsible for ensuring that animals are properly slaughtered according to Islamic law must check all these procedures.

According to Muhammad (2007), non-Muslims most likely think that this method of slaughter is cruel to animals, believing that they will suffer and bleed to death. However, the Islamic principles of slaughter clearly state that the knife used must be very sharp to ensure a quick, deep and clean cut through the vital anatomy of the neck of a *halal* species animal. It is mainly directed at the trachea, oesophagus and major blood vessels. For animal welfare reasons, the knife should not be sharpened in front of the animal (Riaz and Chaudry 2004; Bonne and Verbeke 2008).

The Islamic method of slaughter has been supported by members of the scientific community (Dabayeh 1998; Aidaros 2005) and the Association of Muslim Lawyers (Muhammad 2007). As Kocturk (2002) explained, with a single stroke of a sharp knife, the jugular vein and the oesophagus are cut to interrupt the flow of blood to the brain and thereby render the animal unconscious almost immediately. This acts as a powerful painkiller and disables the sensory centre. According to Aidaros (2005), the immediate cutting of the vessels of the neck during *halal* slaughter causes ischaemia of the brain and makes the animal insensitive to pain. This method results in a rapid gush of blood which drains out from the animal's body. Bleeding ensures the meat is of good quality. As Kocturk (2002) further emphasized, the rules for *halal* slaughter are based on the dual principles of effectively draining the animal's blood without inflicting unnecessary suffering. Here, humane treatment is required in the prohibition of strangling, striking, piercing or goring animals in the attempt to cause injury until they die.

The importance of *halal* for cultural sustainability

Although the focus on sustainability in the context of tourism and hospitality often affects the environmental and economic dimensions of sustainable development (Hall and Lew 1998; Gössling *et al.* 2009; Hall 2011), social and cultural traditions and understandings are also resources that need to be preserved for future generations (Littig and Grießler 2005). Indeed, Littig and Grießler (2005) reasoned that the encouragement of sustainability ought to be directed towards the relationship between nature and society. The provision of food is therefore a matter of economic, environmental *and* cultural sustainability; Reynolds (1993) suggested that eating habits must be viewed as a matter of culture. Therefore, the maintenance of traditional foodways should be regarded as a significant component of cultural sustainability, especially given their role not only as a factor in cultural identity but also their centrality to religious faith. Indeed, the promotion of some religious foodways and the values associated with them have been identified as a potentially important ethical basis for sustainable consumption practices (Bonne and Verbeke 2008; Finch 2010).

Faith clearly influences both the quantitative and qualitative aspects of consumption and material culture and, therefore, environmental stewardship and sustainability. Parker-Jenkins (2008) highlighted that the beliefs and practices of Muslims are influenced by their religious affiliation which leads to commitment to their community and a strong sense of religious values and tradition. Naeem (2003) added that the concepts of *halal* and *haram* constitute a powerful codified system which guides various practices of Muslims and makes Islam a complete way of life. For example, the Prophet Muhammad tells us, 'It is difficult, for a man laden with riches, to climb the steep path that leadeth to bliss' (Al-Suhrawardy 1990: 110). Bonne and Verbeke (2008: 36) note that, 'As a product attribute, "halal" refers to the nature, origin, and the processing method of the food product, which entails similarities with organic foods and foods produced taking animal welfare or sustainability issues into account'. Indeed, Islam promotes modesty and temperance in every aspect that is guided by the *Al-Quran* (Nicolaou *et al.* 2009).

Al-Nahdi *et al.* (2009) stressed that for Muslims *halal* represents by far the most important element in food consumption especially as the obligation to religious needs is the main criterion for becoming a good Muslim (Dahalan 2008). Similarly, Al-Harran and Low (2008) stressed that the rationale of a Muslim consumer when buying a *halal* product results from the commitment to Islamic principles and teachings apart from need for the product. Above all, the way food is grown, distributed and eaten also profoundly affects the environmental, social, spiritual and economic well-being of the community (Feenstra 1997; Naeem 2003).

Demand for *halal* food

The majority of Muslims in Malaysia regard *halal* as the supreme factor in consumption (Al-Nahdi *et al.* 2009). As Muslims, they believe that food has significant effects on their spiritual and physical well-being. Thus, they believe that failure to follow Islamic law will affect their destiny in the afterlife. It is therefore necessary for Muslims to monitor carefully the food that they eat and its source within the food supply chain. Increased international trade and globalization have also contributed to the demand for *halal* food and it is fast becoming a new market force and identifier and gaining entrance into non-Muslim markets and countries (Mohd Yusoff 2004; Muhammad 2007; Al-Harran and Low 2008).

The total world Muslim population is estimated to be 1.8 billion people and the market for *halal* products is worth approximately US$560 billion a year (Wan Omar *et al.* 2008), making Muslims an increasingly significant market for the food industry. Since the late 1980s South East Asian and Middle Eastern countries have witnessed the Westernization of the food service industry (Riaz and Chaudry 2004). Global food service giants such as McDonald's and Kentucky Fried Chicken are now regular features of the food service landscape. Western food companies have therefore had to comply with the local *halal* requirements to compete and be successful (Dana and Vignali 1998; Hall and Mitchell 2000; Hazair 2007).

Malaysian *halal* certification

The certification of *halal* food has been conducted in Malaysia since 1982 (Department of Islamic Development Malaysia (JAKIM) 2010). The enormous economic potential of worldwide demand for *halal* food has also been a driver for certification; the goal of making Malaysia a *halal* food hub is explicitly mentioned in national plans (National SME Development Council 2006). According to Abdul Talib *et al.* (2008: 3):

> Malaysia has developed *halal* certification; a total quality health and sanitary system that involves adopting procedure for slaughtering, processing and other related operations as outlined by Islamic rules. It certifies raw materials, ingredients and products based on quality, sanitary and safety considerations. This broad-based system certified is not only limited to meat and poultry products, but also cut across other consumer items such as pharmaceuticals, toiletries, cosmetics and confectionery.

In most countries *halal* certification and regulation are undertaken at the provincial or state government level or by non-governmental organizations (NGOs), usually in conjunction with national or regional government food labelling and advertising law. Malaysia is therefore one of the few countries in the world where the national government provides the regulatory framework for promoting the *halal* certification process on products and services. Domestically, local state government agencies including the Islamic Religious Council and Islamic Religious Department have also been given the authority by JAKIM to award *halal* certificates with the same logo as that provided by JAKIM but with different state names. The National SME Development Council (2006) reported that the Codex Alimentarius Commission, which is responsible, under the United Nations, for regulations on food preparation globally, has cited Malaysia as a good example in the world in terms of the justification for *halal* food certification.

Mohd Yusoff (2004) defined *halal* certification as the examination of food processes in terms of preparation, slaughter, cleaning, processing, handling, disinfecting, storing, transport and management practices. The application of *halal* should apply to all stages of processing 'from farm to table'. In fact, *halal* certification provides some significant commercial benefits, including consumer confidence where it allows purchases to make an informed choice. For example, a study by Wan Hassan and Hall (2003) on the demand for *halal* food by Muslim travellers in New Zealand stated that, as with any certification system involving consumers, the confidence of the consumer is of prime importance. The other benefit is competitive advantage as manufacturers can use it as a marketing tool to secure bigger market share as *halal* food is suitable for both Muslims and non-Muslims (Mohd Yusoff 2004; Al-Nahdi *et al.* 2009).

The Malaysian Standard MS 1500, 'General Guidelines on the Production, Preparation, Handling and Storage of *Halal* Food', prescribes the practical guidelines for the food industry on the preparation and handling of *halal* food and serves as a basic requirement for food products and the food trade or business in Malaysia (Mohd Daud 2004). It is used together with MS1480:1999, 'Food Safety According to Hazard Analysis and Critical Control Point (HACCP), and MS1514:2001, 'General Principles of Food Hygiene', to set out the necessary hygiene conditions for producing food suitable for consumption from primary production to the final consumer (Abdul Talib *et al.* 2008). According to Mohd Daud (2004), Malaysian Standard MS 1500, 'General Guidelines on the Production, Preparation, Handling and Storage of *Halal* Food', prescribes the practical guidelines for the food industry on *halal* conformance. In addition, the HACCP and *halal* system work together to ensure that a product is safe and can be consumed by anyone including non-Muslims.

Products from other countries are issued *halal* certificates by bodies accredited by JAKIM and other related Malaysian government bodies such as the Department of Veterinary Services, Food Safety and Quality Division, and the Ministry of Health Malaysia which is responsible for issuing the HACCP certificate (Din 2006). In addition, the Malaysian standard for *halal* certification is being developed to potentially act as a benchmark for a global *halal* standard not only for food but also for pharmaceuticals, cosmetics and preservatives although international *halal* standardization is hard to achieve (Mohd Yusoff 2004). Nevertheless, the development of *halal* certification and authority provisions may be internationally attractive. For example, there have been cases in the UK of reported malpractices in trading *halal* meat, including the introduction into the food chain of meat that is unfit for human consumption (Pointing and Teinaz 2004). Any food that is liable to cause ill health (e.g. food unfit for human consumption) cannot be considered *halal*, wholesome or as good *Tayyab/Toyyiban*. The Muslim Council of Britain (MCB) has even suggested that up to 90 per cent of the meat and poultry sold as *halal* in the United Kingdom has been sold illegally and not slaughtered in accordance with Islamic law (Ahmed 2008).

Malaysia has developed its industrial relations with regard to *halal* food through such agencies as JAKIM, the Department of Standards Malaysia, the Institute of Islamic Understanding Malaysia and the Malaysian Institute of Industrial Research and Standard (SIRIM). As a result, a comprehensive *halal* food standard called MS1500:2004 has been developed (Abdul Talib *et al.* 2008). This standard makes a compulsory requirement for physical separation of *halal* and *haram* during production, preparation, handling and storage activities (Mohd Janis 2004). All the products need to be labelled clearly to avoid being mixed or contaminated with non-*halal* products.

Attitudes towards *halal* certification in Malaysian restaurants

In food service terms, *halal* clearly affects quality and hygiene compliance in food manufacturing practices as well as restaurant food service. The issue of the role of *halal* in hospitality and tourism operations is of increasing significance for any food service businesses, given both the sheer size of the Islamic market and also its growing internationalization as a result of tourism and migration. Yet despite the growing importance of *halal* food there is very little discussion of the topic in the food service and hospitality literature (Wan Hassan and Hall 2003; Syed Marzuki *et al.* 2012a, 2012b), and most of the English language studies have focused on *halal* meat (Martini and Chee 2001; Waarden 2004; Bonne and Verbeke 2008), which is only one albeit significant dimension of *halal* food (Mohamed Nasir and Pereira 2008).

This chapter reports the results of a survey of the expectations of restaurant managers towards *halal* certification in Malaysia. This is believed to be the first such comprehensive study of restaurants and *halal* food certification anywhere in the world. The survey was designed to measure perceptions of *halal* certification, both in general and in the context of Malaysia. All items were measured using five-point Likert scales that were anchored from 'strongly agree' to 'strongly disagree'. A draft survey instrument was developed and pretested by the researchers. The cover page of the survey outlined the voluntary nature of the study, informed participants that their responses would remain anonymous, and provided the instructions for returning the survey in the self-addressed envelope provided. A mail survey was chosen due to its low cost and ability to reach a geographically widespread sample. No incentives were provided in order to encourage participation.

In July 2009, 2,080 questionnaires were mailed to restaurants throughout Malaysia. Restaurants were selected using systematic random sampling, where every fourth restaurant was selected from a list of 8,320 provided by the Companies Commission of Malaysia. The survey period was concluded in September 2009 after follow-ups were conducted to non-respondents. A total of 643 restaurant mangers completed the mail survey, thus giving an effective response rate of 30.9 per cent.

Table 14.1 summarizes the business profile of respondents. Kuala Lumpur and Selangor had the highest number of respondents. The majority of respondents (85.69 per cent) had worked in their current position for less than five years, and none of the participants had worked more than 30 years. Similar results were found for the food service industry, with 381 of the respondents (59.25 per cent) having worked in the sector for less than five years and none having experience of 30 years and above. More than 50 per cent of the participants came from *halal* certified restaurants (57.70 per cent), followed by restaurants that were non-certified but claimed to serve *halal* food (33.13 per cent) and the remainder (9.18 per cent) from non-*halal* restaurants.

A total of 643 restaurant managers participated in the mail survey and most of them belonged to the 21–30 years old age group (Table 14.2). The number of male respondents was higher than the female respondents with 397 and 246 respectively. The majority of participants were Muslim (61.59 per cent), followed by Buddhist (24.73 per cent), Christian (5.75 per cent), Hindu (4.04 per cent) and other religions (3.89 per cent). Most of the respondents involved in this study possessed the academic qualification of secondary school (23.95 per cent), diploma (33.44 per cent) and bachelor degree (19.60 per cent). The rest of the respondents held a Master's degree (2.64 per cent), with other qualifications at 7.93 per cent.

Perceptions of *halal* certification in general have raised many interesting and new findings. The results in Table 14.3 show that respondents perceived that *halal* certification meant that all food sources are *halal* certified with a high mean value of 4.41. It was believed that this improved the confidence level among Muslim customers (mean value of 4.40). Being a *halal*-certified restaurant means that it conforms to the *halal* standard (4.39), thus ensuring trust (4.37). Trust has been an important subject matter in academic research on *halal* foods and their certification (Abdul Latif 2006; Dahalan 2008; Al-Nahdi *et al.* 2009). As discussed above, *halal* food is a sensitive matter to Muslims. A Muslim must have no doubts as to whether food may be considered *halal*; otherwise it is *haram* or not to be consumed.

Restaurant managers also perceived that *halal* certification had a positive impact on customer satisfaction, contributing to an increase in demand particularly from Muslim customers (4.30) and providing customers with peace of mind during the dining experience (4.29). Like trust and confidence, having emotional calm (Johns and Howard 1998) or peace of mind is essential for the Muslim dining experience (see also Bonne and Verbeke 2008; Mohamed Nasir and Pereira 2008).

The findings also show that the majority of respondents believed that *halal* certification benefits everyone who visit, their eating premises (mean value of

Table 14.1 Summary of business demographics

Business demographic variables	Categories	Frequency	Percentage
City/state	Kuala Lumpur	215	33.44
	Selangor	238	37.01
	Perak	13	2.02
	Pulau Pinang	38	5.91
	Kedah	16	2.49
	Perlis	2	0.31
	Kelantan	2	0.31
	Terengganu	3	0.47
	Pahang	23	3.58
	Johor	38	5.91
	Melaka	23	3.58
	Negeri Sembilan	21	3.27
	Sabah	10	1.56
	Sarawak	1	0.16
	Total	643	100.00
Seating capacity	Below than 50	171	26.59
	51–100	280	43.55
	101–150	111	17.26
	151–200	41	6.38
	More than 200	40	6.22
	Total	643	100.00
Number of employees	Below than 10	319	49.51
	11–20	233	36.24
	21–30	50	7.78
	31–40	18	2.80
	More than 40	23	3.58
	Total	643	100.00
Number of years working in current position	Less than 5 years	551	85.69
	6–10 years	69	10.73
	11–20 years	22	3.42
	21–30 years	1	0.16
	More than 30 years	0	0.00
	Total	643	100.00
Number of years working in food service industry	Less than 5 years	381	59.25
	6–10 years	153	23.79
	11–20 years	97	15.09
	21–30 years	12	1.87
	More than 30 years	0	0.00
	Total	643	100.00
Type of eating establishment	Certified *Halal*	643	100.00
	Halal Claimant	213	33.13
	Non *Halal*	59	9.18
	Total	643	100.00

Table 14.2 Summary of respondent demographics

Personal demographic variables	Categories	Frequency	Percentage
Age	Below 21	32	4.98
	21–30	339	52.72
	31–40	187	29.08
	41–50	61	9.49
	51–60	20	3.11
	61 and above	4	0.62
	Total	643	100.00
Gender	Male	397	61.74
	Female	246	38.26
	Total	643	100.00
Religion	Buddhist	159	24.73
	Christian	37	5.75
	Hindu	26	4.04
	Muslim	396	61.59
	Other	25	3.89
	Total	643	100.00
Race	Chinese	189	29.39
	Indian	37	5.75
	Malay	359	55.83
	Other	58	9.02
	Total	643	100.00
Educational background	Doctor of Philosophy	0	0.00
	Master's degree	17	2.64
	Bachelor degree	126	19.60
	Diploma	215	33.44
	Certificate	80	12.44
	Secondary school	154	23.95
	Other	51	7.93
	Total	643	100.00

4.28). It was believed by respondents that apart from the issue of food a *halal*-certified eating establishment in one way or another can generate a harmonious environment where Muslims and non-Muslims can share the same food and eat at the same table (Wan Hassan and Hall 2003; Mohamed Nasir and Pereira 2008). Although there may be several issues with respect to 'defensive dining' (Mohamed Nasir and Pereira 2008), where devout and practising Muslims might find themselves in an uncomfortable situation when dining publicly (in restaurants, food courts and individual booths) and conflicts with Islamic dietary restrictions might occur, the findings revealed Muslims and non-Muslims were not separated and no one was excluded from a *halal*-certified restaurant.

Halal certification has certain attributes and Table 14.3 indicates that responses have high mean values, including hygiene (4.17), safety (4.17), food

Table 14.3 Descriptive statistics for perceptions of *Halal* certification in general

Questions I think halal certification in restaurants . . .	N	Mean	SD	Skewness	Std. Error
signifies all food sources are *halal* certified	643	4.41	0.80	−1.46	0.10
increases confidence level among the Muslim customers	643	4.40	0.81	−1.59	0.10
signifies conformance to *halal* standard	643	4.39	0.74	−1.33	0.10
signifies trust	643	4.37	0.80	−1.38	0.10
has a positive impact on customer satisfaction	643	4.30	0.79	−1.10	0.10
increases demand from the Muslim customers	643	4.30	0.84	−1.23	0.10
provides customers with peace of mind during the dining experience	643	4.29	0.80	−0.99	0.10
benefits everyone	643	4.28	0.89	−1.34	0.10
relies on trust on the suppliers when purchasing the food items	643	4.23	0.81	−1.13	0.10
signifies hygienic	643	4.17	0.93	−1.17	0.10
signifies safety	643	4.17	0.91	−1.17	0.10
signifies food quality	643	4.12	0.99	−1.25	0.10
signifies healthy food	643	4.07	1.00	−1.13	0.10
signifies authenticity	643	4.00	0.93	−0.87	0.10
signifies taste genuikeness	643	3.94	1.00	−0.86	0.10
gives competitive advantage over non-certified *halal* restaurants	643	3.93	1.04	−0.78	0.10
acts as a marketing strategy tool	643	3.91	1.01	−0.97	0.10
is a trademark establishment	643	3.88	1.04	−0.82	0.10
attracts the tourism market	643	3.85	1.01	−0.65	0.10
increases confidence level among the non-Muslim customers	643	3.61	1.03	−0.32	0.10
increases demand from the non-Muslim customers	643	3.56	1.02	−0.28	0.10
Valid N (listwise)	643				

quality (4.12), healthy food (4.07) and authenticity (4.00). *Halal* food must come from *halal* food preparation and the *halal* food supply chain. Restaurant managers from *halal*-certified and *halal*-claimant restaurants agreed that they trusted their suppliers (mean value of 4.23). Mohd Yusoff (2004) also emphasized that in order for the manufacturers to comply with *halal* certification, they are obliged to act responsibly to maintain the *halal* status of the food they produce. In addition, cleanliness and hygiene are closely related and affect personal hygiene, attire, equipment and working environment. Pang and Toh (2008), in their study on hawker food industry in Malaysia, reported that hygiene is very important in Islam, given that some parts of the body must be washed before prayers. In fact, this ablution process takes place almost every time before a Muslim performs his daily prayer.

Restaurant managers who participated in the mail survey strongly agreed that *halal* certification signifies safety. Such results are supported by the literature on the importance of certification for food safety (Mohd Yusoff 2004; Riaz and Chaudry 2004). The emphasis on bodily cleanliness and hygiene by some Muslim hawkers may even have a significant effect on the higher food safety performance standard of this religious group compared to others (Pang and Toh 2008).

Halal certification is seen as a source of competitive advantage (3.93) over non-*halal*-certified restaurants. Therefore, marketing plays a vital part in attracting customers, particularly Muslims, with restaurant managers agreeing that *halal* certification acts as a marketing strategy tool (mean value of 3.91). Al-Nahdi *et al.* (2009) suggested that marketing communication tools need to be employed in order to advertise and promote a *halal* restaurant and highlight that eating premises with *halal* certification follow Islamic principles. *Halal* certification is also generally accepted by the respondents as a way to gain confidence and build trust not only in the food service but also in the tourism industry (Josiam *et al.* 2007). Respondents also perceived that *halal* certification could be a way of appealing to Muslim tourists from the Middle East and other parts of the world (mean value of 3.85). However, respondents were less sure that *halal* certification could generate confidence and demand among non-Muslims (mean values of 3.61 and 3.56 respectively).

Discussion

Conforming to *halal* standards and procedures is a must in a *halal* eating environment in order to guarantee the welfare of Muslim customers. In Islam, eating is considered a matter of worship of God, like ritual prayers, whether or not the food has been changed to suit a new environment (Riaz and Chaudry 2004). Muslims must not have doubts about their food but if uncertainty arises, they must leave the food immediately so as not to eat prohibited food. Here, trust plays a vital role when deciding to visit an eating place.

Halal is about trust, responsibility, respect and strict compliance with other food certifications like kosher, organic and Genetically Modified Organisms

(GMO). Trust and perception appear to be very important factors when a customer decides to patronize a particular vendor. Mohamed Nasir and Pereira (2008) found that a large majority of respondents indicated that when they were in doubt regarding *halal* status, they would not visit an eating establishment. They require what Shafie and Othman (2006) describe as 'peace of mind', meaning that Muslim, must know that they are obeying Islamic dietary laws. The results of this study indicate that respondents believed that *halal* certification meant that a restaurant is complying with Islamic dietary laws (Waarden 2004). The importance of trust in a restaurant and its supply chain repeats the findings of other studies on *halal* food, products and restaurants (Aliman and Othman 2007; Dahalan 2008; Wan Omar *et al.* 2008; Al-Nahdi *et al.* 2009). A large majority of restaurant managers who participated in the survey envisaged that *halal* certification would represent the whole restaurant experience. The clear *halal* logo at the entrance means that not only is the food served *halal* but the entire process will be *halal* as well.

Given that Muslim consumers must be certain that they are buying genuine *halal* products, then trust is arguably an even more important purchasing issue than price (Ahmed 2008). The results of the survey reported here suggest that consumers choose certification as a value while sustaining an enjoyable dining experience. Every step from 'farm to table' appears to be critical (Abdul Talib *et al.* 2008). *Halal* certification is therefore a clear example of what Kirwan (2006) describes as face-to-face interactions between producers and consumers where authenticity and trust are co-produced by both parties. Peri (2006) argued that trust is expressed as a relationship between people, not as a relationship between a person and a product. Personal trust guarantees food quality, with trusted people supplying food based on professional competence and moral reliability. Food certification therefore acts as a further guarantee for consumers in obtaining quality foods (Peri 2006). A similar observation was made by De Jonge *et al.* (2008) who noted that consumers place great trust in institutions that have a responsibility for guaranteeing food safety, for instance farmers, retailers, manufacturers and regulators. Trust in these cases extends to certification brands, regulatory bodies, processes and implementation.

Food traceability aims to create a standardized locational information system that includes all food at all stages of production, from farm to fork (Popper 2007). Islamic dietary laws proceed from a set of principles, standards and rules applied throughout the production and distribution process (Bonne and Verbeke 2008). The concerns of Muslims over the *halal* nature of their food is part of a broader public concern with respect to food product traceability and food quality (Farm and Jacoby 2005; Kirwan 2006; Popper 2007). Traceability and food safety are interrelated and often lead to closer links among value chain members (Grunert 2005). However, this requires good communication and cooperation between members as intelligence on consumer demand has to travel all the way back to agricultural producers.

Interestingly, *halal* certification is also viewed by respondents having marketing aspects that act as a strategic tool to persuade customers to purchase from their restaurants. Restaurant managers regarded *halal* certification as a trademark giving a winning value over non-certified restaurants. *Halal* certification by restaurants was also regarded as reinforcing government efforts to promote Malaysia as both a *halal* food hub and a destination for Muslim tourists (Wan Omar *et al.* 2008). Above all, the *halal* food supply chain is the basis on which the *halal* standard delivers trusted *halal* food to customers.

Conclusions

This study provides evidence that *halal* certification serves as a sign of trust restaurant customers that the whole food system is *halal*. JAKIM is now implementing a single *halal* logo for its products and services to avoid confusion (Ngah 2010). The main objective is to give assurance to Muslim consumers that food and services comply with Islamic law.

In the commercial restaurant sector managers who operate *halal* restaurants must be fully aware that their whole process must follow standards of *halal* and *haram*. Restaurants with a *halal* status create trust and confidence for Muslim customers and also for their community. Moreover, it is believed that *halal* certification simultaneously promotes cleanliness, safety and food quality and offers marketing benefits for the domestic and international tourism industry. This enhances the wider market and promotes return patronage, thereby substantially contributing to the sustainability of individual businesses.

Islamic dietary laws instruct Muslims to eat food that is good and pure according to the *Al-Quran* and *hadith*. It also offers Muslims freedom to eat and drink a wide range of foods they like on condition that it is not *haram*. A good Muslim must be absolutely certain that the food he or she intends to eat is *halal*. In relation to the findings, most of the restaurant managers agreed that trust is an essential element in the food service industry. Therefore, *halal* certification is seen as a means to build trust among Muslims that food with that status is consumable.

As with other religious, e.g. kosher, and secular food supply chain concerns, e.g. organic, carbon content, or GE free, every step from farm to fork must follow *halal* rules and standards as this increases the confidence level of consumers, including restaurant patrons. The *halal* concept is vital for the cultural sustainability of Muslims although *halal* certification means that all such foods are fit for human consumption (Mohd Yusoff 2004; Riaz and Chaudry 2004; Abdul Talib *et al.* 2008). *Halal* restaurant certification is also important economically both with respect to increasing Muslim customer confidence and in terms of attracting Muslim tourists from other countries. Certification is likely to be a significant contributor to the economic sustainability of Malaysian tourism. However, further research needs to be conducted on the extent to which *halal* certification may also contribute to environmental sustainability as *halal* consumption clearly favours some consumption and production practices over others. Nevertheless, most fundamentally, the study highlights the importance of understanding different foodways and the regulatory and institutional processes, including religious practices, that surround them, the better to understand the culturally constructed dimensions of sustainability in the hospitality and tourism industries.

Acknowledgements

Research for this chapter was funded by the Ministry of Higher Education Malaysia, Universiti Teknologi Mara, the University of Canterbury and the New Zealand Asian Studies Society.

References

Abdul Latif, M. (2006) Training on Halal Procedures and Standards. Online. Available: www.afmaasia.org/malaysia_2006/Annex-4.pdf (accessed 10 March 2008).

Abdul Talib, H.H., Mohd Ali, K.A. and Jamaludin, K.R. (2008) 'Quality assurance in halal food manufacturing in Malaysia: a preliminary study', paper presented at the International Conference on Mechanical & Manufacturing Engineering (ICME), Johor Bahru, Malaysia.

Ahmed, A. (2008) 'Marketing of *halal* meat in the United Kingdom', *British Food Journal*, 110(7): 655–70.

Aidaros, H. (2005) 'Global perspectives – the Middle East: Egypt', *Revue Scientifique et Technique – Office International*, 24(2): 589–96.

Al-Harran, S. and Low, P. (2008) 'Marketing of *halal* products: the way forward', *The Halal Journal*, 42–4.

Aliman, N.K. and Othman, M.N. (2007) 'Purchasing local and foreign brands: what Product Attributes Matter?' paper presented at the 13th Asia Pacific Management Conference, Melbourne, Australia.

Al-Nahdi, M.T.S.M., Ismail, I., Haron, H. and Islam, M.A. (2009) *'Intention to patronage halal restaurants among Malaysian Muslims – an issue of halal perception'*, paper presented at the Global Business Summit Conference.

Al-Qaradawi, Y. (1980) *The Lawful and the Prohibited in Islam Al-Halal Wal-Haram Fil Islam*, Indianapolis, Ind.: American Trust Publications.

Al-Suhrawardy, A.S. (1990) *The Sayings of Muhammad*, New York: Carol Publishing Group.

Bonne, K. and Verbeke, W. (2008) 'Religious values informing *halal* meat production and the control and delivery of *halal* credence quality', *Agriculture and Human Values*, 25: 35–47.

Bonne, K., Vermier, I., Bergeaud-Blackler, F. and Verbeke, W. (2007) 'Determinants of *halal* meat consumption in France', *British Food Journal*, 109(5): 367–86.

Dabayeh, A. (1998) Halal Slaughter. Online. Available: www.islamicvoice.com/may.98/ CHILD.HTM (accessed 23 June 2010).

Dahalan, Z. (2008) 'Kecenderungan Umat Islam Terhadap Konsep Pemakanan Halal: Kajian Di UiTM Pulau Pinang' [The tendency of Muslims towards halal food concept: a study in UiTM Pulau Pinang], paper presented at the ECER Regional Conference, Kelantan, Malaysia.

Dana, L. and Vignali, C. (1998) 'Introductory cases', *British Food Journal*, 100(2): 49–57.

De Jonge, J., Van Trijp, H., Goddard, E. and Frewer, L. (2008) 'Consumer confidence in

272   *S.Z. Syed Marzuki* et al.

the safety of food in Canada and the Netherlands: the validation of a generic framework', *Food Quality and Preference*, 19: 439–51.

Department of Standards Malaysia (2004) *Halal Food – Production, Preparation, Handling and Storage: General Guidelines, First Revision*, Selangor: Department of Standards Malaysia.

Din, S. (2006) *Trading Halal Commodities: Opportunities and Challenges for the Muslim World*, Kuala Lumpur: Universiti Teknologi Malaysia.

Farm, S.S. and Jacoby, L. (2005) *Feasibility of Marketing Traditionally Slaughtered and Processed Meat to Economically and Culturally Diverse Families, Food Markets and Restaurants*, Madison: Wisconsin Department of Agriculture, Trade and Consumer Protection.

Feenstra, G.W. (1997) 'Local food systems and sustainable communities', *American Journal of Alternative Agriculture*, 12(1): 28–36.

Finch, M.L. (2010) 'Food, taste, and American religions', *Religion Compass*, 4(1): 39–50.

Gössling, S., Hall, C.M. and Weaver, D.B. (2009) 'Sustainable tourism futures: perspectives on systems, restructuring and innovations', in S. Gössling, C.M. Hall and D.B. Weaver (eds) *Sustainable Tourism Futures*, New York: Routledge.

Grunert, K.G. (2005) 'Food quality and safety: consumer perception and demand', *European Review of Agricultural Economics*, 32(3): 369–91.

Hall, C.M. (2011) 'Policy learning and policy failure in sustainable tourism governance: from first and second to third order change?', *Journal of Sustainable Tourism*, 19: 649–71.

Hall, C.M. and Lew, A. (1998) 'The geography of sustainable tourism development: an introduction', in C.M. Hall and A. Lew (eds) *Sustainable Tourism Development: Geographical Perspectives*, London: Addison-Wesley Longman.

Hall, C.M. and Mitchell, R. (2000) 'We are what we eat: food, tourism and globalization', *Tourism, Culture and Communication*, 2(1): 29–37.

Hazair, H.P. (2007) More to Trade than Getting Halal Seal. Online. Available: www.bruneitimes.com.bn/business/2007/08/21/more_to_trade_than_getting_halal_seal (accessed 11 September 2007).

JAKIM (2010) *Sejarah* Halal [Halal History]. Online. Available: www.*halal*.gov.my/v2/index.php?ty=content_view&id=AUS-20090312113707&type=PRO (accessed 18 August 2010).

Johns, N. and Howard, A. (1998) 'Customer expectations versus perceptions of service performance in the food service industry', *International Journal of Service Industry Management*, 9(3): 248–65.

Josiam, B.M., Sohail, S.M. and Monteiro, P.A. (2007) 'Curry cuisine: perceptions of Indian restaurants in Malaysia', *Tourismos: An International Multidisciplinary Journal of Tourism*, 2(2): 25–37.

Kirwan, J. (2006) 'The interpersonal world of direct marketing: examining conventions of quality at UK farmers' markets', *Journal of Rural Studies*, 22: 301–12.

Kocturk, T.O. (2002) 'Food rules in the Koran', *Scandinavian Journal of Nutrition*, 46(3): 137–39.

Littig, B. and Grießler, E. (2005) 'Social sustainability: a catchword between political pragmatism and social theory', *International Journal Sustainable Development*, 8(1/2): 65–79.

Martini, F. and Chee, W.T. (2001) 'Restaurants in Little India, Singapore: a study of spatial organization and pragmatic cultural change', *SOJOURN*, 16(1), 147–61.

Mohamed Nasir, K. and Pereira, A.A. (2008) 'Defensive dining: notes on the public dining experiences in Singapore', *Contemporary Islam*, 2: 61–73.

Mohd Daud, R. (2004) 'HACCP system for food safety', *Standards & Quality News*, 11: 8–9.

Mohd Janis, Z. (2004) '*Halal* food – production, preparation, handling and storage', *Standard & Quality News*, 11: 2–3.

Mohd Yusoff, H. (2004) '*Halal* certification scheme', *Standard & Quality News*, 11: 4–5.

Muhammad, R. (2007) 'Re-branding *Halal*', *The Halal Journal*, May–June: 32, 34.

Naeem, A.G. (2003) 'The role of culture and religion in the management of diabetes: a study of Kashmiri men in Leeds', *The Journal of the Royal Society for the Promotion of Health*, 123(2): 110–16.

National SME Development Council (2006) Moving Forward. Chapter 8: Potential Growth Areas for SMEs. Online. Available: www.bnm.gov.my/files/publication/sme/en/2006/chap_8.pdf (accessed 6 July 2008).

Ngah, N. (2010) Hanya JAKIM, JAIN keluar sijil *halal* [*Halal* Certification Will only be Issued by JAKIM and JAIN]. Online. Available: www.bharian.com.my/bharian/articles/HanyaJAKIM_JAINkeluarsijil*halal*/Article/ (accessed 26 July 2010).

Nicolaou, M., Doak, C.M., Dam, R.M. v., Brug, J., Stronks, K. and Seidell, J.C. (2009) 'Cultural and social influences on food consumption in Dutch residents of Turkish and Moroccan origin: a qualitative study', *Journal of Nutrition Education and Behaviour*, 41(4): 232–41.

Pang, F. and Toh, P.S. (2008) 'Hawker food industry: food safety/public health strategies in Malaysia', *Nutrition & Food Science*, 38(1): 41–51.

Parker-Jenkins, M. (2008) 'Achieving cultural sustainability?: The phenomenon of Jewish and Muslim schools in England and Wales', in Z. Bekerman and E. Kopelowitz (eds) *Cultural Education – Cultural Sustainability: Minority, Diaspora, Indigenous and Ethno-Religious Groups in Multicultural Societies*, New York: Routledge.

Peri, C. (2006) 'The universe of food quality', *Food Quality and Preference*, 17(1/2): 3–8.

Pointing, J. and Teinaz, Y. (2004) 'Halal meat and food crime in the UK', paper presented at the International *Halal* Food Seminar, Islamic University College of Malaysia.

Popper, D.E. (2007) 'Traceability: tracking and privacy in the food system', *The Geographical Review*, 97(3): 365–88.

Regenstein, J.M., Chaudry, M.M. and Regenstein, C.E. (2003) 'The kosher and *Halal* food laws', *Comprehensive Reviews in Food Science and Food Safety*, 2: 111–27.

Reynolds, P.C. (1993) 'Food and tourism: towards an understanding of sustainable culture', *Journal of Sustainable Tourism*, 1(1): 48–54.

Riaz, M.N. and Chaudry, M.M. (2004) *Halal Food Production*, Boca Raton: CRC Press.

Shafie, S. and Othman, M.N. (2006) Halal *Certification: International Marketing Issues and Challenges*. Online. Available: www.ctwcongress.de/ifsam/download/track13/pap00226.pdf (accessed 8 October 2007).

Syed Marzuki, S.Z., Hall, C.M. and Ballantine. P.W. (2012a) 'Restaurant managers' perspectives on halal certification', *Journal of Islamic Marketing*, 3(1), 47–58.

Syed Marzuki, S.Z., Hall, C.M. and Ballantine. P.W. (2012b) 'Restaurant manager expectations toward halal certification in Malaysia', *Journal of Foodservice Business Research*, 15(2), DOI: 10.1080/15378020.2012.677654.

Waarden, F. v. (2004) 'A treatise on taste, traditions, transactions, trust and tragedies'. paper presented at the conference European Food Regulation: The Politics of Contested Governance, University of California, Berkeley.

Wan Hassan, W.M. and Hall, C.M. (2003) 'The demand for *halal* food among Muslim travellers in New Zealand', in C.M. Hall, L. Sharples, R. Mitchell, N. Macionis and B. Cambourne (eds) *Food Tourism Around the World: Development, management and markets*, Oxford: Butterworth-Heinemann.

Wan Omar, W.M., Muhammad, M.Z. and Che Omar, A. (2008) 'An analysis of the Muslim consumers' attitudes towards "Halal" food products in Kelantan', paper presented at the ECER Regional Conference 2008, Kelantan, Malaysia.

15 Heritage cuisines, regional identity and sustainable tourism

Dallen J. Timothy and Amos S. Ron

Introduction

Food, cuisine and culinary traditions are among the most foundational elements of culture. While there is a long tradition of identifying many places with their traditional foods, cuisine is becoming an ever more important part of the contemporary cultural heritage of regions and countries. Regional cuisines enhance a destination's image abroad, they are often exported and replicated overseas, and many locations promote their culinary heritage as a means of creating a place-bound image and firming up their own cultural identities. Much research has documented the great pride with which many a region or country has preserved its gastronomical heritage (Gillespie 2001) and used it as a tool for socio-economic development through tourism (Boniface 2003; Long 2004).

Culinary tourism is a growing element of cultural tourism because, as Wolf (2008) notes, cuisine is a manifestation of culture and helps countries and regions define what they are and what it means to be from there. In doing so, either naturally and organically or intentionally through promotional campaigns, group and individual identities are formulated or enhanced, and destinations can become more empowered as they seek to develop tourism. The purpose of this chapter is to examine the role of cuisine as an important part of cultural heritage in the advancement of community empowerment, which is one of the most salient constituent parts of sustainability in tourism. The chapter first discusses the notion of destination empowerment, followed by an examination of cuisine as a marker of social identity and how traditional gastronomy can help empower destinations so that they can work better towards achieving the goals of sustainability.

Empowerment and sustainability

The concept of empowerment has received considerable attention from development specialists in the tourism context in recent years. Empowerment is now seen as one of the ultimate requirements for communities to achieve any degree of social, ecological or economic sustainability through tourism. Among the most identifiable principles of sustainable tourism are ecological and cultural integrity, social equity, holistic development, community harmony and balanced growth (Bramwell and Lane 1993).

In contrast to boosterist traditions of mass marketing to mass tourists, which rarely, if ever, upheld the goals of sustainability, since the 1990s development specialists have boldly suggested that more careful promotion is needed and alternatives to mass tourism are required if the resources upon which tourism is based are to remain viable in the long term. One aspect of these calls for more responsible and sustainable approaches to tourism is community-based, or participatory, planning and development. Since the 1970s, considerable attention has been devoted to understanding who should be involved in tourism development and planning, who the stakeholders are, and what role community members have to play in tourism development efforts.

Overwhelmingly, the conclusion has been that decision-making power needs to be decentralized away from the political and moneyed elites to the grassroots level, including the people on the ground who live and work in the destinations tourists visit. Many observers have argued that community-based, participatory growth, where the control of decision-making lies in the hands of all stakeholders, is the most sustainable approach to tourism, because it supports the principles of sustainability (those mentioned above) best (Okazaki 2008; Simpson 2001; Timothy 1999, 2002). The process of reassigning authority to communities and their stakeholders is known as empowerment and involves many elements of sustainable tourism by building community solidarity, providing economic opportunities, and enabling people who might have been voiceless in the past to have a voice in decision-making. This has more promise of building harmony and cooperation, equitable relationships between tourism and its stakeholders, and assuring higher levels of cultural preservation as communities come together to work for the common good of residents and the resources upon which their tourism is based. It can be argued that, in most cases at least, the most sustainable destinations are the most empowered destinations where people are invested with agency to control their own futures and those of their communities. True empowerment puts power squarely in the hands of the people most affected by tourism so that they own both the solutions and the challenges associated with it.

From the perspective of tourist destinations, observers have suggested several different types of empowerment that help communities cope with tourism and realize its potential in more responsible ways. Scheyvens (1999, 2002, 2003) is one of the most astute investigators of tourism destination empowerment. Based partially upon the works of Friedmann (1992), Scheyvens (1999) provides a useful framework for understanding community-based empowerment and assessing its success. She identifies four types of empowerment and disempowerment – empowerment when communities experience positive changes from tourism, and disempowerment when tourism brings with it the negative implications that have long been bemoaned in the tourism literature. The four types of empowerment include economic, social, psychological and political. These are not mutually exclusive, and there is heavy connectivity between them.

Economic empowerment exists in a destination when jobs are created via tourism and result in regular, reliable and lasting incomes for community members (Scheyvens 1999). This type of equity is also supported as entrepreneurial opportunities are open and available, and the fiscal benefits of tourism permeate the community so that as many stakeholders as desire such benefits can acquire them. Disadvantaged populations in many parts of the world are especially prone to economic exclusion through either official policies or traditional cultural practices. True economic empowerment can exist only when such 'marginal' peoples receive the benefits they desire from tourism as well (Timothy 1999, 2002).

Social empowerment entails communities having a sense of common purpose and solidarity, and an environment where cooperation and cohesion prevail through the development of tourism (Scheyvens 1999). Earnings from tourism are critical in helping fund social development and improved quality of life, such as clean water, enhanced health care and better educational opportunities (Harrison 2008; Scheyvens 2011). Strong community organizations are important in furthering the idea of social empowerment as they help facilitate improved standards of living and community cohesion. Timothy (2007) argues that indigenous participation in tourism development is a crucial part of social empowerment, for native knowledge is an indissoluble part of sustainable development because of its problem-solving capabilities and general harmony with nature and cultural heritage (Faust and Smardon 2001; Johnston 2003). As individuals become empowered, they see themselves as part of a larger whole, where common social needs outweigh individual needs, and a desire grows to participate more in developing responsible forms of tourism in their community.

Collective esteem, community pride and individual sense of worth are essential elements of psychological empowerment. Destinations that are psychologically empowered rejoice in their cultural traditions and happily share them with tourists. Powerful communities are optimistic about the future, relatively self-reliant and have faith in their citizens (Scheyvens 1999). This may lead to a widespread desire to preserve native heritages. Maintaining a group cultural identity through various means such as tourism is an important element of this as well. Elements of culture that are on the verge of disappearing can be salvaged with tourism earnings, as well as community pride in the past that drives residents to share their heritage with outsiders (Timothy 2007).

Traditionally, the definition of political empowerment is that destinations and their various stakeholders, particularly residents, can voice their opinions and concerns in the tourism planning and development process. Timothy (2007) takes this a step further though, by suggesting that the most empowered societies are those who truly own the benefits and costs of tourism and who are able to instigate tourism growth or reject it when it is imposed upon them. The most disempowered people in any given society should be among the most important stakeholders of all: ethnic minorities and the poor, for it is often these groups that suffer the brunt of tourism's negative impacts.

Cuisine and identity

Culture is generally defined as learned knowledge, as opposed to biological inclinations, and includes everything which members of any given society think, do and have, and which can be learned and shared (Ferraro and Andreatta 2009; Moore 1998). Thus, it includes material and non-material elements, such as beliefs, art, morals, customs, laws, behaviours, values, traditions and folklore, language and foodways. From this perspective, the need for food is biological, but the ways in which food is harvested, prepared and consumed are cultural.

As one of the most salient manifestations of traditional culture, and an important element of intangible heritage, cuisine and foodways are crucial building blocks of regional or national identity. In Israel, for example, foodways and food events (e.g. olive festivals) are developed in rural areas by destination marketing organizations as a means of counteracting agricultural decline. Such endeavours help solidify the Israeli identity while creating income for rural parts of the country. Gastronomical traditions reflect a variety of socio-ecological conditions that are inherent in definitions of place and ethnic identity. Inter-generational customs, struggles to subdue nature, cultural norms and values, influences on other elements of heritage, the veracity of geography and location, and temporal refinement are all representative of these conditions. Food traditions envelop many heritage elements, including indigenous peoples and their folklore, living conditions, celebrations and rituals, religious rites, interpersonal relationships, familial habits, recipes and customary cooking accoutrements (Timothy 2011).

There is also an overarching ecological inevitability regarding how foodways develop. The natural environment has in large part controlled the evolution of regional cuisines. Food traditions are limited or upheld by the environment where they originated. In the Middle East, for instance, foodways have long been determined by arid climates, based upon xerophytic staples that can endure dry environments (Heine 2004). The fare of islands or places near bodies of water has revolved around marine food sources. Portuguese, Spanish and Mexican coastal areas, for example, have provided the essential ocean-based ingredients for much of those countries' most famous dishes. The foods of the Caribbean and Pacific islands are also based largely on abundant seafood in many forms and root crops that grow well in sandy soils. In the Arctic regions of the world, native peoples have always depended on meat and other animal products for their survival: whales, walruses, seals, caribou, Arctic birds and polar bears. Traditionally, fruit and vegetables were almost unheard of, and to this day many northern peoples shy away from imported produce and continue to consume primarily animal-based diets (Lougheed 2010).

From a cultural perspective, what people eat defines who they are or are not. Cuisine and eating habits are closely linked to ethnic behaviours and religious beliefs (Heine 2004; Kittler and Sucher 2008). In most societies, eating traditions and culinary specialties developed from a wide range of cultural practices. Religion and spirituality played a crucial role in developing food practices. Offerings to gods or natural forces were important in most indigenous societies as a way of appeasing the deity or showing gratitude for blessings. Coming-of-age ceremonies and hunting rituals were also influential in the types of food prepared, as various food sources and meals had different meanings and societal values. Cuisines have been instrumental in forming group identity in a variety of ways, including cultural or ethnic cohesiveness, attachment to place, building nationalism, enhancing nostalgia and helping diasporic groups preserve their connections to the homeland.

Through centuries of human history, regional cuisines developed by way of the natural and cultural influences noted above – the same influences that determined many other elements of culture (e.g. dress, religion, music). Food provides nourishment to the body and functions as an important medium of communication that is rich in symbols and meaning (Wilk 1999).

Types of foods consumed, how foods are eaten and how often, and with whom (Ferraro and Andreatta 2009) have all been party to defining ethnicity and cultural identity. This has led to entire societies coalescing around not only food but also beliefs, languages, folklore, architecture and music to form distinctive and defining group characteristics. Because it is one of the most salient markers of cultural expression (Tellström *et al.* 2005), food became one of the defining symbols of culture, which 'tie[s] together people who otherwise might not be part of a unified group' (Ferraro and Andreatta 2009: 29). In Mexico, the beginning of the mestizo Mexican identity, as opposed to Native American or European, was 'the "happy encounter" between corn tortillas and pork sausage that produced the first taco' (Pilcher 1996: 193). Cuisine, thus, was a 'particularly potent symbol of ... group identity, forming one of the foundations of both individuality and a sense of common membership in a larger, bounded group' (Wilk 1999: 244).

Place is another salient element of cuisine and identity. Because of the peculiarities of place, from both natural and cultural perspectives, gastronomies developed in different ways in different places and continue to this day to be one of the most important identifiers of uniqueness of place and sense of place. From a culinary perspective, place can be viewed from a variety of different scales, but primarily we see them as regional or national. Even within countries there are many different kinds of regional cuisine based largely upon the crops and animals grown and the social history of the people. As such, cuisine has been crucial to the development of regional identities for centuries (Parasecoli 2004), particularly since so many different regions express their individuality through food (Cusack 2000). Culinary skills and practices, in the words of Bessière (1998: 29), have differentiated 'one area from another. They are an integral part of individual, collective and territorial identity construction'.

The relationship between food and place is critical in formulating cultural and ethnic identities (Feagan 2007), and the uniqueness of place-bound cuisine is what creates a sense of continuity and connectedness with the past for many people. Because gastronomy is so intimately connected to place and environment (Everett and Aitchison 2008), it is one of the most crucial forces connecting people to their primordial homelands (Timothy and Ron 2010).

Because of their unifying capability, culinary traditions have also played an important role in nation-building. Throughout history, cuisine has been identified as a means of solidifying national identity and building solidarity within countries (Narayan 1995). A national cuisine usually evolves by usurping and amassing various regional recipes that reflect 'long and complex culinary histories as well as domestic ideologies' (Cusack 2000: 207). Together with flags, coats of arms and national anthems, cuisine forms an important part of national culture (Cusack 2000) and has historically even helped in formulating the nation-state. Parasecoli (2004) noted how Italian cuisine helped in the creation of the Italian state during the eighteenth and nineteenth centuries. This is largely because of the important stories told by food, and because so many common elements in Italian cooking helped create a national ethos that united the Italian peoples.

In the case of Mexico, food has long played both a divisive and a uniting role in the process of national development. In colonial Mexico, food was an important marker of social and political status. The indigenous population were labelled the lower-class 'people of the corn', because of the native propensity to consume maize-based foodstuffs, while the Europeans were the wheat-eating nobility. Native dishes were despised by the colonial elites. Eventually, after independence, these food-based social divisions faded, and a mixed mestizo cuisine emerged to help congeal a national Mexican identity (Pilcher 1996). Through the nineteenth and early twentieth centuries, and after considerable debate among various elements of Mexican society (e.g. cultural specialists, chefs, cookbook authors, agriculturists), Mexico's culinary culture began to accept both corn and wheat. While corn and wheat created the divisive element of culinary history in Mexico, the chilli was the only ingredient that pervaded the tastes of both the Europeans and the natives. This mix and, according to many observers and activists, the heavy use of chillies, became the crux of what constituted Mexican cuisine and distinguished it from European fare (Pilcher 1996). Thus, while food divided the indigenes from the colonizers in the beginning, it resulted in a unified vision of statehood and helped create a sense of national solidarity.

Foodways are also directly tied to the ideas of memory and nostalgia, or a longing for something from one's past either directly through personal experience or indirectly through stories and folklore. Memories are often constructed through cuisine, and food as an agent of memory can trigger positive or negative recollections that one would want to continue or obstruct (Holtzman 2006). According to Suen (2007), cuisine is essential to keeping the Chinese memory alive in multicultural Singapore.

Agritourism too has developed in large part because of a need for people to relive memories of earlier times spent on a farm, picking and eating the wholesome foods of their youth (Che 2006). Pick-your-own farms are important for many people in reliving their own agrarian past or sharing the sources of food with the next generation (Timothy and Ron 2009). These journeys of nostalgia permit people to taste the foods they once knew and they also function to help people learn to prepare the traditional foods of their societies (Che 2006; Crouch 2003).

Cultural identity, attachment to place, nation-building and nostalgia through cuisine traditions are all critical in understanding the plight of diasporic peoples across the globe. Ethnic cuisine is one of the most important cultural markers, together with language, music, holidays and ceremonies, that helps diasporic groups and other immigrants to fight the forces of acculturation and cultural assimilation to maintain their identity and connections to the homeland (Thursby 2004; Sukovic *et al.* 2011; Kaftanoglu and Timothy, in press). Among diasporic peoples, food is closely linked to memory. Their ethnic identities, memories of the motherland and attachments to place are performed and maintained through food perhaps more than any other cultural marker (Holtzman 2006). According to Holtzman (2006: 367), the tastes and fragrances of the homeland afford a 'temporary return to a time when their lives were not fragmented' where food becomes 'a nexus of nostalgia and diasporic identity'.

Given these realities of place and culture, certain foods and ingredients have become well connected with particular regions, forming a gastronomy-driven heritage identity that often translates into tourism potential. For many travellers, cuisine is a very important part of their experience, as it helps distinguish one destination from another. In some cases, people travel specifically to partake of a region's food and drink. According to Parasecoli (2004), food is one of the main reasons why many Americans travel to Italy, given its culinary reputation and Americans' love of Italian food. Many destinations have attempted to capitalize on their epicurean advantages by marketing themselves as food destinations or highlighting their heritage cuisines as an important part of their tourism product and brand image (Hjalager and Corigliano 2000; Hall *et al.* 2003; du Rand and Heath 2006; Tellström *et al.* 2006; Okumus *et al.* 2007; Warde 2009). Cuisine heritage sometimes evolves organically and brands destinations as dietary 'other places', while in many cases it is used intentionally to enhance an image or create a new identity (Bessière 2001; Chuang 2009; Lin *et al.* 2011). Many regions and countries devote considerable attention to national and ethnic cuisines in their tourism planning exercises as well (Schlüter and Ellul 2008).

Foodways and cuisine are becoming a more common medium for creating destination images and identities. Both perceived images, or people's perceptions about a particular place, and projected images, those images created by media and other information sources (Lin *et al.* 2011), are important for destinations that are trying to utilize gastronomy as a tourist attraction. Fox (2007) identified several ways in which a sound gastronomical identity can be created and maintained as a way of promoting tourist destinations: differentiation (uniqueness), aestheticization (playing on emotions, pleasures, desires and states of mind), authentication (genuineness and tradition), symbolization (symbols of local identity) and rejuvenation (refresh images of destinations).

'Ethnic foods' are also becoming more popular in the Western world. One of the main reasons for this growing popularity is that ethnic foods are often seen as being healthier and more natural. Some of Western Europeans' and North

Americans' favourite ethnic foods are Mexican, Chinese, Thai, Middle Eastern and Indian, although in most instances these foreign foods rarely resemble the original fares of the lands where they originated (Germann Molz 2004). Through diasporic migrations, ethnic foods spread from their original hearths to other regions of the globe. Through this process and others (e.g. exploration and colonialism), traditional foods were introduced to outsiders, many of whom acquired a taste for the unfamiliar flavours. At times, dishes were amended to suit the tastes of people in the immigrants' adopted homeland and their rejection of key ingredients (e.g. taboos against eating horse or dog meat in the United States), or original ingredients were replaced by others because the originals were unavailable in the new country. Thus, tastes tended to change through time and acculturation, and the masses became accustomed to non-original versions of ethnic cuisines.

In this regard, ethnic cuisines can hardly be considered truly authentic, given the evolutionary nature of food, both in the homeland and abroad. In the places of origin, the most authentic foods might, in some cases, be unappealing to tourists. Furthermore, few truly authentic dishes exist anywhere in the world because of colonial, immigration and globalization influences (Hall and Mitchell 2000; Fox 2007; Hirsch 2011). Diners in their own home regions often eat at ethnic restaurants with preconceived notions about authentic foods, which are often reinforced through restaurant ambience, menu selection and ingredients (Germann Molz 2004). Authenticity is an elusive concept, with some observers suggesting that it can be measured empirically and experienced objectively, while others criticize the notion, suggesting that authenticity is a subjective idea that differs from person to person and place to place (Timothy 2011).

Perhaps a better concept which seems to allow more external influences on foodways is 'traditional cuisines'. In contemporary tourism there is a growing interest in traditional cuisines as part of a more authentic travel experience (Bessière 1998). Vernacular landscapes, or elements of the ordinary landscape, are becoming a more important element of the tourism product, as opposed to heritages that focus only on the ruling classes. This new trend highlights many traditional agricultural practices and products, so that the range of food is expanding, and customary ingredients, preparation methods and recipes are being offered to tourists instead of the homogenized styles to which they have become accustomed. The element of nostalgia comes into play as destinations and their associated gastronomies are played up to epitomize good old times and good old food against bad new food (Fox 2007).

Some traditional dishes are seen as 'gross food' by outsiders, although many are now more willing to try them as part of a more embedded cultural experience. Gross food, or 'scary food', as Gyimóthy and Mykletun (2009) describe it, can be an important point of pride for destination residents as they proudly serve their freakish specialties to tourists. The municipality of Voss, Norway, for example, takes great pride in serving its traditional salted, smoked and cooked sheep's head, split in half and served on a platter. It is marketed as a nostalgic or 'authentic' rural dish and a 'challenging culinary trophy appealing to thrill seeking consumers' (Gyimóthy and Mykletun 2009: 253).

Heritage cuisine and empowerment

The regional identities that heritage cuisines help to create are essential building blocks to empower communities socially, psychologically, economically and politically. Strong regional or national identities embedded in a cultural past, such as with foodways, is important in empowering destination communities as they demonstrate to tourists their heritage and their traditions, as well as their ability to adapt to the modern world. As Warde (2009: 153) noted, cuisine is not simply about cooking; it includes 'all that the composition of meals entails for a social collectivity – tools, recipes, condiments, typical ingredients and organization of eating'. As noted at the outset, cuisines are related to history and reflect longevity, familiarity, development and authenticity. Gastronomy is 'identified in terms of place of origin and presented as evolving from spatially specific traditions' (Warde 2009: 153).

Figure 15.1 illustrates the relationships between regional identity created through culinary heritage and the four types of empowerment described at the outset of the chapter. The figure suggests that regional identities, as described in the previous section, provide the foundation or the linking threads that facilitate the empowerment of communities as they share their culinary heritage with outsiders. The societal cohesiveness inherent in the formulation of regional identities leads to more empowered communities. This, then, leads to more sustainable destinations via heritage cuisines. The following sections highlight in more detail the forms of empowerment as they pertain specifically to cuisine-based cultural tourism.

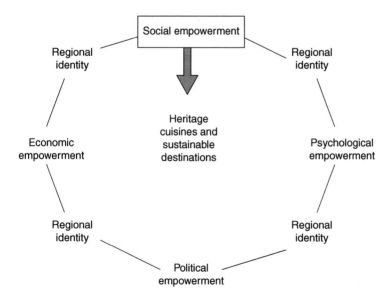

Figure 15.1 The relationships between regional identity created through culinary heritage and the four types of empowerment.

Social and psychological empowerment

The social and place-based identities that heritage cuisines help create are extremely formidable in forwarding social and psychological empowerment. Many regional foodways have their roots in the types of subsistence foods once prepared by indigenous peoples (Kuhnlein *et al.* 2009). Indigenous knowledge comes to the fore as traditional gastronomy is developed and shared with tourists, and often native peoples are consulted as cuisines become refined and they are relied upon to help identify national dishes and traditional ingredients in regional foods.

As the Mexican example described earlier demonstrates (Pilcher 1996), national and regional pride and solidarity are enhanced as gastronomy-based identities help establish national dishes and highlight the native and colonial influences that created them. The 'valorization' of culinary heritage inspires collective initiatives and local action for the greater good of society (Bessière 1998). It helps build solidarity, common purpose and community pride as traditional fare is enjoyed by local residents and shared with tourists. The Norwegian example of *smalahove* (cooked sheep's head) illustrates how a traditional food can become a tourist attraction in its own right. The notion that trophy-hunting thrill-seekers are both repulsed and attracted by such a dish is a considerable point of pride and unifying force for the residents of Voss (Gyimóthy and Mykletun 2009).

In common with other elements of culture, tourism can help maintain culinary heritage that is on the verge of disappearing or help resurrect foods that might have already disappeared. In Taiwan, tourism and the development of haute cuisine have been an important motive for restoring ethnic foods that have already disappeared, especially regional fare that reflects the construction of the Taiwanese national identity (Chuang 2009). Maintaining cooking methods and ingredients is an empowering task that often requires a great deal of collaboration in destination communities to assure that traditional methods and recipes are preserved (Sukovic *et al.* 2011). Local food also plays a key role in helping conserve traditional heritage, skills and ways of life (Everett and Aitchison 2008) – all very important elements of community empowerment and sustainable tourism. Heritage cuisines and their consumption by tourists can also help train younger generations to maintain knowledge about foodways and traditional cooking methods (Everett and Aitchison 2008).

Economic empowerment

Tourism based wholly or partly on culinary heritage has the potential to help rural regeneration in economically depressed areas (Bessière 2001; Hjalager and Richards 2002; Everett and Aitchison 2008; Hall and Sharples 2008). In addition to job creation, the collaborative effects brought about through cuisine-induced identities can have a residual effect of stretching the economic benefits of tourism more equitably throughout a tourist destination. Much of this is currently being accomplished through culinary routes that link different sites together to form a network of cuisine heritage places that provides a more regional experience and gets tourist traffic visiting more locations (Meyer-Cech 2003; Croce and Perri 2010; Timothy and Boyd forthcoming).

As more sectors of society, including indigenes and other traditionally marginalized populations, become involved in helping to create an image and regional identity through culinary heritage, entrepreneurial opportunities arise for people involved in agriculture and fishing, as well as food service industries. Thus, more people might become involved in providing cultural experiences, including cuisine, to tourists.

Political empowerment

The final form of empowerment is political empowerment, which encompasses all other forms to some degree. As already discussed at the outset, political empowerment primarily means communities and all their stakeholders having a voice in development efforts. This includes ethnic minorities and other individuals who have rarely had a voice in tourism planning efforts. In addition, recent debates on the subject take this a step further to suggest that having a voice is not enough; instead, stakeholders should be empowered enough to initiate development projects or reject those that have been suggested. In short, political empowerment is the form that allows destination residents to matter in policy- and decision-making for tourism.

This translates well into the domain of culinary heritage. As alluded to already in the social empowerment section, minorities and other 'marginal' peoples can become more politically empowered through their cuisine. The 'cuisines of poverty' have become synonymous in Israel with the struggling Arab population, who have had little voice in their development since the early twentieth century. Gvion (2009) sees cuisine in Israel as a tool that has empowered Arabs in the broader Israeli society, wherein Israeli consumers have become dependent upon Arab gastronomy and Arab restaurateurs for much of today's 'Israeli' cuisine. For example, Hirsch (2011) argues that the recent 'gourmetization' of hummus in Israel reflects the re-emergence of Arab identity after many years of control by Israel. Hummus, an originally Arab dish has, in Hirsch's (2011: 620) words, come to be the 'foremost signifier of Israeliness'. In this sense, the Arab population of Israel have created a sense of national belonging within the Israeli state (Ron 2010).

Another perspective is ethnic groups using regional ethnic cuisines to make their mark in the larger society to which they belong. The success of indigenous Ainu food in Tokyo and other parts of Japan (Watson 2007) helps the Ainu assert their own distinct identity within the larger Japanese state, so that a sense of autonomy and image of individuality are created. Lappish food is served in Rovaniemi, Finland, near the Arctic Circle, not only to demarcate the city's inclusion in the traditional Sami territory, but also to assert the Sami national identity among the tourists and residents in the area. Heritage cuisine is thus used to solidify ethnic identities and autonomy in a political way and provides a showcase for cultural groups that are often forgotten in the national tourism narratives of Japan and Finland.

All of these forms of empowerment are important elements in growing more sustainable forms of tourism through culinary heritage. The Virginia Department of Historic Resources (2001: 6) outlines several ways in which destinations can benefit from cultural tourism. Because cuisine is such an important part of a region's heritage, by extension the same can be elucidated when heritage cuisines are a focus of tourism. First, sharing culinary heritage with tourists can help protect tangible and intangible resources, not only through the income earned from tourism, but also through community solidarity. Destination residents become involved in efforts to promote and preserve when they are able to relate to their personal, familial, community or regional heritage. This community cohesion motivates people to safeguard their shared resources and practise good stewardship. Second, enhancing the role of heritage cuisines educates residents and tourists about an area's cultural traditions and history. Third, heritage cuisines build closer and stronger communities as respect is instilled in citizens, community pride is boosted, and quality of life is improved. Finally, it provides considerable economic benefits, such as new employment opportunities, economic diversity, entrepreneurialism and increased regional revenue. Thus, cultural heritage in general, and heritage cuisines in particular, have the potential to uphold many of the principles of sustainability as destinations become empowered in part at least by the identities and solidarity created via their culinary heritage.

Conclusion

As part of the current wave of scholarly attention being devoted to intangible heritage (e.g. beliefs, social mores, folklore, celebrations, smells, sounds, flavours and scenery) (Boswell 2008; González 2008; Park 2011; Smith and Akagawa 2009; Taylor 2009) and the heritagization of ordinary landscapes (Timothy 2011), culinary heritage has moved into the spotlight as an important tourism product and a salient cultural building block of regional and national identity.

The Slow Food movement, which began in Europe and is spreading throughout the world, is another manifestation of the democratization of culinary heritage that slants towards sustainable communities as authentic, traditional and local foods are grown, prepared and served (Miele and Murdoch 2002; Hall 2006, 2012). Vernacular foods, traditional gastronomy and peasant dishes are seen not only as emerging tourism products but also as tools for building nationalism and collective social identities that can contribute to more sustainable tourist destinations through the empowerment of communities. As cultural and regional identities emerge, they empower communities socially, psychologically, economically and politically, so that destination residents come together in unity to work for a common cause. In doing so, they support harmony, balance and equity, and they have a better chance of ensuring the long-term viability of their cultural resources for tourism.

References

Bessière, J. (1998) 'Local development and heritage: traditional food and cuisine as tourist attractions in rural areas', *Sociologia Ruralis*, 38(1): 21–34.

Bessière, J. (2001) 'The role of rural gastronomy in tourism', in L. Roberts and D. Hall (eds) *Rural Tourism and Recreation: Principles to Practice*, Wallingford: CAB International.

Boniface, P. (2003) *Tasting Tourism: Travelling for Food and Drink*, Aldershot: Ashgate.

Boswell, R. (2008) 'Scents of identity: fragrance as heritage in Zanzibar', *Journal of Contemporary African Studies*, 26(3): 295–311.

Bramwell, B. and Lane, B. (1993) 'Sustainable tourism: an evolving global approach', *Journal of Sustainable Tourism*, 1(1): 1–5.

Che, D. (2006) 'Select Michigan: local food production, food safety, culinary heritage, and branding in Michigan agritourism', *Tourism Review International*, 9(4): 349–63.

Chuang, H.T. (2009) 'The rise of culinary tourism and its transformation of food cultures: the national cuisine of Taiwan', *Copenhagen Journal of Asian Studies*, 27(2): 84–108.

Croce, E. and Perri, G. (2010) *Food and Wine Tourism: Integrating Food, Travel and Territory*, Wallingford: CAB International.

Crouch, D. (2003) *The Art of Allotments: Culture and Cultivation*, Nottingham: Five Leaves Publications.

Cusack, I. (2000) 'African cuisines: recipes for nation building?', *Journal of African Cultural Studies*, 13(2): 207–25.

du Rand, G.E. and Heath, E. (2006) 'Towards a framework for food tourism as an element of destination marketing', *Current Issues in Tourism*, 9(3): 206–34.

Everett, S. and Aitchison, C. (2008) 'The role of food tourism in sustaining regional identity: a case study of Cornwall, South West England', *Journal of Sustainable Tourism*, 16(2): 150–67.

Faust, B.B. and Smardon, R.C. (2001) 'Introduction and overview – environmental knowledge, rights, and ethics: co-managing with communities', *Environmental Science and Policy*, 4: 147–51.

Feagan, R. (2007) 'The place of food: mapping out the "local" in local food systems', *Progress in Human Geography*, 31(1): 23–42.

Ferraro, G. and Andreatta, S. (2009) *Cultural Anthropology: An Applied Perspective*, 8th edn, Belmont, Calif.: Wadworth.

Fox, R. (2007) 'Reinventing the gastronomic identity of Croatian tourist destinations', *Hospitality Management*, 26: 546–59.

Friedmann, J. (1992) *Empowerment: The Politics of Alternative Development*, Cambridge: Blackwell.

Germann Molz, J. (2004) 'Tasting an imagined Thailand: authenticity and culinary tourism in Thai restaurants', in L.M. Long (ed.) *Culinary Tourism*, Lexington: University Press of Kentucky.

Gillespie, C. (2001) *European Gastronomy into the 21st Century*, Oxford: Butterworth-Heinemann.

González, M.V. (2008) 'Intangible heritage tourism and identity', *Tourism Management*, 29(4): 807–10.

Gvion, L. (2009) 'Narrating modernity and tradition: the case of Palestinian food in Israel', *Identities: Global Studies in Culture and Power*, 16(4): 391–413.

Gyimóthy, S. and Mykletun, R.J. (2009) 'Scary food: commodifying culinary heritage as meal adventures in tourism', *Journal of Vacation Marketing*, 15(3): 259–73.

Hall, C.M. (2006) 'Culinary tourism and regional development: from slow food to slow tourism?', *Tourism Review International*, 9: 303–5.

Hall, C.M. (2012) 'The contradictions and paradoxes of slow food: environmental change, sustainability and the conservation of taste', in S. Fullagar, K. Markwell and E. Wilson (eds) *Slow Tourism: Experiences and Mobilities*, Bristol: Channel View.

Hall, C.M. and Mitchell, R. (2000) ' "We are what we eat": food, tourism, and globalization', *Tourism, Culture and Communication*, 2(1): 29–37.

Hall, C.M. and Sharples, L. (eds) (2008) *Food and Wine Festivals and Events Around the World: Development, Management and Markets*, Oxford: Butterworth-Heinemann.

Hall, C.M., Sharples, L., Mitchell, R., Macionis, N. and Cambourne, B. (eds) (2003) *Food Tourism Around the World: Development, Management and Markets*, Oxford: Butterworth-Heinemann.

Harrison, D. (2008) 'Pro-poor tourism: a critique', *Third World Quarterly*, 29(5): 851–68.

Heine, P. (2004) *Food Culture in the Near East, Middle East, and North Africa*, Westport, Conn.: Greenwood Press.

Hirsch, D. (2011) ' "Hummus is best when it's fresh and made by Arabs": the gourmetization of hummus in Israel and the return of the repressed Arab', *American Ethnologist*, 38(4): 617–30.

Hjalager, A.M. and Corigliano, M.A. (2000) 'Food for tourists – determinants of an image', *International Journal of Tourism Research*, 2: 281–93.

Hjalager, A.M. and Richards, G. (eds) (2002) *Tourism and Gastronomy*, London: Routledge.

Holtzman, J.D. (2006) 'Food and memory', *Annual Review of Anthropology*, 35: 361–78.

Johnston, A.M. (2003) 'Self-determination: exercising indigenous rights in tourism', in S. Singh, D.J. Timothy and R.K. Dowling (eds) *Tourism in Destination Communities*, Wallingford: CAB International.

Kaftanoglu, B. and Timothy, D.J. (in press) 'Return travel, assimilation and cultural maintenance: an example of Turkish-Americans in Arizona', *Tourism Analysis*.

Kittler, P.G. and Sucher, K.P. (2008) *Food and Culture*, 5th edn, Belmont, Calif.: Thomson.

Kuhnlein, H.V., Erasmus, B. and Spigelski, D. (2009) *Indigenous Peoples' Food Systems: The Many Dimensions of Culture, Diversity and Environment for Nutrition and Health*, Wallingford: CAB International.

Lin, Y.C., Pearson, T.E. and Cai, L.A. (2011) 'Food as a form of destination identity: a tourism destination brand perspective', *Tourism and Hospitality Research*, 11(1): 30–48.

Long, L.M. (ed.) (2004) *Culinary Tourism*, Lexington: University Press of Kentucky.

Lougheed, T. (2010) 'The changing landscape of Arctic traditional food', *Environmental Health Perspectives*, 118(9): 386–93.

Miele, M. and Murdock, I. (2002) 'The practical aesthetics of traditional cuisines: slow food in Tuscany', *Sociologia Ruralis*, 42(4): 312–28.

Moore, A. (1998) *Cultural Anthropology: The Field Study of Human Beings*, 2nd edn, San Diego, Calif.: Collegiate Press.

Meyer-Cech, K. (2003) 'Food trails in Austria', in C.M. Hall, L. Sharples, R. Mitchell, N. Macionis and B. Cambourne (eds) *Food Tourism Around the World: Development, Management and Markets*, Oxford: Butterworth-Heinemann.

Narayan, U. (1995) 'Eating cultures: incorporation, identity and Indian food', *Social Identities*, 1(1): 63–86.

Okazaki, E. (2008) 'A community-based tourism model: its conception and use', *Journal of Sustainable Tourism*, 16(5): 511–29.

Okumus, B., Okumus, F. and McKercher, B. (2007) 'Incorporating local and international cuisines in the marketing of tourism destinations: the cases of Hong Kong and Turkey', *Tourism Management*, 28(1): 253–61.

Parasecoli, F. (2004) *Food Culture in Italy*, Westport, Conn.: Greenwood Press.

Park, H.Y. (2011) 'Shared national memory as intangible heritage: re-imagining two Koreas as one nation', *Annals of Tourism Research*, 38: 520–39.

Pilcher, J.M. (1996) 'Tamales or timbales: cuisine and the formation of Mexican national identity, 1821–1911', *The Americas*, 53(2): 193–216.

Ron, A.S. (2010) 'Review of Stein's *Itineraries in Conflict: Israelis, Palestinians and the Political Lives of Tourism*', *Journal of Israeli History*, 29(2): 237–9.

Scheyvens, R. (1999) 'Ecotourism and the empowerment of local communities', *Tourism Management*, 20: 245–9.

Scheyvens, R. (2002) *Tourism for Development: Empowering Communities*, Harlow: Prentice Hall.

Scheyvens, R. (2003) 'Local involvement in managing tourism', in S. Singh, D.J. Timothy and R.K. Dowling (eds) *Tourism in Destination Communities*, Wallingford: CAB International.

Scheyvens, R. (2011) *Tourism and Poverty*. London: Routledge.

Schlüter, R.G. and Ellul, D.T. (2008) 'Gastronomía y turismo en Argentina: Polo gastronómico Tomás Jofré', *PASOS: Revista de Turismo y Patrimonio Cultural*, 6(2): 249–68.

Simpson, K. (2001) 'Strategic planning and community involvement as contributors to sustainable tourism development', *Current Issues in Tourism*, 4(1): 3–41.

Smith, L. and Akagawa, N. (eds) (2009) *Intangible Heritage*, London: Routledge.

Suen, W.H. (2007) 'A taste of the past: historically themed restaurants and social memory in Singapore', in S.C.H. Cheung and T. Chee-Beng (eds) *Food and Foodways in Asia: Resource, Tradition and Cooking*, London: Routledge.

Sukovic, M., Sharf, B.F., Sharkey, J.R. and St John, J. (2011) 'Seasoning for the soul: empowerment through food preparation among Mexican women in the Texas *colonias*', *Food and Foodways*, 19(3): 228–47.

Taylor, M.N. (2009) 'Intangible heritage governance, cultural diversity, ethno-nationalism', *Focaal*, 55: 41–58.

Tellström, R., Gustafsson, I.B. and Mossberg, L. (2005) 'Local food cultures in the Swedish rural economy', *Sociologia Ruralis*, 45(4): 346–59.

Tellström, R., Gustafsson, I.B. and Mossberg, L. (2006) 'Consuming heritage: the use of local food culture in branding', *Place Branding*, 2(2): 130–43.

Thursby, J.S. (2004) 'Culinary tourism among Basques and Basque Americans: maintenance and inventions', in L.M. Long (ed.) *Culinary Tourism*, Lexington: University Press of Kentucky.

Timothy, D.J. (1999) 'Participatory planning: a view of tourism in Indonesia', *Annals of Tourism Research*, 26(2): 371–91.

Timothy, D.J. (2002) 'Tourism and community development issues', in R. Sharpley and D.J. Telfer (eds) *Tourism and Development: Concepts and Issues*, Clevedon: Channel View Publications.

Timothy, D.J. (2007) 'Empowerment and stakeholder participation in tourism destination communities', in A. Church and T. Coles (eds) *Tourism, Power and Space*, London: Routledge.

Timothy, D.J. (2011) *Cultural Heritage and Tourism: An Introduction*, Bristol: Channel View.

Timothy, D.J. and Boyd, S.W. (forthcoming) *Cultural Routes, Nature Trails and Scenic Byways: Tourism and Linear Resources*, Bristol: Channel View.

Timothy, D.J. and Ron, A.S. (2009) Farmers for a day: agricultural heritage and nostalgia in rural Israel. Paper presented at the annual conference of the Association of American Geographers, Las Vegas, Nevada, 26 March.

Timothy, D.J. and Ron, A.S. (2010) The Land of Milk and Honey: Biblical foods and Holy Land tourism. Paper presented at the conference Sustainable Food in Tourism and Hospitality, Kalmar, Sweden, 30 September.

Virginia Department of Historic Resources (2001) *Tourism Handbook: Putting Virginia's History to Work*, Richmond: Virginia Department of Historic Resources.

Warde, A. (2009) 'Imagining British cuisine: representations of culinary identity in the *Good Food Guide*, 1951–2007', *Food, Culture and Society*, 12(2): 151–71.

Watson, M.K. (2007) 'Indigenous food and foodways: mapping the production of Ainu food in Tokyo', in S.C.H. Cheung and T. Chee-Beng (eds) *Food and Foodways in Asia: Resource, Tradition and Cooking*, London: Routledge.

Wilk, R.R. (1999) '"Real Belizean food": building local identity in the transnational Caribbean', *American Anthropologist*, 101(2): 244–55.

Wolf, E. (2008) 'Culinary tourism – a hot and fresh idea', *TourismReview.com*, December: 5–6. Online. Available: www.tourism-review.com/travel-tourism-magazine-culinary-tourism-a-hot-fresh-idea-article677 (accessed 1 April 2012).

Part IV
Conclusion

16 Reimagining sustainable culinary systems

The future of culinary systems

C. Michael Hall and Stefan Gössling

Introduction

In discussing the ways in which sustainability in agri-food systems could be achieved by 2030 given the scale and rate of global environmental change and global population growth, Green *et al.* (2003: 157) emphasised that any critique 'has to confront the obvious problems of industrialized agriculture and its associated consumption patterns'. In many ways the same can be argued of tourism, given the need to confront its own industrialised system and growing consumption in the face of global change (Gössling *et al.* 2009; Hall 2010a, 2011a; Gössling *et al.* 2012b; Scott *et al.* 2012; see also Chapter 1 above). According to the UN World Tourism Organisation (2011) international tourist arrivals are forecast to increase by an average 3.3 per cent a year between 2010 and 2030 and to reach 1.8 billion by 2030. This means that arrivals are projected to pass the 1 billion mark in 2012, up from 940 million in 2010. However, it should also be noted that international tourism only accounts for approximately 16 per cent of all tourist mobility, the remainder being domestic tourism activity. If this same ratio is maintained, by 2030 there will be 11.25 billion domestic tourism trips a year, a figure well in excess of a tourist trip per person expected to be on the planet then.

The modern agri-food system, along with the tourist system, particularly as it exists in the developed countries or the North, has provided consumers with an unparalleled range of products, available virtually all year round, and at prices that account for historically unprecedented minor shares of household budgets (Sage 2012). Both food and tourists are travelling longer distances at lower per unit costs (Hall 2005). Restaurant diners in a major metropolitan centre can, if they are willing to pay the price, eat produce that was harvested or caught on the other side of the world only 24 or 36 hours previously. In the same way, it is now possible to fly from one side of the world to the other on commercial flights in a day. Such opportunities present the possibility of new product developments, new consumption experiences and opportunities, and new profits. Indeed, the interrelationship between tourism and food is often promoted as creating enormous opportunities for business and for economic development (OECD 2012). So why the concern?

Constructing culinary systems

Following on from the culinary systems approach adopted in Chapter 1 above, we can highlight how critique of the sustainability of such systems arises from concerns with respect not only to global environmental change but also to the way in which the culinary system has been socially constructed. Food is deeply personal because of the way in which it directly affects the body (Harvey *et al.* 2004). It should therefore be no surprise that because of this concerns are often expressed about the extent to which what one eats contributes to health and well-being (including religious well-being as noted in Chapter 14 above), and does not carry disease, pollutants or other contaminants. Food safety and associated risk reduction strategies have therefore become highly significant issues with respect to consumer purchasing and the food supply chain overall (Sage 2012). However, these are also highly complex issues, especially with respect to the trade-offs that can take place between different ways of framing personal and collective food security. Quality is not something that can be considered solely as being inherent to a food product (Harvey *et al.* 2004). It is something that must be understood within particular contexts.

> Different people in different situations bring into play a collective knowledge, of which taste is a result. In other words, taste is a way of building relationships, with things and with people; it is not simply a property of goods, not is it a competence of people.
>
> (Teil and Hennion 2004: 25)

A number of the chapters in this book are grounded in concerns over the qualities of food, and whether it is authentic (e.g. chapters 5 and 15), certified (e.g. chapter 14), local (e.g. chapters 2, 8, 9) or sustainable (e.g. chapters 10, 12). Indeed, many of the chapters bring together food and tourism as part of the development of alternative food networks that have emerged from consumer concern over

> human health and food safety, as well as other, wider ethical considerations (animal welfare, fair trade, sustainability). Such developments have demonstrated that food markets are not the result of some 'invisible' hand external to the social world, but result from the active construction of networks by various actors in the food chain.
>
> (Sage 2012: 272)

They also often represent not just the relocalising of food with respect to the embrace of local food initiatives (Feagan 2007) and alternative economic spaces (Fuller *et al.* 2010), such as local food networks (Chapter 2 above), protected food designations (Chapter 4 above), farmers' markets (Chapter 5 above) and Slow Food (Chapter 10 above) but also the resocialising, whereby consumers make conscious ethical choices as to what they purchase, where they travel and what they eat (Lang 2010; Hall 2011b). Nevertheless, such ethical decisions also need to marry with the way in which the culinary system is constructed and can be potentially transformed; here many of the chapters posit the place-bound nature of alternative food networks as a more sustainable alternative to the highly globalised food and, to a lesser extent, tourism industries. But, as noted in Chapter 1 above, there are different understandings not only of what sustainability is but how it may be achieved.

Reimagining culinary systems

One of the difficulties in seeking to transform culinary systems is that what may be proposed as an approach to sustainability (see Table 1.9 above) in one context, may not work in another. Indeed, some approaches, such as fair trade, have even been criticised for failing to acknowledge the wishes of workers in producer countries (Sage 2012). As Green *et al.* (2003: 157) highlight with respect to strategies, some may even be

> unhelpful when presented without clear indications of how they might fit into a variety of different socio-economic contexts, including their suitability at different geographical scales (that is, local, regional, global, etc.) and their implications for the kinds of technological innovation that is currently being pursued. In global society, uneven development is the norm. It seems reasonable to suggest that within one country there will be different strategies; some foods produced by one, others by another strategy; and there will also be great differences between countries, even for the same foods. In addition, whatever the differences between agricultural systems there will be substantial variety in methods of distribution and food preferences.

At one level, Green *et al.* (2003) are certainly correct in their argument: social and economic processes, such as globalisation, consumerism or even neoliberalism, are always uneven in space and time. However, the relative utility of different strategies to achieve sustainable culinary systems still have another benchmark to achieve and that is the extent to which they actually halt or potentially even reverse processes of global environmental change.

The notion of sustainable culinary systems used in Chapter 1 above, *combining concerns for present and future generations, a sustainable culinary system must be able to demonstrate that it can optimize food output and consumption without compromising the stock of natural capital and ecosystem services*, draws upon the notion of a steady-state economy (Goodland and Daly 1996). In tourism this has been defined as tourism development without growth in throughput of matter and energy beyond regenerative and absorptive capacities (Hall 2009). Although often referred to as a service industry, tourism's impacts are clearly not intangible or negligible, as evidenced by the role of tourism and hospitality within the food system and its contribution to global environmental change (Scott *et al.* 2012). In order to reduce their environmental footprint, food and tourism need to become part of a circular economy rather than a linear one, so that inputs of virgin raw material and energy and outputs in the form of emissions and waste requiring disposal are reduced (Hall 2010b). Such a change is often categorised as sustainable consumption.

The four approaches to sustainable culinary systems outlined in Table 1.9 ('business as usual' (BAU), 'green growth', 'steady-state' and 'traditional sustainable') all take different approaches to the sustainability question. There are arguably two main approaches to encouraging sustainable consumption and production in culinary systems for tourism and hospitality (illustrated in Figure 16.1). First is the *efficiency* approach, which seeks to reduce the rate of consumption by using materials more productively. Eco-efficiency stresses the technological link between value creation in economic activities and environmental quality. This approach places more focus on recycling, using energy more efficiently, eco-innovation, and reducing emissions, but otherwise operating in a 'business as usual' manner. Examples of this include efforts to reduce the amount of food waste or using less energy to produce the same food output. The second approach may be broadly referred to as 'slow consumption', and includes consumer activism as well as industry and public policy initiatives designed to reduce the amount and the rate of throughput via changing consumption behaviours and patterns and even the nature of economic relationships as well as production processes and systems. Innovations in this sphere are often substantially different in character and focus more on social and environmental goals or are more well-being-driven than purely profit-driven. Indeed, many of the innovations, including some discussed in the chapters in this book, are more system or social innovations (Hall and Williams 2008). Examples of the slow consumption or 'steady-state' approach include (Seyfang 2006; Hall 2007a, 2009, 2010b; Maye *et al.* 2007; Lang *et al.* 2009; Pinkerton and Hopkins 2009; Fuller *et al.* 2010):

- the development of environmental standards at the community, regional, national and international scales that aim to reduce throughput (also potentially utilised under the efficiency approach);
- the adoption of lifecycle thinking and analysis (cradle-to-cradle) in determining infrastructure and product life spans (also potentially available under the efficiency approach);
- relocalisation schemes such as farmers' markets and 'local diets' that reinforce the potential economic, social and environmental benefits of purchasing, consuming and producing locally, as well as travelling locally;
- ethical consumption which includes fair trade, local and organic purchasing, and Slow Food, of which all are significant for the hospitality sector, as well as low carbon travel, staycations, and local tourism; and
- consumer citizenship activities such as anti-consumerism, consumer rights, boycotts and culture jamming, which may include 'downsizing', 'voluntary simplicity' and focus on living better by consuming less and the satisfaction of non-material needs including leisure.

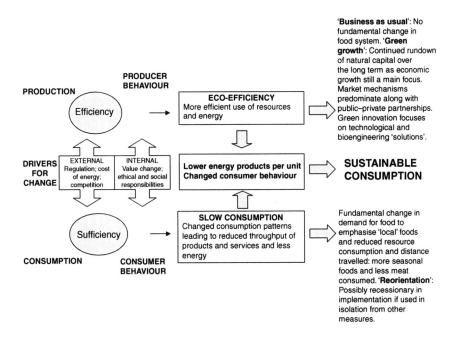

Figure 16.1 Efficiency and sufficiency in sustainable culinary systems (source: after Hall 2007a).

The BAU approach to sustainable food systems is arguably not an appropriate choice for a sustainable future. Although humanity may be fed and continue to travel, it only does so at the cost of enormous global environmental change, including substantial species loss, as well as the creation of further divisions between rich and poor. The long-term implications for humanity are also debatable given the loss of natural capital and the creation of a greenhouse world. The green growth approach seeks to continue the goal of growing the economy while contributing to environmental conservation. In order to achieve this it proposes a market-oriented approach that focuses on greater efficiencies through technical and biological innovation. For example, the World Economic Forum (2009) focus on developing a 'low carbon' travel and tourism industry is geared towards technological innovation and change rather than shifting consumer demand or regulatory strategies (see Gössling 2010). Yet the technological solution is extremely questionable as 'technological progress does not reconcile the conflict between economic growth and biodiversity conservation because it arises only in tandem with the conflict' (Czech 2003: 1456). Indeed, this issue is central to the problems posed by the forecasts for future tourism growth highlighted at the beginning of this chapter. Although it may be possible to achieve greater efficiencies in, for example, energy consumption per tourist trip, the overall number of tourist trips continues to grow in absolute terms at a rate faster than any achievement in efficiency, meaning that use of energy along with rates of emissions continue to grow (Scott *et al.* 2012). This paradox has long been recognised, except perhaps by those who continue to advocate the green growth approach. As Czech (2006: 1563) commented,

> The nineteenth-century economist, William Stanley Jevons, noted in 'The Coal Question' that every increment of additional efficiency in coal extraction and utilization was met with an increment of additional coal extracted and consumed. 'Jevons Paradox' helps illustrate the chicken-or-egg nature of economic growth and technological progress. As long as economic growth is the goal, technological progress will not result in biodiversity conservation; rather, an expansion of the human niche and the consumption of more natural resources will result.

In contrast, the 'steady-state' and 'traditional sustainable' approaches focus more on *sufficiency* in the culinary system and, while recognising the importance of efficiency in production systems, stress sufficiency via changing consumer behaviour, including the overall level or rate of demand, and slowing the overall rate of consumption. The 'traditional sustainable' strategy (Green *et al.* 2003) utilises some of these measures but it is primarily focused on rural areas in the global South, or less developed countries. In addition, it also includes some elements of the green growth approach. Such a strategy may have some merits in terms of achieving a sustainable transition (Gössling *et al.* 2012a) of culinary systems. However, it does not really deal with the reality of the growing urbanisation of the world's population or with the extent of the environmental impact of pro-poor tourism strategies (Hall 2007b). In contrast the 'steady-state' strategy of the establishment of alternative food networks aims at transforming culinary systems in both rural and urban centres.

The emergent property of alternative food networks, as illustrated in many of the chapters in this volume, is that they convey 'a sense of flux, of dynamism and of *social* possibility' (Sage 2012: 273). They are more social and system innovations that focus on notions of well-being than purely profit- or market-driven. Although sometimes dismissed as not being able to compete with the conventional agri-food system approach in terms of production, within the approach there is a strong focus on the development of urban agricultural opportunities as well as the applicability of organic growing and local food networks to higher-latitude areas and more marginal growing regions (Coleman 2009). In place of the anonymous and standardised supply chains of BAU, alternative food networks offer a mechanism to reconnect with the producer and place of production as a result of their focus on food quality, tradition, artisan nature and direct marketing (Skuras *et al.* 2006; Sims 2009, 2010). Above all, as Sage (2012: 274) emphasises, they restore 'the central importance of provenance as a vital ingredient of decent food'.

A further point of differentiation between the different approaches is the role of the state in food systems. In the BAU and green growth approaches the primary role of the state is to intervene to enable markets to work and, in the case of green growth also to enter into public–private partnerships that often allow the private sector to occupy spaces of regulation and governance that were previously clearly in the public domain and not necessarily operated on a 'for profit basis'. In contrast, the traditional sustainable and steady-state approaches tend to advocate a far more direct role of the state so as to intervene in the public and environment's interest. Subsidies and start-up funds may be seen as appropriate for the development of networks and even businesses that promote local alternative food networks and local food security. In North America Food Policy Councils have been a public–private initiative that has often had great success in promoting new initiatives (see Chapter 3 above), while in Europe there has often been far more active intervention by the state (see chapters 2 and 10 above). Intervention often also includes creating structures for certification programmes (Chapter 14 above) as well as regional promotion, the latter being one of the most common areas of state funding and promotion as it is accepted by green growth advocates as well (du Rand and Heath 2006; see also above, Chapter 2 on Sweden, Chapter 4 on Norway, Chapter 7 on Japan and Chapter 9 on Canada and Japan). Nevertheless, the regulatory and governance frameworks created by the state, and the relative role of market initiatives, will undoubtedly be a major issue with respect to food in the future.

So what will the future be? Green *et al.* (2003) suggest that there will be a mixture of various strategies since they are applicable at different levels and to different global and national regions, and envisage 'the co-existence of local, "short", supply chains for some foods (for example, in the UK, local "farm-house" animal products) and global supply chains of foods not locally available (for example, in the UK, rice)' (Green *et al.* 2003: 157). Some of the chapters in this book suggest that this is already occurring, e.g. Chapter 2 on 'local' food networks in Sweden. Such a strategy may also be appropriate as part of transition management to sustainability (Gössling *et al.* 2012a). Nevertheless, caution must also be stressed in the potential dominance of large capital in any transition process. As Sage (2012) observes with respect to the market and corporate power of the conventional agri-food system, it is

> dominant, resourceful and capable of continuous reinvention, especially in the way that it has sought to appropriate the language of alternative practices ('local', 'organic', and with pictures of its specialist suppliers posted on the supermarket walls), remains monolithically corporate and still preoccupied by low cost.
>
> (Sage 2012: 273)

Indeed, despite much talk by lead organisations about tourism and hospitality being vital for a sustainable future as well as a media image of higher-end restaurants and food, the reality is that most food provision in tourism is currently unsustainable as it is based on purchases of the cheapest foodstuffs. Such an approach only continues to favour the lowest common denominator (direct cost minimisation) approach to food without consideration of the externalities that arise from such supply chains. Yes, there are exceptions in terms of the purchasing policies of some hotels and accommodation providers as well as restaurants, as detailed in some of the chapters in this book, but they are the exception rather than the rule. If tourism really does seek to pay more than lip service to the notion of sustainability it needs to start addressing the notion of cost in a much more considered manner and encourage more responsible purchasing behaviour, and the role of tourism and hospitality in the sustainability of culinary systems is a good place to start.

Research needs

This book is only a starting point in exploring the interrelationships between food and tourism from the perspective of sustainability. In seeking to extend our understanding of culinary systems and the actors and stakeholders within them it is important that empirical research is undertaken so as to underpin more strategic and policy-oriented writing that aims to influence decision-making and development trajectories. Significant issues include the need for studies that look at the acceptance and expectation of higher-quality foods in tourism, and the willingness to pay for these. Indeed, there is a wide range of consumer-oriented studies that would be valuable to undertake in a number of different cultural, regional and economic settings. These include the role of food in travel decision-making and during the trip; the most highly demanded food experiences; and the role for local food products in travel experiences. Of course not everyone wants to eat regional specialties all the time but everyone has to eat, therefore studies of the food chain need to identify the way in which local supply can be enhanced especially during periods that are otherwise regarded as being out of season for growing and/or tourism.

The food development potentials of destinations, including with regard to regional networks, are an ever more important issue for the creation of positive regional multipliers especially during periods of economic recession. Therefore, there is a need for better understanding of network relationships in different settings, product development, and consumer education and knowledge. This also requires a more transparent approach to understanding the barriers to sustainable innovation and ecological and social entrepreneurship in tourism and hospitality, including the institutional barriers that may favour certain paradigms of sustainable development over others, or the corporate agri-food system over smaller producers. This also includes the need for more research on social and system innovation practices rather than those that can be patented. Perhaps most fundamentally there is also the need to acknowledge that consumers have the right to know where their food has come from and the relative environmental, social and economic impacts of their being able to eat it.

Conclusions

The role of tourism and hospitality in culinary systems is relatively unacknowledged. As this book has shown, they have a major economic and environmental role in the food chain. The act of 'eating out' has far greater consequences than most people would believe. However, the role of tourism and hospitality is full of paradoxes. As in general with respect to tourism's role in globalisation, local culinary systems either can be valued and reinforced as a result of tourism and hospitality activities or they can be lost as part of a broader process of meeting the perceived needs of tourists and guests. Similarly, in the case of the promotion of the culinary products of the Island of Funen in Denmark, Askegaard and Kjeldgaard (2007) illustrated that marketing may not only represent a homogenization of culture through global corporate business but can also promote the principles of marketing and branding that can be used in the service of creating sustainable small-scale production–consumption relations and, therefore, local cultural sustainability.

The book has also noted that the grounds of what constitutes quality is primarily contingent, contextual and fluid, specific to time and space, and hence culture and institutions. Different 'orders of worth', such as aesthetic, religious, economic, environmental and ethical understandings, also become integral to the claims made for quality and how they are interrogated. Most importantly, there is no single common metric or analytic process of judgement with which to establish that some food is quality food (Harvey *et al.* 2004). Yet, at the same time, alternative food networks have certain qualities of food at their core. Moreover, it can also be argued that the measure of the negative externalities of food is a quality that should be integral to promoting sustainability and reducing the decline of natural capital, although perhaps the decision to recognise that quality is as much a decision about values as it is about quality per se.

In addition, as highlighted throughout the book in various chapters, many businesses and regions as well as even sectors in some cases operate in multiple frameworks of sustainable culinary systems, connecting, if not embracing, both the local and the global, green growth as well as organics, as they seek to be 'competitive' which in many cases really means staying in business and earning an appropriate income level rather than seeking to grow per se. Whether such strategies are readily achievable with respect to both economic and sustainability goals in the longer term remains to be seen. Yet, given the importance of 'diversity' to ecosystems and to innovative economies and communities, perhaps advocating a single strategy for all destinations and locations may be counterproductive for the sustainability of both culinary and environmental systems at least in the shorter term (Green *et al.* 2003). Nevertheless, the 'tensions' as well as areas of agreement between different approaches are worthy of study, especially if they provide greater clarity as to what it is we wish to sustain and how we will achieve it (Sonnino and Marsden 2006). Moreover, areas of common ground may also provide an important starting point for the development of transition frameworks that set in place new development trajectories (Gössling *et al.* 2012a), although, without care, such 'common ground' potentially also offers a space in which the dominant market-driven approaches overwhelm the articulation of alternative perspectives and spaces (Fuller *et al.* 2010). As Sage (2012: 295) records, 'A sustainable food network really does offer the potential to create a viable parallel to the prevailing agri-food system, recognising that, in practice, a high degree of *hybridity* will probably arise (as companies make efforts to improve their environmental performance.'

To be truly sustainable and to meet the challenge of global change, sustainability must refer to qualities of human well-being, economic justice and ecological integrity (Leach *et al.* 2010) not just 'efficiency', 'reductions in emissions per unit', 'green growth' or 'sustainable growth'. Otherwise the environment usually reflects 'its capture by powerful interests for their own ends, and should be resisted' (Sage 2012: 290). Such sentiments apply to the operation of culinary systems, the policies of the states that govern them, and the educational and research institutions that support, reflect and critique them. And so we resist.

References

Askegaard, S. and Kjeldgaard, D. (2007) 'Here, there, and everywhere: Place branding and gastronomical globalization in a macromarketing perspective', *Journal of Macromarketing*, 27(2): 138–47.

Coleman, E. (2009) *The Winter Harvest Handbook. Year-Round Vegetable Production Using Deep-Organic Techniques and Unheated Greenhouses*, White River Junction, Vt.: Chelsea Green Publishing.

Czech, B. (2003) 'Technological progress and biodiversity conservation: A dollar spent, a dollar burned', *Conservation Biology*, 17: 1455–7.

Czech, B. (2006) 'If Rome is burning, why are we fiddling?', *Conservation Biology*, 20: 1563–5.

du Rand, G.E. and Heath, E. (2006) 'Towards a framework for food tourism as an element of destination marketing', *Current Issues in Tourism*, 9(3): 206–34.

Feagan, R. (2007) 'The place of food: Mapping out the "local" in local food systems', *Progress in Human Geography*, 31(1): 23–42.

Fuller, D., Jonas, A.E.G. and Lee, R. (eds) (2010) *Interrogating Alterity: Alternative Economic and Political Spaces*, Farnham: Ashgate.

Goodland, R. and Daly, H. (1996) 'Environmental sustainability: Universal and non-negotiable', *Ecological Applications*, 6(4): 1002–17.

Green, K., Harvey, M. and McMeekin, A. (2003) 'Transformations in food consumption and production systems', *Journal of Environmental Policy & Planning*, 5(2): 145–63.

Gössling, S. (2010) *Carbon Management in Tourism: Mitigating the Impacts on Climate Change*, London: Routledge.

Gössling, S., Ceron, J.-P., Dubois, G. and Hall, C.M. (2009) 'Hypermobile travellers', in S. Gössling and P. Upham (eds) *Climate Change and Aviation*, London: Earthscan.

Gössling, S., Hall, C.M., Ekström, F., Brudvik Engeset, A. and Aall, C. (2012a) 'Transition management for sustainable tourism', *Journal of Sustainable Tourism*, DOI: 10.1080/09669582.2012.699062.

Gössling, S., Peeters, P., Hall, C.M., Dubois, G., Ceron, J.P., Lehmann, L. and Scott, D. (2012b) 'Tourism and water use: Supply, demand, and security. An international review', *Tourism Management*, 33: 1–15.

Hall, C.M. (2005) *Tourism: Rethinking the Social Science of Mobility*. Harlow: Pearson.

Hall, C.M. (2007a) The Possibilities of Slow Tourism: Can the Slow Movement Help Develop Sustainable Forms of Tourism Consumption? Paper presented at Achieving Sustainable Tourism, Helsingborg, Sweden, 11–14 September.

Hall, C.M. (2007b) 'Pro-poor tourism: Do "tourism exchanges benefit primarily the countries of the South"?' *Current Issues in Tourism*, 10: 111–18.

Hall, C.M. (2009) 'Degrowing tourism: Décroissance, sustainable consumption and steady-state tourism', *Anatolia: An International Journal of Tourism and Hospitality Research*, 20(1), 46–61.

Hall, C.M. (2010a) 'Tourism and biodiversity: More significant than climate change?', *Journal of Heritage Tourism*, 5: 253–66.

Hall, C.M. (2010b) 'Changing paradigms and global change: From sustainable to steady-state tourism', *Tourism Recreation Research*, 35(2): 131–45.

Hall, C.M. (2011a) 'Policy learning and policy failure in sustainable tourism governance: From first and second to third order change?', *Journal of Sustainable Tourism*, 19(4–5): 649–71.

Hall, C.M. (2011b) 'Consumerism, tourism and voluntary simplicity: We all have to consume, but do we really have to travel so much to be happy?', *Tourism Recreation Research*, 36(3): 298–303.

Hall, C.M. and Williams, A. (2008) *Tourism and Innovation*, London: Routledge.

Harvey, M., McMeekin, A. and Warde, A. (2004) 'Conclusion: quality and processes of qualification', in M. Harvey, A. McMeekin and A. Warde (eds) *Qualities of Food*, Manchester: Manchester University Press.

Lang, T. (2010) 'From "value-for-money" to "values-for-money"? Ethical food and policy in Europe', *Environment and Planning A*, 42: 1814–32.

Lang, T., Barling, D. and Caraher, M. (2009) *Food Policy: Integrating Health, Environment and Society*. Oxford: Oxford University Press.

Leach, M., Scoones, I. and Stirling, A. (2010) *Dynamic Sustainabilities: Technology, Environment, Social Justice*, London: Earthscan.

Maye, D., Holloway, L. and Kneafsey, M. (eds) (2007) *Alternative Food Geographies: Representation and Practice*, Oxford: Elsevier.

OECD (2012) *Food and the Tourism Experience: The OECD–Korea Workshop*, OECD Studies on Tourism, Paris: OECD Publishing.

Pinkerton, T. and Hopkins, R. (2009) *Local Food: How to Make it Happen in Your Community*, Totnes: Green Books.

Sage, C. (2012) *Environment and Food*, London: Routledge.

Scott, D., Gössling, S. and Hall, C.M. (2012) *Tourism and Climate Change: Impacts, Adaptation and Mitigation*, London: Routledge.

Seyfang, G. (2006) 'Ecological citizenship and sustainable consumption: Examining local organic food networks', *Journal of Rural Studies*, 22(4): 383–95.

Sims, R. (2009) 'Food, place and authenticity: Local food and the sustainable tourism experience', *Journal of Sustainable Tourism*, 17(3): 321–36.

Sims, R. (2010) 'Putting place on the menu: The negotiation of locality in UK food tourism, from production to consumption', *Journal of Rural Studies*, 26: 105–15.

Skuras, D., Dimara, E. and Petrou, A. (2006) 'Rural tourism and visitors' expenditures for local food products', *Regional Studies*, 40: 769–79.

Sonnino, R. and Marsden, T. (2006) 'Beyond the divide: Rethinking relationships between alternative and conventional food networks in Europe', *Journal of Economic Geography*, 6(2): 181–99.

Teil, G. and Hennion, A. (2004) 'Discovering quality or performing taste? A sociology of the amateur', in M. Harvey, A. McMeekin and A. Warde (eds) *Qualities of Food*, Manchester: Manchester University Press.

United Nations World Tourism Organization (2011) International tourists to hit 1.8

billion by 2030, UNWTO Press Release, PR11079, 11 October 2011, Madrid: UNWTO. Online. Available: http://media.unwto.org/en/press-release/2011–10–11/ international-tourists-hit-18-billion-2030 (accessed 1 April 2012).

World Economic Forum (2009) *Towards a Low Carbon Travel & Tourism Sector*, Davos: World Economic Forum.

Index

Page numbers in *italics* denote tables, those in **bold** denote figures.